The Chatto Book of
GHOSTS

BY THE SAME AUTHOR

The Macmillan Dictionary of Women's Biography

George Eliot

Elizabeth Gaskell: A Habit of Stories

The Chatto Book of
GHOSTS

Edited, with an Introduction by
JENNY UGLOW

He always half suspected that something would get him.

THURBER

Chatto & Windus
LONDON

First published in Great Britain 1994

1 3 5 7 9 10 8 6 4 2

© Selection and Introduction, Jenny Uglow 1994

Jenny Uglow has asserted her right under
the Copyright, Designs and Patents Act, 1988
to be identified as the author of this work

Published in 1994 by
Chatto & Windus Limited
Random House, 20 Vauxhall Bridge Road,
London SW1V 2SA

Random House Australia (Pty) Limited
20 Alfred Street, Milsons Point, Sydney,
New South Wales 2061, Australia

Random House New Zealand Limited
18 Poland Road, Glenfield
Auckland 10, New Zealand

Random House South Africa (Pty) Limited
PO Box 337, Bergvlei, South Africa

Random House UK Limited Reg. No. 954009

A CIP catalogue record for this book
is available from the British Library

ISBN 0 7011 6147 7

Typography by Humphrey Stone
Photoset by SX Composing, Raleigh, Essex
Printed in Great Britain by Clays Ltd, St Ives plc

Contents

For Hermione

Introduction

The distance that the dead have gone
Does not at first appear –
Their coming back seems possible
For many an ardent year.

And then, that we have followed them,
We more than half suspect,
So intimate have we become
With their dear retrospect.

EMILY DICKINSON

For as long as men and women have buried their dead, they have imagined their return. For as long as they have told stories, composed prayers or sung songs they have summoned the ghosts in words. Ghosts stalk world literature, speaking to the living, carrying fears and longings through the ages and allowing us to step, hesitantly, across the threshold of the known. Why do they hold us in thrall?

After chasing shades from *Gilgamesh* to *Ghostbusters*, I have come to see their symbolic power as twofold. They fill the void of absence created by the death of others, giving shape to shock, loss, anger, bafflement, love and grief. At the same time, they conjure our own end: the terrible, paradoxical dream of 'waking up' dead, the recoil from the cold grave and the burning fire. This is the message of the spirit who makes Eliphaz' bones shake and his hair stand on end, who says that all men must perish: 'they die, even without wisdom'. Yet even here they offer comfort. If ghosts rise from the grave, to die cannot be the end: non-existence is hard to conceive and even (especially) when religious faith has gone people cling to the promise of some kind of afterlife. Hence the circular tension. Ghosts console, terrify, console: we need them and shun them, summon and exorcise, with equal force.

We enjoy them too. We may not *believe* in ghosts, but we happily suspend all disbelief, fictional and logical, at the words 'It was a dark, dark night': we know that those scoffers and sneerers and sceptical narrators will soon be proved wrong. Jokes about ghosts are as old as the hills. White forms, winding sheets, rattling chains and creaking doors are the stuff of comedy as well as horror. But the jokes may also be a means of self-protection, a way of averting evil, of defusing uncontrollable anger and dread. Like bad dreams told over breakfast, ghosts in poetry, drama and fiction let us confront and shape the unmanageable. We *want* to feel afraid, to experience that delicious, vertiginous thrill – like looking down from a high cliff at a swirling sea below, while knowing that a sturdy parapet, the rules of the genre itself, will stop us falling.

My own interest in ghosts sprang initially from a fondness for the traditional British and American ghost stories of the nineteenth and twentieth centuries. I was particularly intrigued by stories written by Victorian women, who seemed, consciously or unconsciously, to be using the form to write about issues which could not be so openly expressed in more realistic genres: the fear of sexual assault (or of their own sexuality), the urge for revenge against men, or the sense of being pushed to the margins, of being out in the cold, peering through the windows of life, a feeling poignantly expressed in this book by Christina Rossetti.

I was struck by the fact that while short stories are constantly anthologised, I could find no collection which brought together ghosts from different literary forms, and from different cultures. When I set out to compile one myself I didn't quite know what I would find, but – thinking of those women writers – I wanted to see if it had always been true that storytellers and singers, poets and priests, dramatists and novelists had used confrontations with the dead to explore the world of the living. My starting point was the imagination, but it soon became clear that all the writings, even apparently neutral anthropological accounts or awestruck 'true encounters', also illuminate assumptions about religion or society: the place of ritual; the burden of history; the deep structures of justice; the enduring power of love.

The focus is on writing in English (and consequently on ghosts within European folklore and the Classical–Judaeo–Christian tradition) since that is the literature I know best, but it includes pieces from every continent, over many centuries. Some are powerful and frightening: some are silly and some are sad. Far from being corralled in a self-contained, self-parodying form, ghosts are dizzying in their contrast and range. The literature is so vast and rich that I had to make some arbitrary rules. I have let in some poltergeists and could not resist a short section on fakes, but I have tried to keep to spirits of the dead as they appear in human form. I tell myself regretfully, for instance, that vampires have a literature of their own; that hunters' stories about ghosts of animals they kill are about relationships with nature, not society; that most of the magnificent African ghosts are evil spirits, not revenants; that I must deal with human encounters not magical transformations and metamorphoses. The borderlines are fluid, though, since ghost tales merge at every turn with other imaginings of the supernatural. The very shape of the traditional ghost story, following the curve of night from the lengthening shadows and sudden chill, through 'dead of night' to cock-crow and the melting dew, is reminiscent of ancient myths about the going down and rising up of the sun, the circle of the seasons and the movement of Earth itself.

This book follows the arc from dusk to dawn, from summoning to exorcism, appearance to vanishing. Within that overall shape, the chapters highlight particular motifs. Ghosts are slippery creatures: they like to walk through walls. The topics sometimes overlap – some 'Harbingers' are also 'Kinfolk', some of the 'Unquiet Dead' are pretty vengeful, and there are great lovers in 'Deadstown' – but the sections almost selected themselves since ghosts fall so clearly into specific groups, themes and story-types. (They also tend to allot themselves to certain forms: 'Love' favours lyrics, 'Nasty Shocks' come in prose.) While there is a forward movement of time in each section, I have steered clear of strict chronological order or tight thematic grouping, partly to avoid implying that writings from widespread cultures are sequential or directly related, and partly because one of the delights of reading about ghosts is precisely the way that themes reoccur in unexpected places.

Many extracts are like a complex latticework, fusing ancient conventions with current fashions and arguments, or blending folk tale with credible psychology. All deliberately imagined spectres have purpose and meaning, unlike the random manifestations seen by ghost hunters, whose very inexplicability is somehow proof of their existence. But even here, descriptions of 'sightings' tend to follow age-old literary patterns. (Believers, of course, would argue that it's the other way round: fiction following 'fact'.) Ghosts are far from fragile: they are strong and resonant, creatures of their time, yet very, very old.

To illustrate this weaving of strands, one ghost wanders freely through this book – Hamlet's father. True to type, the King of Denmark appears at midnight and vanishes at dawn, and Shakespeare includes formulae fixed in contemporary lore such as the protective charm, 'Angels and ministers of grace defend us', or Horatio's threefold invocation to the ghost to speak and his refusal to do so except to the person he seeks. But is he a soul in Purgatory, to be pitied and helped by the living, as the Catholics of 1600 would say? Or is he a Hellish figure bent on murder and ruin, as the Protestants would claim, arguing that ghosts were popish devices to manipulate the credulous, and that apparitions must be either demonic or angelic, or illusions? Is he a classical ghost of revenge, or is he a projection of Hamlet's own melancholy, the paralysing memory of a powerful father? All these, and more.

A character from an age of faith, Hamlet accepts the existence of the ghost without doubt. Today, although that automatic acceptance has vanished many people would still sympathise with Madame du Deffand, who said she did not believe in ghosts, 'but I am afraid of them'. Once the subject is raised people talk graphically about ghosts they have seen, or friends of friends have seen. It seems inadequate to speak of illusions, born of the atmosphere of a particular place or the desire of the seer, or to suggest, as Francisco does in *The White Devil*, that they merely illustrate the power of our imaginations:

> Thought, as a subtle juggler, makes us deem
> Things supernatural, which yet have cause
> Common as sickness.

Under the heading 'Is there anybody there?', puzzled thinkers tackle the question of whether ghosts exist, and why we believe in them. What are they? Where do they come from? As a worried Dr Johnson and a cynical Byron remind us, the urge to believe is very strong. Argument becomes entangled with intuition, the *feeling* of fear precedes the reasoning. Writers suggest, or dramatise, a variety of reasons: the reluctance of the soul to leave the body, the desire to hold on to loved ones, the fear of desolate places and unknown frontiers, the lure of a romantic (and Romantic) past. The handing down of the tales through the generations itself helps to enforce belief: learned in infancy, they give shape to the child's night terrors, inhabiting the shadows on the stairs or under the bed. Later they allow us to glimpse the gaps in the real, uncovering, in Charlotte Brontë's vivid image, those places where 'knottings and catchings occur – sudden breaks leave damage in the web', and showing us in Henry James's phrase, the 'underside of the tapestry'.

Although authors from the eighteenth century onwards often begin by assuming scepticism, their solid settings or sensible narrators merely help to seduce the reader: William Golding may be right to suggest that in an age of science and materialism, people are still instinctively drawn to an older, stranger, more spiritual model of the cosmos. Even if we can't accept the supernatural we may recognise these ghosts, not as spirits of the dead but as spectres within ourselves. The horror of *The Turn of the Screw*, said Virginia Woolf, 'comes from the force with which it makes us realise the power that our minds possess for such excursions into the darkness; when certain lights sink or certain barriers are lowered, the ghosts of the mind, untracked desires, indistinct intimations, are seen to be a large company'. As Freud acknowledges, and Beckett shows, the uncanny induces an awed, horrified fascination.

*

We may not agree where apparitions come from, but come they do, like sorrows, in battalions. The section on 'Appearances' is deliberately diverse, reflecting a wide range of literary forms as well cultural and religious attitudes. The dead walk upon the earth in all shapes, sizes, languages and genres. Some drive coaches, others take trains: some sport gilt sandals, others come draped in decomposing flesh.

Many early ghosts are wandering spirits who cannot find peace unless the living help them, often debarred from rest because their bodies lie unburied, or their funeral rites unfulfilled. This is the plight of Elpenor, as Odysseus explains (in Chapman's translation):

> His body in the broad-waid earth as yet
> Unmournd, unburied by us, since we swet
> With other urgent labours.

Stories of the 'Grateful Dead' are found across the world from India to Iceland. Long after formal belief has gone they surface in odd places: in the Jesuit Noël Taillepied's attack on heresy, in the fantastical play within a play in Peele's *Old Wives' Tale*, in the Grimm brothers' story 'The Wilful Child', its explanation lost, its solution horrible.

Far back in time it seems that all the dead were thought by nature to be restless, as unquenchable as the buried, dark side of ourselves. In the Old Testament or the Odyssey, in the ancient Chinese tales or the angry ghosts of India and Japan, the dead are dangerous. They mutter beneath the ground, they require blood and sacrifices, they must be appeased. They do not like their state. They can be very nasty indeed, especially when their life or death has been violent. Even when they are not malign, they are wistful and jealous of the living: 'I would rather be a paid servant in a poor man's house and be above ground,' sighs Achilles, 'than be King of Kings among the dead.' They want to come back.

To keep them away (and stop them collecting their living friends and relatives) requires ceremonies and tricks, like those described in the extraordinary list from *The Golden Bough*. In the Middle East and Europe, some of these rituals provide the earliest ghost literature, such as the urgent Egyptian prayer for the safety of a child. It may have been to make the threat of return bearable that ghosts were pinned down to special days, like the Roman feast of the Lemurae whose rituals are described by Ovid, or much later, to the Christian Hallowe'en. On such days they are expected, even tolerated – as long as they go away again. Demons become ancestors: death can be domesticated. At the Greek festival of the Anthesteria, for example, the dear departed were affectionately invited home for a day, offered some porridge and then politely (but *extremely* clearly) told to vanish till next year. (Not unlike a British family Christmas.)

The recent dead are depicted as particularly prone to reappear. Stories and poems from all ages describe that irrational sense of nearness expressed by Emily Dickinson: 'The distance that the dead have gone / Does not at first appear'. Their presence curls so strongly about daily life that it is not surprising to find that custom, folklore and religion frequently define a set period of separation, which does not necessarily coincide with that of mourning, but is just as formal: three days, nine days, a month, a year and a day. During that time, spirits hover near, often by the grave that holds their body. Some do not want to leave and must be frightened off or fought. Some want to go and are held back:

> The twelvemonth and the day being gone
> The ghost began to greet:
> 'Your salten tears they trickle down,
> They wet my winding sheet.'

Often, however, the dead do not linger. Instead they set off on a journey, crossing the Styx or Acheron, riding across the Asian plains, sailing to Valhalla, walking barefoot across the thorns of Whinny Moor, trekking into the snows of the Arctic. (Such journeys lie submerged in later tales, particularly those of the sea and the ghost ship.) And if the living chance to meet them as they travel on their way, as the Inuit Tannaaluk does, the encounter can certainly be startling.

The pieces which describe the time of lingering or passage are often particularly touching, for these ghosts are as transient as the living. They are still strongly individual, not at all like the story-book legionaries doomed to clank about for centuries on Hadrian's Wall or the standard cowled figure in the cloister. For them, time is short and must be used. Buried treasure, or anything hidden, always brings uneasy sleep and one of my favourites among the English folk tales collected by Kathleen Briggs is of the old man who just nips back to tell his daughter 'I put it on the shelf'.

Purposeful ghosts come back to give all sorts of messages but are especially insistent if they have an uneasy conscience, or a strong sense of being wronged. As several pieces in the chapter on guilt show, in periods when belief in an afterlife is general, and your fate in that world depends on your performance in this, it is vital to come back and put wrongs right. Thus the sermons of Medieval Europe are full of ghosts, illustrating the doctrines of Purgatory, and the possibility of confession and contrition even after death. The crime might be murder, theft, arson or simply appearing wrongly dressed before St Peter. Although the mournful visitant is usually aided by the living and finds his way to heaven, this is not always the case: sometimes greed from an ill-gotten legacy is greater than the wish to save father from the flames. Gradually the Purgatorial stories of exposure, guilt, confession and reparation merge with the simpler, less doctrinal belief, roundly stated by Chaucer's Chanticleer (with sophisticated irony in the context of the tale as a whole) that 'Murder will out' and in this secular form the evidence of ghosts is even cited in trials. The Roman and Jacobean ghosts who howl for revenge are rather different, and far more dangerous, for they cry for blood rather than justice, and call on men rather than God or the Law, engendering a continuity not of justice, but of outrage.

The dead may be dangerous but they are also wise. They *are* the history of the nation, the tribe, the family; this is why they can so readily embody the lost values or violent cycles of history itself, in the writing of Yeats, say, or Geoffrey Hill. The dead can explain the past and foretell the future. Legends of returning heroes and protective spirits emphasise this aspect, blending, in Christian tradition, with visions of the Saints, in Celtic stories with tales of the fairies. New heroic ghosts may be invoked for new conditions and new battles; Johnny Appleseed for the farmers, Joe Hill for the workers, Roger Casement for the Irish cause, the jolly swagman for the wild colonial boys. At some points, too, particularly when men are in extremis the figure of the ghost merges with the numinous 'other', a mysterious, consoling companion – as in war, or in the strange experience of Shackleton in the Antarctic, which prompted T. S. Eliot's, 'Who is the third . . . ?'.

From the oldest stories of all, where women and men deliberately seek the dead in the underworld, to win their advice or use their power, a lineage of poetic guides loops down, from Homer, Virgil and Dante to Eliot, Joyce and Heaney. The epics and sagas, both rich in ghosts, are communal modes, giving imaginative shape to the history of their audience. More intimate, but also strongly linked to the sense of community, are the folk tales, like those John Aubrey remembered in his seventeenth-century childhood, handed down from mother to daughter, told around the fire on a winter's night, the warmth of the hearth defying the blackness without. Victorian magazine stories were often read aloud to the family and their modern descendants still have an aura of performance where the effect on the audience is all, its success judged by the open-mouthed suspense, the final laugh or shudder.

The 'ghost story', however, is only a small part of the legacy: from the earliest surviving writing to the present day the public forms – epic, drama, folk tale, film – have been accompanied by the most intimate and private. The great cry of the Bronze Age goddess Ishtar, battering on the gates of the underworld, is matched by the voice of an unknown

Egyptian woman, frustrated that she can no longer manage her household without her husband – 'Listen to me,' she cries. Today's film monsters may make millions scream, but a poet's 'watchful poltergeist' can still express the deepest personal loss.

These private forms cluster towards the end of the book, in the sections on kinfolk and love. Although their origins and genres are diverse, and their expression is clearly determined by their period, the chorus of voices suggests that the phrase 'common humanity' does have some meaning: the agony of a mother over her dead child two thousand years ago, for example, speaks directly to a parent today. While recognising conventional tropes, it is moving to find that the gestures of loss are so similar, as a Japanese farmer, a Trojan hero, an English Puritan, a French poet, all stretch out empty arms to a much-loved being who now eludes, and will ever elude, their embrace. Aeons of ballads about loss – of the living as well as the dead – lie behind Tennyson's lines:

> O that 'twere possible
> After long grief and pain
> To find the arms of my true love
> Round me once again!

One of the unexpected joys of compiling this anthology has been a sense of closeness to the past, of hearing the tongues of the speechless dead, of recognising, in Eliot's words, 'The eyes of a familiar compound ghost / Both intimate and unidentifiable'. Perhaps this is the power of literature itself: the old texts are the true ghosts, at once dead, yet vividly alive.

Another surprise has been noting the great flexibility of traditional ghost genres. The medieval exempla now seem comic, but the comedy springs from our modern disbelief: at the time they were accepted as grave warnings, or consoling promises of grace. Like the secular stories, they implied that familiar structures of justice or morality still held true beyond the grave. One can see Gothic writing as subversive and this is true in so far as it provides a critique of established hierarchies, but on the whole tales of ghosts, whether written or oral, tend to be reactionary, emphasising the strength and continuity of underlying social structures and ideologies.

This conservatism even runs through nineteenth-century spiritualism, with its underlying assumption of the centrality of the family – although sometimes the identification of the spirit world with this is blessedly ludicrous. The middle-class manners of the age, for example (the real cement of society), passed into the Other Realm, as well as the Aunts and Uncles, and a report of planchette-writing in 1889, quoted by

R. C. Finucane in his excellent survey, *Appearances of the Dead*, shows long-dead spirits to be perfectly aware of inviolable Victorian meal-times:

> The board moved after a short pause and one preliminary circling.
> 'David – David – David – dead 143 years.'
> The butler at this moment announced lunch, and Mr Wedgwood said to the spirit, 'Will you go on for us afterwards, as we must break off now?'
> 'I will try.'

Literary ghosts are just as cooperative, keeping their traditional elements while dressing in the language of their age. Authors can take an image like spectral restlessness and adapt it wittily, or movingly, to their time: Pope writes of vanity and dullness, Frances Harper of slavery, Judith Wright of a dead astronaut, endlessly circling the globe. Ghosts have no respect for division of 'high' and 'low' culture. In the English-speaking world alone it is fascinating to follow the evolving forms, from medieval moral tales and earthy ballads to vengeful Renaissance dramas, past the impassioned theological debates of the seventeenth century to the earnest rationalism and robust satire of the eighteenth. Almost in reaction comes a resurgence of the supernatural in Gothic and Romantic writing, and a passionate antiquarianism so that the birth of a cheap periodical press quickly fosters the peculiar mix of gloom, sentiment, piety and humour that decks the Victorian Christmas, flying in the face of loss of faith. A change of tone in 1890s 'decadence' shows the influence of Poe and Baudelaire, while an unhappy combination of Empire and anthropology bring a rash of 'savage' stories, suggestive of Conradian guilt and fear in lands which colonialists claim to 'master'. Other popular forms emerge, musical-hall spooks, flimsy Edwardian wraiths and Wellsian comedies, giving way, suddenly and shockingly, to the sad, graphic ghosts of the First World War.

Looking back, one can see great 'specialists' in ghosts at this uneasy time: Yeats, Hardy, Kipling, Henry James, Edith Wharton, Walter de la Mare, T. S. Eliot. Today ghosts are everywhere, on the page and on the screen. Some step briskly out of past centuries, like the devastating Cynthia of Propertius, resurrected with all her fire and scorn by Robert Lowell. Others are very much of our time. Guilty ghosts take on the colouring of the age: to the Mormon writer Orson Scott Card, for instance, the idea of transplants suggests a macabre, blasphemous parody of Christian belief. Gothic and folk tale acquire new sexual–political dimensions in Angela Carter, Isabel Allende or Michèle Roberts. Caribbean, Classical and British ghosts meet in Derek Walcott's *Omeros*. Cybernetics offer ghost-like immortality in William

Gibson's fiction. The congregation of the dead, so voluble in *Ulysses*, assume a blackly comic guise in Amos Tutuola's *The Palm Wine Drinkard*.

My ghost hunting has brought many incidental pleasures: discovering versions of the Orpheus and Eurydice story in North America, Japan and India; reading the great Elizabethan and Augustan translations of the classics; laughing aloud at *Don Juan*, at Dickens's 'rapper' in the railway carriage, at Thomas Hood, Thurber or Flann O'Brien; rediscovering the fine stories of Algernon Blackwood, Willa Cather or Elizabeth Bowen; being moved by the sombre, tender ghosts of modern writing. Sadly, one can only squash so many spectres into a single book (and recent wraiths come expensive). I am conscious of the hundreds left out, thumping on the gate or loitering in the lane, but this, it seems, has always been so:

> As thicke as leavs do fall in awtum frost,
> as thicke as lytle byrds in flocks do flye
> whom winters cold makes seeke a warmer coast,
> so stood the sowls that did for passage cry.
> The sullen syre admitts not evry ghost,
> but unto dyvers passage doth deny.
>
> HARINGTON'S *Aeneid*

If a favourite spirit is denied, I ask indulgence, and hope that you enjoy, as much as I have, the Ghosts that Have Got In.

Prologue

It is wonderful that five thousand years have
now elapsed since the creation of the world and
still it is undecided whether or not there has
ever been an instance of the spirit of any person
appearing after death. All argument is against it;
but all belief is for it.

SAMUEL JOHNSON

Just sit right down and begin'

The story had held us, round the fire, sufficiently breathless, but except the obvious remark that it was gruesome, as, on Christmas eve in an old house, a strange tale should essentially be, I remember no comment uttered till somebody happened to say that it was the only case he had met in which such a visitation had fallen on a child. The case, I may mention, was that of an apparition in just such an old house as had gathered us for the occasion – an appearance, of a dreadful kind, to a little boy sleeping in the room with his mother and waking her up in the terror of it; waking her not to dissipate his dread and soothe him to sleep again, but to encounter also, herself, before she had succeeded in doing so, the same sight that had shaken him. It was this observation that drew from Douglas – not immediately, but later in the evening – a reply that had the interesting consequence to which I call attention. Someone else told a story not particularly effective, which I saw he was not following. This I took for a sign that he had himself something to produce and that we should only have to wait. We waited in fact till two nights later; but that same evening, before we scattered, he brought out what was in his mind.

'I quite agree – in regard to Griffin's ghost, or whatever it was – that its appearing first to the little boy, at so tender an age, adds a particular touch. But it's not the first occurrence of its charming kind that I know to have involved a child. If the child gives the effect another turn of the screw, what do you say to *two* children – ?'

'We say, of course,' somebody exclaimed, 'that they give two turns! Also that we want to hear about them.'

I can see Douglas there before the fire, to which he had got up to present his back, looking down at his interlocutor with his hands in his pockets. 'Nobody but me, till now, has ever heard. It's quite too horrible.' This, naturally, was declared by several voices to give the thing the utmost price, and our friend, with quiet art, prepared his triumph by turning his eyes over the rest of us and going on: 'It's beyond everything. Nothing at all that I know touches it.'

'For sheer terror?' I remember asking.

He seemed to say it was not so simple as that: to be really at a loss how to qualify it. He passed his hand over his eyes, made a little wincing grimace. 'For dreadful – dreadfulness!'

'Oh, how delicious!' cried one of the women.

He took no notice of her; he looked at me, but as if, instead of me, he saw what he spoke of. 'For general uncanny ugliness and horror and pain.'

'Well then,' I said, 'just sit right down and begin.'

From *The Turn of the Screw* by Henry James, 1898

One

SUMMONINGS

At the essential landscape stare, stare
Till your eyes foist a vision dazzling on the wind:
Whatever lost ghosts flare,
Damned, howling in their shrouds across the moor
Rave on the leash of the starving mind
Which peoples the bare room, the blank, untenanted air.

SYLVIA PLATH

The Descent of Ishtar to the Underworld

To Kurnugi, land of no return,
Ishtar daughter of Sin was determined to go;
The daughter of Sin was determined to go
To the dark house, dwelling of Erkalla's god,
To the house which those who enter cannot leave,
On the road where travelling is one-way only,
To the house where those who enter are deprived of light,
Where dust is their food, clay their bread.
They see no light, they dwell in darkness,
They are clothed like birds, with feathers.
Over the door and the bolt, dust as settled.
Ishtar, when she arrived at the gate of Kurnugi,
Addressed her words to the keeper of the gate,
   'Here gatekeeper, open your gate for me,
   Open your gate for me to come in!
   If you do not open the gate for me to come in,
   I shall smash the door and shatter the bolt,
   I shall smash the doorpost and overturn the doors,
   I shall raise up the dead and they shall eat the living:
   The dead shall outnumber the living!

From 'The Descent of Ishtar to the Underworld' (Late Bronze Age),
translated from the Akkadian by Stephanie Dalley

'Listen to me!'

A Twelfth Dynasty period [c.1800–2000 BC] 'letter to the dead' on a small red pottery bowl, from the widow Dedi to her husband, the priest Antef:

As for this servant-girl Imiu who is sick: you're not fighting for her, night and day, against every man who's harming her and against every woman. Why do you want ruin at your own front door? Take up the fight again today so her household may be safe, and a libation of water be poured out for you. If you don't help, your house will be destroyed. Is it just that you're not recognizing your own household's servant girl? Fight for her! Watch over her! Save her from those doing her harm! Then your house and your children will be safe. Listen to me!

From *Egyptian Letters to the Dead*, by Sir Alan H. Gardiner and Kurt Sethe, 1928

The Witch of Endor

Now Samuel was dead, and all Israel had lamented him, and buried him in Ramah, even in his own city. And Saul had put away those that had familiar spirits, and the wizards, out of the land.

And the Philistines gathered themselves together, and came and pitched in Shunem: and Saul gathered all Israel together, and they pitched in Gilboa.

And when Saul saw the host of the Philistines, he was afraid, and his heart greatly trembled.

And when Saul enquired of the LORD, the LORD answered him not, neither by dreams, nor by Urim, nor by prophets.

Then said Saul unto his servants, Seek me a woman that hath a familiar spirit, that I may go to her, and enquire of her. And his servants said to him, Behold, *there is* a woman that hath a familiar spirit at Endor.

And Saul disguised himself, and put on other raiment, and he went, and two men with him, and they came to the woman by night: and he said, I pray thee, divine unto me by the familiar spirit, and bring me *him* up, whom I shall name unto thee.

And the woman said unto him, Behold, thou knowest what Saul hath done, how he hath cut off those that have familiar spirits, and the wizards, out of the land: wherefore then layest thou a snare for my life, to cause me to die?

And Saul sware to her by the LORD, saying, *As* the LORD liveth, there shall no punishment happen to thee for this thing.

Then said the woman, Whom shall I bring up unto thee? And he said, Bring me up Samuel.

And when the woman saw Samuel, she cried with a loud voice: and the woman spake to Saul, saying, Why hast thou deceived me? for thou *art* Saul.

And the king said unto her, Be not afraid: for what sawest thou? And the woman said unto Saul, I saw gods ascending out of the earth.

And he said unto her, What form *is* he of? And she said, An old man cometh up; and he *is* covered with a mantle. And Saul perceived that it *was* Samuel, and he stooped with *his* face to the ground, and bowed himself.

And Samuel said to Saul, Why hast thou disquieted me, to bring me up? And Saul answered, I am sore distressed; for the Philistines make war against me, and God is departed from me, and answereth me no more, neither by prophets, nor by dreams: therefore I have called thee, that thou mayest make known unto me what I shall do.

Then said Samuel, Wherefore then dost thou ask of me, seeing the LORD is departed from thee, and is become thine enemy?

And the LORD hath done to him, as he spake by me: for the LORD hath rent the kingdom out of thine hand, and given it to thy neighbour, *even* to David:

Because thou obeyedst not the voice of the LORD, nor executedst his fierce wrath upon Amalek, therefore hath the LORD done this thing unto thee this day.

Moreover the LORD will also deliver Israel with thee into the hand of the Philistines: and to morrow *shalt* thou and thy sons *be* with me: the LORD also shall deliver the host of Israel into the hand of the Philistines.

Then Saul fell straightway all along on the earth, and was sore afraid, because of the words of Samuel; and there was no strength in him; for he had eaten no bread all the day, nor all the night.

And the woman came unto Saul, and saw that he was sore troubled, and said unto him, Behold, thine handmaid hath obeyed thy voice, and I have put my life in my hand, and have hearkened unto thy words which thou spakest unto me.

Now therefore, I pray thee, hearken thou also unto the voice of thine handmaid, and let me set a morsel of bread before thee; and eat, that thou mayest have strength, when thou goest on thy way.

But he refused, and said, I will not eat. But his servants, together with the woman, compelled him; and he hearkened unto their voice. So he arose from the earth, and sat upon the bed.

And the woman had a fat calf in the house; and she hasted, and killed it, and took flour, and kneaded *it*, and did bake unleavened bread thereof:

And she brought *it* before Saul, and before his servants; and they did eat. Then they rose up, and went away that night.

From I *Samuel* XXVII

Odysseus calls Tiresias

Here drew we up our ship, our sheepe with-drew,
And walkt the shore till we attaind the view
Of that sad region Circe had foreshow'd;
And then the sacred offerings, to be vow'd,
Eurylochus and Perimedes bore.
When I my sword drew, and earth's wombe did gore
Till I a pit digg'd of a cubite round,
Which with the liquid sacrifice we crown'd –
First, honey mixt with wine, then sweete wine neate,

Then water powr'd in, last the flowre of wheate.
Much I impurtun'd then the weake-neckt dead,
And vowd, when I the barren soile should tread
Of cliffie Ithaca, amidst my hall
To kill a Heifer, my cleare best of all,
And give in offering on a Pile composd
Of all the choise goods my whole house enclosd –
And to Tiresias himselfe alone
A sheepe cole-blacke and the selectest one
Of all my flockes. When to the powres beneath,
The sacred nation that survive with Death,
My prayrs and vowes had done devotions fit,
I tooke the offrings, and upon the pit
Bereft their lives. Out gusht the sable blood,
And round about me fled out of the flood
The Soules of the deceast. There cluster'd then
Youths, and their wives, much suffering aged men,
Soft tender virgins that but new came there
By timelesse death, and greene their sorrowes were.
There men at Armes, with armors all embrew'd,
Wounded with lances and with faulchions hew'd,
In numbers up and downe the ditch did stalke,
And threw unmeasur'd cries about their walke,
So horrid that a bloodlesse feare surprisde
My daunted spirits. Straight then I advisde
My friends to flay the slaughter'd sacrifice,
Put them in fire, and to the Deities,
Sterne Pluto and Persephone, apply
Excitefull prayrs. Then I drew I from my Thy
My well-edg'd sword, stept in, and firmely stood
Betwixt the prease of shadowes and the blood,
And would not suffer any one to dip
Within our offring his unsolide lip
Before Tiresias, that did all controule.

From *Homer's Odysses*, ninth century BC,
translated from the Greek by George Chapman, 1614–15

Lucian's liars

'Immediately after Glaucias' father died and he acquired the property, he fell in love with Chrysis, the wife of Demeas. I was in his employ as his tutor in philosophy, and if that love-affair had not kept him too busy, he would have known all the teachings of the Peripatetic school, for even at eighteen he was solving fallacies and had completed the course of lectures on natural philosophy. At his wit's end, however, with his love-affair, he told me the whole story; and as was natural, since I was his tutor, I brought him that Hyperborean magician at a fee of four minas down (it was necessary to pay something in advance towards the cost of the victims) and sixteen if he should obtain Chrysis. The man waited for the moon to wax, as it is then, for the most part, that such rites are performed; and after digging a pit in an open court of the house, at about midnight, he first summoned up for us Alexicles, Glaucias' father, who had died seven months before. The old gentleman was indignant over the love-affair and flew into a passion, but at length he permitted him to go on with it after all. Next he brought up Hecate, who fetched Cerberus with her, and he drew down the moon, a many-shaped spectacle, appearing differently at different times; for at first she exhibited the form of a woman, then she turned into a handsome bull, and then she looked like a puppy. Finally, the Hyperborean made a little Cupid out of clay and said: "Go and fetch Chrysis." The clay took wing, and before long Chrysis stood on the threshold knocking at the door, came in and embraced Glaucias as if she loved him furiously, and remained with him until we heard the cocks crowing. Then the moon flew up to the sky, Hecate plunged beneath the earth, the other phantasms disappeared, and we sent Chrysis home at just about dawn. If you had seen that, Tychiades, you would no longer have doubted that there is much good in spells.'

'Quite so,' said I, 'I should have believed if I had seen it, but as things are I may perhaps be pardoned if I am not able to see as clearly as you. However, I know the Chrysis whom you speak of, an amorous dame and an accessible one, and I do not see why you needed the clay messenger and the Hyperborean magician and the moon in person to fetch her, when for twenty drachmas she could have been brought to the Hyperboreans! The woman is very susceptible to that spell, and her case is the opposite to that of ghosts; if they hear a chink of bronze or iron, they take flight, so you say, but as for her, if silver chinks anywhere, she goes toward the sound. Besides, I am surprised at the magician himself, if he was able to have the love of the richest women and get whole talents from them, and yet made Glaucias fascinating, penny-wise that he is, for four minas.'

From the *Philopseudes* of Lucian, second century AD, translated from the Greek by A. H. Harman

Tsunemasa

GYŌKEI: I am Gyōkei, priest of the imperial temple Ninnaji. You must know that there was a certain prince of the House of Taira named Tsunemasa, Lord of Tajima, who since his boyhood has enjoyed beyond all precedent the favour of our master the Emperor. But now he has been killed at the Battle of the Western Seas.

It was to this Tsunemasa in his lifetime that the Emperor had given the lute called Green Hill. And now my master bids me take it and dedicate it to Buddha, performing a liturgy of flutes and strings for the salvation of Tsunemasa's soul. And that was my purpose in gathering these musicians together.

Truly it is said that strangers who shelter under the same tree or draw water from the same pool will be friends in another life. How much the more must intercourse of many years, kindness and favour so deep . . .

> Surely they will be heard,
> The prayers that all night long
> With due performances of rites
> I have reverently repeated in this Palace
> For the salvation of Tsunemasa
> And for the awakening of his soul.

CHORUS: And, more than all, we dedicate
> The lute Green Hill for this man;
> The pipe and flute are joined to sounds of prayer.
> For night and day the Gate of Law
> Stands open and the Universal Road
> Rejects no wayfarer.

TSUNEMASA (*speaking off the stage*): 'The wind blowing through withered trees: rain from a cloudless sky.
> The moon shining on level sands: frost on a summer's night.'
> Frost lying . . . but I, because I could not lie at rest,
> Am coming back to the World for a while,
> Like a shadow that steals over the grass.
> I am like dews that in the morning
> Still cling to the grasses. Oh pitiful the longing
> That has beset me!

GYŌKEI: How strange! Within the flame of our candle that is burning low because the night is far spent, suddenly I seemed to see a man's shadow dimly appearing. Who can be here?

TSUNEMASA *(his shadow disappearing)*: I am the ghost of Tsunemasa. The sound of your prayers has brought me in visible shape before you.

GYŌKEI: 'I am the ghost of Tsunemasa,' he said, but when I looked to where the voice had sounded nothing was there, neither substance nor shadow!

TSUNEMASA: Only a voice,

GYŌKEI: A dim voice whispers where the shadow of a man
    Visibly lay, but when I looked

TSUNEMASA: It had vanished –

GYŌKEI: This flickering form ...

TSUNEMASA: Like haze over the fields.

CHORUS: Only as a tricking magic,
    A bodiless vision,
    Can he hover in the world of his lifetime,
    Swift-changing Tsunemasa.
    By this name we call him, yet of the body
    That men named so, what is left but longing?
    What but the longing to look again, through the wall of death,
    On one he loved?
    'Sooner shall the waters in its garden cease to flow
    Than I grow weary of living in the Palace of my Lord.'
    Like a dream he has come,
    Like a morning dream.

From *Tsunemasa*, Nôh play, by Seami, mid-fourteenth century,
translated from the Japanese by Arthur Waley

An experiment of the dead

First fast and praie three daies, and absteine thee from all filthinesse; go to one that is new buried, such a one as killed himselfe or destroied himselfe wilfullie: or else get thee promise of one that shalbe hanged, and let him sweare an oth to thee, after his bodie is dead, that his spirit shall come to thee, and doo thee true service, at thy commandements, in all daies, houres, and minuts ...

The maister standing at the head of the grave, his fellow having in his hands the candle and the stone, must begin the conjuration as followeth, and the spirit will appeare to you in the christall stone, in a faire forme of a child of twelve yeares of age. And when he is in, feele

the stone, and it will be hot; and feare nothing, for he or shee will shew
manie delusions, to drive you from your worke. Feare God, but feare
him not. This is to constraine him, as followeth.

I conjure thee spirit *N.* by the living God, the true God, and by the
holie God, and by their vertues and powers which have created both
thee and me, and all the world. I conjure thee *N.* by these holie names
of God, *Tetragrammaton* ✤ *Adonay* ✤ *Algramay* ✤ *Saday* ✤ *Saboath* ✤
Planaboth ✤ *Panthon* ✤ *Craton* ✤ *Neupmaton* ✤ *Deus* ✤ *Homo* ✤ *Omnipo-*
tens ✤ *Sempiturnus* ✤ *Ysus* ✤ *Terra* ✤ *Unigenitus* ✤ *Salvator* ✤ *Via* ✤ *Vita*
✤ *Manus* ✤ *Fons* ✤ *Origo* ✤ *Filius* ✤

I conjure thee *N.* by the vertues and powers of all the riall names and
words of the living God of me pronounced, that thou be obedient unto
me and to my words rehearsed. If thou refuse this to doo, I by the holie
trinitie, and their vertues and powers doo condemne thee thou spirit *N.*
into the place where there is no hope of remedie or rest, but everlasting
horror and paine there dwelling, and a place where is paine upon paine,
dailie, horriblie, and tementablie, thy paine to be there augmented as
the starres in the heaven, and as the gravell or sand in the sea.

From *The Discoverie of Witchcraft* by Reginald Scot, 1584

'To fashion my revenge'

To fashion my revenge more seriously,
Let me remember my dead sister's face:
Call for her picture? no, I'll close mine eyes,
And in a melancholic thought I'll frame

(*Enter* ISABELLA's *ghost.*)
Her figure 'fore me. Now I ha 't: – how strong
Imagination words! how she can frame
Things which are not! Methinks she stands afore me,
And by the quick idea of my mind,
Were my skill pregnant, I could draw her picture.
Thought, as a subtle juggler, makes us deem
Things supernatural, which yet have cause
Common as sickness. 'Tis my melancholy. –

How cam'st thou by thy death? – How idle am I
To question mine own idleness! – Did ever
Man dream awake till now? – Remove this object;
Out of my brain with 't! What have I to do
With tombs, or death-beds, funerals, or tears,

That have to meditate upon revenge?

(Exit Ghost.)
So, now 'tis ended, like an old wives' story:

From *The White Devil* by John Webster, *c.*1608

Glubbdubdrib

Glubbdubdrib, as nearly as I can interpret the word, signifies the Island of *Sorcerers* or *Magicians*. It is about one third as large as the Isle of Wight, and extremely fruitful: it is governed by the head of a certain tribe, who are all magicians.

The Governor and his family are served and attended by domestics of a kind somewhat unusual. By his skill in necromancy, he hath power of calling whom he pleaseth from the dead, and commanding their service for twenty-four hours, but no longer; nor can he call the same persons up again in less than three months, except upon very extraordinary occasions.

We continued in the island for ten days, most part of every day with the Governor, and at night in our lodging. I soon grew so familiarized to the sight of spirits, that after the third or fourth time they gave me no emotion at all; or if I had any apprehensions left, my curiosity prevailed over them. For his Highness the Governor ordered me to call up whatever persons I would choose to name, and in whatever numbers among all the dead from the beginning of the world to the present time, and command them to answer any questions I should think fit to ask; with this condition, that my questions must be confined within the compass of the times they lived in. And one thing I might depend upon, that they would certainly tell me truth, for lying was a talent of no use in the lower world.

I made my humble acknowledgements to his Highness for so great a favour. We were in a chamber, from whence there was a fair prospect into the park. And because my first inclination was to be entertained with scenes of pomp and magnificence, I desired to see Alexander the Great, at the head of his army just after the battle of Arbela, which upon a motion of the Governor's finger immediately appeared in a large field under the window, where we stood. Alexander was called up into the room: it was with great difficulty that I understood his Greek, and had but little of my own. He assured me upon his honour that he was not poisoned, but died of a fever by excessive drinking.

I saw Cæsar and Pompey at the head of their troops, just ready to engage. I saw the former in his last great triumph. I desired that the Senate of Rome might appear before me in one large chamber, and a modern representative, in counterview, in another. The first seemed to be an assembly of heroes and demigods; the other a knot of pedlars, pickpockets, highwaymen and bullies.

It would be tedious to trouble the reader with relating what vast numbers of illustrious persons were called up, to gratify that insatiable desire I had to see the world in every period of antiquity placed before me. I chiefly fed mine eyes with beholding the destroyers of tyrants and usurpers, and the restorers of liberty to oppressed and injured nations. But it is impossible to express the satisfaction I received in my own mind, after such a manner as to make it a suitable entertainment to the reader.

From *Travels into Several Remote Nations of the World . . .*
By Captain Lemuel Gulliver by Jonathan Swift, 1726

A lesson in belief

As Will Gordon, the tinkler, was sitting with his family in his original but wretched cottage, called Thief's Hole, one winter night, the dialogue chanced to turn on the subject of apparitions, when his son-in-law, Hob, remarked, that he wondered how any reasonable being could be so absurd as to entertain a dread of apparitions.

'Aye, aye, lad,' says old Will, 'Nae doubt ye're a verra bauld chiel, but ma courage has been rather longer tried than yours, an' it was never doubtit yet. For a' that, I hae heard the goodwife there tell a story that frightit me sae ill I hardly kend what I was doing. Aye, whether I was fa'ing off the stool, or sitting still on 't, or sinkin down through the grund or rising up i' the air.'

'Sic nonsense! sickan absurdity!' exclaimed Hobby, 'I wa like to hae a touch o' thae kind o' feelings for aince in my life. Ane might be feared for a human creature that has power to hurt ane, but why ony man should be afraid of a shadow, a mere vision of a human creature, I never can comprehend. If my wife, there, war to hae the luck to dee, an' her ghaist to appear to me, I wa be nae mair feared for it than I'm for that shadow o' hers on the wa'.'

'O but ye ken there's nae body has ha'f the currage that ye hae. Ye wadna be feared, aw daursay, an' the deil an' aw his awgents war gaun to come in. Goodwife, tell us the story o' the Barber o' Duncow.'

'Ohon an' it's een lang sin I tried to tell that tale, Willie,' said old

[13]

Raighel, with a grin and a snivel, 'but sin ye desyre me, I'll e'en try't. It has only ae ill clag till't that story, an' it's this: when any body hears it, an disna believe it, the murdered woman is sure to come in.'

'What d'ye say?' cried Hob, in manifest alarm, 'plague on the auld randy, gie us nae sickan story as that, for I assure you I winna believe it.'

'Aye, but it will make nae odds to you, though the ghaist *war* to come in, ye ken,' said old Will, with a malicious grin.

'This is the hale story of the barber; but the most curious part is, that if the tale be accurately tould, and one of the hearers or more should doubt of its verity, the ghost o' poor Grizel to this day comes in in the same guise, and gives its testimony. An' mair by token, I hae a test to try you a' wi'.' She took a lammer bead out o' her pocket, and held it to her own ear, then to the baby's on her knee – the lurcher began to bristle and look frightened, uttering short, smothered barks, the pup followed the example – 'Hush! what's that at the door?' –

From 'The Barber of Duncow' by James Hogg, 1831

'You who dare'

Owls or spectres, thick they flee;
Nightmare upon horror broods;
Hooded laughter, monkish glee,
    Gaps the vital air.
Enter these enchanted woods
    You who dare.

You must love the light so well
That no darkness will seem fell.
Love it so you could accost
Fellowly a livid ghost.
Whish! the phantom wisps away,
Owns him smoke to cocks of day.

From 'The Woods of Westermain' by George Meredith, 1883

Cathy

'How did she die?' he resumed, at last – fain, notwithstanding his hardihood, to have a support behind him, for, after the struggle, he trembled, in spite of himself, to his very finger-ends.

'Poor wretch!' I thought; 'you have a heart and nerves the same as your brother men! Why should you be anxious to conceal them? your pride cannot blind God! You tempt him to wring them, till he forces a cry of humiliation!'

'Quietly as a lamb!' I answered, aloud. 'She drew a sigh, and stretched herself, like a child reviving, and sinking again to sleep; and five minutes after I felt one little pulse at her heart, and nothing more!'

'And – did she ever mention me?' he asked, hesitatingly, as if he dreaded the answer to his question would introduce details that he could not bear to hear.

'Her senses never returned – she recognised nobody from the time you left her,' I said. 'She lies with a sweet smile on her face; and her latest ideas wandered back to pleasant early days. Her life closed in a gentle dream – may she wake as kindly in the other world!'

'May she wake in torment!' he cried, with frightful vehemence, stamping his foot, and groaning in a sudden paroxysm of ungovernable passion. 'Why, she's a liar to the end! Where is she? Not *there* – not in heaven – not perished – where? Oh! you said you cared nothing for my sufferings! And I pray one prayer – I repeat it till my tongue stiffens – Catherine Earnshaw, may you not rest, as long as I am living! You said I killed you – haunt me then! The murdered *do* haunt their murderers. I believe – I know that ghosts *have* wandered on earth. Be with me always – take any form – drive me mad! only *do* not leave me in this abyss, where I cannot find you! Oh God! it is unutterable! I *cannot* live without my life! I *cannot* live without my soul!'

He dashed his head against the knotted trunk; and, lifting up his eyes, howled, not like a man, but like a savage beast getting goaded to death with knives and spears.

From *Wuthering Heights* by Emily Brontë, 1847

'How pure at heart'

How pure at heart and sound in head,
    With what divine affections bold
    Should be the man whose thought would hold
An hour's communion with the dead.

In vain shalt thou, or any, call
    The spirits from their golden day,
    Except, like them, thou too canst say,
My spirit is at peace with all.

[15]

They haunt the silence of the breast,
   Imagination calm and fair,
   The memory like a cloudless air,
The conscience as a sea at rest:

But when the heart is full of din,
   And doubt beside the portal waits,
   They can but listen at the gates,
And hear the household jar within.

From *In Memoriam* by Alfred Lord Tennyson, 1850

The fellow-traveller

That opposite man had had, through the night – as that opposite man always has – several legs too many, and all of them too long. In addition to this unreasonable conduct (which was only to be expected of him), he had had a pencil and a pocket-book, and had been perpetually listening and taking notes. . . .

At first I was alarmed, for an Express lunatic and no communication with the guard, is a serious position. The thought came to my relief that the gentleman might be what is popularly called a Rapper: one of a sect for (some of) whom I have the highest respect, but whom I don't believe in. I was going to ask him the question, when he took the bread out of my mouth.

'You will excuse me,' said the gentleman contemptuously, 'if I am too much in advance of common humanity to trouble myself at all about it. I have passed the night – as indeed I pass the whole of my time now – in spiritual intercourse.'

'O!' said I, something snappishly.

'The conferences of the night began,' continued the gentleman, turning several leaves of his note-book, 'with this message: "Evil communications corrupt good manners."'

'Sound,' said I; 'but, absolutely new?'

'New from spirits,' returned the gentleman.

I could only repeat my rather snappish 'O!' and ask if I might be favoured with the last communication.

'"A bird in the hand,"' said the gentleman, reading his last entry with great solemnity, '"is worth two in the Bosh."'

'Truly I am of the same opinion,' said I; 'but shouldn't it be Bush?'

'It came to me, Bosh,' returned the gentleman.

The gentleman then informed me that the spirit of Socrates had delivered this special revelation in the course of the night. 'My friend, I hope you are pretty well. There are two in this railway carriage. How do you do? There are seventeen thousand four hundred and seventy-nine spirits here, but you cannot see them. Pythagoras is here. He is not at liberty to mention it, but hopes you like travelling.' Galileo likewise had dropped in, with this scientific intelligence. 'I am glad to see you, *amico. Come sta?* Water will freeze when it is cold enough. *Addio!*' In the course of the night, also, the following phenomena had occurred. Bishop Butler had insisted on spelling his name, 'Bubler,' for which offence against orthography and good manners he had been dismissed as out of temper. John Milton (suspected of wilful mystification) had repudiated the authorship of Paradise Lost, and had introduced, as joint authors of that poem, two Unknown gentlemen, respectively named Grungers and Scadgingtone. And Prince Arthur, nephew of King John of England, had described himself as tolerably comfortable in the seventh circle, where he was learning to paint on velvet, under the direction of Mrs Trimmer and Mary Queen of Scots.

From 'The Haunted House' by Charles Dickens, 1859

Mesmerism

All I believed is true!
  I am able yet
  All I want, to get
By a method as strange as new:
Dare I trust the same to you?

If at night, when doors are shut,
  And the wood-worm picks,
  And the death-watch ticks,
And the bar has a flag of smut,
And a cat's in the water-butt –

And the socket floats and flares,
  And the house-beams groan,
  And a foot unknown
Is surmised on the garret-stairs,
And the locks slip unawares –

And the spider, to serve his ends,
  By a sudden thread,
  Arms and legs outspread,
On the table's midst descends,
Comes to find, God knows what friends! –

If since eve drew in, I say,
  I have sat and brought
  (So to speak) my thought
To bear on the woman away,
Till I felt my hair turn grey –

I, still with a gesture fit
  Of my hands that best
  Do my soul's behest,
Pointing the power from it,
While myself do steadfast sit –

Steadfast and still the same
  On my object bent,
  While the hands give vent
To my ardour and my aim
And break into very flame –

Then I reach, I must believe,
  Not her soul in vain,
  For to me again
It reaches, and past retrieve
Is wound in the toils I weave;

And must follow as I require,
  As befits a thrall,
  Bringing flesh and all,
Essence and earth-attire,
To the source of the tractile fire:

Till the house called hers, not mine,
  With a growing weight
  Seems to suffocate
If she break not its leaden line
And escape from its close confine . . .

'Now – now' – the door is heard!
  Hark, the stairs! and near –
  Nearer – and here –
'Now!' and at call the third
She enters without a word.

On doth she march and on
  To the fancied shape;

It is, past escape,
      Herself, now: the dream is done
      And the shadow and she are one.

First I will pray. Do Thou
      That ownest the soul,
      Yet wilt grant control
To another, nor disallow
For a time, restrain me now!

I admonish me while I may,
      Not to squander guilt,
      Since require Thou wilt
At my hand its price one day!
What the price is, who can say?

From 'Mesmerism' by Robert Browning, 1855

'Oh, Whistle, and I'll come to you, My Lad'

As he went along the passages he met the boots of the Globe, who stopped and said:

'Beg your pardon, sir, but as I was a-brushing your coat just now there was somethink fell out of the pocket. I put in on your chest of drawers, sir, in your room, sir – a piece of a pipe or somethink of that, sir. Thank you, sir. You'll find it on your chest of drawers, sir – yes, sir. Good night, sir.'

The speech served to remind Parkins of his little discovery of that afternoon. It was with some considerable curiosity that he turned it over by the light of his candles. It was of bronze, he now saw, and was shaped very much after the manner of the modern dog-whistle; in fact it was – yes, certainly it was – actually no more nor less than a whistle. He put it to his lips, but it was quite full of a fine, caked-up sand or earth, which would not yield to knocking, but must be loosened with a knife. Tidy as ever in his habits, Parkins cleared out the earth on to a piece of paper, and took the latter to the window to empty it out. The night was clear and bright, as he saw when he had opened the casement, and he stopped for an instant to look at the sea and note a belated wanderer stationed on the shore in front of the inn. Then he shut the window, a little surprised at the late hours people kept at Burnstow, and took his whistle to the light again. Why, surely there were marks on it, and not merely marks, but letters! A very little rubbing rendered the deeply-cut inscription quite legible, but the Professor had to confess, after some earnest thought, that the meaning of it was as obscure to him as the writing on the wall to Belshazzar. There were legends both on the front and on the back of the whistle. The one read thus:

FLA

FUR   BIS

FLE

The other:

Ψ QUIS EST ISTE QUI UENIT Ψ

'I ought to be able to make it out,' he thought; 'but I suppose I am a little rusty in my Latin. When I come to think of it, I don't believe I even know the word for a whistle. The long one does seem simple enough. It ought to mean, "Who is this who is coming?" Well, the best way to find out is evidently to whistle for him.'

He blew tentatively and stopped suddenly, startled and yet pleased at the note he had elicited. It had a quality of infinite distance in it, and, soft as it was, he somehow felt it must be audible for miles round. It was a sound, too, that seemed to have the power (which many scents possess) of forming pictures in the brain. He saw quite clearly for a moment a vision of a wide, dark expanse at night, with a fresh wind blowing, and in the midst a lonely figure – how employed, he could not tell. Perhaps he would have seen more had not the picture been broken by the sudden surge of a gust of wind against his casement, so sudden that it made him look up, just in time to see the white glint of a sea-bird's wing somewhere outside the dark panes.

The sound of the whistle had so fascinated him that he could not help trying it once more, this time more boldly. The note was little, if at all, louder than before, and repetition broke the illusion – no picture followed, as he had half hoped it might. 'But what is this? Goodness! what force the wind can get up in a few minutes! What a tremendous gust! There! I knew that window-fastening was no use! Ah! I thought so – both candles out. It's enough to tear the room to pieces.'

The first thing was to get the window shut. While you might count twenty Parkins was struggling with the small casement, and felt almost as if he were pushing back a sturdy burglar, so strong was the pressure. It slackened all at once, and the window banged to and latched itself. Now to relight the candles and see what damage, if any, had been done. No, nothing seemed amiss; no glass even was broken in the casement. But the noise had evidently roused at least one member of the household: the Colonel was to be heard stumping in his stockinged feet on the floor above, and growling.

Quickly as it had risen, the wind did not fall at once. On it went, moaning and rushing past the house, at times rising to a cry so desolate that, as Parkins disinterestedly said, it might have made fanciful people feel quite uncomfortable; even the unimaginative, he thought after a quarter of an hour, might be happier without it.

Whether it was the wind, or the excitement of golf, or of the researches in the preceptory that kept Parkins awake, he was not sure. Awake he remained, in any case, long enough to fancy (as I am afraid I often do myself under such conditions) that he was the victim of all manner of fatal disorders: he would lie counting the beats of his heart, convinced that it was going to stop work every moment, and would entertain grave suspicions of his lungs, brain, liver, etc. – suspicions which he was sure would be dispelled by the return of daylight, but which until then refused to be put aside. He found a little vicarious comfort in the idea that someone else was in the same boat. A near neighbour (in the darkness it was not easy to tell his direction) was tossing and rustling in his bed, too.

The next stage was that Parkins shut his eyes and determined to give sleep every chance. Here again over-excitement asserted itself in another form – that of making pictures. *Experto crede*, pictures do come to the closed eyes of one trying to sleep, and are often so little to his taste that he must open his eyes and disperse them.

Parkins's experience on this occasion was a very distressing one. He found that the picture which presented itself to him was continuous. When he opened his eyes, of course, it went; but when he shut them once more it framed itself afresh, and acted itself out again, neither quicker nor slower than before. What he saw was this:

A long stretch of shore – shingle edged by sand, and intersected at short intervals with black groynes running down to the water – a scene, in fact, so like that of his afternoon's walk that, in the absence of any landmark, it could not be distinguished therefrom. The light was obscure, conveying an impression of gathering storm, late winter evening, and slight cold rain. On this bleak stage at first no actor was visible. Then, in the distance, a bobbing black object appeared; a moment more, and it was a man running, jumping, clambering over the groynes, and every few seconds looking eagerly back. The nearer he came the more obvious it was that he was not only anxious, but even terribly frightened, though his face was not to be distinguished. He was, moreover, almost at the end of his strength. On he came; each successive obstacle seemed to cause him more difficulty than the last. 'Will he get over this next one?' thought Parkins; 'it seems a little higher than the others.' Yes; half climbing, half throwing himself, he did get over, and fell all in a heap on the other side (the side nearest to the spectator). There, as if really unable to get up again, he remained crouching under the groyne, looking up in an attitude of painful anxiety.

So far no cause whatever for the fear of the runner had been shown; but now there began to be seen, far up the shore, a little flicker of something light-coloured moving to and fro with great swiftness and irregularity. Rapidly growing larger, it, too, declared itself as a figure in pale, fluttering draperies, ill-defined. There was something about its motion which made Parkins very unwilling to see it at close quarters. It would stop, raise arms, bow itself toward the sand, then run stooping across the beach to the water-edge and back again; and then, rising upright, once more continue its course forward at a speed that was startling and terrifying. The moment came when the pursuer was hovering about from left to right only a few yards beyond the groyne where the runner lay in hiding. After two or three ineffectual castings hither and thither it came to a stop, stood upright, with arms raised high, and then darted straight forward towards the groyne. . . .

From 'Oh, Whistle, and I'll Come to You, My Lad' by M. R. James, 1904

All Souls' Night

Midnight has come, and the great Christ Church Bell
And many a lesser bell sound through the room;
And it is All Souls' Night,
And two long glasses brimmed with muscatel
Bubble upon the table. A ghost may come;
For it is a ghost's right,
His element is so fine
Being sharpened by his death,
To drink from the wine-breath
While our gross palates drink from the whole wine.

*

But names are nothing. What matters who it be,
So that his elements have grown so fine
The fume of muscatel
Can give his sharpened palate ecstasy.
No living man can drink from the whole wine.
I have mummy truths to tell
Whereat the living mock,
Though not for sober ear,
For maybe all that hear
Should laugh and weep an hour upon the clock.

Such thought – such thought have I that hold it tight
Till meditation master all its parts,
Nothing can stay my glance
Until that glance run in the world's despite

To where the damned have howled away their hearts,
And where the blessed dance;
Such thought, that in it bound
I need no other thing,
Wound in mind's wandering
As mummies in the mummy-cloth are wound.

W. B. Yeats, 1920

To Call up the Shades

One candle is enough. Its gentle light
will be more suitable, will be more gracious
when the Shades come, the Shades of Love.

One candle is enough. Tonight the room
should not have too much light. In deep reverie,
all receptiveness, and with the gentle light –
in this deep reverie I'll form visions
to call up the Shades, the Shades of Love.

C. P. Cavafy, 1920

'Always'

MADAME ARCATI: Now there are one or two things that I should like to explain, so will you all listen attentively.

RUTH: Of course.

MADAME ARCATI: Presently, when the music begins, I am going to switch out the lights. I may then either walk about the room for a little or lie down flat – in due course I shall draw up this dear little stool and join you at the table – I shall place myself between you and your wife, Mr Condomine, and rest my hands lightly upon yours – I must ask you not to address me or move or do anything in the least distracting – is that quite, quite clear?

CHARLES: Perfectly.

MADAME ARCATI: Of course, I cannot guarantee that anything will happen at all – Daphne may be unavailable – she had a head cold very recently, and was rather under the weather, poor child. On the other hand, a great many things might occur – one of you might

[23]

have an emanation, for instance, or we might contact a poltergeist which would be extremely destructive and noisy. . . .

RUTH (*anxiously*): In what way destructive?

MADAME ARCATI: They throw things, you know.

RUTH: I didn't know.

MADAME ARCATI: But we must cross that bridge when we come to it, mustn't we?

CHARLES: Certainly – by all means.

MADAME ARCATI: Fortunately an Elemental at this time of the year is most unlikely. . . .

RUTH: What do Elementals do?

MADAME ARCATI: Oh, my dear, one can never tell – they're dreadfully unpredictable . . . usually they take the form of a very cold wind. . . .

MRS BRADMAN: I don't think I shall like that –

MADAME ARCATI: Occasionally reaching almost hurricane velocity –

RUTH: You don't think it would be a good idea to take the more breakable ornaments off the mantelpiece before we start?

MADAME ARCATI (*indulgently*): That really is not necessary, Mrs Condomine – I assure you I have my own methods of dealing with Elementals.

RUTH: I'm so glad.

MADAME ARCATI: Now then – are you ready to empty your minds?

DR BRADMAN: Do you mean we're to try to think of nothing?

MADAME ARCATI: Absolutely nothing, Dr Bradman. Concentrate on a space or a nondescript colour, that's really the best way. . . .

DR BRADMAN: I'll do my damndest.

MADAME ARCATI: Good work! I will now start the music.

(*She goes to the gramophone, puts on the record of* 'Always', *and begins to walk about the room; occasionally she moves into an abortive little dance step, and once, on passing a mirror on the mantelpiece, she surveys herself critically for a moment and adjusts her hair. Then with sudden speed, she runs across the room and switches off the lights.*)

MRS BRADMAN: Oh, dear!

MADAME ARCATI: Quiet – please. . . .

(*Presently in the gloom* MADAME ARCATI, *after wandering about a little, draws up a stool and sits at the table between* CHARLES *and* RUTH. *The gramophone record comes to an end. There is dead silence.*)

Is there anyone there? . . . (*A long pause.*) . . . Is there anyone there? . . . (*Another longer pause.*) . . . One rap for yes – two raps for no – now then – Is there anyone there? . . .

(*After a shorter pause, the table gives a little bump.*)

MRS BRADMAN (*involuntarily*): Oh!

MADAME ARCATI: Sshh! . . . Is that you, Daphne? (*The table gives a louder bump.*) Is your cold better, dear? (*The table gives two loud bumps very quickly.)* Oh, I'm so sorry – are you doing anything for it? *(The table bumps several times.)* I'm afraid she's rather fretful. . . . *(There is a silence.)* Is there anyone there who wishes to speak to anyone here? *(After a pause the table gives one bump.)* Ah! Now we're getting somewhere. . . . No, Daphne, don't do that, dear, you're hurting me . . . Daphne, dear, please . . . Oh, oh, oh! . . . be good, there's a dear child. . . . You say there is someone there who wishes to speak to someone here? *(One bump.)* Is it me? *(Two sharp bumps.)* Is it Dr Bradman? *(Two bumps.)* Is it Mrs Bradman? *(Two bumps.)* Is it Mrs Condomine? *(Several very loud bumps, which continue until* MADAME ARCATI *shouts it down.)* Stop it! Behave yourself! Is it Mr Condomine? *(There is dead silence for a moment, and then a very loud single bump.)* There's someone who wishes to speak to you, Mr Condomine. . . .

CHARLES: Tell them to leave a message.

(The table bangs about loudly.)

MADAME ARCATI: I really must ask you not to be flippant, Mr Condomine . . .

RUTH: Charles, how can you be so idiotic – you'll spoil everything.

CHARLES: I'm sorry – it slipped out.

MADAME ARCATI: Do you know anybody who has passed over recently?

CHARLES: Not recently, except my cousin in the Civil Service, and he wouldn't be likely to want to communicate with me – we haven't spoken for years.

MADAME ARCATI *(hysterically)*: Are you Mr Condomine's cousin in the Civil Service? *(The table bumps violently several times.)* I'm afraid we've drawn a blank. . . . Can't you think of anyone else? Rack your brains. . . .

RUTH *(helpfully)*: It might be old Mrs Plummett, you know – she died on Whit Monday. . . .

CHARLES: I can't imagine why old Mrs Plummett should wish to talk to me – we had very little in common.

RUTH: It's worth trying, anyhow.

MADAME ARCATI: Are you old Mrs Plummett? *(The table remains still.)*

RUTH: She was very deaf – perhaps you'd better shout –

MADAME ARCATI *(shouting)*: Are you old Mrs Plummett? *(Nothing happens.)* There's nobody there at all.

MRS BRADMAN: How disappointing – just as we were getting on so nicely.

DR BRADMAN: Violet, be quiet.

MADAME ARCATI *(rises)*: Well, I'm afraid there's nothing for it but for me to go into a trance. I had hoped to avoid it because it's so exhausting – however, what must be must be. Excuse me a moment while I start the gramophone again. *(She comes to gramophone.)*

CHARLES *(in a strained voice)*: Not 'Always' – don't play 'Always' –

[25]

RUTH: Why ever not, Charles? Don't be absurd.

MADAME ARCATI (*gently*): I'm afraid I must – it would be imprudent to change horses in midstream if you know what I mean. . . . (*She restarts the gramophone.*)

CHARLES: Have it your own way.

(MADAME ARCATI *starts to moan and comes back slowly to stool and sits – then in the darkness a child's voice is heard reciting rather breathlessly:* 'Little Tommy Tucker'.)

DR BRADMAN: That would be Daphne – she ought to have had her adenoids out.

MRS BRADMAN: George – please –

(MADAME ARCATI *suddenly gives a loud scream and falls off the stool on to the floor.*)

CHARLES: Good God!

RUTH: Keep still, Charles. . . .

(CHARLES *subsides. Everyone sits in silence for a moment, then the table starts bouncing about.*)

MRS BRADMAN: It's trying to get away . . . I can't hold it. . . .

RUTH: Press down hard.

(*The table falls over with a crash.*)

There now!

MRS BRADMAN: Ought we to pick it up or leave it where it is?

DR BRADMAN: How the hell do I know?

MRS BRADMAN: There's no need to snap at me.

(*A perfectly strange and very charming voice says:*
'Leave it where it is.')

CHARLES: Who said that?

RUTH: Who said what?

CHARLES: Somebody said: 'Leave it where it is.'

RUTH: Nonsense, dear.

CHARLES: I heard it distinctly.

RUTH: Well, nobody else did – did they?

MRS BRADMAN: I never heard a sound.

CHARLES: It was you, Ruth – you're playing tricks.

RUTH: I'm not doing anything of the sort. I haven't uttered.

(*There is another pause, and then the voice says:*
'Good evening, Charles.')

CHARLES (*very agitated*): Ventriloquism – that's what it is – ventriloquism. . . .

RUTH (*irritably*): What is the matter with you?

CHARLES: You must have heard that – one of you must have heard that!

RUTH: Heard *what*?

CHARLES: You mean to sit there solemnly and tell me that none of you heard anything at all?

DR BRADMAN: I certainly didn't.

MRS BRADMAN: Neither did I – I wish I had. I should love to hear something.

RUTH: It's you who are playing the tricks, Charles – you're acting to try to frighten us . . .

CHARLES *(breathlessly)*: I'm not – I swear I'm not.

(The voice speaks again. It says: 'It's difficult to think of what to say after seven years, but I suppose good evening is as good as anything else.'*)*

CHARLES *(intensely)*: Who are you?

(The voice says: 'Elvira, of course – don't be so silly.' . . .*)*

*(*CHARLES *rises and goes to light-switch centre, then down stage right to fireplace. Others all rise.* MADAME ARCATI *on floor.)*

CHARLES: I can't bear this for another minute. . . . *(He rises violently.)* Get up, everybody – the entertainment's over.'

(He rushes across the room and switches on the lights.)

From *Blithe Spirit* by Noël Coward, 1941

The Call

From our low seat beside the fire
Where we have dozed and dreamed and watched the glow
Or raked the ashes, stopping so
We scarcely saw the sun or rain
Above, or looked much higher
Than this same quiet red or burned-out fire.
    To-night we heard a call,
    A rattle on the window-pane,
    A voice on the sharp air,
And felt a breath stirring our hair,
A flame within us: Something swift and tall
Swept in and out and that was all.
Was it a bright or a dark angel? Who can know?
It left no mark upon the snow,
But suddenly it snapped the chain
Unbarred, flung wide the door
Which will not shut again;
And so we cannot sit here any more.
We must arise and go:
The world is cold without
And dark and hedged about

With mystery and enmity and doubt,
But we must go
Though yet we do not know
Who called, or what marks we shall leave upon the snow.

Charlotte Mew, 1916

The Wit

'Wait. Let me think a minute,' you said.
And in the minute we saw:
Eve and Newton with an apple apiece,
and Moses with the Law,
Socrates, who scratched his curly head,
and many more from Greece,
all coming hurrying up to now,
bid by your crinkled brow.

But then you made a brilliant pun.
We gave a thunderclap of laughter.
Flustered, your helpers vanished one by one;
and through the conversational spaces, after,
we caught, – back, back, far, far, –
the glinting birthday of a fractious star.

Elizabeth Bishop, 1956

Two

'IS THERE ANYBODY THERE?'

I merely mean to say what Johnson said,
  That in the course of some six thousand years,
All nations have believed that from the dead
  A visitant at intervals appears;
And what is strangest upon this strange head,
  Is, that whatever bar the reason rears
'Gainst such belief, there's something stronger still
  In its behalf, let those deny who will.

LORD BYRON

GHOST, *n.* The outward and visible sign of an inward fear . . .
  Accounting for the uncommon behaviour of ghosts, Heine
  mentions somebody's ingenious theory to the effect that
  they are as much afraid of us as we of them. Not quite,
if I may judge from such tables of comparative speed as I am
  able to compile from memories of my own experience.

AMBROSE BIERCE

House of umbrage, house of fear,
House of multiplying air

House of memories that grow
Like shadows out of Allan Poe.

DEREK WALCOTT

'A Converse of Spirits'

As there is a Converse of Spirits, an Intelligence, or call it what you please, between our Spirits embodied and cased up in Flesh, and the Spirits unembodied; ... why should it be thought so strange a thing, that those Spirits should be able to take upon them an Out-side or Case? ... If they can assume a visible Form, as I see no Reason to say they cannot, there is no room then to doubt of the Reality of their appearing; because what *may be* we cannot but believe sometimes *has been*, as what *has been*, we are sure may be.

From 'An Essay on the History and Reality of Apparitions'
by Daniel Defoe, 1727

'What is a ghost?'

– He will have it that *Hamlet* is a ghoststory, John Eglinton said for Mr Best's behoof. Like the fat boy in Pickwick he wants to make our flesh creep.

List! List! O List!

My flesh hears him: creeping, hears.

If thou didst ever . . .

– What is a ghost? Stephen said with tingling energy. One who has faded into impalpability through death, through absence, through change of manners. Elizabethan London lay as far from Stratford as corrupt Paris lies from virgin Dublin. Who is the ghost from *limbo patrum*, returning to the world that has forgotten him? Who is king Hamlet?

From *Ulysses* by James Joyce, 1922

Unheimlich . . .

Heimlich, adj., subst. *Heimlichkeit* (pl. *Heimlichkeiten*): I. Also *heimelich, heimelig*, belonging to the house, not strange, familiar, tame, intimate, friendly, etc. . . .

Note especially the negative '*un-*': eerie, weird, arousing gruesome fear: 'Seeming quite *unheimlich* and ghostly to him.' 'The *unheimlich*, fearful hours of night.' 'I had already long since felt an *unheimlich*, even

[30]

gruesome feeling.' 'Now I am beginning to have an *unheimlich* feeling.' ... 'Feels an *unheimlich* horror.' '*Unheimlich* and motionless like a stone image.' 'The *unheimlich* mist called hill-fog.' 'These pale youths are *unheimlich* and are brewing heaven knows what mischief.' ' *"Unheimlich" is the name for everything that ought to have remained ... secret and hidden but has come to light'* (Schelling).

Many people experience the feeling in the highest degree in relation to death and dead bodies, to the return of the dead, and to spirits and ghosts. As we have seen, some languages in use to-day can only render the German expression 'an *unheimlich* house' by 'a *haunted* house'. We might indeed have begun our investigation with this example, perhaps the most striking of all, of something uncanny, but we refrained from doing so because the uncanny in it is too much intermixed with what is purely gruesome and is in part overlaid by it. There is scarcely any other matter, however, upon which our thoughts and feelings have changed so little since the very earliest times, and in which discarded forms have been so completely preserved under a thin disguise, as our relation to death. Two things account for our conservatism: the strength of our original emotional reaction to death and the insufficiency of our scientific knowledge about it. Biology has not yet been able to decide whether death is the inevitable fate of every living being or whether it is only a regular but yet perhaps avoidable event in life. It is true that the statement 'All men are mortal' is paraded in text-books of logic as an example of a general proposition; but no human being really grasps it, and our unconscious has as little use now as it ever had for the idea of its own mortality. Religions continue to dispute the importance of the undeniable fact of individual death and to postulate a life after death; civil governments still believe that they cannot maintain moral order among the living if they do not uphold the prospect of a better life hereafter as a recompense for mundane existence. In our great cities, placards announce lectures that undertake to tell us how to get into touch with the souls of the departed; and it cannot be denied that not a few of the most able and penetrating minds among our men of science have come to the conclusion, especially towards the close of their own lives, that a contact of this kind is not impossible. Since almost all of us still think as savages do on this topic, it is no matter for surprise that the primitive fear of the dead is still so strong within us and always ready to come to the surface on any provocation. Most likely our fear still implies the old belief that the dead man becomes the enemy of his survivor and seeks to carry him off to share his new life with him. Considering our unchanged attitude towards death, we might rather enquire what has become of the repression, which is the necessary condition of a primitive feeling recurring in the shape of

[31]

something uncanny. But repression is there, too. All supposedly educated people have ceased to believe officially that the dead can become
visible as spirits, and have made any such appearances dependent on
improbable and remote conditions; their emotional attitude towards
their dead, moreover, once a highly ambiguous and ambivalent one,
has been toned down in the higher strata of the mind into an un-
ambiguous feeling of piety.

From 'The Uncanny' by Sigmund Freud, 1919

'Fear came upon me'

Then Eliphaz the Temanite answered and said . . .
Now a thing was secretly brought to me, and mine ear received a
little thereof.
In thoughts from the visions of the night, when deep sleep falleth on
men,
Fear came upon me, and trembling, which made all my bones to
shake.
Then a spirit passed before my face; the hair of my flesh stood up:
It stood still, but I could not discern the form thereof: an image *was*
before mine eyes, *there was* silence, and I heard a voice, *saying*,
Shall mortal man be more just than God? shall a man be more pure
than his maker?
Behold, he put no trust in his servants; and his angels he charged
with folly:
How much less *in* them that dwell in houses of clay, whose foundation *is* in the dust, *which* are crushed before the moth?
They are destroyed from morning to evening: they perish for ever
without any regarding *it*.
Doth not their excellency *which is* in them go away? they die, even
without wisdom.

Job, iv, 11–21

Babylon

When the owl raised its melancholy voice in the darkness the listener
heard the spirit of a departed mother crying for her child. Ghosts and
evil spirits wandered through the streets in darkness; they haunted

empty houses; they fluttered through the evening air as bats; they hastened, moaning dismally, across barren wastes searching for food or lay in wait for travellers; they came as roaring lions and howling jackals, hungering for human flesh.

From *Myths of Babylonia and Assyria* by Donald Mackenzie, 1913

The reluctant soul

'I think, if when it departs from the body it is defiled and impure, because it was always with the body and cared for it and loved it and was fascinated by it and its desires and pleasures, so that it thought nothing was true except the corporeal, which one can touch and see and drink and eat and employ in the pleasures of love, and if it is accustomed to hate and fear and avoid that which is shadowy and invisible to the eyes but is intelligible and tangible to philosophy – do you think a soul in this condition will depart pure and uncontaminated?'

'By no means,' said he.

'But it will be interpenetrated, I suppose, with the corporeal which intercourse and communion with the body have made a part of its nature because the body has been its constant companion and the object of its care?'

'Certainly.'

'And, my friend, we must believe that the corporeal is burdensome and heavy and earthly and visible. And such a soul is weighed down by this and is dragged back into the visible world, through fear of the invisible and of the other world, and so, as they say, it flits about the monuments and the tombs, where shadowy shapes of souls have been seen, figures of those souls which were not set free in purity but retain something of the visible; and this is why they are seen.'

'That is likely, Socrates.'

'It is likely, Cebes. And it is likely that those are not the souls of the good, but those of the base, which are compelled to flit about such places as a punishment for their former evil mode of life. And they flit about until through the desire of the corporeal which clings to them they are again imprisoned in a body. And they are likely to be imprisoned in natures which correspond to the practices of their former life. . . .'

From the *Phaedo* of Plato, fourth century BC,
translated by Harold Fowler

Animula, vagula, blandula

The Emperor Hadrian to his soul

Little soul so sleek and strong
Flesh's guest and friend also
Where departing will you wander
Growing paler now and languid
And not joking as you used to?

Translated by Stevie Smith, 1966

Cassius explains to Brutus

One night very late (when all the camp took quiet rest) as he was in his tent with a little light, thinking of weighty matters, he thought he heard one come in to him, and, casting his eye towards the door of his tent, that he saw a wonderful strange and monstrous shape of a body coming towards him, and said never a word. So Brutus boldly asked what he was, a god or a man, and what cause brought him thither. The spirit answered him, 'I am thy evil spirit, Brutus: and thou shalt see me by the city of Philippi.' Brutus, being no otherwise afraid, replied again unto it: 'Well, then I shall see thee again.' The spirit presently vanished away, and Brutus called his men unto him, who told him that they heard no noise, nor saw anything at all. Thereupon Brutus returned again to think on his matters as he did before: and when the day broke he went unto Cassius, to tell him what vision had appeared unto him in the night. Cassius being in opinion an Epicurean, and reasoning thereon with Brutus, spoke to him touching the vision thus. 'In our sect, Brutus, we have an opinion, that we do not always feel or see that which we suppose we do both see and feel: but that our senses being credulous, and therefore easily abused (when they are idle and unoccupied in their own objects), are induced to imagine they see and conjecture that which they in truth do not. For our mind is quick and cunning to work (without either cause or matter) anything in the imagination whatsoever. And therefore the imagination is resembled to clay, and the mind to the potter: who without any other cause than his fancy and pleasure, changeth it into what fashion and form he will

From 'Brutus' in *The Lives of the Emperors* by Plutarch, first century AD, translated from the Latin by Thomas North, 1599

Of visions, noises, apparitions, and imagined sounds, and of other illusions, of wandering soules: with a confutation thereof.

Manie thorough melancholie doo imagine, that they see or heare visions, spirits, ghosts, strange noises, &c: as I have alreadie prooved before, at large. Manie againe thorough feare proceeding from a cowardlie nature and complexion, or from an effeminate and fond bringing up, are timerous and afraid of spirits, and bugs, &c. Some through imperfection of sight also are afraid of their owne shadowes, and (as *Aristotle* saith) see themselves sometimes as it were in a glasse. And some through weaknesse of bodie have such unperfect imaginations. Droonken men also sometimes suppose they see trees walke, &c: according to that which *Salomon* saith to the droonkards; Thine eies shall see strange visions, and mervellous appearances.

In all ages moonks and preests have abused and bewitched the world with counterfet visions; which proceeded through idlenes, and restraint of marriage, wherby they grew hot and lecherous, and therefore devised such meanes to compasse and obteine their loves. And the simple people being then so superstitious, would never seeme to mistrust, that such holie men would make them cuckholds, but forsooke their beds in that case, and gave roome to the cleargie. Item, little children have beene so scared with their mothers maids, that they could never after endure to be in the darke alone, for feare of bugs.

From *The Discoverie of Witchcraft* by Reginald Scot, 1584

'A questionable shape'

HORATIO: Look, my lord, it comes.
HAMLET: Angels and ministers of grace defend us!
    Be thou a spirit of health or goblin damn'd,
    Bring with thee airs from heaven or blasts from hell,
    Be thy intents wicked or charitable,
    Thou comest in such a questionable shape
    That I will speak to thee: I'll call thee Hamlet,
    King, father; royal Dane, O! answer me:
    Let me not burst in ignorance; but tell
    Why thy canoniz'd bones, hearsed in death,
    Have burst their cerements; why the sepulchre,
    Wherein we saw thee quietly inurn'd,

Hath op'd his ponderous and marble jaws,
To cast thee up again. What may this mean,
That thou, dead corse, again in complete steel
Revisit'st thus the glimpses of the moon,
Making night hideous; and we fools of nature
So horridly to shake our disposition
With thoughts beyond the reaches of our souls?
Say, why is this? wherefore? what should we do?

From *Hamlet* by William Shakespeare, 1603–4

'Devils'

Those apparitions and ghosts of departed persons are not the wandering souls of men, but the unquiet walks of Devils, prompting and
suggesting unto mischief, blood, and villainy.

From *Religio Medici* by Sir Thomas Browne, 1643

Old wives' tales

When I was a child (and so before the Civill Warres), the fashion was
for old women and mayds to tell fabulous stories nighttimes, of
Sprights and walking of ghosts, &c. This was derived down from
mother to daughter, from the Monkish Ballance which upheld Holy
Church, for the Divines say, Deny Spirits, you are an Atheist. When
the warres came, and with them Liberty of Conscience and Liberty of
inquisition, the phantoms vanished. Now children feare no such things,
having heard not of them; and are not checked with such feares.

John Aubrey, 1690

'Dangerous drugs'

The only supernatural agents which can in any manner be allowed to
us moderns are ghosts; but of these I would advise an author to be extremely sparing. These are indeed like arsenic, and other dangerous
drugs in physic, to be used with the utmost caution; nor would I advise
the introduction of them at all in those works, or by those authors to

which, or to whom a horse-laugh in the reader, would be any great pre-
judice or mortification.

As soon as the play, which was *Hamlet Prince of Denmark*, began, Partridge was all attention, nor did he break silence till the entrance of the
ghost; upon which he asked Jones, 'What man that was in the strange
dress; something,' said he, 'like what I have seen in a picture. Sure it is
not armour, is it?' Jones answered, 'That is the ghost.' To which Partridge replied with a smile, 'Persuade me to that, sir, if you can. Though
I can't say I ever actually saw a ghost in my life, yet I am certain I
should know one, if I saw him, better than that comes to. No, no, sir,
ghosts don't appear in such dresses as that, neither.' In this mistake,
which caused much laughter in the neighbourhood of Partridge, he was
suffered to continue, 'till the scene between the ghost and Hamlet,
when Partridge gave that credit to Mr Garrick, which he had denied to
Jones, and fell into so violent a trembling, that his knees knocked
against each other. Jones asked him what was the matter, and whether
he was afraid of the warrior upon the stage? 'O la! sir,' said he, 'I perceive now it is what you told me. I am not afraid of anything; for I
know it is but a play: and if it was really a ghost, it could do no harm at
such a distance, and in so much company; and yet if I was frightened, I
am not the only person.' 'Why, who,' cries Jones, 'dost thou take to be
such a coward here besides thyself?' 'Nay, you may call me coward if
you will; but if that little man there upon the stage is not frightened, I
never saw any man frightened in my life . . .'
    . . . He durst not go to bed all that night, for fear of the ghost; and for
many nights after, sweat two or three hours before he went to sleep,
with the same apprehensions, and waked several times in great horrors,
crying out, 'Lord have mercy upon us! there it is.'

From Tom Jones by Henry Fielding, 1749

'Astonishment'

I have spoken with some on the third day after their death. Three of
these spirits had been known to me in the world, and I told them that
funeral arrangements were then being made for burying their bodies;
the expression I used was 'for burying *them*,' and at this they were
struck with astonishment; they declared that they were alive, and that
their friends were only burying that which had served them for a body
in the world. They afterwards wondered exceedingly that during their
life in the body they had not believed in such a life after death, and

were especially amazed that hardly any within the Church have this belief.

Those who in the world have not believed that the soul has any life subsequent to the life of the body, are exceedingly ashamed when they find that they are alive after death.

From *Heaven and Hell* by Emanuel Swedenborg, 1758, translated from the Latin for the Swedenborg Society, 1859–64

At the Great Pyramid

'Pekuah,' said the princess, 'of what art thou afraid?' 'Of the narrow entrance,' answered the lady, 'and of the dreadful gloom. I dare not enter a place which must surely be inhabited by unquiet souls. The original possessors of these dreadful vaults will start up before us, and perhaps shut us in for ever.' She spoke, and threw her arms round the neck of her mistress.

'If all your fear be of apparitions,' said the prince, 'I will promise you safety: there is no danger from the dead: he that is once buried will be seen no more.'

'That the dead are seen no more,' said Imlac, 'I will not undertake to maintain, against the concurrent and unvaried testimony of all ages, and of all nations. There is no people, rude or learned, among whom apparitions of the dead are not related and believed. This opinion, which perhaps prevails as far as human nature is diffused, could become universal only by its truth: those that never heard of one another would not have agreed in a tale which nothing but experience can make credible. That it is doubted by single cavillers, can very little weaken the general evidence; and some who deny it with their tongues confess it by their fears.

'Yet I do not mean to add new terrors to those which have already seized upon Pekuah. There can be no reason why spectres should haunt the Pyramid more than other places, or why they should have power or will to hunt innocence and purity. Our entrance is no violation of their privileges; we can take nothing from then, how then can we offend them?'

From *Rasselas* by Samuel Johnson, 1759

The Indian Burying Ground

In spite of all the learned have said,
I still my old opinion keep;

[38]

The posture, that we give the dead,
Points out the soul's eternal sleep.

Not so the ancients of these lands –
The Indian, when from life released,
Again is seated with his friends,
And shares again the joyous feast.

His imaged birds, and painted bowl,
And venison, for a journey dressed,
Bespeak the nature of the soul,
Activity, that knows no rest.

His bow, for action ready bent,
And arrows, with a head of stone,
Can only mean that life is spent,
And not the old ideas gone.

Thou, stranger, that shalt come this way,
No fraud upon the dead commit –
Observe the swelling turf, and say
They do not lie, but here they sit.

Here still a lofty rock remains,
On which the curious eye may trace
(Now wasted, half, by wearing rains)
The fancies of a ruder race.

Here still an aged elm aspires,
Beneath whose far-projecting shade
(And which the shepherd still admires)
The children of the forest played!

There oft a restless Indian queen
(Pale Shebah, with her braided hair)
And many a barbarous form is seen
To chide the man that lingers there.

By midnight moons, o'er moistening dews,
In habit for the chase arrayed,
The hunter still the deer pursues,
The hunter and the deer, a shade!

And long shall timorous fancy see
The painted chief, and pointed spear,

And Reason's self shall bow the knee
To shadows and delusions here.

Philip Freneau, 1788

'Their own proper likeness'

Disembodied Spirits, however, more often manifest themselves in their
own proper mortal likeness than under any hideous or horrible aspect.
Sometimes they are encountered on a high road as walking, or riding.
It is true that it has been recorded that a ghost will appear in a flame of
fire, very ghastly; or all covered with wounds and blood; or again horribly mangled with the bowels gushing out and ripped from the belly.
Sometimes only a hand appears, or a shadowy form, or it may be some
sign or token, some object dear to the departed, is indicated. Sometimes, indeed, the apparition seems like a bundle of blazing straw; or,
again, merely a muffled voice is heard.

From 'A Treatise of Ghosts' by Father Noël Taillepied, 1588,
translated by M. Summers

Of the Politics of Fashion

Ghosts commonly appear in the same dress they usually wore whilst
living; though they are sometimes clothed all in white; but that is
chiefly the churchyard ghosts who have no particular business, but
seem to appear *pro bono publico*, or to scare drunken rustics from tum-
bling over their graves ... Dragging chains is not the fashion of
English ghosts, chains and black vestments being chiefly the accoutre-
ments of foreign spectres, seen in arbitrary governments; dead or alive,
English spirits are free.

Captain Francis Grose, 1775

Coleridge reads the Arabian Nights

And then I found the Arabian Nights' Entertainments, one tale of
which (the tale of a man who was compelled to seek for a pure virgin)
made so deep an impression on me (I had read it in the evening while
my mother was mending stockings), that I was haunted by spectres,
whenever I was in the dark; and I distinctly remember the anxious and

fearful eagerness with which I used to watch the window in which the books lay, and whenever the sun lay upon them, I would seize it, carry it by the wall, and bask and read. My father found out the effect which these books had produced, and burnt them.

Samuel Taylor Coleridge to Thomas Poole, 1797

Night Terrors

In my father's book-closet the history of the Bible by Stackhouse occupied a distinguished station. The pictures with which it abounds – one of the ark, in particular, and another of Solomon's temple, delineated with all the fidelity of ocular admeasurement, as if the artist had been upon the spot – attracted my childish attention. There was a picture, too, of the Witch raising up Samuel, which I wish that I had never seen. ... That detestable picture!

I was dreadfully alive to nervous terrors. The night-time, solitude, and the dark, were my hell. The sufferings I endured in this nature would justify the expression. I never laid my head on my pillow, I suppose, from the fourth to the seventh or eighth year of my life – so far as memory serves in things so long ago – without an assurance, which realized its own prophecy, of seeing some frightful spectre. Be old Stackhouse then acquitted in part, if I say, that to this picture of the Witch raising up Samuel – (O that old man covered with a mantle!) – I owe – not my midnight terrors, the hell of my infancy – but the shape and manner of their visitation ... It was he who dressed up for me a hag that nightly sate upon my pillow – a sure bedfellow, when my aunt or my maid was far from me. All day long, while the book was permitted me, I dreamed waking over his delineation, and at night (if I may use so bold an expression) awoke into sleep, and found the vision true. I durst not, even in the day-light, once enter the chamber where I slept, without my face turned to the window, aversely from the bed where my witch-ridden pillow was. Parents do not know what they do when they leave tender babes alone to go to sleep in the dark. The feeling about for a friendly arm – the hoping for a familiar voice – when they wake screaming – and find none to soothe them – what a terrible shaking it is to their poor nerves! The keeping them up till midnight, through candle-light and the unwholesome hours, as they are called, – would, I am satisfied, in a medical point of view, prove the better caution.

From *The Essays of Elia* by Charles Lamb, 1823

'The credence they in childhood gain'd'

Though now the sun was o'er the hill,
In this dark spot 'twas twilight still,
Save that on Greta's farther side
Some straggling beams through copsewood glide;
And wild and savage contrast made
That dingle's deep and funeral shade,
With the bright tints of early day,
Which, glimmering through the ivy spray,
On the opposing summit lay.

The lated peasant shunn'd the dell;
For Superstition wont to tell
Of many a grisly sound and sight,
Scaring its path at dead of night.
When Christmas logs blaze high and wide,
Such wonders speed the festal tide;
While Curiosity and Fear,
Pleasure and Pain, sit crouching near,
Till childhood's cheek no longer glows,
And village maidens lose the rose.
The thrilling interest rises higher,
The circle closes nigh and nigher,
And shuddering glance is cast behind,
As louder moans the wintry wind.
Believe, that fitting scene was laid
For such wild tales in Mortham glade;
For who had seen, on Greta's side,
By that dim light fierce Bertram stride,
In such a spot, at such an hour, –
If touch'd by Superstition's power,
Might well have deem'd that Hell had given
A murderer's ghost to upper Heaven,
While Wilfrid's form had seem'd to glide
Like his pale victim by his side.

Nor think to village swains alone
Are these unearthly terrors known;
For not to rank nor sex confined
Is this vain ague of the mind:
Heart firm as steel, as marble hard,
'Gainst faith, and love, and pity barr'd,
Have quaked, like aspen leaves in May,

Beneath its universal sway.
Bertram had listed many a tale
Of wonder in his native dale,
That in his secret soul retain'd
The credence they in childhood gain'd.

From 'Rokeby' by Sir Walter Scott, 1813

Shadow March

All round the house is the jet-black night;
    It stares through the window-pane;
It crawls in the corners, hiding from the light,
    And it moves with the moving flame.

Now my little heart goes a-beating like a drum,
    With the breath of the Bogie in my hair;
And all round the candle the crooked shadows come
    And go marching along up the stair.

The shadow of the balusters, the shadow of the lamp,
    The shadow of the child that goes to bed –
All the wicked shadows coming, tramp, tramp, tramp,
    With the black night overhead.

From 'North West Passage' in *A Child's Garden of Verses*
by Robert Louis Stevenson, 1883

The Stay-Puft Man

As bizarre as it was, I wanted the film to say something about life –
even if it was subliminal. I knew if I could just harmonize it in my own
mind, I'd feel a lot better about it. Finally, I found some symbolism in
the fact that the whole world of the paranormal seems to represent
people's abstract fears – people need a place to put all that nameless
dread and so they put it into ghosts and things unseen. But the real
source of that dread is in very real things like violence and death and
economic uncertainty. So it seemed to me very appropriate that when
our monster finally appeared, it turned out to be marshmallow – that,
literally and figuratively, our biggest fear of the unknown was as insub-
stantial as marshmallow.

Harold Ramis, in *making Ghostbusters* by D. Shay, 1985

'A dead wall'

The future is like a dead wall or a thick mist hiding all objects from our view; the past is alive and stirring with objects, bright or solemn, and of unfading interest.

From *Table-Talk* by William Hazlitt, 1821–2

'Grim reader!'

Grim reader! did you ever see a ghost?
    No; but you have heard – I understand – be dumb!
And don't regret the time you may have lost,
    For you have got that pleasure still to come:
And do not think I mean to sneer at most
    Of these things, or by ridicule benumb
That source of the sublime and the mysterious: –
For certain reasons my belief is serious.

Serious? You laugh; – you may: that will I not;
    My smiles must be sincere or not at all.
I say I do believe a haunted spot
    Exists – and where? That shall I not recall,
Because I'd rather it should be forgot,
    'Shadows the soul of Richard' may appal.
In short, upon that subject I've some qualms very
Like those of the philosopher of Malmsbury.

The night – (I sing by night – sometimes an owl,
    And now and then a nightingale) – is dim.
And the loud shriek of sage Minerva's fowl
    Rattles around me her discordant hymn:
Old portraits from old walls upon me scowl –
    I wish to heaven they would not look so grim;
The dying embers dwindle in the grate –
I think too that I have sat up too late:

And therefore, though 'tis by no means my way
    To rhyme at noon – when I have other things
To think of, if I ever think – I say
    I feel some chilly midnight shudderings,
And prudently postpone, until mid-day,

Treating a topic which, alas! but brings
Shadows; – but you must be in my condition
Before you learn to call this superstition.

Between two worlds life hovers like a star,
     'Twixt night and morn, upon the horizon's verge.
How little do we know that which we are!
     How less what we may be! The eternal surge
Of time and tide rolls on, and bears afar
     Our bubbles; as the old burst, new emerge,
Lash'd from the foam of ages; while the graves
Of empires heave but like some passing waves.

From *Don Juan* by Lord Byron, 1819–24

'An actual authentic Ghost'

Again, could anything be more miraculous than an actual authentic
Ghost? The English Johnson longed, all his life, to see one; but could
not, though he went to Cock Lane, and thence to the church-vaults,
and tapped on coffins. Foolish Doctor! Did he never, with the mind's
eye as well as with the body's, look round him into that full tide of
human Life he so loved; did he never so much as look into Himself?
The good Doctor was a Ghost, as actual and authentic as heart could
wish; well-nigh a million of Ghosts were travelling the streets by his
side. Once more I say, sweep away the illusion of Time: compress the
threescore years into three minutes: what else was he, what else are
we? Are we not Spirits, that are shaped into a body, into an Appearance; and that fade away again into air and Invisibility? This is no
metaphor, it is a simple scientific *fact*: we start out of Nothingness, take
figure, and are Apparitions; round us, as round the veriest spectre, is
Eternity; and to Eternity minutes are as years and æons. Come there
not tones of Love and Faith, as from celestial harp-strings, like the
Song of beatified Souls? And again, do not we squeak and jibber (in our
discordant, screech-owlish debatings and recriminatings); and glide
bodeful, and feeble, and fearful; or uproar (*poltern*), and revel in our
mad Dance of the Dead, – till the scent of the morning air summons us
to our still Home; and dreamy Night becomes awake and Day? Where
now is Alexander of Macedon: does the steel Host, that yelled in fierce
battle-shouts at Issus and Arbela, remain behind him; or have they all
vanished utterly, even as perturbed Goblins must? Napoleon too, and
his Moscow Retreats and Austerlitz Campaigns! Was it all other than
the veriest Spectre-hunt; which has now, with its howling tumult that

made Night hideous, flitted away? – Ghosts! There are nigh a thousand-million walking the Earth openly at noontide; some half-hundred have vanished from it, some half-hundred have arisen in it, ere thy watch ticks once.

O Heaven, it is mysterious, it is awful to consider that we not only carry each a future Ghost within him; but are, in very deed, Ghosts!

From Sartor Resartus by Thomas Carlyle, 1833–4

'So-called hauntings'

With regard to some so-called *hauntings*, there seems reason to believe that the invisible guest was formerly a dweller upon earth, in the flesh, who is prevented by some circumstance which we are not qualified to explain, from pursuing the destiny of the human race, by entering freely into the next state prepared for him. He is like an unfortunate caterpillar that cannot entirely free itself from the integuments of its reptile life which chain it to the earth, whilst its fluttering wings vainly seek to bear it into the region to which it now belongs.

From The Nightside of Nature by Catharine Crowe, 1849

The Raven

Once upon a midnight dreary, while I pondered, weak and weary,
Over many a quaint and curious volume of forgotten lore –
While I nodded, nearly napping, suddenly there came a tapping,
As of someone gently rapping, rapping at my chamber door.
''Tis some visiter,' I muttered, 'tapping at my chamber door –
    Only this and nothing more.'

Ah, distinctly I remember it was in the bleak December,
And each separate dying ember wrought its ghost upon the floor.
Eagerly I wished the morrow; – vainly I had sought to borrow
From my books surcease of sorrow – sorrow for the lost Lenore –
For the rare and radiant maiden whom the angels name Lenore –
    Nameless here for evermore.

And the silken sad uncertain rustling of each purple curtain
Thrilled me – filled me with fantastic terrors never felt before;
So that now, to still the beating of my heart, I stood repeating,
''Tis some visiter entreating entrance at my chamber door –

Some late visiter entreating entrance at my chamber door; –
    This it is and nothing more.'

Presently my soul grew stronger; hesitating then no longer,
'Sir,' said I, 'or Madam, truly your forgiveness I implore;
But the fact is I was napping, and so gently you came rapping,
And so faintly you came tapping, tapping at my chamber door,
That I scarce was sure I heard you –' here I opened wide the door; –
    Darkness there and nothing more.

Deep into that darkness peering, long I stood there wondering,
    fearing,
Doubting, dreaming dreams no mortals ever dared to dream
    before;
But the silence was unbroken, and the stillness gave no token;
And the only word there spoken was the whispered word,
    'Lenore?'
This I whispered, and an echo murmured back the word,
    'Lenore!' –
    Merely this, and nothing more.

From 'The Raven' by Edgar Allan Poe, 1845

'A ghostly, dismantled old quarto'

When I first saw the table, dingy and dusty, in the furthest corner of the old hopper-shaped garret, and set out with broken, be-crusted old purple vials and flasks, and a ghostly, dismantled old quarto, it seemed just such a necromantic little old table as might have belonged to Friar Bacon. . . . I took particular satisfaction in my table, as a night reading-table. At a ladies' fair, I bought me a beautifully worked reading-cushion, and, with elbow leaning thereon, and hand shading my eyes from the light, spent many a long hour – nobody by, but the queer old book I had brought down from the garret . . .

It was late on a Saturday night in December. In the little old cedar-parlor, before the little old apple-tree table, I was sitting up, as usual, alone. I had made more than one effort to get up and go to bed; but I could not. I was, in fact, under a sort of fascination. Somehow, too, certain reasonable opinions of mine seemed not so reasonable as before. I felt nervous. The truth was, that though, in my previous night-readings, Cotton Mather had but amused me, upon this particular night he terrified me. A thousand times I had laughed at such stories. Old wives' fables, I thought, however entertaining. But now, how different. They began to put on the aspect of reality. Now, for the first time it struck me that this was no romantic Mrs Radcliffe, who had written the 'Magnalia', but a practical, hard-working, earnest, upright man, a learned doctor, too, as well as a good Christian and orthodox clergyman. What possible motive could such a man have to deceive? His style had all the plainness and unpoetic boldness of truth. In the most straightforward way, he laid before me detailed accounts of New England witchcraft, each important item corroborated by respectable townsfolk, and, of not a few of the most surprising, he himself had been eye-witness. Cotton Mather testified whereof he had seen. But, is it possible? I asked myself. Then I remembered that Dr Johnson, the matter-of-fact compiler of a dictionary, had been a believer in ghosts, besides many other sound, worthy men. Yielding to the fascination, I read deeper and deeper into the night. At last, I found myself starting at the least chance sound, and yet wishing that it were not so very still.

A tumbler of warm punch stood by my side, with which beverage, in a moderate way, I was accustomed to treat myself every Saturday night ...

But, upon the night in question, I found myself wishing that, instead of my usual mild mixture, I had concocted some potent draught. I felt the need of stimulus. I wanted something to hearten me against Cotton Mather – doleful, ghostly, ghastly Cotton Mather. I grew more and more nervous. Nothing but fascination kept me from fleeing the room. The candles burnt low, with long snuffs, and huge winding-sheets. But I durst not raise the snuffers to them. It would make too much noise. And yet, previously, I had been wishing for noise. I read on and on. My hair began to have a sensation. My eyes felt strained; they pained me. I was conscious of it. I knew I was injuring them. I knew I should rue this abuse of them next day; but I read on and on. I could not help it. The skinny hand was on me.

From 'The Apple-Tree Table, or Original Spiritual Manifestations'
by Herman Melville, 1856

'The dead face'

The tableau of Hermione was doubly striking from its dissimilarity with what had gone before: it was answering perfectly, and a murmur of applause had been gradually suppressed while Leontes gave his permission that Paulina should exercise her utmost art and make the statue move.

Hermione, her arm resting on a pillar, was elevated by about six inches, which she counted on as a means of showing her pretty foot and instep, when at the given signal she should advance and descend.

'Music, awake her, strike!' said Paulina (Mrs Davilow, who by special entreaty had consented to take the part in a white burnous and hood).

Herr Klesmer, who had been good-natured enough to seat himself at the piano, struck a thunderous chord – but in the same instant, and before Hermione had put forth her foot, the movable panel, which was on a line with the piano, flew open on the right opposite the stage and disclosed the picture of the dead face and the fleeing figure, brought out in pale definiteness by the position of the waxlights. Everyone was startled, but all eyes in the act of turning towards the opened panel were recalled by a piercing cry from Gwendolen, who stood without change of attitude, but with a change of expression that was terrifying in its terror. She looked like a statue into which a soul of Fear had entered: her pallid lips were parted; her eyes, usually narrowed under their long lashes, were dilated and fixed. Her mother, less surprised than alarmed, rushed towards her, and Rex too could not help going to her side. But the touch of her mother's arm had the effect of an electric charge; Gwendolen fell on her knees and put her hands before her face. She was still trembling, but mute, and it seemed that she had self-consciousness enough to aim at controlling her signs of terror, for she presently allowed herself to be raised from her kneeling posture and led away, while the company were relieving their minds by explanation.

'A magnificent bit of *plastik* that!' said Klesmer to Miss Arrowpoint. And a quick fire of undertoned question and answer went round.

'Was it part of the play?'

'Oh no, surely not. Miss Harleth was too much affected. A sensitive creature!'

'Dear me! I was not aware that there was a painting behind that panel; were you?'

'No; how should I? Some eccentricity in one of the Earl's family long ago, I suppose.'

'How very painful! Pray shut it up.'

'Was the door locked? It is very mysterious. It must be the spirits.'

'But there is no medium present.'

'How do you know that? We must conclude that there is, when such things happen.'

'Oh, the door was not locked; it was probably the sudden vibration from the piano that sent it open.'

This conclusion came from Mr Gascoigne, who begged Miss Merry if possible to get the key. But this readiness to explain the mystery was thought by Mrs Vulcany unbecoming in a clergyman, and she observed in an undertone that Mr Gascoigne was always a little too worldly for her taste. However, the key was produced, and the rector turned it in the lock with an emphasis rather offensively rationalising – as who should say, 'It will not start open again' – putting the key in his pocket as a security.

From Daniel Deronda by George Eliot, 1876

Subversion

MRS ALVING: I'm haunted by ghosts. When I heard Regina and Osvald out there, it was just as if there were ghosts before my very eyes. But I'm inclined to think that we're all ghosts, Pastor Manders; it's not only the things that we've inherited from our fathers and mothers that live on in us, but all sorts of old dead ideas and old dead beliefs, and things of that sort. They're not actually alive in us, but they're rooted there all the same, and we can't rid ourselves of them. I've only to pick up a newspaper, and when I read it I seem to see ghosts gliding between the lines. I should think there must be ghosts all over the country – as countless as grains of sand. And we are, all of us, so pitifully afraid of the light.

PASTOR MANDERS: Ah! So there we have the fruits of your reading – and fine fruits they are, upon my word! Oh, these terrible, subversive, free-thinking books!

From Ghosts by Henrik Ibsen, 1881, translated by Peter Watts

Duppy

Now we come to a tragedy. Selina is drowned, and they sing smoothly and flowingly:–

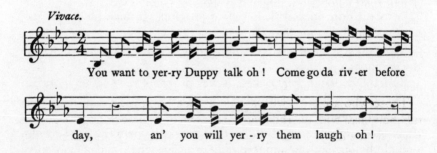

Vivace.

You want to yer-ry Duppy talk oh! Come go da riv-er before day, an' you will yer-ry them laugh oh!

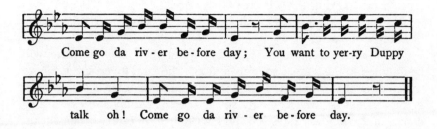

Come go da riv-er be-fore day; You want to yer-ry Duppy
talk oh! Come go da riv-er be-fore day.

Everybody in Jamaica believes in Duppy, and many women and children will not go out at night for fear of meeting one.

A man, they say, has two spirits, one from God and the other not from God. The one from God is good, and the one not from God may be either good or bad. During sleep, these spirits leave the body and go to other people's houses in search of food. Being shadows themselves, they feed on the shadow of food and on the smell of food. They are seldom far apart, and the heavenly spirit can always prevent the earthly spirit from doing harm. At death the God-given spirit flies up upon a tree, and goes to heaven the third day. The other spirit remains on earth as Duppy. Its abiding place is the grave of the dead man, but it wanders about at night as it did when he was alive. A good Duppy will watch over and protect the living. A bad Duppy tries to frighten and harm people, which it is able to do now that it has lost the restraining influence of its former companion, the heavenly spirit. It can assume any sort of shape, appearing sometimes as a man, sometimes as an animal. If it is a very bad Duppy, it makes the place where it is unbearably hot . . .

A Duppy of one's own family is worse than a stranger's, and the 'baddest' of all is Coolie Duppy. One of the most dreaded Duppies is 'Rolling (i.e. roaring) Calf'. It goes about making a hideous noise, and clanking a chain. 'If Rolling Calf catch you, give you one lick, you dead.' Your only chance is to run, and you must keep on 'cutting ten' (making the sign of the cross), and the pursuing monster has to go round that place ten times. 'Shop-keeper and butcher', so goes local tradition 'tief too much (rob their customers very much) and when they dead they turn Rolling Calf.'

Those who are born with a caul can see Duppy. So can those who rub their faces with the rheum from the eye of a horse or dog, and those who cut their eye-lashes. Every Duppy walks two feet above the ground, floating in the air. If a child is not christened before it is six months old, Duppy will carry it away into the bush. To avoid this, a Bible and pair of scissors are laid on the child's pillow. The scissors are a protection, owing to their cross-like form.

Such are the main beliefs with regard to this remarkable superstition of Duppy on earth.

This, however, is not all. At the day of judgment the two spirits will be reunited to the body, and in many cases the God-given spirit will go to hell after all. I often ask my boys which of these three is themselves? Is it the body? Is it the heavenly spirit? Is it the earthly spirit? But they do not understand the question and have no sort of reply. When I ask if it is not hard that the heavenly spirit after its sojourn in heaven should go to hell, they laugh.

From *Jamaican Song and Story*, collected by Walter Jekyll, 1907

The trembling of the earth

(WOYZECK *and* ANDRES *are in a copse, cutting firewood.*)

WOYZECK: That's the place, Andres – that patch there, do you see? where the toadstools are growing – that's where this head comes rolling down at dusk. A bloke picked it up once, thought it was a hedgehog; three days and three nights after, they were laying him out in the shavings. *(Softly)* Freemasons, Andres, that's what it is: freemasons. – Sssh!

ANDRES *(singing)*: Two old hares were feeding,
Nibbling the juicy, juicy grass –

WOYZECK: Hush! Something's happening!

ANDRES: Nibbling the juicy, juicy grass
    Till the roots were bleeding.

WOYZECK: It's behind me – no, it's underneath. *(He stamps on the ground.)* Hollow – do you hear that? It's all hollow down there. Free-masons!

ANDRES: I don't like it.

WOYZECK: So queer and still. Like holding your breath. – Andres!

ANDRES: Yes?

WOYZECK: Say something. *(He stares around him.)* Isn't it bright, Andres! A great fire going round the sky, and a blaring under the earth like trombones. It's coming nearer! Quick, don't look behind you! *(Pulls him into the thicket.)*

ANDRES *(after a pause)*: Can you hear it now, Woyzeck?

WOYZECK: No, it's still; everything's still, as if the world had died.

From *Woyzeck* by Georg Büchner, 1909, translated by John Holmstrom

The Way Through the Woods

They shut the road through the woods
Seventy years ago.
Weather and rain have undone it again,
And now you would never know
There was once a road through the woods
Before they planted the trees.
It is underneath the coppice and heath
And the thin anemones.
Only the keeper sees
That, where the ring-dove broods,
And the badgers roll at ease,
There was once a road through the woods.

Yet, if you enter the woods
Of a summer evening late,
When the night-air cools on the trout-ringed pools
Where the otter whistles his mate,
(They fear not men in the woods,
Because they see so few.)
You will hear the beat of a horse's feet,
And the swish of a skirt in the dew,
Steadily cantering through
The misty solitudes,

As though they perfectly knew
The old lost road through the woods . . .
But there is no road through the woods.

From *Rewards and Fairies* by Rudyard Kipling, 1910

The Taxis

In the first taxi he was alone tra-la,
No extras on the clock. He tipped ninepence
But the cabby, while he thanked him, looked askance
As though to suggest someone had bummed a ride.

In the second taxi he was alone tra-la
But the clock showed sixpence extra; he tipped according
And the cabby from his muffler said: 'Make sure
You have left nothing behind tra-la between you.'

In the third taxi he was alone tra-la
But the tip-up seats were down and there was an extra
Charge of one-and-sixpence and an odd
Scent that reminded him of a trip to Cannes.

As for the fourth taxi, he was alone
Tra-la when he hailed it but the cabby looked
Through him and said: 'I can't tra-la well take
So many people, not to speak of the dog.'

Louis MacNeice, 1961

'Not Watt . . .'

. . . It is hard to believe that the face of Watt, dreadful and all as it was
at the time, was dreadful and all enough to cause a powerful lymphatic
man like Micks to recoil to the wall with his hands to his face, as if to
ward off a blow, or press back a cry, in the way he did, and to turn pale,
for he turned pale, very properly. For Watt's face, dreadful and all as it
undoubtedly was, especially when it wore this particular expression,
was scarcely as dreadful and all as all that. Nor was Micks a little girl,
or an innocent little choirboy, no, but a big placid man, who had seen
something of the world, both at home, and abroad. What may it then
have been, if not Watt's face, that so repelled Micks, and drained

his cheeks, of their natural high colour? The greatcoat? The hat? The shoe and boot? Yes, the shoe and boot perhaps, taken together, so brown, so peeping, so sharp and blunt, heel to heel in obscene attention splayed, and so brown, such a brown. Or was it not perhaps something that was not Watt, nor of Watt, but behind Watt, or beside Watt, or before Watt, or beneath Watt, or above Watt, or about Watt, a shade uncast, a light unshed, or the grey air aswirl with vain entelechies?

From Watt by Samuel Beckett, 1963

The Garden by the Graveyard

We had a garden at the back of the house, not large, but with lawn, flowers, and a few trees. In daylight the trees leaned out over the churchyard or over the path through it and the stones were nothing but stones. But as the sun went down behind the church tower, the stones became stiller than stone – as if they were waiting. When the sun had gone down I did not look at the churchyard at all. I knew how the stones were lengthening, lifting and peering blankly, inscrutably, over the wall. As I went indoors, if I dared a backward glance, or climbed towards the little shot window, I saw how they did indeed peer; but up, always over my shoulder or my head, crowded, still, other. Then I would go quickly to my father or my mother or my brother for human company by the fire.

One afternoon I was sitting on the wall that divided our garden from the churchyard. Eight, was I, perhaps, or nine? Or older even? There is nothing by which I can tell. I contemplated the stones a few feet away and saw suddenly that several of them were flat up against our wall. I remember knowing then that I had seen and thought enough. My nights were miserable as it was, with every sort of apprehension given a label, and these even so only outliers of a central, not-comprehended dark. But the sun shone on the wall and I watched the inside of my head go on and take step after logical step. At which end of a grave does a stone stand? I remembered the sexton, Mr Baker, calling them headstones and I made the final deduction that the dead lay, their heads under our wall, the rest of them projecting from their own place into our garden, their feet, their knees even, tucked under our lawn.

Logic is insistent. I recall an awareness at that moment that I was being foolish; that the demonstration of this proposition would do no one any good and me a great deal of harm. The lawn, almost the only uncontaminated place in that ancient neighbourhood, had been sunny and innocent until my deliberate exercise of logic had invited the enemy in.

What was that enemy? I cannot tell. He came with darkness and he reduced me to a shuddering terror that was incurable because it was indescribable. In daylight I thought of the Roman remains that had been dug up under the church as the oldest things near, sane things from sane people like myself. But at night, the Norman door and pillar, even the flint wall of our cellar, were older, far older, were rooted in the darkness under the earth.

How could I talk to [my parents] about darkness and the irrational? They knew so much, had such certainties, were backing all the obvious winners. I floated in their world, holding on to a casual hand, sometimes sinking again in the dark. Then I found Edgar Allan Poe's *Tales of Mystery and Imagination*. I read them with a sort of shackled fascination and recognized their quality, knew they were reports, knew that he and I had been in the same place.

But my career was to be a scientific one. Science was busy clearing up the universe. There was no place in this exquisitely logical universe for the terrors of darkness. There was darkness, of course, but it was just darkness, the absence of light; had none of the looming terror which I knew night-long in my very bones. God might have been a help but we had thrown Him out, along with Imperialism, Toryism, the Exploitation of Women, War and the Church of England. I nodded agreement, was precocious with the catch-phrases of progress; but even in daylight now, the dead under the wall drew up the green coverlet of our grass and lay back with a heart-squeezing grin. Though cosmology was driving away the shadows of our ignorance, though bones were exhibited under glass, though the march of science was irresistible, its path did not lie through my particular darkness.

From 'The Ladder and the Tree' by William Golding, 1965

'Not as we are but as we must appear'

Not as we are but as we must appear,
Contractual ghosts of pity; not as we
Desire life but as they would have us live,
Set apart in timeless colloquy.
So it is required; so we bear witness,
Despite ourselves, to what is beyond us,
Each distant sphere of harmony forever

Poised, unanswerable. If it is without
Consequence when we vaunt and suffer, or
If it is not, all echoes are the same
In such eternity. Then tell me, love,
How that should comfort us – or anyone
Dragged half-unnerved out of this worldly place,
Crying to the end 'I have not finished'.

Sonnet 8 of 'Funeral Music', from *King Log* by Geoffrey Hill, 1968

They are alive

They are alive,
here
as long as you remember them,

at a distance,
shrouded,
saying something –

they're walking behind the hedge,
you almost reach them
or the wind,

pale, like linen.

Bo Carpelan, Finland, 1983; translated from the Swedish by Anne Born

The Absences

Tree crickets tap tap tap. They are tunnelling
their way out of the dark; when they break through,
their dry husk will be planets. Little sheep-bells
clink. The sheep are finding their way down
through clouds, and fence by fence into the distance
dogs bark, clearing ditches, marking farms.
Much that is living here goes into the mouth
of night or issues from it. I sleep, and silence
climbs into my ear, the land blacks out, all
that was delicate and sharp subdued with fog.
The dead are buried in us. We dream them
as they dreamed us and woke and found us

flesh. Their bones rise through us. These are your eyes:
you will see a new world through them. This is your tongue
speaking. These are your hands, even in sleep
alert like animals. Stumbling on
down known paths through blackberry canes I happen
on details that insist. They scratch, they drag
their small hooks, they whiplash. They draw blood.

From 'Elegy The Absences, G M, 1896–1964' by David Malouf

Hauntings

This is the greatest sadness, like Handel
Ascending a staircase to loud tribute
That is already worms although
We have to pretend that it is music.
And other sadnesses: that she
Whose whole existence is an answer
Has questions of her own that strike
Us dumb. Only our smile survives,
To haunt our quiet retreat from life,
And that abundant love bred out
Of loneliness which merely puzzles
Its busy, sensual, happy victims.

Inside a piano in a cottage
A mile out of the nearest village
A spirit in the jangling strings
Practises ascending thirds in
Moments of calculated stillness:
Not Peter Lorre's scampering hand,
Nor the ghost-print of Cage prepared
For his strange business, nor even Handel
Reduced to such vague finger-stirrings
As an ecto-presence might manifest,
Like picking the nose, but a ditsy shrew
To whom is allowed its privacy.

Do all such hauntings have precise
Explanations? Only the failure
That makes us feel pursued is never
Exorcised, for we ourselves
Become the terrible excuse

That it projects, our shadow-play,
Our mirror, our familiar.
Out there, though, every kind of music
Is ready to recreate the worldly

Heartache or triumph it once became,
And having once become it, will
Again do so, and yet again.

John Fuller, 1991

The Wall

It was a changeable house. Sometimes it felt safe as a church, and
sometimes it shivered then cracked apart.

A sloping blue slate roof held it down. Turrets at the four corners
wore pointed blue hats. The many eyes of the house were blinded by
white shutters.

What bounded the house was skin. A wall of gristle a soldier could
tear open with his bare hands. Antoinette laughed. She was buried in
the cellar under a heap of sand. Her mouth was stuffed full of torn-up
letters and broken glass but she was tunnelling her way out like a mole.
Her mouth bled from the corners. She laughed a guttural laugh, a Nazi
laugh.

The house was strict. The rules indicated the forbidden places. Chief
of these was the bedroom at the back on the first floor, at the top of the
kitchen stairs.

The rules said you mustn't go there. It was for your own protection.
Each time Léonie tried she had to halt. The terror was so strong. It
pushed her away, wouldn't let her come near. Behind the terror was
something evil which stank and snarled and wanted to fix her in its
embrace. Better to flee, to clatter back across the bare plank floor of the
landing, find the headlong stairs and fall down them. Better to stay at
the front of the house.

Antoinette was dead, which was why they had buried her in the cellar. She moved under the heap of sand. She clutched her red handbag,
which was full of shreds of dead flesh. She was trying to get out, to
hang two red petticoats on the washing-line in the orchard. Sooner or
later she would batter down the cellar door and burst up through it on
her dead and bleeding feet.

The deadness and the evil and the stink were inside Léonie. She
rushed up the cellar steps, magically she erupted into her own bed in
the dark, the smell of warm blood, soaked sawdust.

Now she was properly awake. She ran to the bathroom to be sick. It was Thérèse she was throwing up. She vomited her forth, desperate to be rid of her and then weak with gasping relief that she was gone.

From *Daughters of the House* by Michèle Roberts, 1992

'There are ghosts and ghosts'

Another dead one; dear Jesus, I do keep on adding to them, don't I? Well, that's life, I suppose. I think of them like the figures in one of Vaublin's twilit landscapes, placed here and there in isolation about the scene, each figure somehow the source of its own illumination, aglow in the midst of shadows, still and speechless, not dead and yet not alive either, waiting perhaps to be brought to some kind of life. That's it, let us have a disquisition, to pass the time and keep ourselves from brooding. Think of a topic. Ghosts, now, why not. I have never been able to understand why ghosts should be considered something to be afraid of; they might be troublesome, a burden to us, perhaps, pawing at us as we try to get on with our poor lives, but not frightening, surely. Yet, though the fresh-made widow weeps and tears her breast, if she were to come home from the cemetery in her weeds and veil and find her husband's spirit sitting large as life in his favourite armchair by the fire she would run into the street gibbering in terror. It makes no sense. I can think of times and circumstances when even the ghosts of complete strangers, no matter how horrid, would be welcomed. The prisoner held in solitary confinement, for instance, would be grateful surely to wake up some fevered night and find a troupe of his predecessors come walking through the wall in their rags and beards and clanking their chains, while Saint Teresa would have been tickled, I suspect, to receive a visit to her interior castle from some long-dead hidalgo of Old Castile. And what of our friend Crusoe in his hut, would he not have been happy to be haunted by the spirits of his drowned shipmates? The ship's doctor could have advised him on his ague, the carpenter on his fencing, while the cabin boy, no matter how fey, surely would have afforded a welcome change of fare from Friday's dusky charms.

There are ghosts and ghosts, of course. Banquo was a dampener on the king's carousings, and Hamlet's father made what I cannot but think were excessive calls on filial piety. Yet, for myself, I know I would be grateful for any intercourse with the dead, no matter how baleful their stares or unavoidable their pale, pointing fingers. I feel I might be able, not to exonerate, but to explain myself, perhaps, to account for my neglectfulness, my failures, the things left unsaid, all those sins against the dead, both of omission and commission, of which I had been guilty while they were still in the land of the living. But more than that, more important than the desire for self-justification, is the conviction that I have, however preposterous it may sound, that there is an onus on us, the living, to conjure up our particular dead. I am certain there is no other form of afterlife for them than this, that they should live in us, and through us. It is our duty. (I like the high moral tone. How dare I, really!)

From *Ghosts* by John Banville, 1993

The Listeners

'Is there anybody there?' said the Traveller,
    Knocking on the moonlit door;
And his horse in the silence champed the grasses
    Of the forest's ferny floor:
And a bird flew up out of the turret,
    Above the Traveller's head:
And he smote upon the door again a second time;
    'Is there anybody there?' he said.
But no one descended to the Traveller;
    No head from the leaf-fringed sill
Leaned over and looked into his grey eyes,
    Where he stood perplexed and still.

But only a host of phantom listeners
    That dwelt in the lone house then
Stood listening in the quiet of the moonlight
    To that voice from the world of men:
Stood thronging the faint moonbeams on the dark stair,
    That goes down to the empty hall,
Hearkening in an air stirred and shaken
    By the lonely Traveller's call.
And he felt in his heart their strangeness,
    Their stillness answering his cry,
While his horse moved, cropping the dark turf,
    'Neath the starred and leafy sky;

For he suddenly smote on the door, even
    Louder, and lifted his head: –
'Tell them I came, and no one answered,
    That I kept my word,' he said.
Never the least stir made the listeners,
    Though every word he spake
Fell echoing through the shadowiness of the still house
    From the one man left awake:
Ay, they heard his foot upon the stirrup,
    And the sound of iron on stone,
And how the silence surged softly backward,
    When the plunging hoofs were gone.

Walter de la Mare, 1912

Under Ben Bulben

Many times man lives and dies
Between his two eternities,
That of race and that of soul,
And ancient Ireland knew it all.
Whether man die in his bed
Or the rifle knocks him dead,
A brief parting from those dear
Is the worst man has to fear.

Though grave-diggers' toil is long,
Sharp their spades, their muscles strong,
They but thrust their buried men
Back in the human mind again.

From 'Under Ben Bulben' by W. B. Yeats, 1938

Three

APPEARANCES

When lo! appear'd along the dusky coasts,
Thin airy shoals of visionary ghosts:
Fair, pensive youths, and soft enamour'd maids;
And wither'd elders, pale and wrinkled shades;
Ghastly with wounds, the forms of warriors slain
Stalk'd with majestic port, a martial train.

ALEXANDER POPE

In the uncertain hour before the morning
 Near the ending of interminable night
 At the recurrent end of the unending...
... I met one walking, loitering and hurried
As if blown towards me like the metal leaves
 Before the urban dawn wind unresisting.

T. S. ELIOT

The Haunted House

I'll never forgit when I was a young kid at home – an' that's been a long time ago – 'bout the only way there was to pass off the time then – there was no TV, no radio – was to go spend bedtime with a neighbor or them come spend bedtime with us. An' the ol' folks sat around an' talked about these ol' ghost stories back yonder, an' I used ta go to bed scared to death to hear them tell about the ol' haunted house.

They couldn't get nobody to stay in that house. Ever'time a person'd go there to spend the night, why, a ha'nt'd run 'em off. So this ol' feller, he decided he'd stay. He wadn't a-scared o' nothin'. So he taken the job, an' built him up a good fire in the fireplace an' had his supper an' got ever'thing ready. Pulled off his coat an' hat; he'd brought his paper along to read an' set down, begin to readin'. The ol' haunt walked around in front of him an' pulled the paper back, said, 'Ain' nobody here tonight but you an' I, are they?'

An' the man said, 'Naw, an' if you wait 'til I get my hat, there won't be nobody here but you!'

Collected by John A. Burrison in *Storytellers:
Folktales and Legends from the South*, 1971

The Dead

I see them, – crowd on crowd they walk the earth,
Dry leafless trees no autumn wind laid bare;
And in their nakedness find cause for mirth,
And all unclad would winter's rudeness dare;
No sap doth through their clattering branches flow,
Whence springing leaves and blossoms bright appear;
Their hearts the living God have ceased to know
Who gives the spring time to th' expectant year;
They mimic life, as if from him to steal
The glow of health to paint the livid cheek;
They borrow words for thoughts they cannot feel,
That with a seeming heart their tongue may speak;
And in their show of life more dead they live
Than those that to the earth with many tears they give.

Jones Very, 1839

The Chapter of Coming Forth by Day

The overseer of the house of the overseer of the seal, Nu, triumphant, saith: –

'The doors of heaven are opened for me, the doors of earth are opened for me, the bars and bolts of Seb are opened for me, and the first temple hath been unfastened for me by the god Petra. Behold, I was guarded and watched, but now I am released . . . and I shall come forth by day into whatsoever place I please. I have gained the mastery over my heart; I have gained the mastery over my breast; I have gained the mastery over my two hands; I have gained the mastery over my two feet; I have gained the mastery over my mouth; I have gained the mastery over my whole body; I have gained the mastery over sepulchral offerings; I have gained the mastery over the waters; I have gained the mastery over the air; I have gained the mastery over the canal; I have gained the mastery over the river and over the land; I have gained the mastery over the furrows; I have gained the mastery over the male workers for me; I have gained the mastery over the female workers for me in the underworld; I have gained the mastery over all the things which were ordered to be done for me upon the earth, according to the entreaty which ye spake for me saying, "Behold, let him live upon the bread of Seb." That which is an abomination unto me, I shall not eat, nay I shall live upon cakes made of white grain, and my ale shall be made of the red grain of Hāpi. In a clean place shall I sit on the ground beneath the foliage of the date palm of the goddess Hathor . . . I shall lift myself up on my left side, and I shall place myself on my right side; I shall lift myself up on my right side, and I shall place myself on my left side. I shall sit down, I shall stand up, and I shall place myself in the path of the wind like a guide who is well prepared.'

RUBRIC: If this composition be known by the deceased he shall come forth by day, and he shall be in a position to journey about over the earth among the living, and he shall never suffer diminution, never never

From *The Egyptian Book of the Dead*, translated by E. A. Wallis Budge, 1899

A Conversation with Achilles

'If you will not accuse me of bragging,' said Apollonius, 'you shall hear everything.'

The rest of the company besought him to tell them all about it, and as

[65]

they were in a mood to listen to him, he said: 'Well, it was not by digging a ditch like Odysseus, nor by tempting souls with the blood of
sheep, that I obtained a conversation with Achilles; but I offered up the
prayer which the Indians say they use in approaching their heroes. "O
Achilles," I said, "most of mankind declare that you are dead, but I cannot agree with them, nor can Pythagoras, my spiritual ancestor. If then
we hold the truth, show to us your own form; for you would profit not
a little by showing yourself to my eyes, if you should be able to use
them to attest your existence." Thereupon a slight earthquake shook
the neighbourhood of the barrow, and a youth issued forth five cubits
high, wearing a cloak of Thessalian fashion; but in appearance he was
by no means the braggart figure which some imagine Achilles to have
been. Though he was stern to look upon, he had never lost his bright
look; and it seems to me that his beauty has never received its meed of
praise, even though Homer dwelt at length upon it; for it was really
beyond the power of words, and it is easier for the singer to ruin his
fame in this respect than to praise him as he deserved. At first sight he
was of the size which I have mentioned, but he grew bigger, till he was
twice as large and even more than that; at any rate he appeared to me
to be twelve cubits high just at that moment when he reached his complete stature, and his beauty grew apace with his length. He told me
then that he had never at any time shorn off his hair, but preserved it
inviolate for the river Spercheus, for this was the river of his first intimacy; but on his cheeks you saw the first down.

'And he addressed me and said: "I am pleased to have met you, since
I have long wanted a man like yourself. For the Thessalians for a long
time past have failed to present their offerings at my tomb, and I do not
yet wish to show my wrath against them; for if I did so, they would
perish more thoroughly than ever the Hellenes did on this spot. . . .
You must go as my envoy to their council in behalf of the object I have
mentioned." "I will be your envoy," I replied, "for the object of my
embassy were to save them from ruin."'

From *The Life of Apollonius* by Flavius Philostratus, *c.*220 BC,
translated by F. C. Conybeare

Of a citizen on whose legs was written, 'Ave Maria'

A certain citizen of Cologne had a habit of always praying when he was
alone. Going to the church or returning, or walking in the court, he
meditated on the angelic salutation. When he was dead, he appeared to
his grand-daughter in a shining dress and all over him and especially
on his boots was written in verse: 'Hail Mary, full of grace etc.' Because

as I have said, he had uttered that verse continually as he walked about, it was seen written more often on his feet. From what has been said we gather that as God punishes a sin according to kind and measure, so also he rewards a good deed, putting the mark of glory most of all on those members by which it was earned.

From *The Dialogue of Miracles* by Caesarius of Heisterbach, c.1220–35, translated by H. von E. Scott and C. C. Swinton Bland.

Of a spirit that helped his master

Richer, a monk of Senones, speaks of a spirit which returned in his time, in the town of Epinal, about the year 1212, in the house of a burgess named Hugh de la Cour, and who, from Christmas to Mid-summer, did a variety of things in that same house, in sight of every body. They could hear him speak, they could see all he did, but nobody could see him. He said, he belonged to Cléxenteine, a village seven leagues from Epinal; and what is also remarkable is, that during the six months he was heard about the house, he did no harm to any one. One day, Hugh having ordered his domestic to saddle his horse, and the valet being busy about something else, deferred doing it, when the spirit did his work, to the great astonishment of all the household. Another time, when Hugh was absent, the spirit asked Stephen, the son-in-law of Hugh, for a penny, to make an offering of it to St. Goëric, the patron saint of Epinal. Stephen presented him with an old denier of Provence; but the spirit refused it, saying, he would have a good denier of Thoulouse. Stephen placed on the threshold of the door a Thoulousian denier, which disappeared immediately; and the following night, a noise, as of a man who was walking therein, was heard in the Church of St. Goëric.

Another time, Hugh having bought some fish to make his family a repast, the spirit transported the fish to the garden which was behind the house, put half of it on a tile, (*scandula*,) and the rest in a mortar, where it was found again. Another time, Hugh desiring to be bled, told his daughter to get ready some bandages. Immediately the spirit went into another room, and fetched a new shirt, which he tore up into several bandages, presented them to the master of the house, and told him to choose the best. Another day, the servant having spread out some linen in the garden to dry, the spirit carried it all up stairs, and folded them more neatly than the cleverest laundress could have done.

From *The Phantom World* by Augustine Calmet, 1746, translated by the Rev. H. Christmas, 1850

In the Lop Nor Desert

If, during the daytime, any persons remain behind on the road, either when overtaken by sleep or detained by their natural occasions, until the caravan has passed a hill and is no longer in sight, they unexpectedly hear themselves called to by their names, and in a tone of voice to which they are accustomed. Supposing the call to proceed from their companions, they are led away by it from the direct road, and not knowing in what direction to advance, are left to perish. In the night-time they are persuaded they hear the march of a large cavalcade on one side or the other of the road, and concluding the noise to be that of the footsteps of their party, they direct theirs to the quarter from whence it seems to proceed; but upon the breaking of day, find they have been misled and drawn into a situation of danger. Sometimes likewise during the day these spirits assume the appearance of their travelling companions, who address them by name and endeavour to conduct them out of the proper road. It is said also that some persons, in their course across the desert, have seen what appeared to them to be a body of armed men advancing towards them, and apprehensive of being attacked and plundered have taken to flight. Losing by this means the right path, and ignorant of the direction they should take to regain it, they have perished miserably of hunger. Marvellous indeed and almost passing belief are the stories related of these spirits of the desert.

From *The Travels of Marco Polo*, c.1290, translated by W. Marsden

'Speak to me'

HORATIO: But, soft! behold! lo! where it comes again.
(Re-enter Ghost)
I'll cross it, though it blast me. Stay, illusion!
If thou hast any sound, or use of voice,
Speak to me:
If there be any good thing to be done,
That may to thee do ease and grace to me,
Speak to me:
If thou art privy to thy country's fate,
Which happily foreknowing may avoid,
O! speak;
Or if thou hast uphoarded in thy life

Extorted treasure in the womb of earth,
For which, they say, you spirits oft walk in death,
Speak of it: stay, and speak!

From *Hamlet, Prince of Denmark* by William Shakespeare, 1603-4

Of speech

1

Anno 1670, not far from Cirencester, was an apparition: being demanded, whether a good spirit, or a bad? returned no answer, but disappeared with a curious perfume and most melodious twang. Mr W. Lilley believes it was a Fairie.

John Aubrey, *Miscellanies*, 1691

2

It has been universally found by experience, as well as affirmed by divers apparitions themselves, that a ghost has not the power to speak till it has been first spoken to. . . . It has not been found that female ghosts are more loquacious than those of the male sex, both being equally restrained by this law.

Captain Francis Grose, 1775

3

In the parish of Trefethin, Monmouthshire, the ghost of a woman given to a loose life appeared to her brother and told him she was in 'a sore, cold place, with a sword over her head.' When the brother advised her to give glory to God, she said she would not and departed.

From *Welsh Folklore* by T. Gwynn Jones, 1930

Nick's Night Out

One learned gentleman, 'a sage, grave man,'
  Talk'd of the Ghost in Hamlet, 'sheath'd in steel' –
His well-read friend, who next to speak began,
  Said, 'That was Poetry, and nothing real';
A third, of more extensive learning, ran
  To Sir George Villiers' Ghost, and Mrs Veal;

[69]

Of sheeted Spectres spoke with shorten'd breath,
And thrice he quoted 'Drelincourt on Death.'

*

'Twas now the very witching time of night,
    When churchyards groan, and graves give up their dead,
And many a mischievous, enfranchised Sprite
    Had long since burst his bonds of stone or lead,
And hurried off, with schoolboy-like delight,
    To play his pranks near some poor wretch's bed,
Sleeping, perhaps serenely as a porpoise,
Nor dreaming of this fiendish Habeas Corpus.

Not so our Nicholas: his meditations
    Still to the same tremendous theme recurr'd,
The same dread subject of the dark narrations,
    Which, back'd with such authority, he'd heard:
Lost in his own horrific contemplations,
    He ponder'd o'er each well-remember'd word;
When at the bed's foot, close beside the post,
He verily believed he saw – a Ghost!

*

All motionless the Spectre stood – and now
    Its rev'rend form more clearly shone confest;
From the pale cheek a beard of purest snow
    Descended o'er its venerable breast;
The thin grey hairs, that crown'd its furrow'd brow,
    Told of years long gone by. – An awful guest
It stood, and with an action of command,
Beckon'd the Cobbler with its wan right hand.

'Whence, and what art thou, Execrable Shape?'
    Nick *might* have cried, could he have found a tongue,
But his distended jaws could only gape,
    And not a sound upon the welkin rung:
His gooseberry orbs seem'd as they would have sprung
    Forth from their sockets – like a frighten'd Ape
He sat upon his haunches, bolt upright,
And shook, and grinn'd, and chatter'd with affright.

And still the shadowy finger, long and lean,
    Now beckon'd Nick, now pointed to the door;
And many an ireful glance, and frown, between,
    The angry visage of the Phantom wore,
As if quite vex'd that Nick would do no more

[70]

Than stare, without e'en asking, 'What d'ye mean?'
Because, as we are told – a sad old joke, too –
Ghosts, like the ladies, 'never speak till spoke to.'

From 'The Ghost' by R. H. Barham, 1820

The Skeleton in Armour

'Speak! speak! thou fearful guest!
Who, with thy hollow breast
Still in rude armour drest,
    Comest to daunt me!
Wrapt not in Eastern balms,
But with thy fleshless palms
Stretched, as if asking alms,
    Why dost thou haunt me?'

Then, from those cavernous eyes
Pale flashes seemed to rise,
As when the Northern skies
    Gleam in December;
And, like the water's flow
Under December's snow,
Came a dull voice of woe
    From the heart's chamber.

'I was a Viking old!
My deeds, though manifold,
No Skald in song has told,
    No Saga taught thee
Take heed, that in thy verse
Thou dost the tale rehearse,
Else dread a dead man's curse!
    For this I sought thee.'...

Henry Wadsworth Longfellow, 1841

Guest

Is the kitchen tap still dripping?
You should always chain the door at nights.
Soon the roof will need repairing.
What's happening these days at the office?

Too much coffee agitates the nerves.
Now don't forget to spray the roses.
Do see the doctor about those twinges.

But tell me where you are? How is it there?
Are you in pain or bliss? And what is bliss?
Are you lonely? Do we live for ever?
How do you pass the time, if time there is?
Does God exist? Is God loving?
Why must his ways be so mysterious?
Is there a purpose in our living?

*

Why won't you speak of things that matter?
You used to be so wise, so serious.
Now all our talk is roofs and roses
Like neighbours chatting at the corner.

Here wisdom is as common as the air,
Great matters are the ground I tread.
Tell me, what weather are you having?
Are the planes still noisy overhead?
Ask my old mates how work is going –

Don't be angry, dear. This hasn't changed:
Those things we lack are what we covet.
I am the guest, the one to be indulged.

D. J. Enright, 1981

Mrs Veal

Above a Twelve Month of the time, Mrs *Bargrave* had been absent from *Dover*, and this last half Year, has been in *Canterbury* about two Months of the time, dwelling in a House of her own.

In this House, on the Eighth of *September* last, *viz.* 1705. She was sitting alone in the Forenoon, thinking over her Unfortunate Life, and arguing her self into a due Resignation to Providence, tho' her condition seem'd hard. And said she, *I have been provided for hitherto, and doubt not but I shall be still; and am well satisfied, that my Afflictions shall end, when it is most fit for me:* And then took up her Sewing-Work, which she had no sooner done, but she hears a Knocking at the Door; she went to see who it was there, and this prov'd to be Mrs *Veal*, her Old Friend, who was in a Riding Habit: At that Moment of Time, the Clock struck Twelve at Noon.

Madam says Mrs *Bargrave*, I am surprized to see you, you have been so long a stranger, but told her, she was glad to see her and offer'd to Salute her, which Mrs *Veal* complyed with, till their Lips almost touched, and then Mrs *Veal* drew her hand cross her own Eyes, and said, *I am not very well*, and so waved it. She told Mrs *Bargrave*, she was going a Journey, and had a great mind to see her first: But says Mrs *Bargrave, how came you to take a Journey alone? I am amaz'd at it, because I know you have so fond a Brother.* O! says Mrs *Veal, I gave my Brother the Slip, and came away, because I had so great a Mind to see you before I took my Journy.* So Mrs *Bargrave* went in with her, into another Room within the first, and Mrs *Veal* sat her self down in an Elbow-chair, in which Mrs *Bargrave* was sitting when she heard Mrs *Veal* Knock. Then says Mrs *Veal, My Dear Friend, I am come to renew our Old Friendship again, and to beg your Pardon for my breach of it, and if you can forgive me you are one of the best of Women.* O! says Mrs *Bargrave, don't mention such a thing, I have not had an uneasie thought about it, I can easily forgive it.* What did you think of me says Mrs *Veal?* Says Mrs *Bargrave, I thought you were like the rest of the World, and that Prosperity had made you forget your self and me.* Then Mrs *Veal* reminded Mrs *Bargrave* of the many Friendly Offices she did her in former Days, and much of the Conversation they had with each other in the time of their Adversity; what Books they Read, and what Comfort in particular they received from *Drelincourt's Book of Death*, which was the best she said on that Subject, was ever Wrote. . . .

As they were admiring Friendship, Mrs *Veal* said, Dear Mrs *Bargrave*, I shall love you for ever: In the Verses, there is twice used the Word *Elysium.* Ah! says Mrs *Veal, These Poets have such Names for Heaven.* She would often draw her Hand cross her own Eyes; and say, Mrs *Bargrave Don't you think I am mightily impaired by my Fits?* No, says Mrs *Bargrave,* I think you look as well as ever I knew you. . . .

Then she said, *she would not take her Leave of her,* and walk'd from Mrs *Bargrave* in her view, till a turning interrupted the sight of her, which was three quarters after One in the Afternoon.

Mrs *Veal* Dyed the 7th of *September* at 12 a Clock at Noon, of her Fits, and had not above four hours Senses before her Death, in which time she received the Sacrament. . . .

This thing has very much affected me, and I am well satisfied, as I am of the best grounded Matter of Fact. And why should we dispute Matter of Fact, because we cannot solve things, of which we can have no certain or demonstrative Notions, seems strange to me: Mrs *Bargrave*'s Authority and Sincerity alone, would have been undoubted in any other Case.

From *A True Relation of the Apparition of One Mrs Veal* by Daniel Defoe, 1706

'Those Graves'

Those Graves, with bending Osier bound,
That nameless heave the crumbled Ground,
Quick to the glancing Thought disclose
Where *Toil* and *Poverty* repose.
   The flat smooth Stones that bear a Name,
The Chissels slender help to Fame,
(Which e'er our Sett of Friends decay
Their frequent Steps may wear away)
A *middle Race* of Mortals own,
Men, half ambitious, all unknown.
   The Marble Tombs that rise on high,
Whose Dead in vaulted Arches lye,
Whose Pillars swell with sculptur'd Stones,
Arms, Angels, Epitaphs and Bones,
These (all the poor Remains of State)
Adorn the *Rich*, or praise the Great;
Who while on Earth in Fame they live,
Are sensless of the Fame they give.
   Ha! while I gaze, pale *Cynthia* fades,
The bursting Earth unveils the Shades!
All slow, and wan, and wrap'd with Shrouds,
They rise in visionary Crouds,
And all with sober Accent cry,
Think, Mortal, what it is to dye.

From 'A Night Piece on Death' by Thomas Parnell, 1722

'Strange Things'

Strange Things, the Neighbours say, have happen'd here:
Wild Shrieks have issu'd from the hollow Tombs,
Dead men have come again, and walk'd about,
And the Great Bell has toll'd, unrung, untouch'd.
(Such Tales their Chear, at Wake or Gossiping,
When it draws near to Witching Time of Night.)
   Oft, in the lone Church-yard at Night I've seen
By Glimpse of Moon-shine, chequering thro' the Trees,
The School-boy with his Satchel in his Hand,

Whistling aloud to bear his Courage up,
And lightly tripping o'er the long flat Stones
(With Nettles skirted, and with Moss o'ergrown,)
That tell in homely Phrase who lie below;
Sudden! he starts, and hears, or thinks he hears
The Sound of something purring at his Heels:
Full fast he flies, and dares not look behind him,
Till out of Breath he overtakes his Fellows;
Who gather round, and wonder at the Tale
Of horrid *Apparition*, tall and ghastly,
That walks at Dead of Night, or takes his Stand
O'er some new-open'd *Grave*; and, strange to tell!
Evanishes at Crowing of the Cock.

From *The Grave* by Robert Blair, 1743

Phantom

All look and likeness caught from earth
All accident of kin and birth,
Had pass'd away. There was no trace
Of aught on that illumined face,

Uprais'd beneath the rifted stone
But of one spirit all her own; –
She, she herself, and only she,
Shone through her body visibly.

Samuel Taylor Coleridge, 1805

'Impressions'

'Monsieur, I tell you every glance you cast from that lattice is a wrong done to the best part of your own nature. To study the human heart thus, is to banquet secretly and sacrilegiously on Eve's apples. I wish you were a Protestant.'

Indifferent to the wish, he smoked on. After a space of smiling yet thoughtful silence, he said, rather suddenly, –

'I have seen other things.'

'What other things?'

[75]

Taking the weed from his lips, he threw the remnant amongst the shrubs, where, for a moment, it lay glowing in the gloom.

'Look at it,' said he: 'is not that spark like an eye watching you and me?'

He took a turn down the walk; presently returning, he went on:–

'I have seen, Miss Lucy, things to me unaccountable, that have made me watch all night for a solution, and I have not yet found it.'

The tone was peculiar; my veins thrilled; he saw me shiver.

'Are you afraid? Whether is it of my words or that red jealous eye just winking itself out?'

'I am cold; the night grows dark and late, and the air is changed; it is time to go in.'

'It is little past eight, but you shall go in soon. Answer me only this question.'

Yet he paused ere he put it. The garden was truly growing dark: dusk had come on with clouds, and drops of rain began to patter through the trees. I hoped he would feel this, but, for the moment, he seemed too much absorbed to be sensible of the change.

"Mademoiselle, do you Protestants believe in the supernatural?"

'There is a difference of theory and belief on this point amongst Protestants as amongst other sects,' I answered. 'Why, monsieur, do you ask such a question?'

'Why do you shrink and speak so faintly? Are you superstitious?'

'I am constitutionally nervous. I dislike the discussion of such subjects. I dislike it the more because –'

'You believe?'

'No: but it has happened to me to experience impressions –'

'Since you came here?'

'Yes; not many months ago.'

'Here – in this house?'

'Yes.'

'Bon! I am glad of it. I knew it somehow, before you told me. I was conscious of rapport between you and myself. You are patient, and I am choleric; you are quiet and pale, and I am tanned and fiery; you are a strict Protestant, and I am a sort of lay Jesuit: but we are alike – there is affinity between us. Do you see it, mademoiselle, when you look in the glass? Do you observe that your forehead is shaped like mine – that your eyes are cut like mine? Do you hear that you have some of my tones of voice? Do you know that you have many of my looks? I perceive all this, and believe that you were born under my star. Yes, you were born under my star! Tremble! for where that is the case with mortals, the threads of their destinies are difficult to disentangle; knottings and catchings occur – sudden breaks leave damage in the web. But these "impressions", as you say, with English caution. I, too, have had my "impressions".'

'Monsieur, tell me them.'

'I desire no better, and intend no less. You know the legend of this house and garden?'

'I know it. Yes. They say that hundreds of years ago a nun was buried here alive at the foot of this very tree, beneath the ground which now bears us.'

'And that in former days a nun's ghost used to come and go here.'

'Monsieur, what if it comes and goes here still?'

'Something comes and goes here: there is a shape frequenting this house by night, different to any forms that show themselves by day. I have indisputably seen a something, more than once; and to me its conventual weeds were a strange sight, saying more than they can do to any other living being. A nun!'

'Monsieur, I too have seen it.'

'I anticipated that. Whether this nun be flesh and blood, or something that remains when blood is dried, and flesh is wasted, her business is as much with you as with me, probably. Well, I mean to make it out; it has baffled me so far, but I mean to follow up the mystery. I mean –'

Instead of telling what he meant, he raised his head suddenly; I made the same movement in the same instant; we both looked to one point – the high tree shadowing the great berceau, and resting some of its boughs on the roof of the first classe. There had been a strange and inexplicable sound from that quarter, as if the arms of that tree had swayed of their own motion, and its weight of foliage had rushed and crushed against the massive trunk. Yes: there scarce stirred a breeze, and that heavy tree was convulsed, whilst the feathery shrubs stood still. For some minutes amongst the wood and leafage a rending and heaving went on. Dark as it was, it seemed to me that something more solid than either night-shadow, or branch-shadow, blackened out of the boles. At last the struggle ceased. What birth succeeded this travail? What Dryad was born of these throes? We watched fixedly. A sudden bell rang in the house – the prayer-bell. Instantly into our alley there came, out of the berceau, an apparition, all black and white. With a sort of angry rush – close, close past our faces – swept swiftly the very NUN herself! Never had I seen her so clearly. She looked tall of stature, and fierce of gesture. As she went, the wind rose sobbing; the rain poured wild and cold; the whole night seemed to feel her.

From *Villette* by Charlotte Brontë, 1853

The child in the snow

The great frost never ceased all this time; and whenever it was a more stormy night than usual, between the gusts, and through the wind, we heard the old lord playing on the great organ. But, old lord, or not, wherever Miss Rosamond went, there I followed; for my love for her, pretty helpless orphan, was stronger than my fear for the grand and terrible sound. Besides, it rested with me to keep her cheerful and merry, as beseemed her age. So we played together, and wandered together, here and there, and everywhere; for I never dared to lose sight of her again in that large and rambling house. And so it happened, that one afternoon, not long before Christmas Day, we were playing together on the billiard-table in the great hall (not that we knew the way of playing, but she liked to roll the smooth ivory balls with her pretty hands, and I liked to do whatever she did); and, by-and-by, without our noticing it, it grew dusk indoors, though it was still light in the open air, and I was thinking of taking her back into the nursery, when, all of a sudden, she cried out:

'Look, Hester! look! there is my poor little girl out in the snow!'

I turned towards the long narrow windows, and there, sure enough, I saw a little girl, less than my Miss Rosamond – dressed all unfit to be out-of-doors such a bitter night – crying, and beating against the window-panes, as if she wanted to be let in. She seemed to sob and wail, till Miss Rosamond could bear it no longer, and was flying to the door to open it, when, all of a sudden, and close up upon us, the great organ pealed out so loud and thundering, it fairly made me tremble; and all the more when I remembered me that, even in the stillness of that dead-cold weather, I had heard no sound of little battering hands upon the window-glass, although the Phantom Child had seemed to put forth all its force; and, although I had seen it wail and cry, no faintest touch of sound had fallen upon my ears. Whether I remembered all this at the very moment, I do not know; the great organ sound had so stunned me into terror; but this I know, I caught up Miss Rosamond before she got the hall door opened, and clutched her, and carried her away, kicking and screaming, into the large bright kitchen, where Dorothy and Agnes were busy with their mince-pies.

'What is the matter with my sweet one?' cried Dorothy, as I bore in Miss Rosamond, who was sobbing as if her heart would break.

'She won't let me open the door for my little girl to come in; and she'll die if she is out on the Fells all night. Cruel, naughty Hester,' she said, slapping me; but she might have struck harder, for I had seen a look of ghastly terror on Dorothy's face, which made my very blood run cold.

'Shut the back-kitchen door fast, and bolt it well,' said she to Agnes.

She said no more; she gave me raisins and almonds to quiet Miss Rosamond: but she sobbed about the little girl in the snow, and would not touch any of the good things. I was thankful when she cried herself to sleep in bed. Then I stole down to the kitchen, and told Dorothy I had made up my mind. I would carry my darling back to my father's house in Applethwaite; where, if we lived humbly, we lived at peace.

From 'The Old Nurse's Story' by Elizabeth Gaskell, 1852

'If one should bring me this report'

If one should bring me this report,
  That thou hadst touch'd the land to-day,
  And I went down unto the quay,
And found thee lying in the port;

And standing, muffled round with woe,
  Should see thy passengers in rank
  Come stepping lightly down the plank,
And beckoning unto those they know;

And if along with these should come
  The man I held as half-divine;
  Should strike a sudden hand in mine,
And ask a thousand things of home;

And I should tell him all my pain,
  And how my life had droop'd of late,
  And he should sorrow o'er my state
And marvel what possess'd my brain;

And I perceived no touch of change,
  No hint of death in all his frame,
  But found him all in all the same,
I should not feel it to be strange.

From *In Memoriam* by Alfred Lord Tennyson, 1850

Hallam returns

She felt a stab of pain, like an icicle between the clutched ribs. She heard the rattle of hail, or rain, suddenly in great gusts on the window-pane, like scattered seed. She felt a sudden weight in the room, a heavy space, as one feels tapping at the door of a house, knowing in advance that it is inhabited, before the foot is heard on the stair, the rustle and clink in the hall. She knew she must not look behind her, and knowing that, began drowsily to hum in her head the richness of 'The Eve of St Agnes':

> Out went the taper as she hurried in;
> Its little smoke, in pallid moonshine, died:
> She clos'd the door, she panted, all akin
> To spirits of the air, and visions wide:
> No uttered syllable, or, woe betide!
> But to her heart, her heart was voluble,
> Paining with eloquence her balmy side;
> As though a tongueless nightingale should swell
> Her throat in vain, and die, heart-stifled, in her dell.

Whatever was behind her sighed, and then drew in its breath, with difficulty. Sophy Sheekhy told him dubiously, 'I *think* you are there. I should like to see you.'

'Perhaps you wouldn't like what you saw,' she heard, or thought she heard.

'Was that you?'

'I said, perhaps you wouldn't like what you saw.'

'It isn't my habit to like or dislike,' she found herself answering.

She took her candle and held it up to the mirror, still filled with the superstitious sense, like those poetic ladies, Madeline, the Lady of Shalott, that she must not look away from the plane of glass. The candle caused a local shimmer and gloom in the depths in which she thought she saw something move.

'We cannot always help ourselves as to that,' he said, much more clearly.

'Please –' she breathed to the glass.

She felt him move in on her, closer, closer. She heard the words of the poem spoken in an ironic, slightly harsh voice.

> Into her dream he melted, as the rose
> Blendeth its odour with the violet. –
> Solution sweet:

Her hand shook, the face behind her bulged and tightened, sagged and reassembled, not pale, but purple-veined, with staring blue eyes and parched thin lips, above a tremulous chin. There was a sudden gust of odour, not rose, not violet, but earth-mould and corruption.

'You see,' said the harsh, small voice. 'I am a dead man, you see.'

Sophy Sheekhy took a breath and turned round. She saw her own little white bed, and a row of doves preening themselves on the cast-iron bedstead. She saw, briefly, a parrot, scarlet and blue, on the windowsill. She saw dark glass, and she saw him, struggling, it seemed to her, to keep his appearance, his sort-of-substance, together, with a kind of deadly defiance.

She knew immediately that he was the man. Not because she recognised him, but because she did not, and yet he fitted the descriptions, the curls, the thin mouth, the bar on the brow. He wore an ancient high-collared shirt, out of fashion when Sophy's mother was a small child, and stained breeches. He stood there, trembling and morose. The trembling was not exactly human. It caused his body to swell and contract as though sucked out of shape and pressed back into it. Sophy took a few steps towards him. She saw that his brows and lashes were caked with clay. He said again, 'I am a dead man.'

He moved away from her, walking like someone finding his feet after a long illness, and sat down on the seat in the window, displacing a number of white birds, who ran fluttering and resettled at the foot of the curtains. Sophy followed him, and stood and considered him. He was very young. His lovers on earth watched and waited for him like some wise god gone before, but this young man was younger than she was herself, and seemed to be in the last stages of exhaustion, owing to his state. She had been told, in the Church of the New Jerusalem, of Swedenborg's encounters with the newly dead, who refused to believe that they were dead, who attended their own funerals with indignant interest. Later, Swedenborg taught, the dead, who took with them into the next world the affections and minds of this terrestrial space, had to find their true selves and their true, their appropriate companions, amongst spirits and angels. They had to learn that they were dead, and then to go on. She said, 'How is it with you? What is your state?'

'As you see me. Baffled and impotent.'

'You are much mourned, much missed. More than any being I know.'

A spasm of anguish twisted the dull red face, and Sophy Sheekhy suddenly felt in her blood and bones that the mourning was painful to him. It dragged him down, or back, or under. He moved his heavy tongue in his mouth, unaccustomed now.

'I walk. Between. Outside. I cannot tell you. I am part of nothing. Impotent and baffled,' he added, quick and articulate suddenly, as though these were words he knew, had tamed doggedly in his mind over the long years. Which might not, of course, appear to him to be years. A thousand ages in thy sight are but an instant gone. She spoke from her heart.

'You are so *young.*'

'I am young. And dead.'

'And not forgotten.'

Again, the same spasm of pain.

'And alone.' The pure self-pity of the young.

'I would like to help you, if I could.'

It was help he appeared to need.

'Hold me,' he said. 'I imagine – you cannot. I am cold. It is dark. Hold me.'

Sophy Sheekhy stood, white.

'You cannot.'

'I will.'

She lay on the white bed, and he walked across to her, in his hesitant, imperfect step, and lay beside her, and she cradled his head and his stench on her cold bosom. She closed her eyes, the better to bear it, and felt his weight, the weight, more or less, of a living man, but a man not breathing, a man inert like a side of beef. Perhaps it would kill her, Sophy Sheekhy thought on the surface of her mind, where the ripples crisped away from the dark pool in a flurry of terror. But the depths of the pool bore her up, her and him both. Sophy Sheekhy and the dead young man. With her chilly lips, carefully, she kissed his cold curls. Could he feel her kiss? Could she warm him?

'Be still,' she said, as she would to a fractious child.

From 'The Conjugial Angel' by A. S. Byatt, 1992

'Of nearness to her Sundered Things'

Of nearness to her sundered Things
The Soul has special times –
When Dimness – looks the Oddity,
Distinctness – easy – seems –

The Shapes we buried dwell about,
Familiar in the Rooms –
Untarnished by the Sepulchre
Our Mouldering Playmate comes –

In just the Jacket that he wore –
Long-buttoned in the Mould
Since we – old mornings, Children – played –
Divided – by a world –

The Grave yields back her Robberies –
The Years of our pilfered Things –
Bright Knots of Apparitions
Salute us, with their wings –

As we – it were – that perished –
Themself – had just remained –
Till we rejoin them – and 'twas They,
And not Ourself – that mourned.

Emily Dickinson, c.1860

Nuit du Walpurgis classique*

C'est plutôt le sabbat du second Faust que l'autre,
Un rhythmique sabbat, rhythmique, extrêmement
Rhythmique. – Imaginez un jardin de Lenôtre,
   Correct, ridicule et charmant.

Des ronds-points; au milieu, des jets d'eau; des allées
Toutes droites; sylvains de marbre; dieux marins
De bronze; çà et là, des Vénus étalées;
   Des quinconces, des boulingrins;

Des châtaigniers; des plants de fleurs formant la dune;
Ici, des rosiers nains qu'un goût docte affila;
Plus loin, des ifs taillés en triangles. La lune
   D'un soir d'éte sur tout cela.

Minuit sonne, et réveille au fond du parc aulique
Un air mélancolique, un sourd, lent et doux air
De chasse: tel, doux, lent, sourd et mélancolique,
   L'air de chasse de *Tannhäuser*.

Des chants voilés de cors lointains, où la tendresse
Des sens étreint l'effroi de l'âme en des accords
Harmonieusement dissonants dans l'ivresse;
   Et voici qu'à l'appel des cors

S'entrelacent soudain des formes toutes blanches,
Diaphanes, et que le clair de lune fait
Opalines parmi l'ombre verte des branches,
   – Un Watteau rêvé par Raffet! –

S'entrelacent parmi l'ombre verte des arbres
D'un geste alangui, plein d'un désespoir profond;

[83]

Puis, autour des massifs, des bronzes et des marbres,
    Très lentement dansent en rond.

– Ces spectres agités, sont-ce donc la pensée
Du poète ivre, ou son regret ou son remords,
Ces spectres agités en tourbe cadencée,
    Ou bien tout simplement des morts?

Sont-ce donc ton remords, ô rêvasseur qu'invite
L'horreur, ou ton regret, ou ta pensée, – hein? – tous
Ces spectres qu'un vertige irrésistible agite,
    Ou bien des morts qui seraient fous? –

N'importe! ils vont toujours, les fébriles fantômes,
Menant leur ronde vaste et morne et tressautant
Comme dans un rayon de soleil des atomes,
    Et s'évaporant à l'instant

Humide et blême où l'aube éteint l'un après l'autre
Les cors, en sorte qu'il ne reste absolument
Plus rien – absolument – qu'un jardin de Lenôtre,
    Correct, ridicule et charmant.

Paul Verlaine, 1866

* (No English verse translation of this 'untranslatable' poem can be found.)

Marie Antoinette?

Beyond the little bridge our pathway led under trees; it skirted a narrow meadow of long grass, bounded on the farther side by trees, and very much overshadowed by trees growing in it. This gave the whole place a sombre look suggestive of dampness, and shut out the view of the house until we were close to it. The house was a square, solidly built small country house – quite different from what I expected. The long windows looking north into the English garden (where we were) were shuttered. There was a terrace round the north and west sides of the house, and on the rough grass, which grew quite up to the terrace, and with her back to it, a lady was sitting, holding out a paper as though to look at it at arm's-length. I supposed her to be sketching, and to have brought her own camp-stool. It seemed as though she must be making a study of trees, for they grew close in front of her, and there seemed to be nothing else to sketch. She saw us, and when we passed close by on her left hand, she turned and looked full at us. It was not a young face, and (though rather pretty) it did not attract me. She had on a shady white hat perched on a good deal of fair hair that fluffed round her forehead. Her light summer dress was arranged on her shoulders in handkerchief fashion, and there was a little line of either green or gold near the edge of the handkerchief, which showed me that it was *over*, not tucked into, her bodice, which was cut low. Her dress was long-waisted, with a good deal of fullness in the skirt, which seemed to be short. I thought she was a tourist, but that her dress was old-fashioned and rather unusual (though people were wearing fichu bodices that summer). I looked straight at her; but some indescribable feeling made me turn away annoyed at her being there.

We went up the steps on to the terrace, my impression being that they led up direct from the English garden; but I was beginning to feel as though we were walking in a dream – the stillness and oppressiveness were so unnatural. Again I saw the lady, this time from behind, and noticed that her fichu was pale green. It was rather a relief to me that Miss Jourdain did not propose to ask her whether we could enter the house from that side.

From *An Adventure* by 'Miss Moberley and Miss Jourdain', 1901

'The mode of appearance'

The mode of appearance and disappearance of apparitions is also various. The ghost is usually either seen on looking round, as a human being might be, or seems to come in at the door. Sometimes it forms gradually out of what at first seems a cloud-like appearance. I do not think there are any cases of its appearing suddenly in a spot which the percipient was actually looking at and perceived to be vacant before. It disappears suddenly in this way sometimes, and sometimes if the percipient looks away for a moment it is gone. Sometimes it vanishes in a cloud-like manner, sometimes, retaining its form, it becomes gradually more and more transparent till it is gone. Frequently it disappears through the door, either with or without apparently opening it, or goes into a room where there is no other exit, and where it is not found.

From *Notes on the Evidence, collected by the Society, for Phantoms of the Dead*,
Mrs H. Sidgwick, Society for Psychical Research, 1885

An insuperable obstacle

There is one insuperable obstacle to a belief in ghosts. A ghost never comes naked: he appears either in a winding-sheet or 'in his habit as he lived.' To believe in him, then, is to believe that not only have the dead the power to make themselves visible after there is nothing left of them, but that the same power inheres in textile fabrics. Supposing the products of the loom to have this ability, what object would they have in exercising it? And why does not the apparition of a suit of clothes sometimes walk abroad without a ghost in it? These be riddles of significance. They reach away down and get a convulsive grasp on the very tap-root of this flourishing faith.

From *The Devil's Dictionary* by Ambrose Bierce, 1913

The Cheltenham ghost

I had gone up to my room, but was not yet in bed, when I heard someone at the door, and went to it, thinking it might be my mother. On opening the door, I saw no one; but on going a few steps along the passage, I saw the figure of a tall lady, dressed in black, standing at the head of the stairs. After a few moments she descended the stairs, and I followed for a short distance, feeling curious what it could be. I had only a small piece of candle, and it suddenly burnt itself out; and being unable to see more, I went back to my room.

The figure was that of a tall lady, dressed in black of a soft woollen material, judging from the slight sound in moving. The face was hidden in a handkerchief held in the right hand. This is all I noticed then; but on further occasions, when I was able to observe her more closely, I saw the upper part of the left side of the forehead, and a little more of the hair above. Her left hand was nearly hidden by her sleeve and a fold of her dress. As she held it down a portion of a widow's cuff was visible on both wrists, so that the whole impression was that of a lady in widow's weeds. There was no cap on the head but a general effect of blackness suggests a bonnet, with long veil or a hood.

Statement of Rosina Despard, Proceedings of the Society
for Psychical Research, 1892

A letter to the Society for Psychical Research

And so it goes, report after report, letter after letter, anxious folk trying in their spidery or stubby or sloppy handwriting – even sending room-diagrams and maps – to convince someone that they really *had* seen an apparition. Sometimes there are arabesque turns to the material: during a church service at Bath College in 1888 while his father was preaching, a percipient saw a naked man wander through the choir and disappear. The writer somewhat curiously adds, 'It might have been a monk.'

From *Appearances of the Dead* by R. C. Finucane, 1982

'The Poplars'

'This gentleman wants to know,' said the landlord, 'if anything's seen at the Poplars.'

''Ooded woman with a howl,' said Ikey, in a state of great freshness.

'Do you mean a cry?'

'I mean a bird, Sir.'

'A hooded woman with an owl. Dear me! Did you ever see her?'

'I seen the howl.'

'Never the woman?'

'Not so plain as the howl, but they always keep together.'

'Has anybody ever seen the woman as plainly as the owl?'

'Lord bless you, Sir! Lots.'

'Who?'

'Lord bless you, Sir! Lots.'

'The general-dealer opposite, for instance, who is opening his shop?'

'Perkins? Bless you, Perkins wouldn't go a-nigh the place. No!' observed the young man, with considerable feeling; 'he an't overwise, an't Perkins, but he an't such a fool as *that*.'

(Here, the landlord murmured his confidence in Perkins's knowing better.)

'Who is – or who was – the hooded woman with the owl? Do you know?'

'Well!' said Ikey, holding up his cap with one hand while he scratched his head with the other, 'they say, in general, that she was murdered, and the howl he 'ooted the while.'

This very concise summary of the facts was all I could learn, except that a young man, as hearty and likely a young man as ever I see, had been took with fits and held down in 'em, after seeing the hooded woman. Also, that a personage, dimly described as 'a hold chap, a sort of one-eyed tramp, answering to the name of Joby, unless you challenged him as Greenwood, and then he said, "Why not? and even if so, mind your own business," had encountered the hooded woman, a matter of five or six times. But, I was not materially assisted by these witnesses: inasmuch as the first was in California, and the last was, as Ikey said (and he was confirmed by the landlord), Anywheres.

From 'The Haunted House' by Charles Dickens, 1859

The Collingham Ghost

I'll tell ye aboot the Collingham ghost,
    An' a rare awd ghost was he;
For he could laugh, an' he could talk,
    An' run, an' jump, an' flee.

He went aboot hither an' thither,
    An' freeten'd some out o' their wits,
He freeten'd the parson as weel as the clerk,
    An' lots beside them into fits. . . .

The parson then, a larnèd man,
    Said he wad conjure the ghost;
He was sure it was nea wandrin' beast,
    But a spirit that was lost.

All languages this parson knew
    That onny man can chat in,
The Ebrew, Greek, an' Irish too,
    As weel as Dutch an' Latin.

O! he could talk an' read an' preach,
    Few men knew mair or better,
An' nearly all the bukes he read
    Were printed in black letter.

He read a neet, he read a day,
    To mak him fit for his wark,
An' when he thowt he was quite up,
    He sent for the awd clerk.

The clerk was quickly by his side,
    He took but little fettlin',

An' awa they went wi' right good will
   To gie the ghost a settlin'.

Aye off they set wi' all their might,
   Nor stopp'd at thin or thick,
The parson wi' his sark an' buke,
   The clerk wi' a thick stick.

At last by t' side o' t' bank they stopp'd,
   Where Wharfe runs murmurin' clear,
A beautiful river breet an' fine,
   As onny in wide Yorkshire.

The parson then began to read,
   An' read full loud an' lang,
The rabbits they ran in an' oot,
   An' wonder'd what was wrang.

The host was listnin' in a hole,
   An' oot he bang'd at last,
The fluttrin' o' his mighty wings,
   Was like a whirlwind blast.

He laughed 'an shooted as he flew,
   Until the wild woods rang;
His who-who-whoop was niver heard
   Sea lood an' clear an' strang.

The parson he fell backwards ower
   Into a bush o' whins,
An' lost his buke, an' rave his sark,
   An' prick'd his hands an' shins.

The clerk he tried to run awa,
   But tumml'd ower his stick,
An' there he made a nasty smell
   While he did yell an' fick.

An' lots o' pranks this ghost he play'd
   That here I darn't tell,
For if I did, folks wad declare
   I was as ill as hissel.

For eighteen months an' mair he stay'd,
   An' just did as he thowt;

For lord nor duke, parson nor clerk,
   He fear'd, nor carèd nowt.

Efter that time he went awa,
   Just when it pleas'd hissel;
But what he was, or whar he com fra,
   Nea mortal man can tell.

Anon., from *Yorkshire Dialect Poems*, edited by F. W. Moorman, 1912

Paddy and the ghost

One feather of the phoenix Paddy wore in his hat, and it was a yard long. . . .

Paddy, the story goes, as he came out of his mother's house looking for the leprechaun, on the famous day on which he ate the phoenix, had not gone twenty yards down the road, the one that goes to Ballyna-clare, when he met a ghost; a poor little lean old thing the colour of the wind, Paddy called it. It was a ghost going down the road, as it probably had done for ages, moved by stray winds or maybe by old passions, whichever would be the most likely to move ghosts; and loitering a little way and then stopping altogether and suddenly going on again. And no one had ever seen him until Paddy ate the phoenix.

'What ails you?' asked Paddy.

'Ah,' said the ghost, 'I bin going up and down this road for longer nor you were in that body, nor your father before you in his. And in all that time I ne'er had a glass of whiskey.'

'Sure, we'll put that right,' said Paddy. 'And how did you come to be loose on the road?'

'Ah,' said the ghost, 'I got to arguing with a man about politics, the way one does; and he was of the opposite persuasion to myself, and he lets out at me in order to illustrate a point, and, begob, that was the end of me.'

And Paddy was just about to call to mind two lads that were very prominent in politics at that time, and to ask him which he was for, when he suddenly recollects that their names would be new to the ghost, so he asks him instead if he was for Cavendish and Bourke, or against them, thinking they would be nearer his time. But all the ghost says to him is: 'Ah, get along with your politics, for I've lost my taste for them.'

'Well, I never knew a man to do that,' said Paddy, 'and to retain his taste for whiskey.'

'Well, it's the way it is,' said the ghost.

'I don't doubt it,' said Paddy, and he went on down the road, heading for Geogehan's public house, and the ghost came with him, running along ahead and lagging behind, just the way that a dog does. And that makes it seem more likely that it was old passions, or whatever whims drive spirits, that moved him along; for he was now going in the opposite direction to the way that he had been going when he met Paddy, which he could not have done if it was the wind that was blowing him, unless it had changed suddenly.

Well, they come to the public house, says the story I heard in Rathallen, and in goes the ghost with Paddy. There were five or six young lads in there at the time, but of course they none of them sees the ghost, never having eaten a phoenix. And Paddy passes the time of day to them and goes up to the bar and asks Geogehan for two small whiskies. And before Geogehan can ask who the second whiskey is for, Paddy turns to the ghost and says: 'Here is a glass of good whiskey, for Mr Geogehan never gives us anything less, and it will be a change for you after the cold of the grave.'

And no sooner has Paddy said that than all the young lads that there were in Geogehan's knew that Paddy was making his remarks to a ghost. They all look more attentively then at the space beside Paddy, to see if they can see anything, but they see nothing at all. And then they look at Paddy to see if he means it, and they see by the solemn face of him that he does. And they see the feather of the phoenix in his hat, as they couldn't very well help doing, for it was over a yard long, and, though they don't know yet that Paddy has eaten it, they see he has been in touch with magical things; and everyone knew that ghosts go down that road, though nobody now alive in Rathallen had seen one, and it seems likely enough that if Paddy didn't get from the phoenix the power to call up ghosts, at any rate the ghost had been attracted to him by the sight of that magical feather.

'And what do you be doing in the long evenings?' said Paddy next.

And whatever the ghost said, nobody knows. But after a while the young lads heard Paddy say: 'Ah, well, I thought maybe you would sleep while the sun was up.'

And to that the ghost unmistakably did not agree, as they could see from Paddy's face; though all he said was: 'B'jabers, but eternity must be a long time.'

And it seemed to the young lads that the ghost agreed to that, though of course they never heard a word that he said, nor could they see a single one of his shadows; and all the while its glass stood untouched beside Paddy's on the counter, whenever Paddy put his down. And the emptier Paddy's glass became, the more he had to say to the ghost. Geogehan was polishing a great many glasses all the time with a cloth, whether they needed to be polished or not, and looking out of the corners of his eyes at the space beside Paddy and saying nothing.

'And how do you occupy yourself?' said Paddy to the ghost.

'Haunting, is it?' he said a moment later. 'Begob, I wouldn't be doing that, for it might be misinterpreted. What I mean is, there is them as might not like it, and might want to be running you out of the place.'

And again it seemed to those from whom I have the story that the ghost disagreed, for Paddy began to excuse and explain himself. 'Ah, sure, I only meant,' he said, 'that there are some young fellows about here that are afraid of nothing, who've shot a policeman before now. And, when they put a man out of the world, would they stop at putting a ghost out of the air? Begob, they might not. Though I say it with all respect to you.'

But the ghost seemed not to be so sure of all that, judging from what Paddy said to it. For his next words were: 'Didn't one of them fight a battle alone with a whole regiment in the very next village last March. Sure, everyone knows it.'

But he seemed to be losing his argument, whatever it was, with the ghost. 'Wasn't the whole village watching the battle?' he protested.

And then he stopped arguing altogether. 'Ah, you wouldn't haunt a man,' he said, 'who'd given you the first drink you'd had in a hundred years, and you lonely on the road. Sure, you'd never do that at all.'

And a little later he said: 'Well, that's all right then. That's all that I meant.'

And one or two of the young lads seemed to get thirsty, and they went to the bar to get another drink from Geogehan. But, however many of them there were standing about, there was always a space by Paddy, on the side that the ghost was standing. And then Paddy had a long talk with the ghost, and sometimes they could guess the ghost's answers and sometimes they couldn't; but it seemed to be all about the Ballynaclare road and the company that was to be found on it, the company of winds and owls and stars, and very often a comet; that is to say one in every forty years or so, which would seem very often to a ghost. And all kinds of things would be running about at night, Paddy said, and the ghost seemed to agree; and he would hear the foxes bark and quite often see a badger, and he would get to know every family of tinkers that ever used that road, and all their donkeys. And what did he think of motors?

And at the word motors, Paddy suddenly stopped, and stood silent and rather surprised. And then he said: 'He's gone.' And the door was ajar and a draught ran through, going the other way. And of course draughts would run in and out of the door of a public house as long as the house remained open, so that to say there was a draught at any particular moment was no use as evidence, and had probably been added to the story after it started; though it is no good saying that in Rathallen, for it is one of their stories, and is much too much valued there for anyone to permit a single word to be taken away from it.

The glass of whiskey that Paddy had got for the ghost remained on the counter for weeks. Nobody moved it and nobody touched the whiskey. It just stayed there until it got broken by accident.

And that is one of the stories they have about Paddy O'Hone. But there are a great many more of them under the deep thatches of Rathallen, if you could only get them out.

From *The Man Who Ate the Phoenix* by Lord Dunsany, 1947

'The element in question'

At ten o'clock that evening the pair separated, as usual, on the upper landing, outside their respective doors, for the night; but Miss Amy had hardly set down her candle on her dressing-table before she was startled by an extraordinary sound, which appeared to proceed not only from her companion's room, but from her companion's throat. It was something she would have described, had she ever described it, as between a gurgle and a shriek, and it brought Amy Frush, after an interval of stricken stillness that gave her just time to say to herself 'Someone under her bed!' breathlessly and bravely back to the landing. She had not reached it, however, before her neighbour, bursting in, met her and stayed her.

'There's someone in my room!'

They held each other. 'But who?'

'A man.'

'Under the bed?'

'No – just standing there.'

They continued to hold each other, but they rocked. 'Standing? Where? How?'

'Why, right in the middle – before my dressing-glass.'

Amy's blanched face by this time matched her mate's, but its terror was enhanced by speculation. 'To look at himself?'

'No – with his back to it. To look at *me*,' poor Susan just audibly breathed. 'To keep me off,' she quavered. 'In strange clothes – of another age; with his head on one side.'

Amy wondered, 'On one side?'

'Awfully!' the refugee declared while, clinging together, they sounded each other.

This, somehow, for Miss Amy, was the convincing touch; and on it, after a moment, she was capable of the effort of darting back to close her own door. 'You'll remain then with me.'

'Oh!' Miss Susan wailed with deep assent; quite as if, had she been a slangy person, she would have ejaculated 'Rather!' So they spent the night together; with the assumption thus marked, from the first, both that it would have been vain to confront their visitor as they didn't even pretend to each other that they would have confronted a house-breaker; and that by leaving the place at his mercy nothing worse could happen than had already happened. It was Miss Amy's approaching the door again as with intent ear and after a hush that had represented between them a deep and extraordinary interchange – it was this that put them promptly face to face with the real character of the occurrence. 'Ah,' Miss Susan, still under her breath, portentously exclaimed, 'it isn't anyone –!'

'No' – her partner was already able magnificently to take her up. 'It isn't anyone –'

'Who can really hurt us' – Miss Susan completed her thought. And Miss Amy, as it proved, had been so indescribably prepared that this thought, before morning, had, in the strangest, finest way, made for itself an admirable place with them. The person the elder of our pair had seen in her room was not – well, just simply was not anyone in from outside. He was a different thing altogether. Miss Amy had felt it as soon as she heard her friend's cry and become aware of her commotion; as soon, at all events, as she saw Miss Susan's face. That was all – and there it was. There had been something hitherto wanting, they felt, to their small state and importance; it was present now, and they were as handsomely conscious of it as if they had previously missed it. The element in question, then, was a third person in their association, a hovering presence for the dark hours, a figure that with its head very much – too much – on one side, could be trusted to look at them out of unnatural places; yet only, it doubtless might be assumed, to look at them. They had it at last – had what was to be had in an old house where many, too many, things had happened, where the very walls they touched and floors they trod could have told secrets and named names, where every surface was a blurred mirror of life and death, of the endured, the remembered, the forgotten. Yes; the place was h— but they stopped at sounding the word. And by morning, wonderful to say, they were used to it – had quite lived into it.

Not only this indeed, but they had their prompt theory. There was a connexion between the finding of the box in the vault and the appearance in Miss Susan's room. The heavy air of the past had been stirred by the bringing to light of what had so long been hidden. The communication of the papers to Mr Patten had had its effect. They faced each other in the morning at breakfast over the certainty that their queer roused inmate was the sign of the violated secret of these relics. No matter; for the sake of the secret they would put up with his attention; and – this, in them, was most beautiful of all – they must, though he was such an addition to their grandeur, keep him quite to themselves. Other people might hear of what was in the letters, but they should never hear of *him*.

From 'The Third Person' by Henry James, 1900

Shadwell Stair

I am the ghost of Shadwell Stair.
    Along the wharves by the water-house,
    And through the dripping slaughter-house,
I am the shadow that walks there.

Yet I have flesh both firm and cool,
    And eyes tumultuous as the gems
    Of moons and lamps in the lapping Thames
When dusk sails wavering down the pool.

Shuddering the purple street-arc burns
    Where I watch always; from the banks
    Dolorously the shipping clanks,
And after me a strange tide turns.

I walk till the stars of London wane
    And dawn creeps up the Shadwell Stair.
    But when the crowing syrens blare
I with another ghost am lain.

Wilfrid Owen, 1918

'What? Dignam dead?'

Now who is that lankylooking galoot over there in the macintosh? Now who is he I'd like to know? Now, I'd give a trifle to know who he is. Always someone turns up you never dreamt of. A fellow could live on his lonesome all his life. Yes, he could. Still he'd have to get someone to sod him after he died though he could dig his own grave. We all do. Only man buries. No ants too. First thing strikes anybody. Bury the dead. Say Robinson Crusoe was true to life. Well then Friday buried him. Every Friday buries a Thursday if you come to look at it.

> O, poor Robinson Crusoe,
> How could you possibly do so?

Poor Dignam! His last lie on the earth in his box. When you think of them all it does seem a waste of wood. All gnawed through. They could invent a handsome bier with a kind of panel sliding let it down that way. Ay but they might object to be buried out of another fellow's. They're so particular. Lay me in my native earth. Bit of clay from the holy land. Only a mother and deadborn child ever buried in the one coffin. I see what it means. I see. To protect him as long as possible even in the earth. The Irishman's house is his coffin. Embalming in catacombs, mummies, the same idea.

Mr Bloom stood far back, his hat in his hand, counting the bared heads. Twelve. I'm thirteen. No. The chap in the macintosh is thirteen. Death's number. Where the deuce did he pop out of? He wasn't in the chapel, that I'll swear. Silly superstition that about thirteen.

From *Ulysses* by James Joyce, 1922

Wessex Heights

There are some heights in Wessex, shaped as if by a kindly hand
For thinking, dreaming, dying on, and at crises when I stand,
Say, on Ingpen Beacon eastward, or on Wylls-Neck westwardly,
I seem where I was before my birth, and after death may be.

In the lowlands I have no comrade, not even the lone man's friend –
He who suffereth long and is kind; accepts what he is too weak to
　　mend:
Down there they are dubious and askance; there nobody thinks as I,
But mind-chains do not clank where one's next neighbour is the sky.

In the towns I am tracked by phantoms having weird detective
　　ways –
Shadows of beings who fellowed with myself of earlier days:
They hang about at places, and they say harsh heavy things –
Men with a frigid sneer, and women with tart disparagings.

Down there I seem to be false to myself, my simple self that was,
And is not now, and I see him watching, wondering what crass
   cause
Can have merged him into such a strange continuator as this,
Who yet has something in common with himself, my chrysalis.

I cannot go to the great grey Plain; there's a figure against the
   moon,
Nobody sees it but I, and it makes my breast beat out of tune;
I cannot go to the tall-spired town, being barred by the forms
   now passed
For everybody but me, in whose long vision they stand there fast.

There's a ghost at Yell'ham Bottom chiding loud at the fall of the
   night,
There's a ghost in Froom-side Vale, thin lipped and vague, in a
   shroud of white,
There is one in the railway-train whenever I do not want it near,
I see its profile against the pane, saying what I would not hear.

As for one rare fair woman, I am now but a thought of hers,
I enter her mind and another thought succeeds me that she
   prefers;
Yet my love for her in its fulness she herself even did not know;
Well, time cures hearts of tenderness, and now I can let her go.

So I am found on Ingpen Beacon, or on Wylls-Neck to the west,
Or else on homely Bulbarrow, or little Pilsdon Crest,
Where men have never cared to haunt, nor women have walked
   with me,
And ghosts then keep their distance; and I know some liberty.

Thomas Hardy, 1914

'La larva'

The garden must once have been much larger, he supposed. The combination of squalor and splendour, so typically Venetian, fascinated
him, and by its likeness to his own case began to draw some of the
soreness from his thoughts. He wandered on, his footsteps getting
slower, towards the great bulk of the palace which blocked the end of

the garden like a cliff. On this the architect had been sparing with ornament; plain spaces of green-grey plaster soared up, relieved only by round-headed windows whose peeling shutters, closed against the heat of the day, had a blind, forbidding look. He began to experience that unaccountable unwillingness to go farther which had visited him once at Highcross Hill and again at the park gate of Anchorstone Hall, and his heart began to pound. But he could not go back, for the gate was locked; he could not climb out, for the walls were high; he must go forward. Hilda was asking for him.

Now he could see, a little to his left, the upper part of the stone staircase, and at its summit the open door which gave on the vestibule of Lady Nelly's room. A short ascent, compared to many Eustace had made, and a gentle gradient, but he shrank from it, and what was his relief, as he passed a clump of bamboos and the full extent of the staircase came into view, to see, stooping down, perhaps in search of something she had dropped, a woman whose dark clothes and self-effacing aspect made him think at once of Lady Nelly's maid. This, then, was the dryad of the garden, this prosaic middle-aged woman, whom the chickens relied on for their food.

He coughed so as not to startle her, and evidently she heard him, for though she did not turn round she stood up, raising her arms in a wide gesture that might have been calling down a blessing or a curse. Then her hands fell to her sides, and slowly she began to mount the stairs.

He followed her to the far end of the gallery to another door, standing half open, from behind which came the strong glare of electric light and the sound of someone moving about. He knocked and went in, and there was the maid on her hands and knees laying out his shoes under a table. He could only see her back and the soles of her felt slippers. 'How quickly she has got to work!' he thought, and then she heard him and turned, and he saw at once that it was Elvira, the dark, pretty housemaid, Elvira. Her face wreathed in smiles, she scrambled to her feet.

'Ah, signore!' she exclaimed, 'Scusi tanto' – but the Signora Contessa, molto, molto dispiacente, had told her to move his things, tutta la sua roba – because of the sposi, the newly married couple, who were coming to-morrow for the grand festa. 'Tutta la casa sarà piena, piena.' Pressing her knuckles together, she indicated that nowhere would there be an inch of room. 'Camera stretta ma carina, non è vero?' she went on chattily, measuring the room with her eye.

Lady Nelly had said he would be like Truth at the bottom of a well. It was certainly a narrow room, compared with his old one, and the two tall windows emphasised its height. He was not so sure that it was pretty. The pale pink pattern round the cornice might have been stencilled on, and the design in the centre of the ceiling was flamboyant and cheap, the kind of thing you might expect to find in an hotel bedroom, recently done up.

The maid followed his eyes anxiously. 'You like?' she said.

Eustace was touched by her solicitude for his comfort, and the presence of a human being suddenly seemed very precious. 'But what have you done with your shawl?' he asked her in Italian.

'My shawl?' she repeated; 'but I have no shawl. Even outside I do not use the shawl, only the older women use it.'

'But you were wearing one just now,' said Eustace, 'when you showed me the way here.'

She gazed at him with round eyes. 'But – scusi – the signore is mistaken. I did not show him the way. I have been in this room for a little half-hour – una mezzoretta – arranging the signore's things.'

'Ah, then it was the Countess's maid; I thought it must have been.'

'Ma no, scusi – Mees Simmonds is out till seven o'clock. Besides, she is English, she does not wear the shawl.'

Eustace's tired mind wanted to shelve the problem, but could not quite dismiss it, and he said casually, 'I saw a lady in black in the garden and she brought me up here.'

Elvira's eyes goggled again, and the hairbrushes she was holding slipped from her fingers to the floor.

'In the garden, signore?'

'Yes, she was looking for something.'

'And she was dressed in black?'

'Yes.'

'And she came into the house?'

'Yes.'

Elvira's whole being seemed to contract with terror.

'Allora, signore, ha visto la larva!' she gasped.

'La larva?' echoed Eustace.

'Si, si, la larva! la larva! E porta sfortuna! Aie, aie!' And with two piercing little screams she rushed from the room.

Eustace dropped into a chair. He had seen the larva, and it brought bad luck. But how could a caterpillar bring bad luck? Anyhow, he had seen no caterpillar. Had the woman in the garden been looking for a caterpillar, perhaps? Larva, larva, it was a Latin word. Groping among his classical studies, his memory brought out something pale with the milky glow of phosphorescence, something in an incomplete, provisional state of being.

Now it came to him. Larva was a ghost. He had seen a ghost.

From *Eustace and Hilda* by L. P. Hartley, 1947

The Visitant

A cloud moved close. The bulk of the wind shifted.
A tree swayed over water.
A voice said:
Stay. Stay by the slip-ooze. Stay.

Dearest tree, I said, may I rest here?
A ripple made a soft reply.
I waited, alert as a dog.
The leech clinging to a stone waited;
And the crab, the quiet breather.

Slow, slow as a fish she came,
Slow as a fish coming forward,
Swaying in a long wave;
Her skirts not touching a leaf,
Her white arms reaching towards me.

She came without sound,
Without brushing the wet stones;
In the soft dark of early evening,
She came,
The wind in her hair,
The moon beginning.

I woke in the first of morning.
Staring at a tree, I felt the pulse of a stone.
Where's she now, I kept saying.
Where's she now, the mountain's downy girl?
But the bright day had no answer.
A wind stirred in a web of appleworms;
The tree, the close willow, swayed.

Theodore Roethke, 1953

Tristessa's house

The dark spaces, full of the desolate scent of time and old perfume, had
the air of a long-abandoned cathedral, for it was just as cold, just as
quiet, and the furniture, on its own, under the influence of the tensions

of its structure, now and then let out a faint, melodious twang as if it had been touched by a ghostly fingernail.

When I heard the faint music the house made by itself, I felt myself already in the presence of Tristessa, as if she were one of those super-sensitive ghosts who manifest their presence by only a sound, an odour, or an impression of themselves that they leave on the air behind them – a sense, a feeling that, for no definable reason, penetrates us with a pure anguish, as if they were telling us, in the only way left to them, that is, by a direct intervention upon our sensibilities, how much, how very much they want to be alive and how impossible it is for them to be so.

From *The Passion of New Eve* by Angela Carter, 1977

The Vanishing Hitchhiker

On this night, as we were driving along – the three of us to the beach – we saw this girl standing by the road, probably a half mile before we got to her. And as we approached we saw that she was seemingly try-ing to stop a car. The wind was blowing, and her long blond hair seemed to flow with the wind along with the soft material of her white dress, if you could picture this. As we got to her she seemed so lonely and we knew that she needed help, so we stopped. And she asked if we could give her a ride to the beach. Naturally, we picked her up, and she began to talk with us as though we had always known her.

We had not driven more than a mile before she said she was hot and wondered if it was all right to lower the window in the car, even though she was the only one with a sleeveless dress on. We felt that something must be wrong with her because we had on wraps, but of course we went along with her, and she did this in a jovial manner. We enjoyed her company to the beach, and when we got there we asked where she was planning to go. And she said, 'Nowhere in particular'; so we asked her if she would like to join us for dancing. She im-mediately said she would love to.

After we arrived at the place where the orchestra was playing, we decided to walk out on the pier; but we were afraid that she would be cold, because even on a summer night it was usually cold to walk out over the water. But she insisted that she wasn't cold at all, that in fact she thought it would be refreshing because she was a little warm.

After we came back to the table where we were sitting, she excused herself to go to the little girls' room, and as soon as she left we saw this bewildered look on the friend of my husband's, who had danced with the girl. As soon as she left the table he said, 'Something is wrong.' He said, 'As soon as I took her hand to dance, it was just like holding a piece of ice.' Said, 'She's isn't warm, she's cold.' Naturally, this stirred up a little excitement in us. She came back to the table. My husband asked her to dance, and he came back to the table and related the same thing to me, that she was so cold: her hands were just like ice.

So, shortly after this, we decided to leave to come home, and we asked her if we could carry her someplace. And she said no, that she was just coming down to enjoy the night, that she would go back with us. And the boy thought that she was very charming, though, and he had asked her where she lived, and she gave him her house number and the street she lived on and told him that it would be all right for him to call if he liked someday. So he wrote her name down; he thought as we came back that when we carried her home he would know how to get back to her house so that he could look her up. But as we approached where we had picked her up, she said, 'You can stop here.' And of course the men just thought that this would be terrible to put a young, charming, beautiful girl out by the road, and they insisted on carrying her home. But she said, 'No, put me out right where you picked me up.' And she made this so definite that there was no other way out.

The next day . . . we got to the place where we picked her up, and, sure enough, this was the name of the street that she lived on. But when we drove up about a mile off the highway we saw the number of the place, and it was a convent. Then we began to wonder if she had slipped out of the convent; maybe this was why she was so mysterious about getting out. Then we thought, No, this couldn't have been true, and after wondering really if we had taken the right number down we decided the only thing to do was to go and ask one of the sisters.

The friend and my husband went to the door, and they asked if this is where Rose White stayed. And the elder sister looked at them, not with wonder, they said, but with concern. And she said, 'Rose White? Yes, come in, my friends.' So they came back to the car to get me, and the three of us went in. And the sister said, 'Where did you know Rose White?'

And we said that actually we did not know her before the night before, that we had met her just the night before.

And she said, 'Would you recognize her picture?' And of course we would. She took down this old album and she said, 'Thumb through here, and find a picture that you think is Rose White.'

So immediately the three of us, still with curiosity, flipped through the pages, and then we saw the beautiful eight-by-ten picture of Rose White and there was no mistake, we knew this was she. We told the sister, 'This is Rose White, that we met last night.'

Then she said, 'My friends, you aren't the first ones who have come here looking for Rose White. But I'd like for you to go with me to where she is.' And she came out and got into the car with us and directed us down the road. We turned off to the left and then we could see this cemetery. We got out, without a speech of thought from anyone; we walked through the cemetery and she came to this tombstone and she said, 'My friends, there is Rose White.' And we saw on the tombstone, 'Rose White.' She had died on the day of her graduation from high school. The day that she died was the very date of the day before. We were so lost in thought, we were so bewildered, until we all just bowed our heads.

We went back to the car, the sister followed, and on the way she told us, 'Yes, Rose White has been seen three other times, and it's always on the date of the day that she was buried. She doesn't come back but once every fifteen years.' And that happened to be the day that we passed.

Joy Hendrix, recorded by Debby Creecy and Sharon McParland, 1971

'The only Ghost I ever saw'

The only Ghost I ever saw
Was dressed in Mechlin – so –
He wore no sandal on his foot –
And stepped like flakes of snow –

His Gait – was soundless, like the Bird –
But rapid – like the Roe –
His fashions, quaint, Mosaic –
Or haply, Mistletoe –

His conversation – seldom –
His laughter, like the Breeze –
That dies away in Dimples
Among the pensive Trees –

Our interview – was transient –
Of me, himself was shy –
And God forbid I look behind –
Since that appalling Day!

Emily Dickinson, c.1861

[103]

Four

THE UNQUIET DEAD

'Rest, rest perturbed spirit'...
Hamlet

O me, why have they not buried me deep enough?
Is it kind to have made me a grave so rough?
Me, that was never a quiet sleeper?
Maybe still I am but half-dead;
Then I cannot be wholly dumb;
I will cry to the steps above my head
And somebody, surely, some kind heart will come
To bury me, bury me
Deeper, ever so little deeper.

ALFRED LORD TENNYSON

'What beck'ning ghost?'

What beck'ning ghost, along the moonlight shade
Invites my step, and points to yonder glade?
'Tis she! – but why that bleeding bosom gor'd,
Why dimly gleams the visionary sword?
Oh ever beauteous, ever friendly! tell,
Is it, in heav'n, a crime to love too well?
To bear too tender, or too firm a heart,
To act a Lover's or a Roman's part?
Is there no bright reversion in the sky,
For those who greatly think, or bravely die?

From 'Elegy to the Memory of an Unfortunate Lady' by Alexander Pope, 1717

The Intermediate State

O nobly-born, when thou art driven hither and thither by the ever-moving wind of *karma*, thine intellect, having no object upon which to rest, will be like a feather tossed about by the wind, riding on the horse of breath. Ceaselessly and involuntarily wilt thou be wandering about. To all those who are weeping thou wilt say, 'Here I am; weep not.' But they not hearing thee, thou wilt think, 'I am dead!' And again, at that time, thou wilt be feeling very miserable. Be not miserable in that way.

There will be a grey twilight-like light, both by night and by day, and at all times. In that kind of Intermediate State thou will be either for one, two, three, four, five, six, or seven weeks, until the forty-ninth day . . .

Thou wilt see thine own home, the attendants, relatives, and the corpse, and think, 'Now I am dead! What shall I do?' and being oppressed with intense sorrow, the thought will occur to thee, 'O what would I not give to possess a body!' And so thinking, thou wilt be wandering hither and thither seeking a body.

Even though thou couldst enter thy dead body nine times over – owing to the long interval which thou hast passed in the *Chönyid Bardo* – it will have been frozen if in winter, been decomposed if in summer, or, otherwise, thy relatives will have cremated it, or interred it, or thrown it into the water, or given it to the birds and beasts of prey. Wherefore finding no place for thyself to enter into, thou wilt be dissatisfied and have the sensation of being squeezed into cracks and crevices amidst rocks and boulders. The experiencing of this sort of misery occurs in the Intermediate State when seeking rebirth. Even though thou seekest a body, thou wilt gain nothing but trouble. Put aside the desire for a body; and permit thy mind to abide in the state of resignation, and act so as to abide therein.

From *The Tibetan Book of the Dead*, translated by the Lāma Kazi Dawa-Sandup

Elpenor

The first that preast in was Elpenor's soule,
His body in the broad-waid earth as yet
Unmourn'd, unburied by us, since we swet
With other urgent labours. Yet his smart
I wept to see, and ru'd it from my heart,
Enquiring how he could before me be
That came by ship? He, mourning, answered me:
'In Circe's house, the spite some Spirit did beare
And the unspeakable good licour there
Hath bene my bane. For being to descend
A ladder much in height, I did not tend
My way well downe, but forwards made a proofe
To tread the rounds, and from the very roofe
Fell on my necke and brake it. And this made
My soule thus visite this infernall shade.
And here, by them that next thy selfe are deare,
Thy Wife and Father, that a little one
Gave food to thee, and by thy onely Sonne
At home behind thee left, Telemachus,
Do not depart by stealth and leave me thus,
Unmourn'd, unburied, lest neglected I
Bring on thy selfe th'incensed Deitie.
I know that, saild from hence, thy ship must touch
On th'Ile Ææa, where vouchsafe thus much,
Good king, that, landed, thou wilt instantly
Bestow on me thy royall memory
To this trace, that my body, armes and all,
May rest consum'd in firie funerall.
And on the fomie shore a Sepulchre
Erect to me, that after times may heare
Of one so haplesse. Let me these implore,
And fixe upon my Sepulcher the Ore
With which alive I shooke the aged seas,

And had of friends the deare societies.'
　　I told the wretched Soule I would fulfill
And execute to th'utmost point his will;
And all the time we sadly talkt, I still
My sword above the blood held, when aside
The Idoll of my friend still amplified
His plaint, as up and downe the shades he err'd.

From *Homer's Odysses*, translated from the Greek by George Chapman, 1614–15

Palinurus

'Cocytus is the deep pool that you see,
The swamp of Styx beyond, infernal power
By which the gods take oath and fear to break it.
All in the nearby crowd you notice here
Are pauper souls, the souls of the unburied.
Charon's the boatman. Those the water bears
Are souls of buried men. He may not take them
Shore to dread shore on the hoarse currents there
Until their bones rest in the grave, or till
They flutter and roam this side a hundred years;
They may have passage then, and may return
To cross the deeps they long for.'
　　　　　　　　　　　　　Anchises' son
Had halted, pondering on so much, and stood
In pity for the souls' hard lot. Among them
He saw two sad ones of unhonored death,
Leucaspis and the Lycian fleet's commander,
Orontës, who had sailed the windy sea
From Troy together, till the Southern gale
Had swamped and whirled them down, both ship and men.
Of a sudden he saw his helmsman, Palinurus,
Going by, who but a few nights before
On course from Libya, as he watched the stars,
Had been pitched overboard astern. As soon
As he made sure of the disconsolate one
In all the gloom, Aeneas called:
　　　　　　　　　　　　　'Which god
Took you away from us and put you under,
Palinurus? Tell me. In this one prophecy
Apollo, who had never played me false,

Falsely foretold you'd be unharmed at sea
And would arrive at the Ausonian coast.
Is the promise kept?'
                        But the shade said:
                                    'Phoebus' caldron
Told you no lie, my captain, and no god
Drowned me at sea. The helm that I hung on to,
Duty bound to keep our ship on course,
By some great shock chanced to be torn away,
And I went with it overboard. I swear
By the rough sea, I feared less for myself
Than for your ship: with rudder gone and steersman
Knocked overboard, it might well come to grief
In big seas running. Three nights, heavy weather
Out of the South on the vast water tossed me.
On the fourth dawn, I sighted Italy
Dimly ahead, as a wave-crest lifted me.
By turns I swam and rested, swam again
And got my footing on the beach, but savages
Attacked me as I clutched at a cliff-top,
Weighted down by my wet clothes. Poor fools,
They took me for a prize and ran me through.
Surf has me now, and sea winds, washing me
Close inshore.
                    By heaven's happy light
And the sweet air, I beg you, by your father,
And by your hopes of Iulus' rising star,
Deliver me from this captivity,
Unconquered friend! Throw earth on me – you can –
Put in to Velia port! Or if there be
Some way to do it, if your goddess mother
Shows a way – and I feel sure you pass
These streams and Stygian marsh by heaven's will –
Give this pour soul your hand, take me across,
Let me at least in death find quiet haven.'
When he had made his plea, the Sibyl said:
'From what source comes this craving, Palinurus?
Would you though still unburied see the Styx
And the grim river of the Eumenides,
Or even the river bank, without a summons?
Abandon hope by prayer to make the gods.
Change their decrees. Hold fast to what I say
To comfort your hard lot: neighboring folk
In cities up and down the coast will be

Induced by portents to appease your bones,
Building a tomb and making offerings there
On a cape forever named for Palinurus.'

From Virgil: *The Aeneid*, first century AD, translated from the Latin
by Robert Fitzgerald

Melissa is cold

Periander, understanding that which had been done and perceiving that
Thrasybulos counselled him to put to death those who were eminent
among his subjects, began then to display all manner of evil treatment
to the citizens of the State; for whatsoever Kypselos had left undone in
killing and driving into exile, this Periander completed. And in one day
he stripped all the wives of the Corinthians of their clothing on account
of his own wife Melissa. For when he had sent messengers to the Thes-
protians on the river Acheron to ask the Oracle of the dead about a
deposit made with him by a guest-friend, Melissa appeared and said she
would not tell in what place the deposit was laid, for she was cold and
had no clothes, since those which he had buried with her were of no
use to her, not having been burnt; and this, she said, would be an evidence to him that she was speaking the truth, namely that when the
oven was cold, Periander had put his loaves into it. When the report of
this was brought back to Periander, the token made him believe,
because he had had commerce with Melissa after she was dead; and
straightway after receiving the message he caused proclamation to be
made that all the wives of the Corinthians should come out to the temple of Hera. They accordingly went as to a festival in their fairest
adornment; and he having set the spearmen of his guard in ambush,
stripped them all alike, both the free women and their attendants; and
having gathered together all their clothes in a place dug out, he set fire
to them, praying at the same time to Melissa. Then after he had done
this and had sent a second time, the apparition of Melissa told him in
what spot he had laid the deposit entrusted to him by his guest-friend.

'Such a thing, ye must know, Lacedemonians, is despotism, and such
are its deeds.'

From Herodotus' *History*, Book V, fifth century BC, translated from the Greek
by G. C. Macaulay

To Licinius Sura

Our leisure gives me the chance to learn and you to teach me; so I should very much like to know whether you think that ghosts exist, and have a form of their own and some sort of supernatural power, or whether they lack substance and reality and take shape only from our fears. . . .

Now consider whether the following story, which I will tell just as it was told to me, is not quite as remarkable and even more terrifying. In Athens there was a large and spacious mansion with the bad reputation of being dangerous to its occupants. At dead of night the clanking of iron and, if you listened carefully, the rattle of chains could be heard, some way off at first, and then close at hand. Then there appeared the spectre of an old man, emaciated and filthy, with a long flowing beard and hair on end, wearing fetters on his legs and shaking the chains on his wrists. The wretched occupants would spend fearful nights awake in terror; lack of sleep led to illness and then death as their dread increased, for even during the day, when the apparition had vanished, the memory of it was in their mind's eye, so that their terror remained after the cause of it had gone. The house was therefore deserted, condemned to stand empty and wholly abandoned to the spectre; but it was advertised as being to let or for sale in case someone was found who knew nothing of its evil reputation.

The philosopher Athenodorus came to Athens and read the notice. His suspicions were aroused when he heard the low price, and the whole story came out on inquiry; but he was none the less, in fact all the more, eager to rent the house. When darkness fell he gave orders that a couch was to be made up for him in the front part of the house, and asked for his notebooks, pen and a lamp. He sent all his servants to the inner rooms, and concentrated his thoughts, eyes and hand on his writing, so that his mind would be occupied and not conjure up the phantom he had heard about nor other imaginary fears. At first there was nothing but the general silence of night; then came the clanking of iron and dragging of chains. He did not look up nor stop writing, but steeled his mind to shut out the sounds. Then the noise grew louder, came nearer, was heard in the doorway, and then inside the room. He looked round, saw and recognized the ghost described to him. It stood and beckoned, as if summoning him. Athenodorus in his turn signed to it to wait a little, and again bent over his notes and pen, while it stood rattling its chains over his head as he wrote. He looked round again and saw it beckoning as before, so without further delay he picked up his lamp and followed. It moved slowly, as if weighed down with chains, and when it turned off into the courtyard of the house it suddenly vanished, leaving him alone. He then picked some plants and leaves and marked the spot. The following day he approached the magistrates, and advised them to give orders for the place to be dug up. There they found bones, twisted round with chains, which were left bare and corroded by the fetters when time and the action of the soil had rotted away the body. The bones were collected and given a public burial, and after the shades had been duly laid to rest the house saw them no more. . . .

From The Letters of the Younger Pliny, c.AD 90, translated from the Latin
by Betty Radice

The appeasing of the dead

Hence when thrice Phosphor shows his gilded face
And fainting stars have thrice to Sol given place,
The night-Lemuria, an old rite, is paid
And dirges to the silent ghosts are said.
Th' old year was short; unknown the *februa* were
And double Janus did not guide the year.
Yet to the dead their gifts they did discharge,
The pious son his father's tomb did purge.
This was in May, from 'majors' first deduced,
In which are some of those old rites still used.
About midnight when sleep and silence fill
The drowsy brains, and dogs and birds are still,
The rite-remembering, ghost-abhorring son
Arises gently, and no shoes puts on.
Then points with his closed fingers and his thumb
Put in the midst, lest ghosts should near him come.
Then in spring-water he his hands doth cleanse,
And first doth roll about his mouth blue beans,
Then o'er his shoulder throws them down; says he:
'These beans I throw my house and self to free.'
Nine times 'tis said. The ghost doth trace his track
And picks them up, if that he looks not back.
Again he washes; then a basin beats;
And so the spirits to leave his house entreats.
Then nine times crying, 'Kindred ghosts, begone,'
He looketh back, and all is purely done.

Our ancestors barred up their temples in
These baleful days, as now is to be seen.

Ill times for widow's wedding, or for maid;
Those that have wedded have not long enjoyed.
And for this cause, if proverbs thou dost weigh,
The proverb says: "'Tis ill to wed in May.'

From the Fasti by Ovid, translated by John Gower, 1640

The Unquiet Grave

O bonny, bonny sang the bird,
    Sat on the coil of hay,
But dowie, dowie was the maid
    That loved the corpse of clay.

'Cold blows the wind on my true love,
    And a few small drops of rain;
I never had but one true love,
    And in greenwood he was slain.

'I'll do as much for my true love
    As any lover may;
I'll sit and mourn all on his grave
    A twelvemonth and a day.'

The twelvemonth and the day being gone,
    The ghost began to greet:
'Your salten tears they trickle down,
    They wet my winding sheet.'

''Tis I, your love, sits on your grave
    And will not let you sleep;
For I crave one kiss of your clay-cold mouth,
    And that is all I seek.'

'O, lily, lily are my lips;
    My breath comes earthy strong;
If you have one kiss of my clay-cold mouth,
    Your time will not be long.'

'Is there any room at your head, Willie?
    Is any room at your feet?
Is any room at your two sides,
    Wherein that I may creep?'

'There is no room at my head, Margret,
    Nor any at my feet;
There is no room at my two sides,
    My coffin's made so meet.'

''Tis down in yonder garden green,
    Love, where we used to walk,
The finest flower that e'er was seen
    Is withered to a stalk.'

'The stalk is withered dry, indeed,
    So will our hearts decay;
O, make yourself content, my love,
    Till Death calls you away.

'But plait a wand of bonny birk,
    And lay it on my breast;
Then get you hame, my May Margret,
    And wish my soul good rest.'

Traditional

The heretics cast out

In the year 1534 the wife of the Provost of the city of Orleans, a woman
who had long been a hot fautress of the Lutherans, lay sick unto death,
and she entreated her husband to bury her as quietly as might be, without any decent ceremonies such as the passing-bell and the knell,
without dishaloof, or reverend following or waking the corpse, nay
even without nocturnals, dirge and requiem.

The husband out of his too fond affection for his wife gave the required promise, and she was interred as he directed in the Franciscan
church, hard by the graves of his father and his grandparents. But on
the following night whilst Matins was being sung in choir, the Spirit of
the dead woman appeared hovering upon the Rood-beam and high in
the vaulting of the Church, making most lamentable moan and outcry.
The religious of the house, shrewdly suspecting that this haunting and
disturbance came from the dead woman who had been buried with
mangled rites and mutilated observance, advised the Provost and his
friends of the matter. It was resolved that the ghost must be exorcized,
for which ceremony there gathered no small crowd of folk. When the
Spirit was adjured to speak the dead woman confessed that she was a

lost soul inasmuch as she had secretly joined the Lutheran heresy. She implored that her body should be taken up and cast forth out of the church in some unconsecrated ground. Whilst the friars were consulting how this might be done without scandal or undue offense certain violent and evilly-disposed men raised a riot against the good fathers and attacked them, using them despitefully, even as the Arian heretics persecuted S. Athanasius of old. John Sleidan has related this circumstance in the Ninth Book of his *General History of the Reformation of the Church*, but with sinuous cunning he has perverted the facts and presents them as he learned them from one of his own sect. So he has written a bouncing lie.

Yet even if it all happened just as he pretends – which was not the case – his narrative is wholly impertinent, for by the laws of Holy Church and by the decrees of the Parliament it is not permitted to give a Lutheran Catholic burial. Those who are manifest and notorious heretics must not be interred with the faithful. So enjoins Pope Innocent III in an Epistle addressed to the Monks of Faenza in 1206, and the Pontiff spoke the decision of many Councils.

S. Gregory in the Fourth Book of his *Dialogues*, says that those who are lost are even more grievously tormented whilst their bodies lie in consecrated ground, and he cites instances of unhappy souls who have appeared and wailing entreated that their carcasses shall be exhumed and cast away in some unhallowed spot far from the sanctuary.

I have thought it well briefly to make mention of these and similar happenings in order that it may be the more plainly proved that ghosts do appear and converse with men.

From *A Treatise of Ghosts* by Father Noël Taillepied, 1588,
translated by M. Summers

A little while since

The Jews of our days believe that after the body of a man is interred, his spirit goes and comes, and departs from the spot where it is destined to visit his body, and to know what passes around him; that it is wandering during a whole year after the death of the body, and that it was during that year of delay that the Pythoness of Endor evoked the soul of Samuel, after which time the evocation would have had no power over his spirit.

The Pagans thought much in the same manner upon it. Lucan introduces Pompey, who consults a witch, and commands her to evoke the soul of a dead man to reveal to him what success he would meet with in his war against Caesar; the poet makes this woman say, 'Shade, obey my spells, for I evoke not a soul from gloomy Tartarus, but one which hath gone down thither a little while since, and which is still at the gate of hell.'

The Egyptians believed that when the spirit of an animal is separated from its body by violence, it does not go to a distance, but remains near it. It is the same with the soul of a man who has died a violent death; it remains near the body – nothing can make it go away; it is retained there by sympathy; several have been seen sighing near their bodies which were interred.

Augustine Calmet, *The Phantom World*, 1746,
translated by Rev. H. Christmas

The Hindu ghosts

Other evil beings are the ghosts of the dead, the *bhūts*, in so far as they are malignant. Such a spirit is that of a man who has died a violent death, whether by suicide, accident, or capital punishment; and the malevolence of a ghost of this type is inevitably increased greatly if he has been denied due funeral rites. Indeed, if a man otherwise free from sin dies without offspring to perform the *śrāddha* for him he is liable to become a *gayāl* or sonless ghost, especially dangerous to the young sons of other people. Many Bīrs are men killed by accident, as by a fall from a tree, by a tiger, and so on. The *bhūts* are particularly feared by women and children, and at the time of marriage, and a woman who weds a second time must take steps to propitiate the spirit of her first husband. *Bhūts* never rest on the ground, which is inimical to them. Hence their shrines are provided with a bamboo or other place to allow them to descend upon it; whereas, on the other hand, people anxious to avoid ill from *bhūts* lie on the ground, as do a bride and bridegroom, or a dying man at the moment of dissolution. Three signs of the nature of a *bhūt* are his lack of shadow, his fear of burning turmeric, and his speaking with a nasal accent. A person beset by them should invoke Kālī, Durgā, and especially Śiva, who is the lord of *bhūts*. The vampire of Europe has a parallel in the *vetāl*, who enters corpses, often being the spirit of a discontented man who chooses such a home instead of re-taining his own body.

The spirits who haunt burning grounds are styled *masān* from the San-skrit *śmaśāna* ('cemetery') and are dangerous to children, whom they afflict with consumption. Among the *bhūts* of the Hills is Airi, the ghost of a man killed in hunting, who goes about with a pack of belled hounds and to meet whom is death. The *acheri* are the ghosts of little girls, living on the mountain-tops, but descending for revels at night. The *baghauts* are the ghosts of men slain by tigers, for whom shrines are erected on the spot of their sad end. Such spirits are dangerous and require careful treatment. Still more perilous is the *churel*. In origin the name seems to have denoted the ghosts of some low caste people, whose spirits are always especially malignant, and whose bodies – like those of suicides in England in former times – are buried face downward to hinder the easy escape of the evil spirit. The modern acceptance of the *churel*, however, is that it is the ghost of a woman who dies while pregnant or in child-birth or before the period of ceremonial impurity has elapsed. Such a ghost may appear beautiful, but it can be recognized by the fact that its feet are turned round. She is apt to captivate handsome young men and take them to her abode, where, if they eat the food she offers, they fall under her power and will not be dismissed until they are grey-haired old men. All sorts of spells are adopted to prevent the ghost of a dead woman from becoming a *churel* and to avert the spirits which threaten evil to children and to mothers.

Ghosts are accustomed to haunt the deserts, where they can be seen and heard at night. They also live in old dwellings, whence the unwillingness in India to demolish ruinous buildings, because the spirits which dwell there may be annoyed and punish the man who destroys their home. Excavators in their explorations have constantly found this difficulty in the way of their work. Other places frequented by *bhūts* are the hearth of the household, the roof of the house, cross-roads, and boundaries; while empty houses and even flowers may be infested by them.

From *Indian Mythology* by A. Berrievale Keith, 1916

The Cleveland Lyke Wake Dirge

This ae night, this ae night,
Every night and all;
Fire and selte and candle-light;
And Christ receive thy saule.

When thou from hence away are passed,
Every night and all;
To Whinny-muir thou comest at last;
And Christ receive thy saule.

If ever thou gavest hosen and shoon,
Every night and all;

Sit thee down and put them on;
And Christ receive thy saule.

If hosen and shoon thou ne'er gavest nane,
Every night and all;
The whins shall pyke thee to the bare bane;
And Christ receive thy saule.

From Whinny-muir when thou mayest pass,
Every night and all;
To Brig of Dread thou comest at last;
And Christ receive thy saule.

If ever thou gave of thy silver and gold,
Every night and all;
At Brig of Dread thou'lt find foothold;
And Christ receive thy saule.

If silver or gold thou ne'er gavest nane,
Every night and all;
Thou'lt tumble down towards hell's flame;
And Christ receive thy saule.

From Brig of Dread when thou mayest pass,
Every night and all;
To Purgatory fire thou comest at last;
And Christ receive thy saule.

If ever thou gavest meat or drink,
Every night and all;
The fire shall never make thee shrink;
And Christ receive thy saule.

If meat or drink thou ne'er gavest nane,
Every night and all;
The fire shall burn thee to the bare bane;
And Christ receive thy saule.

This ae night, this ae night,
Every night and all;
Fire and selte and candle-light;
And Christ receive thy saule.

Traditional North Country ballad

Whinny Moor

Old people will tell you that after death the soul passes over
Whinny-moore, a place full of whins and brambles, and . . .
would be met by an old man carrying a huge bundle of boots; and
if among these could be found a pair which the bare-footed soul
had given away during life, the old man gave them to the soul to
protect its feet whilst crossing the thorny moor.

I was back walking on Lothersdale Moor,
through ling, blackthorn and blips of sheepshit,
over dry-stone walls and up kestrels' airstreams,
back with the becks and original sources,
to land on the fell road under Pinhaw
beside the steamed-up hatchback of a Ford.

The driver's window opened as I stood there.
'Tha'll catch thi death – get in an warm thisen'
said the heathery face, open, bloodshot,
leaning across to unlock the other door.
I limped around and took my seat beside him,
cupping my bones around his leather flask.

That highland nip restored me to the land
of the living and I warmed to my tale:
how I had hiked the backs of the Pennine Way,
leaving at dawn from Todmorden to end –
'down there, see, if this mist would just clear up
a bit' – in the shade of Thornton church.

He glanced, disbelieving, at my plimsolls,
frayed and holy with a flapping sole.
He was a rep for Peter Lord, he said,
nodding behind him at the bootful of boots.
'Ah've worked in shoes near alf a century
an sin all t'flippin lot go reet down'ill.'

Then he asked who I was. 'Morrison, eh,
a name for up ere. I knew thi father well
an t'ole surgery in Water Street.
E did is best by Earby, wi disease an that,
aye an thi mother too, deliverin bairns.
Ad thi no mind to follow in their shoes?

'Ere, ave another swig – tha's like a sheet
what started out as peachy then lost
its colourin in t'wash. Ah tell thi what:
you tek these pumps off me to elp thi ome.
They're seconds, any road, an just your size,
an tha's some sloggin still to Thornton.'

Then I was out beside him shaking hands
as he clattered off across a cattle grid,
turning left down to Elslack by the pines.
He should have come out by the Tempest
but the roak was too mawky to see beyond
the reservoir and he vanished in thin air.

That cardboard box was all I had to show
for our meeting, its pair of char-black pumps
like the ones I'd brought from school for Jeffrey Holmes
the Christmas break after his accident,
the lorry that flicked him from his bicycle
turning my mate into a sickbed ghost.

I laced the eyelets for the journey on
across the bogs and sandylands of moor.
Beside the ink-blot of a rookery
I could make out the nib of Thornton church,
and up behind, like an act of kindness,
a perched, solitary, whitewashed farm.

And in the gorse and peat and heather-scorch
his voice came back again like judgement,
the voice of the tarns with their millstones,
a cairn of slingshot stopping me in my tracks
until the wind brought the grit of a Hargreaves
or one of the Barnoldswick MacBrides:

Get on wi thee, stuck there in t'eather
maunderin and moulderin like a corpse.
What odds would it ave made tha stayin put?
Didst think tha could cure us like thi father?
If tha'd not buggered off at twenty
tha'd as like be a boss at Silentnight,

layin us off wi no brass or future
in this valley of dead vases an mills.

Lest they return

It is often supposed that the spirits of persons who have recently
departed this life are apt to carry off with them to the world of the dead
the souls of their surviving relations ... Among the Yorubas of West
Africa, when one of twins dies, the mother carries about, along with the
surviving child, a small wooden figure roughly fashioned in human
shape and of the sex of the dead twin. This figure is intended not
merely to keep the live child from pining for its lost comrade, but also
to give the spirit of the dead child something into which it can enter
without disturbing its little brother or sister. Among the Tschwi of
West Africa a lady observed a sickly child with an image beside it
which she took for a doll. But it was no doll, it was an effigy of the
child's dead twin which was being kept near the survivor as a habitation for the little ghost, lest it should wander homeless and, feeling
lonely, call its companion away after it along the dark road of death.

From *The Golden Bough* by J. G. Frazer, 1911

Isa

A man had three sons, and decided to divide his money among them
during his life-time, because he foresaw that they would otherwise
quarrel over it. The two older sons received ninety-nine rupees each,
but for the youngest there were only eight rupees left. This young
man, Isa was his name, asked his father why he received so little. The
father answered: 'All receiving is from God. He will give you suste-
nance. Use your common sense.' Isa then decided to set out on a safari
to try his luck. He asked his father's blessing and departed. He travelled
for many days, until he came to a cemetery. There he saw a group of
men who put down a dead body and went away, leaving the body lying
there. Isa called after them, saying: 'Why is this man not buried?' One
of the men replied: 'There is no money for a burial.' Isa said: 'My father
told me to use my common sense, and my common sense tells me that
it is not proper to abandon a dead man along the road. Go and bury this
man, that his soul may have peace.' The men did so, and Isa paid what
he possessed to give the dead man a proper funeral.

After that, he continued his safari until he came to a river. There he found a man washing clothes, and as soon as the man saw him, he called him: 'Isa, Isa, come here, I have an important message for you. Travel along this river until you come to a city. In that city there lives a sultan who is gravely ill. All the learned doctors have been called to his bedside, but in vain. Go the palace and say that you can cure the sultan. Here is a medicine that will restore his health.' Isa did as the washerman told him and he was admitted to the ailing sultan. He administered the washerman's medicine, and to everybody's surprise the sultan rose from his couch; his disease had vanished. The sultan was overjoyed at this, and gave his daughter in marriage to Isa, making him his successor. Later, Isa again met the man who was washing clothes by the river. He said: 'You are a good man, for you gave all your money to redeem me and pay for a proper funeral. Without you I would still be lying rotting on the ground.'

Jan Knappert, *Myths and Legends of the Swahili*, 1978

The grateful corpse

A rich hero buys a corpse from creditors who were objecting to its being buried, and has it interred. The dead man appears to his benefactor in a dream and promises him success, on condition that the advantages gained are shared fairly between the two of them. The hero soon wins the love of a princess, whom he rescues from many dangers with the help of his supernatural protector. The question now arises: must the princess be shared? She, as it happens, is bewitched, half woman, half dragon or snake. The dead man claims his share; the hero agrees and his partner, pleased by his fairness, takes only the diabolical part, leaving the hero a humanized wife.

From *Tristes Tropiques* by Claude Lévi-Strauss, 1955, translated from the French by John and Doreen Weightman

Jack and the Wandering Knight

(Enter WIGGEN, COREBUS, CHURCHWARDEN *and* SEXTON.*)*
WIGGEN: You may be ashamed, you whoreson scald Sexton and Churchwarden (if you had any shame in those shameless faces of yours) to let a poor man lie so long above ground unburied. A rot on you all, that have no more compassion of a good fellow when he is gone!

CHURCHWARDEN: What, would you have us to bury him, and to answer it ourselves to the parish?

SEXTON: Parish me no parishes! Pay me my fees, and let the rest run on in the quarter's accounts, and put it down for one of your good deeds, a God's name; for I am not one that curiously stands upon merits.

COREBUS: You whoreson sodden-headed sheep's face! Shall a good fellow do less service and more honesty to the parish, and will you not, when he is dead, let him have Christmas burial?

WIGGEN: Peace, Corebus! As sure as Jack was Jack, the frollic'st franion amongst you, and I Wiggen, his sweet sworn brother, Jack shall have his funerals – or some of them shall lie on God's dear earth for it, that's once!

CHURCHWARDEN: Wiggen, I hope thou wilt do no more than thou dar'st answer.

WIGGEN: Sir, sir! dare or dare not! more or less! answer or not answer! do this or have this!

SEXTON: Help, help, help! Wiggen sets upon the parish with a pikestaff!

(EUMENIDES awakes and comes to them.)

EUMENIDES: Hold thy hands, good fellow.

COREBUS: Can you blame him, sir, if he take Jack's part against this shake-rotten parish that will not bury Jack?

EUMENIDES: Why, what was that Jack?

COREBUS: Who, Jack, sir? Who, our Jack, sir? As good a fellow as ever trod upon neat's leather.

[The quarrel continues]

EUMENIDES *(the wandering knight)*: This fellow does but the part of a friend, to seek to bury his friend. How much will bury him?

WIGGEN: Faith, about some fifteen or sixteen shillings will bestow him honestly.

SEXTON: Ay, even thereabouts, sir.

EUMENIDES: Here, hold it, then. *(Aside)* And I have left me but one poor three half-pence. Now do I remember the words the old man spake at the cross:
    'Bestow all thou hast', (and this is all)
    'Till dead men's bones comes at thy call.'
Here, hold it. *(Gives money.)* And so, farewell.

WIGGEN: God, and all good, be with you, sir.

[Miraculous adventures follow, in which a young man named Jack becomes Eumenides' servant. In a final test of his promise to divide everything with him, Eumenides is about to kill the woman he loves, until Jack stops him.]

JACK: Stay, master! It is sufficient I have tried your constancy. Do you now remember since you paid for the burying of a poor fellow?

EUMENIDES: Ay, very well, Jack.

JACK: Then, master, thank that good deed for this good turn. And so, God be with you all!

(JACK *leaps down in the ground.*)

EUMENIDES: Jack, what, art thou gone? Then, farewell, Jack. –
Come, brothers, and my beauteous Delia,
Erestus, and thy dear Venelia.
We will to Thessaly with joyful hearts.

ALL: Agreed. We follow thee and Delia.

Exeunt omnes (except MADGE, FROLIC *and* FANTASTIC*).*

FANTASTIC: What, gammer, asleep?

MADGE: By the mass, son, 'tis almost day; and my windows shuts at the cock's crow.

FROLIC: Do you hear, gammer? Methinks this Jack bore a great sway amongst them.

MADGE: O, man, this was the ghost of the poor man that they kept such a coil to bury, and that makes him to help the wandering knight so much. But, come, let us in. We will have a cup of ale and a toast this morning – and so depart.

FANTASTIC: Then you have made an end of your tale, gammer?

MADGE: Yes, faith. When this was done, I took a piece of bread and cheese, and came my way. And so shall you have too, before you go, to your breakfast. (*Exeunt.*)

From *The Old Wives' Tale* by George Peele, c.1592–3

The horses of the Oghuz Turks

After the dead man has been interred and his tomb roofed over with a 'kind of clay dome' his companions,

'betaking themselves to his horses. . . . kill a hundred, two hundred or (only) one of them according to their quantities. They eat the flesh of these except the head, legs, hide and tail which they suspend on wood. And they say: "These are the horses on which he shall ride to Paradise". . . . And sometimes they neglect to kill the horses for a day or two, and an old man, one of their elders, will exhort them saying: "I saw so and so, (meaning the dead man) in my sleep and he said to me: 'As you see, my companions have got ahead of me and my feet are sore from following them. I cannot catch up with them and have been left all alone.' Upon this they betake themselves to the horses, kill them and hang them up alongside his tomb. And after a day or two the old man goes to them and says: 'I saw so-and-so and he said: "Tell my family and my companions that I have caught up with those that got ahead of me and have rested from my weariness."'

From the account of Ibn Fadlan, 16th century, translated by J. A. Boyle

Tannaaluk: Soul Restoration

Death, in Tikigaq's view, was a two-stage process. After biological death, the spirit *(ilitqusiq)* stayed near the body for four or five days in a condition called *siññiktaq*, 'supernatural sleep.' If a shaman or some other adept intervened during this period, body and spirit could be reconciled and life renewed. During or just after siññiktaq, the dead traveled east beyond the Kuukpak River 'toward daylight.'

Tannaaluk was at Kuukpak, alone, by himself. He spent his time fishing. He lived at Kuukpak in the autumn when the ice was forming. Tannaaluk was a man. He lived at Kuukpak because he liked being alone.

And one day when he returned to his iglu from fishing, he saw that his skylight was lit up. Tannaaluk said to himself, 'I must have a visitor. Someone must have come from Tikigaq.'

Tannaaluk was bringing home the fish he had caught in a seal-skin bag. He was carrying home frozen fish. Tannaaluk was sure he had a visitor, because his iglu skylight was lit up; he saw this as he approached it.

And when Tannaaluk entered his iglu, he found a woman there. She was sitting there covered with something.

And this was a dead woman. Not long before, Tannaaluk had learned that a woman in Tikigaq was sick. Tannaaluk had heard about the woman.

This woman in the iglu was covered with something. A dead woman had come into the iglu.

And when Tannaaluk entered, he brought fish with him, so his visitor could eat *quaq* ('raw frozen fish').

Tannaaluk started to eat. And as he ate, he threw a fish to the woman. But when it hit her the fish bounced back at him, alive and writhing. Tannaaluk did this for some time, but the fish kept bouncing back to him alive.

Later in the evening Tannaaluk said to the woman, 'Why are you

[125]

covered up? It doesn't look good.' So he grabbed the skin she was wrapped in [caribou skin] and threw it out into the entrance passage.

But every time he threw the skin into the passage, it returned to the house and landed where it had been before. Tannaaluk went on trying to throw away the skin, but it always came back to him in the iglu.

Then Tannaaluk said, 'You're my only visitor, and you can't even speak to me!' That is what he said.

They spent the evening together. And Tannaaluk tried to find out what was happening at Tikigaq: but she didn't reply to his questions. When it was late Tannaaluk said to her, 'Since you're not doing anything, we will go to bed.'

It was then that Tannaaluk found the woman was frozen. So he said, 'Come to bed with me.' And he took her to bed and undressed her.

(It was said in the past that when a person dies they use a certain path [from Tikigaq] to go upriver. They used to say that the dead all take the same trail toward Kuukpak. They go straight through Kanigaluk. They don't go around it. This dead woman had taken that trail and passed the place where Tannaaluk was living.)

Tannaaluk went to bed with the woman, but she was frozen stiff. And at first when he lay down with her Tannaaluk found her very cold; in fact, her body was frozen. So he started thawing her. (Some of the stories are like this, but I won't leave anything out.)

Tannaaluk knew this was a woman, so he got on top of her. All night he made love to her. He pulled out his penis when it started freezing inside her. But he continued all night.

Finally Tannaaluk thawed the woman out, and when she had warmed up he saw that she could move her joints. But the woman still wasn't breathing. When she was completely thawed, and no longer stiff, her corpse came alive.

The woman came alive, and at last she spoke to Tannaaluk. 'Come back to Tikigaq with me!' she said. But Tannaaluk refused: he didn't want to go to Tikigaq.

'We can get there fast,' she said, 'by the path I came on. When we get to Tikigaq, we'll live together, because you brought me to life again. I won't go back to my husband.'

The woman wanted Tannaaluk for her husband. '*Naami!* No!' Tannaaluk didn't want to leave Kuukpak. The woman tried talking him into it because he had restored her to life. But Tannaaluk just went to bed and to sleep.

Tannaaluk slept. And while he was asleep, he started to feel cold, and he woke up. He found he was in the entrance passage. The woman had swept him out into the passage as she was leaving the iglu.

That's why Tannaaluk didn't get a wife for himself. It was his own fault; he refused to take that woman when she passed through Kuukpak. He could certainly have had that woman.

When Tannaaluk woke up he was sorry, but the woman had gone already. A corpse had travelled through his iglu, while he was living at Kuukpak.

When Tannaaluk went to Tikigaq, he told the woman's husband what had happened, and the man was sorry. 'If you had agreed to have her as your wife, she would be alive now,' he said to Tannaaluk. Instead, she passed on because he had refused her. The story ends here.

From *The Things That Are Said of Us*, told by Asatchaq, translated from the Inupiaq by Tukummiq and Tom Lowenstein, 1992

Mary Lee of Carelha'

'Twas late, late on a Sabbath night!
At the hour of the ghost, and the restless sprite!
The mass at Carelha' had been read,
And all the mourners were bound to bed,
When a foot was heard on the paved floor,
And a gentle rap came to the door.

   O God! that such a rap should be
So fraught with ambiguity!
A dim haze clouded every sight;
Each hair had life and stood upright;
No sound was heard throughout the hall,
But the beat of the heart and the cricket's call;
So deep the silence imposed by fear,
That a vacant buzz sung in the ear.

   The lady of Carelha' first broke
The breathless hush, and thus she spoke.
'Christ be our shield! – who walks so late,
And knocks so gently at my gate?
I felt a pang – it was not dread –
It was the memory of the dead!
O! death is a dull and dreamless sleep!
The mould is heavy, the grave is deep!
Else I had weened that foot so free
The step and the foot of my Mary Lee!
And I had weened that gentle knell
From the light hand of my daughter fell!
The grave is deep, it may not be!
Haste porter – haste to the door and see.'

He took the key with an eye of doubt,
He lifted the lamp and he looked about;
His lips a silent prayer addressed,
And the cross was signed upon his breast;
Thus mailed within the armour of God,
All ghostly to the door he strode.
He wrenched the bolt with grating din,
He lifted the latch – but none came in!
He thrust out his lamp, and he thrust out his head,
And he saw the face and the robes of the dead!
One sob he heaved, and tried to fly,
But he sunk on the earth, and the form came bye.

She entered the hall, she stood in the door,
Till one by one dropt on the floor,
The blooming maiden, and matron old,
The friar gray, and the yeoman bold.
It was like a scene on the Border green,
When the arrows fly and pierce unseen;
And nought was heard within the hall,
But Aves, vows, and groans withal.
The lady of Carel' stood alone,
But moveless as a statue of stone.

'O! lady mother, thy fears forego;
Why all this terror and this woe?
But late when I was in this place,
Thou would'st not look me in the face;
O! why do you blench at sight of me?
I am thy own child, thy Mary Lee.'

'I saw thee dead and cold as clay;
I watched thy corpse for many a day;
I saw thee laid in the grave at rest;
I strewed the flowers upon thy breast;
And I saw the mould heaped over thee –
Thou art not my child, my Mary Lee.'

O'er Mary's face amazement spread;
She knew not that she had been dead;
She gazed in mood irresolute:
Both stood agast, and both were mute.

'Speak thou loved form – *my* glass is run,
I nothing dread beneath the sun,
Why come'st thou in thy winding-sheet,
Thy life-blood streaming to thy feet?
The grave-rose that my own hands made,
I see upon thy bosom spread;
The kerchief that my own hands bound,
I see still tied thy temples round;
The golden rings, and bracelet bands,
Are still upon thy bloody hands.
From earthly hope all desperate driven,
I nothing fear beneath high heaven;
Give me thy hand and speak to me,
If thou art indeed my Mary Lee. . . .'

From 'Pilgrims of the Sun' by James Hogg, 1815

The Shroud

A mother had a dear little boy of seven years old. He was so sweet and pretty that no one could look at him without loving him. To her he was dearer and more precious than anything on earth. It happened that the little boy fell suddenly ill and God took him. The mother was inconsolable, and she wept bitter tears night and day. After he was buried the child appeared in the night at the place where in life he had sat or played, and then vanished when morning came.

As his mother never ceased to mourn and cry, he came one night in his little shroud, and a wreath on his head, and sat at the foot of her bed.

'Mother,' he said, 'do stop crying; otherwise I can't rest in my coffin, for my shroud is so wet with your tears which fall on it.'

On hearing this his mother looked frightened and cried no more. And the next night the child came again, holding in his hand a little light.

'Look,' he said, 'now my shroud is nearly dry, and I can rest in my grave.'

After that the mother asked God to comfort her in her grief, and bore it with patience and resignation.

The child never appeared again, but slept peacefully in his earthy little bed.

From *Grimm's Fairy Stories* (1812–15), translated by Beatrice Marshall

The Wilful Child

There was once a child who was so wilful that she would do nothing her mother told her. For this reason God was not pleased with the child, and let her fall sick. No doctor came to her, and she soon lay on her deathbed. When she was buried and the earth spread over her, one of her arms was stretched forth and came through. More earth was then thrown on the grave, but still the arm showed. Then the mother went herself to the grave and struck the little arm with a scythe, and after that the child rested in peace beneath the earth.

From *Grimm's Fairy Stories* (1812–15), translated by Beatrice Marshall

The Dead Man's Arm

It was the custom in a certain village, whenever a man died, for his sister to keep watch over his grave three nights in a row. If a girl should die the watch would be kept by her brother. A certain maiden died, and her brother, a strapping youth who was afraid of nothing under the sun, went to the cemetery for the usual vigil.

At the stroke of midnight three dead men arose from their graves and asked, 'How about a game?'

'Why not?' he answered. 'But where do you want to play?'

'We always play in church.'

They entered the church and showed him to an underground crypt packed with rotting coffins and a jumble of human bones. They picked up some of the bones and a skull and went back upstairs into church, where they stood the bones in a straight line on the floor. 'These are our ninepins.' They picked up the skull. 'This is our ball.' And they began bowling.

'Do you want to play for money?'

'Certainly!'

The young man bowled with the skull and was so good at it that he won each time and took every cent the dead men had. As soon as they ran out of money they carried ball and ninepins back to the crypt and retreated to their graves.

The second night the dead man wanted to play the return game, staking rings and gold teeth, and again the youth won everything. The third night they played still another round, at the end of which the men said, to the youth, 'You've won again, and we have nothing left to give you. But since gaming debts are settled on the spot, we shall give you this dead man's arm, which is well preserved although a bit dry and will come in handier than a sword. No matter what enemy you touch with it, the arm will grab him around the chest and throw him down dead, even if he is a giant.'

The dead man departed and left the young man standing there with that arm in his hand.

The next morning he took to his father the money and the gold won at ninepins and said, 'Dear Father, I'm going out into the world and seek my fortune.' His father gave him his blessing and the young man departed, with the dead man's arm hidden under his cloak.

From *Italian Folklore* by Italo Calvino, 1956, translated from the Italian
by George Martin

The Saints whose Grave-stones Moved

To' Panjang or 'Father Lanky' (as he is generally called) was one of the earliest apostles of Islam in the State of Pătāni and enjoyed a great reputation. At length however Sah Nyāya the Unjust King came to the throne and requested To' Panjang to assist in casting some cannon, the copper being placed in his charge for the purpose. But one day a foreign merchant came to visit him and begged for a portion of the copper, which the Saint gave him, intending no harm thereby. Taxed by the Raja with stealing his copper, To' Panjang admitted his mistake and was condemned to die the death. A pupil of his own was chosen to execute the sentence, but refused to do so, whereupon both master and pupil were strangled and their bodies thrown into the Patāni River, which then escaped to the sea in the neighbourhood of Jámbu. But when they were thrown into the river the two corpses instead of sinking stood miraculously upright in the water, and in this position travelled continually against the stream, both at flood and ebb. At length however the Raja commanded the remains of both saints to be buried ashore, but as often as the bodies were measured for their shrouds, so often they kept outgrowing them. At length therefore a goat was sacrificed and the shrouds having then been measured again were at last found to be of the correct length. The burial therefore was completed; but up to this day the grave-stones of both saints continue to make miraculous movements in proof of the divine nature of To' Panjang and his pupil.

Translated from the Malay by Walter Skeat in
Fables and Folk Tales from an Eastern Forest, 1901

Of a monk who was not allowed to enter paradise because he had thrown off his cowl when dying

A few years before in the kingdom of France in a certain house of the Cistercian Order a monk of good life was suffering from a very painful illness. Being tortured by the double heat of his fever and the air, he begged the infirmarian to allow him to take off his habit and to put on a scapular. He in pity for the sick man allowed him, but as he was going away he came back and found the sick man dead. A little disturbed at this he closed the cell, took off the scapular, put on the hood again and laid him on the mat, afterwards beating the board. He was carried into the oratory and the next night, as the monks were reading the psalms round the body according to custom, he sat up on the bier and looking round called to the monks. They in terror fled into the dormitory except the sub-prior who had greater courage, and he said: 'Be not afraid; I am that brother of yours that was dead and have come to life again. Call the abbot to me.' Meantime the monks who had fled, let it be known that the dead man had risen, and there was a great commotion in the dormitory, and a gathering of the brothers. The abbot went to the bier and the man said: 'Lord, I confess to you that I died in such and such a way; but being taken by the angels to paradise, when I thought I could enter freely, S. Benedict came to the door and said, "Who are you?" And when I answered that I was a monk of the Cistercian order, the saint rejoined: "Certainly you are not. If you are a monk, where is your habit? This is a place for rest, and are you going to enter in your working dress?" After I had gone round the walls of that blessed mansion, through the windows I saw some older men of venerable appearance, and one of them looking kinder than the rest, I begged him to intercede for me. On his interposition I was allowed to return to the body, that resuming my habit I might attain to the promised state of bliss.' After hearing this the abbot took off the habit in which the man was lying and put on him again that which he had stripped off in his sickness. And so having received his blessing, he expired again.

From *The Dialogue of Miracles* by Caesarius of Heisterbach, c.1220–35,
translated by H. von E. Scott and C. C. Swinton Bland

Thorgunna

In the summer that Christianity was adopted by law in Iceland, a ship from Dublin put in at Snæfell Ness. Most of the crew came from Ireland and the Hebrides, but there were some Norwegians too. They lay at Rif for a good part of the summer, then with a fair wind sailed up the fjord to Dogurdar Ness, where a number of people from the neighbourhood came to trade with them.

There was a Hebridean woman on board called Thorgunna, and the crew said she had some valuable things with her, difficult to get in Iceland. When Thurid of Frodriver heard about it, she was very keen to see all this finery, for she was a vain woman and extremely fond of elegant clothes and rich adornment.

[When Thorgunna dies she makes Thurid's husband, Thorodd, promise to burn the rich hangings on her bed, and not to let his wife have them. Thurid persuades him to let her keep them and so, on the night of Thorgunna's funeral, the omens, deaths and hauntings begin.]

Soon people started dying one after another, six of them in all. This was just about the beginning of Advent, but in those days people in Iceland didn't observe the fast . . .

MORE GHOSTS

Next morning Thorodd and his men put out from Ness with their dried fish, and they were all drowned off Enni. The boat and the fish were washed ashore there, but the bodies were never found.

When the news came to Frodriver, Kjartan and Thurid invited their neighbours to a funeral feast, at which they used the Christmas ale. On the first evening of the feast, when all the guests were seated, Thorodd and his companions came into the room drenched to the skin. Everyone welcomed Thorodd and his men, and thought this a happy omen because in those days it was believed that drowned people had been well received by the sea-goddess, Ran, if they came to their own funeral feast. At that time a good many heathen beliefs still prevailed, though people were baptized and supposed to be Christians. Thorodd and his men walked across the main room, which had two doors, and into the living-room. They ignored the greetings people gave them and sat down at the fire. The people ran out of the living-room, but Thorodd and his men stayed on until the fire began to burn very low, then went away. As long as the funeral feast lasted this continued: every evening the drowned men would come to the fire. It gave people at the feast plenty to talk about, but some of them thought it would stop once the feast was over.

After the feast all the guests went back home and the place seemed rather dull without them. In the evening after the guests had gone the fire in the living-room was lit as usual, and as soon as it was ablaze, Thorodd and his companions came in, all of them soaking wet. They sat down at the fire and began squeezing the water out of their clothes. No sooner had they taken their seats than Thorir Wood-Leg and his six companions came into the room, all of them covered with earth. They started shaking the dirt out of their clothes and throwing mud at Thorodd and his men. The people ran out of the room, as you would expect, and that evening they had to do without light, heating-stones, and everything else the fire provided. Next evening they lit a fire in another room, hoping the dead men would not come there, but things turned out otherwise. Everything happened just as before, and both parties came to sit by the fire. On the third evening, Kjartan suggested they should light a long-fire in the living room, and another in a separate room for the household, so they tried that. As it turned out, Thorodd and the other dead men came and sat at the long-fire, while the living sat at the smaller one, and so it continued throughout the Christmas season . . .

There had been thirty servants there in the autumn, but eighteen of them died, five more ran away, and by midwinter there were only seven of them left.

THE GHOSTS ARE BANISHED

After these weird events had been going on for some time, Kjartan set off one day over to Helgafell to see his uncle Snorri and ask his advice about what should be done to put an end to them. At that time there was a priest staying at Helgafell, sent to Snorri by Gizur the White. Snorri asked the priest to go with Kjartan to Frodriver along with his son Thord the Cat and six other people. They must burn the canopy from Thorgunna's bed, said Snorri, and then summons all the dead to a door-court. After that the priest was to sing Mass, consecrate water, and hear people's confessions. They rode over to Frodriver, and on the way there they asked the neighbours to come with them.

It was Candlemas Eve when they came to Frodriver, and the fire had just been lit. Thurid had been taken with the same illness as those who had died. Kjartan went straight into the living-room and saw Thorodd and the other dead people sitting by the fire as usual. He pulled down the canopy from Thorgunna's bed, plucked a brand from the fire, then went out and burnt to ashes all the bed-furnishings that had once belonged to Thorgunna.

Next Kjartan summonsed Thorir Wood-Leg, and Thord the Cat summonsed Thorodd for trespassing on the home and robbing people of life and health. All the dead ones at the fire were summonsed in the same way. Then the door-court was held and charges made, the proper procedure of ordinary lawcourts being observed throughout. The jury was appointed, testimony was taken, and the cases were summed up and referred for judgment. As sentence was being passed on Thorir Wood-Leg, he rose to his feet. 'I sat here as long as people would let me,' he said, then went out through the other door where the court was not being held.

After that, sentence was passed on the shepherd, and he stood up.
'I'll go now,' he said, 'and it seems I should have gone sooner.'

When Thorgrima Witch-Face heard her sentence, she stood up, too.
'I stayed as long as you let me,' she said.

So they all were sentenced one after another; and as they were sentenced, they got up, made some such remark, and left the room. It was clear that none of them wanted to go.

Thorodd was the last to be sentenced. When he heard the judgment, he stood up. 'There's no peace here,' he said, 'we'd best all be on our way.' And with that he walked out.

Then Kjartan and the others went back inside, and the priest carried holy water and sacred relics to every corner of the house. Next day he sang all the prayers and celebrated Mass with great solemnity, and there were no more dead men haunting Frodriver after that. Thurid began to improve and got well again. In the spring after all these strange events Kjartan engaged new servants. He farmed at Frodriver for a long time, and people thought him a very courageous man.

From the *Eyrbyggia Saga*, mid-thirteenth century, translated from the Icelandic
by Hermann Pálsson and Paul Edwards

Ladies

When other Ladies to the Groves go down,
Corinna still, and *Fulvia* stay in Town;
Those Ghosts of Beauty ling'ring here reside,
And haunt the Places where their Honour dy'd.

Alexander Pope, *Miscellanies*, 1732

'Some heard a voice'

Some heard a voice in Branksome Hall,
Some saw a sight, not seen by all:
That dreadful voice was heard by some,
Cry, with loud summons, 'GYLDIN, COME!'
    And on the spot where burst the brand,
      Just where the page had flung him down,
    Some saw an arm, and some a hand,
      And some the waving of a gown.
The guests in silence pray'd and shook,
And terror dimm'd each lofty look.

But none of all the astonish'd train
Was so dismay'd as Deloraine;
His blood did freeze, his brain did burn,
'Twas fear'd his mind would ne'er return;
For he was speechless, ghastly wan,
Like him of whom the story ran,
    Who spoke the spectre-hound in Man.
At length, by fits, he darkly told,
With broken hint, and shuddering cold –
    That he had seen, right certainly,
A shape with amice wrapp'd around,
With a wrought Spanish baldric bound,
    Like a pilgrim from beyond the sea;
And knew – but how it matter'd not –
It was the wizard, Michael Scott.

The anxious crowd, with horror pale,
All trembling, heard the wondrous tale;
    No sound was made, no word was spoke,
    Till noble Angus silence broke;
        And he a solemn sacred plight
    Did to St Bride of Douglas make,
    That he a pilgrimage would take
    To Melrose Abbey, for the sake
        Of Michael's restless sprite.
Then each, to ease his troubled breast
To some bless'd saint his prayers address'd:
Some to St Moden made their vows,
Some to St Mary of the Lowes,
Some to the Holy Rood of Lisle,
Some to our Ladye of the Isle;
Each did his patron witness make,
That he such a pilgrimage would take,
And monks should sing, and bells should toll,
All for the weal of Michael's soul.

                    From 'The Lay of the Last Minstrel' by Sir Walter Scott, 1805

Waltzing Matilda

Once a jolly swagman camped by a billabong,
    Under the shade of a coolabah tree;

And he sang as he watched and waited till his billy boiled,
  'You'll come a-waltzing Matilda with me!'

'Waltzing Matilda, Waltzing Matilda,
  You'll come a-waltzing Matilda with me,'
And he sang as he watched and waited till his billy boiled,
  'You'll come a-waltzing Matilda with me.'

Down came a jumbuck to drink at the billabong,
  Up jumped the swagman and grabbed him with glee;
And he sang as he shoved that jumbuck in his tucker-bag,
  'You'll come a-waltzing Matilda with me.'

'Waltzing Matilda, Waltzing Matilda,
  You'll come a-waltzing Matilda with me,'
And he sang as he shoved that jumbuck in his tucker-bag,
  'You'll come a-waltzing Matilda with me.'

Up rode the squatter mounted on his thoroughbred;
  Down came the troopers – one, two and three.
'Whose the jolly jumbuck you've got in your tucker-bag?
  You'll come a-waltzing Matilda with me.'

'Waltzing Matilda, Waltzing Matilda,
  You'll come a-waltzing Matilda with me,
Whose the jolly jumbuck you've got in your tucker-bag?
  'You'll come a-waltzing Matilda with me.'

Up jumped the swagman, sprang into the billabong,
  'You'll never catch me alive,' said he.
And his ghost may be heard as you pass by that billabong
  'Who'll come a-waltzing Matilda with me?'

'Waltzing Matilda, Waltzing Matilda,
  You'll come a-waltzing Matilda with me,'
And his ghost may be heard as you pass by that billabong,
  'Who'll come a-waltzing Matilda with me?'

1903 version

Old Sykes's Wife

In a secluded dell, on the banks of Mellor Brook, not far from the
famous Old Hall of Samlesbury, stands a lonely farmhouse which was

occupied for many generations by a family named Sykes. They gave their name to the homestead, or *vice versa*, on its being cleared from the forest; and from the fact of the pastures lying at a short distance from a broad and deep portion of the brook, it became generally known by the name of Sykes Lumb Farm. The Sykes, however, have long since become extinct; but the doings of one of the race have passed into tradition, and will, no doubt, be handed down to many future generations.

It is said that one of the latest occupiers of the farm had become very rich, partly by the constant hoarding of his ancestors, partly by the thrift of his too covetous wife, but much more by having discovered the hidden treasures of some former possessor. Be this as it may, civil troubles arose, and the Wars of the Roses exhausted not only the wealth but the population of Lancashire. Old Sykes's wife had neither son nor daughter. Her husband was too old to be called off to the wars; and hence her only anxiety was lest some lawless marauders should seize upon their stores . . . The treasure was therefore carefully secured in earthenware jars, and was then buried deep beneath the roots of an apple-tree in the orchard.

The farm passed into other hands, and Old Sykes's wife might have been forgotten had not her ghost, unable to find rest, continued occasionally to visit the old farmhouse. Many a time, in the dusk of the evening, have the neighbouring peasants met an old wrinkled woman dressed in ancient garb, passing along the gloomy road which leads across the Lumb, but fear always prevents them from speaking. She never lifted her head, but helped herself noiselessly along, by means of a crooked stick, which bore no resemblance to those then in use. At times she was seen in the old barn, on other occasions in the house, but more frequently in the orchard, standing by an apple-tree which still flourished over the place where the buried treasure was afterwards said to have been found. Generations passed away, and still her visits continued. One informant minutely described her withered visage, her short quaintly-cut gown, her striped petticoat, and her stick. He was so much alarmed that he ran away from the place, notwithstanding that he had engaged to perform some urgent work. 'She was not there,' he gravely said, 'when I went to pluck an apple, but no sooner did I raise my hand towards the fruit, than she made her appearance just before me.' At last, it is said, an occupier of the farm, when somewhat elated by liquor, ventured to question her as to the reasons of her visits. She returned no answer, but after moving slowly towards the stump of an old apple-tree, she pointed significantly towards a portion of the orchard which had never been disturbed. On search being made, the treasure was found deep down in the earth, and as the soil was being removed, the venerable looking shade was seen standing on the edge of the trench. When the last jar was lifted out, an unearthly smile passed over her withered features; her bodily form became less and less distinct, until at last it disappeared altogether. Since then the old farmhouse has ceased to be haunted. Old Sykes's wife is believed to have found eternal rest; – but there are yet many, both old and young, who walk with quickened pace past the Lumb whenever they are belated, fearful lest they should be once more confronted with the dreaded form of its unearthly visitor.

From *Traditions of Lancashire* by John Harland, 1829

'I will, I will, I will!'

An old woman of Sexhow, near Stokesley, appeared after her death to a farmer of the place, and informed him that beneath a certain tree in his apple orchard he would find a hoard of gold and silver which she had buried there; the silver he was to keep for his trouble, but the gold he was to give to a niece of hers living in great poverty. The farmer went to the spot indicated, found the money, and kept it all to himself. But from that day his conscience gave him no rest, and every night, at home or abroad, old Nanny's ghost dogged his steps. At last one evening the neighbours heard him returning from Stokesley Market very late; his horse was galloping furiously, and as he passed a neighbour's house, its inmates heard him screaming out, 'I will, I will, I will!' But when the horse reached the farm all was still, for the rider was a corpse.

From T. F. Thistleton-Dyer, *The Ghost World*, 1893

Anything hidden

Anything hidden before death, especially money, is said to cause haunting, and country people are still careful not to hide even a tool in case it makes them uneasy after death. A friend told me once that she was walking out one evening when an old neighbour passed her, and said, 'Tell my girl it's on the top shelf'. 'Very well', she said, and only when she had walked on did she remember that the old man had died the week before. However, she went to the daughter and told her, and the daughter said, 'Oh, that's where it is, is it?' She was too polite to ask what 'it' was, so heard no more of the matter.

From *A Dictionary of British Folk-Tales* by Katharine M. Briggs, 1971

Business as usual

For *some* Victorian ghosts it was business as usual: they requested delivery of messages, advised where their bodies might be discovered, sought payment of old debts, satisfied vows to return, and reminded the living to keep their word. Finally, they also indicated where to find lost goods which, as the following narration suggests, might not always be treasure-trove. William White moved into a cottage in the village of Berwick, on the Sussex downs, some time after the death (in 1855) of the previous tenant, Mr Henry Duty. One day, as White washed his hands in the kitchen, the dead Mr Duty stood before him. Speechless at first, White finally remembered what to do in such situations, intoning 'In the Name of the Father, of the Son, and of the Holy Ghost what troublest thou Mr Duty?' In reply to the ancient adjuration the spirit told Mr White that he had buried some seed potatoes, indicated their location, then vanished.

From *Appearances of the Dead* by R. C. Finucane, 1982

Homesickness

The souls of the dead who may happen to die abroad, greatly desire to rest in Ireland. And the relations deem it their duty to bring back the body to be laid in Irish earth. But even then the dead will not rest peaceably unless laid with their forefathers and their own people, and not amongst strangers.

A young girl happened to die of a fever while away on a visit to some friends, and her father thought it safer not to bring her home, but to have her buried in the nearest churchyard. However, a few nights after his return home, he was awakened by a mournful wail at the window, and a voice cried, 'I am alone; I am alone; I am alone!' Then the poor father knew well what it meant, and he prayed in the name of God that the spirit of his dead child might rest in peace until the morning. And when the day broke he arose and set off to the strange burial ground, and there he drew the coffin from the earth, and had it carried all the way back from Cork to Mayo; and after he had laid the dead in the old graveyard beside his people and his kindred, the spirit of his child had rest, and the mournful cry was no more heard in the night.

From *Ancient Legends of Ireland* by Lady Wilde, 1887

Bury Me in a Free Land

Make me a grave where'er you will,
In a lowly plain or a lofty hill;
Make it among earth's humblest graves,
But not in a land where men are slaves.

I could not rest, if around my grave
I heard the steps of a trembling slave;
His shadow above my silent tomb
Would make it a place of fearful gloom.

I could not sleep, if I heard the tread
Of a coffle-gang to the shambles led,
And the mother's shriek of wild despair
Rise, like a curse, on the trembling air.

I could not rest, if I saw the lash
Drinking her blood at each fearful gash;
And I saw her babes torn from her breast,
Like trembling doves from their parent nest.

I'd shudder and start, if I heard the bay
Of a bloodhound seizing his human prey;
And I heard the captive plead in vain,
As they bound, afresh, his galling chain.

If I saw young girls from their mother's arms
Bartered and sold for their youthful charms,
My eye would flash with a mournful flame,
My death-pale cheek grow red with shame.

I would sleep, dear friends, where bloated Might
Can rob no man of his dearest right;
My rest shall be calm in any grave
Where none can call his brother a slave.

I ask no monument, proud and high,
To arrest the gaze of the passers by;
All that my yearning spirit craves
Is – *Bury me not in a land of slaves!*

Frances Harper, 1854

When the little parade finally started I got a hammer and some pliers and nails out of my truck for emergencies and followed along the sidewalk with Joe Copper. It was a good thing I did, because one yoke of oxen ran away and smashed a car, which in turn smashed the Seal of Ohio, but not beyond a few hasty repairs. I also had to grab a State trooper to help me because our tree had to go way round the traffic lights instead of under them, and at the street corners people were crowded far into the street and had to be pushed back. When I took up farming I didn't know it was going to involve handling people at parades, but then I didn't know much about it.

And it was worth it, all right. It was all worth it. A few hasty glances back at our float proved that. At the end of that silly little parade our great tree, with its leaves and apples shining in the sunlight, was really something. And Mr Locksley wasn't there any more. Standing there before the tree in the little nursery leaning on his staff, with his Bible in his hand, looking out remotely in his incomparable dignity and beauty at the clapping crowd and staring, awe-struck children, was Johnny Appleseed himself. It sent a shiver down more spines than mine.

When we reached the end I was in a bit of a daze, but I remembered that someone had said Johnny could be got on the radio in front of the courthouse. This seemed a bit out of key, but I remembered that farm organizations, like all others, can use good publicity, and I knew that Mr Locksley could dominate any situation. The old Negro with the peg leg knew where to take the team and float, and I got Mr Locksley off the float and we hurried silently through the crowd. When we got near the courthouse the crowd was so thick that we couldn't make any headway. An old newspaper editor I know, who has a bad heart at that, saw our plight and jammed his way through ahead of us like a trooper. The announcer saw us and made a few remarks, and then Johnny Appleseed was standing there before a microphone. Once again that strange thing happened, and quiet spread out a little way.

'My name is Johnny Appleseed,' he said. 'I lived in this part of the country a long time ago, when it had hardly been touched. I liked the Indians and I liked the white people and I liked the animals, and I didn't hurt any of them. I planted seeds and set out apple trees for the settlers, and I took care of them. I told the people about God, and I tried to be a good man myself. I tried to be a good American, on this land we had found. Maybe I was, a little. Maybe I'm not dead yet.'

With that he turned away, and after a minute there was a kind of exclamation from the crowd, mixed with clapping. Then he got down from the platform and gave the seedlings he had left to the children in the crowd, until they were all gone.

Then I found Mr Locksley, and we smiled at each other a little wearily and shook hands and found our cars and went home.

This all happened a year ago, and Peggy and I have seen all these people again and again since then, and we haven't heard one word said about it. I feel sure that there has been little or no talk about it of any kind. I feel equally sure that there has been some tall thinking about it. To what effect, I don't know. But in another hundred and fifty years we may not miss the big parade, and in another hundred and fifty years we may still be producing the real thing.

From 'The Return of Johnny Appleseed' by Charles Allen Smart, 1939

Joe Hill

I dreamed I saw Joe Hill last night
    Alive as you and me.
Says I, 'But Joe, you're ten years dead.'
    'I never died,' says he.
    'I never died,' says he.

'In Salt Lake, Joe, by God,' says I,
    Him standing by my bed,
'They framed you on a murder charge.'
    Says Joe, 'But I ain't dead.'
    Says Joe, 'But I ain't dead.'

'The copper bosses killed you, Joe.
    They shot you, Joe,' says I.
'Takes more than guns to kill a man,'
    Says Joe, 'I didn't die.'
    Says Joe, 'I didn't die.'

And standing there as big as life
    And smiling with his eyes,
Joe says, 'What they forgot to kill
    Went on to organize.
    Went on to organize.'

'Joe Hill ain't dead,' he says to me,
    'Joe Hill ain't never died.
Where working men are out on strike
    Joe Hill is at their side.
    Joe Hill is at their side.'

'From San Diego up to Maine
  In every mine and mill,
Where workers strike and organize,'
  Says he, 'You'll find Joe Hill.'
  Says he, 'You'll find Joe Hill.'

I dreamed I saw Joe Hill last night
  Alive as you and me.
Says I, 'But Joe, you're ten years dead.'
  'I never died,' says he.
  'I never died,' says he.

A song in tribute to Joe Hill, song-writer leader of the IWW – Industrial
Workers of the World – executed for murder in Salt Lake City, 1915, aged 30.
Words by Alfred Hayes, c.1935. The night before his death Hill sent a telegram
to IWW headquarters: 'Don't waste time mourning. Organize.'

The Ghost of Roger Casement

O what has made that sudden noise?
What on the threshold stands?
It never crossed the sea because
John Bull and the sea are friends;
But this is not the old sea
Nor this the old seashore.
What gave that roar of mockery,
That roar in the sea's roar?
The ghost of Roger Casement
Is beating on the door.

John Bull has stood for Parliament,
A dog must have his day,
The country thinks no end of him,
For he knows how to say,
At a beanfeast or a banquet,
That all must hang their trust
Upon the British Empire,
Upon the Church of Christ.
The ghost of Roger Casement
Is beating on the door.

John Bull has gone to India
And all must pay him heed,
For histories are there to prove
That none of another breed
Has had a like inheritance,
Or sucked such milk as he,
And there's no luck about a house
If it lack honesty.
The ghost of Roger Casement
Is beating on the door.

I poked about a village church
And found his family tomb
And copied out what I could read
In that religious gloom;
Found many a famous man there;
But fame and virtue rot.
Draw round, beloved and bitter men,
Draw round and raise a shout;
The ghost of Roger Casement
Is beating on the door.

W. B. Yeats, 1936

Blok

A weak shaft of light through the blackness of hell is
your voice under the rumble of exploding shells

in that thunder like a seraph he is announcing
in a toneless voice, from somewhere else, some

ancient misty morning he inhabits, how he
loved us, who are blind and nameless who

share the blue cloak of sinful treachery
and more tenderly than anyone loved the woman who

sank more daringly than any into the night of evil,
and of his love for you, Russia, which he cannot end.

And he draws an absent-minded finger along
his temple all the time he tells us of

[145]

the days that wait for us, how God will deceive us.
We shall call for the sun and it will not rise.

He spoke like a solitary prisoner
(or perhaps a child speaking to himself)

so that over the whole square the sacred
heart of Alexander Blok appeared to us.

From *Poems for Alexander Blok* by Marina Tsvetayeva, 1921,
translated from the Russian by Elaine Feinstein

The Dead Astronaut

I circle still. You showed me love when time began;
and when this flesh had burned away, my bones
melted to nothing and eternity,
I cried to taste Time and your clay again.
I saw you veiled in air, impeccable Mary,
ageless Earth, clothed in old imagery.
There'd be no stone of you I would not kiss.

But I go blowing weightless in light's ways –
a hollow wingless seed, a seed of death –
and my eternity has no nights or days.
I circle you forever, visible Earth
who separate dark from light. You, you alone,
fabricate diamonds in your sightless stone
and make the universe into a truth.

Had I heart, eyes – as I am charred and blind –
I'd watch forever your altering light and dark –
your circling seasons, your renewing meaning.
Those words I used! Do you know you focus there
all of this space, the dream of the dumb sleeper
who is the axis of the galaxies?
Because of you, for you alone
this terrible sun began his endless shining.

Give me your night. I burn.

Judith Wright, 1970

Five

GUILT AND REPARATION

On Twelfth Night the dead walk, and on every
tile of the house a soul is sitting, waiting
for your prayers to take it out of purgatory.

IRISH SAYING

'They tell of Pausanias'

They tell of Pausanias, that when he was in Byzantium, he solicited a young lady of a noble family in the city, whose name was Cleonice, to debauch her. Her parents, dreading his cruelty, were forced to consent, and so abandoned their daughter to his wishes. The daughter asked the servants outside the chamber to put out all the lights; so that approaching silently and in the dark towards his bed, she stumbled upon the lamp, which she overturned. Pausanias, who was fallen asleep, awakened, and startled with the noise, thought an assassin had taken that dead time of night to murder him, so that hastily snatching up his poniard that lay by him, he struck the girl, who fell with the blow, and died. After this, he never had rest, but was continually haunted by her, and saw an apparition visiting him in his sleep, and addressing him with these angry words:—

> 'Go on thy way, unto the evil end,
> That doth on lust and violence attend.'

This was one of the chief occasions of indignation against him among the confederates, who now, joining their resentments and forces with Cimon's, besieged him in Byzantium. He escaped out of their hands, and, continuing, as it is said, to be disturbed by the apparition, fled to the oracle of the dead at Heraclea, raised the ghost of Cleonice, and entreated her to be reconciled. Accordingly she appeared to him, and answered that, as soon as he came to Sparta, he should speedily be freed from all evils; obscurely foretelling, it would seem, his imminent death. This story is related by many authors.

From 'Cimon' in *Plutarch's Lives*, c.AD 100, translated by A. H. Clough, 1864

'Murder will out'

Oon of the gretteste auctour that men rede
Seith thus: that whilom two felawes wente
On pilgrimage, in a ful goode entente;
And happed so, they coomen in a toun
Wher as ther was swich congregacioun
Of peple, and eek so streit of herbergage,
That they ne founde as muche as cotage
In which they bothe myghte ylogged bee.
Wherfore they mosten of necessitee,

As for that nyght, departen compaignye;
And ech of hem gooth to his hostelrye,
And took his loggyng, as it wolde falle.
That oon of hem was logged in a stalle,
Fer in a yeerd, with oxen of the plough;
That oother man was logged wel ynough.
As was his aventure or his fortune,
That us governeth alle as in commune.

And so bifel that, longe er it were day,
This man mette in his bed, ther as he lay,
How that his felawe gan upon hym calle,
And seyde, 'Allas! for in an oxes stalle
This nyght I shal be mordred ther I lye.
Now help me, deere brother, or I dye.
In alle haste com to me!' he sayde.
This man out of his sleep for feere abrayde;

But whan that he was wakened of his sleep,
He turned hym, and took of this no keep.
Hym thoughte his dreem nas but a vanitee.
Thus twies in his slepyng dremed hee;
And atte thridde thyme yet his felawe
Cam, as hym thoughte, and seide, 'I am now slawe.
Bihoold my bloody woundes depe and wyde!
Arys up erly in the morwe tyde,
And at the west gate of the toun,' quod he,
'A carte ful of dong ther shaltow se,
In which my body is hid ful prively;
Do thilke carte arresten boldely.
My gold caused my mordre, sooth to sayn.'
And tolde hym every point how he was slayn,
With a ful pitous face, pale of hewe.
And truste wel, his dreem he foond ful trewe,
For on the morwe, as soone as it was day,
To his felawes in he took the way;
And whan that he cam to this oxes stalle,
After his felawe he bigan to calle.

The hostiler answerede hym anon,
And seyde, 'Sire, your felawe is agon.
As soone as day he wente out of the toun.'

This man gan fallen in suspecioun,
Remembrynge on his dremes that he mette,
And forth he gooth – no lenger wolde he lette –
Unto the west gate of the toun, and fond
A dong-carte, wente as it were to donge lond,

That was arrayed in that same wise
As ye han herd the dede man devyse.
And with an hardy herte he gan to crye
Vengeance and justice of this felonye.
'My felawe mordred is this same nyght,
And in this carte he lith gapyng upright.
I crye out on the ministres,' quod he,
'That sholden kepe and reulen this citee.
Harrow! allas! heere lith my felawe slayn!'
What sholde I moore unto this tale sayn?
The people out sterte and caste the cart to grounde,
And in the myddel of the dong they founde
The dede man, that mordred was al newe.
    O blisful God, that art so just and trewe,
Lo, how that thou biwreyest mordre alway!
Mordre wol out, that se we day by day.
Mordre is so wlatsom and abhomynable
To God, that is so just and resonable,
That he ne wol nat suffre it heled be,
Though it abyde a yeer, or two, or thre.
Mordre wol out, this my conclusioun.
And right anon, ministres of that toun
Han hent the carter and so soore hym pyned,
And eek the hostiler so soore engyned,
That they biknewe hire wikkednesse anon,
And were anhanged by the nekke-bon.

Chanticleer's story, from 'The Nun's Priest's Tale' by Geoffrey Chaucer, c.1393

The Twa Sisters of Binnorie

There were twa sisters sat in a bower,
    Edinbro', Edinbro',
There came a knight to be their wooer.
    Stirling for aye!
He courted the elder with glove and ring,
But he loved the younger beyond all thing.
    Bonny St Johnstone stands on Tay.

He courted the elder with glove and ring,
But he loved the younger beyond all thing;
He courted the elder with brooch and knife,
But he loved the younger as his life.

[150]

The elder she was vexéd sair
And sair envied her sister fair.
'O sister, come to the river-strand
And watch the boats as they row to land.'

She's ta'en her by the milk-white hand
And led her down to the river strand;
The younger she stood on a stane
And the elder sister threw her in.

'O sister, sister, give me your hand
And I'll make you heir to all my land;
O sister, sister, save my life
And I swear I'll never be no man's wife.'

'Foul fall the hand that I should take –
It twined me out of my wardle's make.
Your cherry cheeks and your yellow hair
Make me go maiden for evermair.'

Sometimes she sank, sometimes she swam,
Until she came to the miller's dam;
'O draw the dam,' cried the miller's son,
'Here's either a mermaid or a swan.'

The miller quickly focht his dam
And there he found a drowned womán;
You could not see her fingers white,
For golden rings that were so gryte.

Then by there came a harper fine
Such as harp to nobles when they dine.
He's ta'en three strands of her yellow hair
And with them strung his harp so rare.

He's done him to her father's hall
And played the harp before them all.
O then, the harp began to sing,
And it's 'farewell, sweetheart,' sang the string.

And syne the harp spake loud and clear,
    Edinbro', Edinbro',
'Farewell, my father and mother dear!'
    Stirling for aye!

[151]

And then as plain as plain could be:
'There sits my sister who drownéd me.'
Bonny St Johnstone stands on Tay.

Scottish ballad

The youth unshriven and in a state of sin

This youth appeared on the morrow of his funeral to a close friend of
his, a scholar likewise, whom he begged to go on his behalf to Rodez
and crave absolution from the holy Bishop. His friend at once set out,
and as he made his way through the mountain passes, dangerous to
tread and slippery with snow, his dead friend went with him guiding
his steps and conversing with him, although he saw no man. The
ghost, indeed, led him safely over the snow and ice, and when he was
come to Rodez he obtained a full absolution from the Bishop, the
Blessed François. On his return the ghost again companioned with and
conducted him with careful steps. As is the Catholic custom in such a
case absolution was given to the dead body, and the Spirit then took
leave of his friend with many tender expressions of gratitude, promising to pray for and assist him.

From *A Treatise of Ghosts* by Father Noël Taillepied, 1588,
translated by M. Summers

'The very painting of your fear'

LADY MACBETH: My royal lord,
You do not give the cheer: the feast is sold
That is not often vouch'd, while 'tis a-making,
'Tis given with welcome: to feed were best at home;
From thence, the sauce to meat is ceremony;
Meeting were bare without it.
MACBETH: Sweet remembrancer!
Now good digestion wait on appetite,
And health on both!
LENNOX: May it please your highness sit?
(The Ghost of BANQUO *enters, and sits in* MACBETH's *place.)*
MACBETH: Here had we now our country's honour roof'd,
Were the grac'd person of our Banquo present;
Who may I rather challenge for unkindness
Than pity for mischance!

ROSS: His absence, sir,
Lays blame upon his promise. Please 't your highness
To grace us with your royal company.
MACBETH: The table's full.
LENNOX: Here is a place reserv'd, sir.
MACBETH: Where?
LENNOX: Here, my good lord. What is 't that moves your highness?
MACBETH: Which of you hath done this?
LORDS: What, my good lord?
MACBETH: Thou canst not say I did it: never shake
Thy gory locks at me.
ROSS: Gentlemen, rise; his highness is not well.
LADY MACBETH: Sit, worthy friends: my lord is often thus,
And hath been from his youth: pray you, keep seat;
The fit is momentary; upon a thought
He will again be well. If much you note him
You shall offend him and extend his passion:
Feed and regard him not. Are you a man?
MACBETH: Ay, and a bold one, that dare look on that
Which might appal the devil.
LADY MACBETH: O proper stuff!
This is the very painting of your fear;
This is the air-drawn dagger which, you said,
Led you to Duncan. O! these flaws and starts –
Impostors to true fear – would well become
A woman's story at a winter's fire,
Authoriz'd by her grandam. Shame itself!
Why do you make such faces? When all's done
You look but on a stool.
MACBETH: Prithee, see there! behold! look! lo! how say you?
Why, what care I? If thou canst nod, speak too.
If charnel-houses and our graves must send
Those that we bury back, our monuments
Shall be the maws of kites. *(Ghost disappears.)*
LADY MACBETH: What! quite unmann'd in folly?
MACBETH: If I stand here, I saw him.
LADY MACBETH: Fie, for shame!
MACBETH: Blood hath been shed ere now, i' the olden time,
Ere human statute purg'd the gentle weal;
Ay, and since too, murders have been perform'd
Too terrible for the ear: the times have been,
That, when the brains were out, the man would die,
And there an end; but now they rise again,
With twenty mortal murders on their crowns,

And push us from our stools: this is more strange
Than such a murder is.

From *Macbeth* by William Shakespeare, *c.*1606

The appearing of a ghost of one Mr Bower *of* Guilford *to an Highway-man in Prison*

About ten Years ago, one Mr *Bower*, an ancient Man, living at *Guilford* in *Surrey*, was upon the High-way, not far from that place, found newly murdered very barbarously, having one great cut cross his Throat, and another down his Breast. Two men were seized upon suspicion, and put into Gaol at *Guilford*, to another who had been committed for Robbing as I suppose. That Night this third Man was awakened about one of the Clock, and greatly terrified with an old Man, who had a great gash cross his Throat almost Ear to Ear, and a wound down his Breast. He also came in stooping, and holding his Hand on his Back. Thus he appeared, but said nothing. The Thief calls to his two new Companions, they grumbled at him, but made no answer.

In the Morning he had retained so lively an impression of what he had seen, that he spoke to them to the same purpose again, and they told him it was nothing but his fancy: But he was so fully persuaded of the reality of the Apparition, that he told others of it, and it came to the Ears of my Friend Mr *Reading*, Justice of the Peace in *Surrey*, and Cousin to the Gentleman that was murdered. . . .

After preliminary Interrogatories, he desired him to tell him what he had seen in the Night, which he immediately did, exactly according to the Relation I gave before: And withal, described the old Gentleman so by his picked Beard, and that he was (as he called it) rough on his Cheeks, and that the Hairs of his Face were black and white. Mr *Reading* saith, that he himself could not have given a more exact Description of Mr *Bower* than this was. He told the Highway-man, that he must give him his Oath, (though that would signify little from such a Rogue) to which the Man readily consented, and took Oath before the Justice of all this.

Mr READING being a very discrete Man, concealed this Story from the Jury at the Assizes, as knowing this would be no Evidence according to our Law. However, the Friends of the Murdered Gentleman had been very inquisitive, and discovered several suspicious Circumstances, one of which was that those two Men had washed their Cloaths, and that some stains of Blood remained. Another, that one of them denied he ever heard that Mr *Bower* was dead, whenas he had in another place confessed it two Hours before. Upon these and such like Evidences, those two were condemn'd and executed, but denied it to the last.

This is the first Story, which I had from Mr *Reading* himself, who is a very honest Person and not credulous.

From *Saducismus Triumphatus* by Joseph Glanvill, 1681

The ghosts in Salem

And another thing that quickned them yet more to Act upon it, was, that the Afflicted were frequently entertained with *Apparitions* of *Ghosts* at the same time that the *Spectres* of the supposed *Witches* troubled them: Which *Ghosts* always cast the Beholders into far more Consternation than any of the *Spectres*; and when they exhibited themselves, they cried out of being *Murdered* by the *Witchcrafts*, or other Violences of the Persons represented in the *Spectres*. Once or Twice these Apparitions were seen by others at the very same time that they shew'd themselves to the *afflicted*; and seldom were they seen at all, but when something unusual and suspicious had attended the Death of the Party thus appearing.

The *afflicted* People many times had never heard any thing before of the Persons appearing in *Ghost*, or of the Persons *accused* by the *Apparitions*; and yet the accused upon Examination have confessed the Murders of those very Persons, though these *accused* also knew nothing of the *Apparitions* that had come in against them; and the *afflicted* Persons likewise, without any private Agreement or Collusion, when successively brought into a Room, have all asserted the same *Apparitions* to be there before them: These *Murders* did seem to call for an Enquiry.

From *Magnalia Christi Americana* by Cotton Mather, 1702

The Gardener's Ghost

Perhaps the latest ghost in a court of justice (except in cases about the letting of haunted houses) 'appeared' at the Aylesbury Petty Sessions on 22nd August, 1829. On 25th October, 1828, William Edden, a market gardener, was found dead, with his ribs broken, in the road between Aylesbury and Thame. One Sewell, in August, 1829, accused a man named Tyler, and both were examined at the Aylesbury Petty Sessions.

Mrs Edden gave evidence that she sent five or six times for Tyler 'to come and see the corpse. . . . I had some particular reasons for sending for him which I never did divulge. . . . I will tell you my reasons, gentlemen, if you ask me, in the face of Tyler, even if my life should be in danger for it.' The reasons were that on the night of her husband's murder, 'something rushed over me, and I thought my husband came by me. I looked up, and I thought I heard the voice of my husband come from near my mahogany table. . . . I thought I saw my husband's apparition, and the man that had done it, and that man was Tyler. . . . I ran out and said, "O dear God! my husband is murdered, and his ribs are broken".'

LORD NUGENT: 'What made you think your husband's ribs were broken?'

'He held up his hands like this, and I saw a hammer, or something like a hammer, and it came into my mind that his ribs were broken.' Sewell stated that the murder was accomplished by means of a hammer.

The prisoners were discharged on 13th September. On 5th March 1830, they were tried at the Buckingham Lent Assizes, were found guilty and were hanged, protesting their innocence, on 8th March 1830.

From *The Book of Dreams and Ghosts* by Andrew Lang, 1897

'My Spectre'

My Spectre around me night & day
Like a Wild beast guards my way
My Emanation far within
Weeps incessantly for my Sin

A Fathomless & boundless deep
There we wander there we weep
On the hungry craving wind
My Spectre follows thee behind

He scents thy footsteps in the snow
Wheresoever thou dost go
Thro the wintry hail & rain
When wilt thou return again

Dost thou not in Pride & Scorn
Fill with tempests all my morn
And with jealousies & fears
Fill my pleasant nights with tears

Seven of my sweet loves thy knife
Has bereaved of their life
Their marble tombs I built with tears
And with cold & shuddering fears

Seven more loves weep night & day
Round the tombs where my loves lay
And seven more loves attend each night
Around my couch with torches bright

And seven more Loves in my bed
Crown with wine my mournful head
Pitying & forgiving all
Thy transgressions great & small

When wilt thou return & view
My loves & them to life renew
When wilt thou return & live
When wilt thou pity as I forgive

Never Never I return
Still for Victory I burn
Living thee alone Ill have
And when dead Ill be thy Grave

Thro the Heaven & Earth & Hell
Thou shalt never never quell
I will fly & thou pursue
Night & Morn the flight renew

Till I turn from Female love
And root up the infernal grove
I shall never worthy be
To step into Eternity

And to end thy cruel mocks
Annihilate thee on the rocks
And another form create
To be subservient to my Fate

Let us agree to give up Love
And root up the infernal grove
Then shall we return & see
The worlds of happy Eternity

& Throughout all Eternity
I forgive you you forgive me
As our Dear Redeemer said
This the Wine & this the Bread

William Blake, 1804

Peter Grimes

With greedy eye he look'd on all he saw,
He knew not justice, and he laugh'd at law;
On all he mark'd he stretch'd his ready hand;
He fish'd by water, and he filch'd by land:
Oft in the night has Peter dropp'd his oar,
Fled from his boat and sought for prey on shore;
Oft up the hedge-row glided, on his back
Bearing the orchard's produce in a sack,
Or farm-yard load, tugg'd fiercely from the stack;
And as these wrongs to greater numbers rose,
The more he look'd on all men as his foes.
 He built a mud-wall'd hovel, where he kept
His various wealth, and there he oft-times slept;
But no success could please his cruel soul,
He wish'd for one to trouble and control;
He wanted some obedient boy to stand
And bear the blow of his outrageous hand;
And hoped to find in some propitious hour
A feeling creature subject to his power.
 Peter had heard there were in London then, –
Still have they being! – workhouse-clearing men,
Who, undisturb'd by feelings just or kind,
Would parish-boys to needy tradesmen bind.

A winter pass'd since Peter saw the town,
And summer-lodgers were again come down;
These, idly curious, with their glasses spied
The ships in bay as anchor'd for the tide, –
The river's craft, – the bustle of the quay, –
And sea-port views, which landmen love to see.
 One, up the river, had a man and boat
Seen day by day, now anchor'd, now afloat;

Fisher he seem'd, yet used no net nor hook;
Of sea-fowl swimming by no heed he took,
But on the gliding waves still fix'd his lazy look:
At certain stations he would view the stream,
As if he stood bewilder'd in a dream,
Or that some power had chain'd him for a time,
To feel a curse or meditate on crime.
　　This known, some curious, some in pity went,
And others question'd – 'Wretch, dost thou repent?' –
He heard, he trembled, and in fear resign'd
His boat: new terror fill'd his restless mind;
Furious he grew, and up the country ran,
And there they seized him – a distemper'd man: –
Him we received, and to a parish-bed,
Follow'd and cursed, the groaning man was led.
　　Here, when they saw him, whom they used to shun,
A lost, lone man, so harass'd and undone;
Our gentle females, ever prompt to feel,
Perceived compassion on their anger steal;
His crimes they could not from their memories blot,
But they were grieved, and trembled at his lot.
　　A priest too came, to whom his words are told;
And all the signs they shudder'd to behold.
　　'Look! look!' they cried; 'his limbs with horror shake,
And as he grinds his teeth, what noise they make!
How glare his angry eyes, and yet he's not awake:
See! what cold drops upon his forehead stand,
And how he clenches that broad bony hand.'
　　The priest attending, found he spoke at times
As one alluding to his fears and crimes:
'It was the fall,' he mutter'd, 'I can show
The manner how – I never struck a blow:' –
And then aloud – 'Unhand me, free my chain;
On oath, he fell – it struck him to the brain: –
Why ask my father? – that old man will swear
Against my life; besides, he wasn't there: –
What, all agreed? – Am I to die to-day? –
My Lord, in mercy, give me time to pray.'
　　Then, as they watch'd him, calmer he became,
And grew so weak he couldn't move his frame,
But murmuring spake, – while they could see and hear
The start of terror and the groan of fear;
See the large dew-beads on his forehead rise,
And the cold death-drop glaze his sunken eyes;

Nor yet he died, but with unwonted force
Seem'd with some fancied being to discourse:
He knew not us, or with accustom'd art
He hid the knowledge, yet exposed his heart;
'Twas part confession and the rest defence,
A madman's tale, with gleams of waking sense.
   'I'll tell you all,' he said, 'the very day
When the old man first placed them in my way:
My father's spirit – he who always tried
To give me trouble, when he lived and died –
When he was gone, he could not be content
To see my days in painful labour spent,
But would appoint his meetings, and he made
Me watch at these, and so neglect my trade.
   ''Twas one hot noon, all silent, still, serene,
No living being had I lately seen;
I paddled up and down and dipp'd my net,
But (such his pleasure) I could nothing get, –
A father's pleasure, when his toil was done,
To plague and torture thus an only son!
And so I sat and look'd upon the stream,
How it ran on, and felt as in a dream:
But dream it was not; no! – I fix'd my eyes
On the mid stream and saw the spirits rise;
I saw my father on the water stand,
And hold a thin pale boy in either hand;
And there they glided ghastly on the top
Of the salt flood, and never touch'd a drop:
I would have struck them, but they knew th'intent,
And smiled upon the oar, and down they went.
   'Now, from that day, whenever I began
To dip my net, there stood the hard old man –
He and those boys: I humbled me and pray'd
They would be gone; – they heeded not, but stay'd:
Nor could I turn, nor would the boat go by,
But gazing on the spirits, there was I:
They bade me leap to death, but I was loth to die:
And every day, as sure as day arose,
Would these three spirits meet me ere the close;
To hear and mark them daily was my doom,
And "Come," they said, with weak, sad voices, "come."
To row away with all my strength I try'd,
But there were they, hard by me in the tide,
The three unbodied forms – and "Come," still "come," they cried.

'Fathers should pity – but this old man shook
His hoary locks, and froze me by a look:
Thrice, when I struck them, through the water came
A hollow groan, that weaken'd all my frame:
"Father!" said I, "have mercy:" – He replied,
I know not what – the angry spirit lied, –
"Didst thou not draw thy knife?" said he: – 'Twas true,
But I had pity and my arm withdrew:
He cried for mercy which I kindly gave,
But he has no compassion in his grave.
    'There were three places, where they ever rose, –
The whole long river has not such as those, –
Places accursed, where, if a man remain,
He'll see the things which strike him to the brain;
And there they made me on my paddle lean,
And look at them for hours; – accursed scene!
When they would glide to that smooth eddy-space,
Then bid me leap and join them in the place;
And at my groans each little villain sprite
Enjoy'd my pains and vanish'd in delight.
    'In one fierce summer-day, when my poor brain
Was burning hot and cruel was my pain,
Then came this father-foe, and there he stood
With his two boys again upon the flood;
There was more mischief in their eyes, more glee
In their pale faces when they glared at me:
Still did they force me on the oar to rest,
And when they saw me fainting and oppress'd,
He, with his hand, the old man, scoop'd the flood,
And there came flame about him mix'd with blood;
He bade me stoop and look upon the place,
Then flung the hot-red liquor in my face;
Burning it blazed, and then I roar'd for pain,
I thought the demons would have turn'd my brain.
    'Still there they stood, and forced me to behold
A place of horrors – they cannot be told –
Where the flood open'd, there I heard the shriek
Of tortured guilt – no earthly tongue can speak:
"All days alike! for ever!" did they say,
"And unremitted torments every day" –
Yes, so they said:' – But here he ceased and gazed
On all around, affrighten'd and amazed;
And still he tried to speak, and look'd in dread
Of frighten'd females gathering round his bed;

Then dropp'd exhausted and appear'd at rest,
Till the strong foe the vital powers possess'd;
Then with an inward, broken voice he cried,
'Again they come,' and mutter'd as he died.

From 'Peter Grimes' in *The Borough* by George Crabbe, 1810

Cain

The scene around was desolate; as far as the eye could reach it was desolate: the bare rocks faced each other, and left a long and wide interval of thin white sand. You might wander on and look round and round, and peep into the crevices of the rocks and discover nothing that acknowledged the influence of the seasons. There was no spring, no summer, no autumn: and the winter's snow, that would have been lovely, fell not on these hot rocks and scorching sands. . . .

It was here that Enos had found the pitcher and cake, and to this place he led his father. But ere they had reached the rock they beheld a human shape: his back was towards them, and they were advancing unperceived, when they heard him smite his breast and cry aloud, 'Woe is me! woe is me! I must never die again, and yet I am perishing with thirst and hunger.'

Pallid, as the reflection of the sheeted lightning on the heavy-sailing night-cloud, became the face of Cain; but the child Enos took hold of the shaggy skin, his father's robe, and raised his eyes to his father, and listening whispered, 'Ere yet I could speak, I am sure, O my father, that I heard that voice. Have not I often said that I remembered a sweet voice? O my father! this is it': and Cain trembled exceedingly. The voice was sweet indeed, but it was thin and querulous, like that of a feeble slave in misery, who despairs altogether, yet can not refrain himself from weeping and lamentation. And, behold! Enos glided forward, and creeping softly round the base of the rock, stood before the stranger, and looked up into his face. And the Shape shrieked, and turned round, and Cain beheld him, that his limbs and his face were those of his brother Abel whom he had killed! And Cain stood like one who struggles in his sleep because of the exceeding terribleness of a dream.

From *The Wanderings of Cain* by Samuel Taylor Coleridge, 1798

A Dree Neet

'T were a dree neet, a dree neet, as t' squire's end drew nigh,
A dree neet, a dree neet, to watch, an' pray, an' sigh.

When t' streeam runs dry, an t' deead leaves fall, an' t' ripe ear
    bends its heead,
An' t' blood wi' lithin' seems fair clogg'd, yan kens yan's neam'd
    wi' t' deead.

When t' een grows dim, an' folk draw nigh frae t' other saade o' t'
    grave,
It's late to square up awd accoonts a gannin' sowl to save.

T' priest may coom, an' t' priest may gan, his weel-worn tale to
    chant,
When t' deeath-smear clems a wrinkled broo, sike disn't fet yan's
    want.

Nea book, nea can'le, bell, nor mass, nea priest iv onny lan',
When t' dree neet cooms, can patch a sowl, or t' totterin' mak to
    stan'.

'T were a dree neet, a dree neet, for a sowl to gan away,
A dree neet, a dree neet, bud a gannin' sowl can't stay.

An' t' winner shuts they rattled sair, an' t' mad wild wind did shill,
An' t' Gabriel ratchets yelp'd aboon, a gannin' sowl to chill.

'T were a dree neet, a dree neet, for deeath to don his cowl,
To staup abroad wi' whimly treead, to claim a gannin' sowl.

Bud laal deeath recks hoo dree t' neet be, or hoo a sowl may pray,
When t' sand runs oot, his sickle reaps; a gannin' sowl can't stay.

'T were a dree neet, a dree neet, ower Whinny-moor to trake,
Wi' shoonless feet, ower flinty steanes, thruf monny a thorny
    brake.

A dree neet, a dree neet, wi' nowt neaways to mark
T' gainest trod to t' Brig o' Deead; a lane lost sowl i' t' dark.

A dree neet, a dree neet, at t' brig foot theer to meet
Laal sowls at he were t' father on, wi' nea good-deame i' seet.

At t' altar steps he niver steead, thof monny a voo he made,
Noo t' debt he awes to monny a lass at t' brig foot mun be paid.

They face him noo wiv other deeds, like black spots on a sheet,
They noo unscape, they egg him on, on t' brig his doom to meet.

Nea doves has sattled on his sill, bud a flittermoose that neet
Cam thrice taames thruf his casement, an' flacker'd roond his feet.

An' thrice taames did a raven croak, an' t' seame-like thrice cam t'
     hoot
Frae t' ullets' tree; doon chimleys three there cam a shrood o'
     soot.

An' roond t' can'le twea taames there cam a dark-wing'd moth to
     t' leet,
Bud t' thod it swirl'd reet into t' fleame, wheer gans his sowl this
     neet.

'T were a dree neet, a dree neet, for yan too late to pray,
A dree neet, a dree neet, but a gannin' sowl can't stay.

Traditional; from *Yorkshire Dialect Poems*, edited by F. W. Moorman, 1917

Marley's ghost

The yard was so dark that even Scrooge, who knew its every stone,
was fain to grope with his hands. The fog and frost so hung about the
black old gateway of the house, that it seemed as if the Genius of the
Weather sat in mournful meditation on the threshold.

Now, it is a fact, that there was nothing at all particular about the
knocker on the door, except that it was very large. It is also a fact, that
Scrooge had seen it, night and morning, during his whole residence in
that place; also that Scrooge had as little of what is called fancy about
him as any man in the city of London, even including – which is a bold
word – the corporation, aldermen, and livery. Let it also be borne in
mind that Scrooge had not bestowed one thought on Marley, since his
last mention of his seven-years' dead partner that afternoon. And then
let any man explain to me, if he can, how it happened that Scrooge,
having his key in the lock of the door, saw in the knocker, without its
undergoing any intermediate process of change – not a knocker, but
Marley's face.

Marley's face. It was not in impenetrable shadow as the other objects in the yard were, but had a dismal light about it, like a bad lobster in a dark cellar. It was not angry or ferocious, but looked at Scrooge as Marley used to look: with ghostly spectacles turned up on its ghostly forehead. The hair was curiously stirred, as if by breath or hot air; and, though the eyes were wide open, they were perfectly motionless. That, and its livid colour, made it horrible; but its horror seemed to be in spite of the face and beyond its control, rather than a part of its own expression.

As Scrooge looked fixedly at this phenomenon, it was a knocker again.

Scrooge fell upon his knees, and clasped his hands before his face.

'Mercy!' he said. 'Dreadful apparition, why do you trouble me?'

'Man of the worldly mind!' replied the Ghost, 'do you believe in me or not?'

'I do,' said Scrooge. 'I must. But why do spirits walk the earth, and why do they come to me?'

'It is required of every man,' the Ghost returned, 'that the spirit within him should walk abroad among his fellow-men, and travel far and wide; and if that spirit goes not forth in life, it is condemned to do so after death. It is doomed to wander through the world – oh, woe is me! – and witness what it cannot share, but might have shared on earth, and turned to happiness!'

Again the spectre raised a cry, and shook its chain and wrung its shadowy hands.

'You are fettered,' said Scrooge, trembling. 'Tell me why?'

'I wear the chain I forged in life,' replied the Ghost. 'I made it link by link, and yard by yard; I girded it on of my own free will, and of my own free will I wore it. Is its pattern strange to *you*?'

Scrooge trembled more and more.

'Or would you know,' pursued the Ghost, 'the weight and length of the strong coil you bear yourself? It was full as heavy and as long as this, seven Christmas Eves ago. You have laboured on it since. It is a ponderous chain!'

Scrooge glanced about him on the floor, in the expectation of finding himself surrounded by some fifty or sixty fathoms of iron cable: but he could see nothing.

'Jacob,' he said, imploringly. 'Old Jacob Marley, tell me more. Speak comfort to me, Jacob!'

'I have none to give,' the Ghost replied. 'It comes from other regions, Ebenezer Scrooge, and is conveyed by other ministers, to other kinds of men.'

'How it is that I appear before you in a shape that you can see, I may not tell. I have sat invisible beside you many and many a day.'

It was not an agreeable idea. Scrooge shivered, and wiped the perspiration from his brow.

'That is no light part of my penance,' pursued the Ghost. 'I am here to-night to warn you, that you have yet a chance and hope of escaping my fate. A chance and hope of my procuring, Ebenezer.'

'You were always a good friend to me,' said Scrooge. 'Thank'ee!'

'You will be haunted,' resumed the Ghost, 'by Three Spirits.'

Scrooge's countenance fell almost as low as the Ghost's had done.

'Is that the chance and hope you mentioned, Jacob?' he demanded, in a faltering voice.

'It is.'

'I – I think I'd rather not,' said Scrooge.

From *A Christmas Carol* by Charles Dickens, 1843

The Haunted Man

A CHRISTMAS STORY

Don't tell me that it wasn't a knocker. I had seen it often enough, and I ought to know. So ought the three-o'clock beer, in dirty high-lows, swinging himself over the railing, or executing a demoniacal jig upon the doorstep; so ought the butcher, although butchers as a general thing are scornful of such trifles; so ought the postman, to whom knockers of the most extravagant description were merely human weaknesses, that were to be pitied and used. And so ought, for the matter of that, etc., etc., etc.

But then it was *such* a knocker. A wild, extravagant, and utterly incomprehensible knocker. A knocker so mysterious and suspicious that Policeman X37, first coming upon it, felt inclined to take it instantly in custody, but compromised with his professional instincts by sharply and sternly noting it with an eye that admitted of no nonsense, but confidently expected to detect its secret yet. An ugly knocker; a knocker with a hard, human face, that was a type of the harder human face within. A human face that held between its teeth a brazen rod. So hereafter, in the mysterious future should be held, etc., etc.

He sat alone in a gloomy library listening to the wind that roared in the chimney. Around him novels and story-books were strewn thickly; in his lap he held one with its pages freshly cut, and turned the leaves wearily until his eyes rested upon a portrait in its frontispiece. And as the wind howled the more fiercely, and the darkness without fell blacker, a strange and fateful likeness to that portrait appeared above

[166]

his chair and leaned upon his shoulder. The Haunted Man gazed at the portrait and sighed. The figure gazed at the portrait and sighed too.

'Here again?' said the Haunted Man.

'Here again,' it repeated in a low voice.

'Another novel?'

'Another novel.'

'The old story?'

'The old story.'

'I see a child,' said the Haunted Man, gazing from the pages of the book into the fire, – 'a most unnatural child, a model infant. It is prematurely old and philosophic. It dies in poverty to slow music. It dies surrounded by luxury to slow music. It dies with an accompaniment of golden water and rattling carts to slow music. Previous to its decease it makes a will; it repeats the Lord's Prayer, it kisses the "boofer lady." That child –'

'Is mine,' said the phantom.

'I see a good woman, undersized. I see several charming women, but they are all undersized. They are more or less imbecile and idiotic, but always fascinating and undersized. They wear coquettish caps and aprons. I observe that feminine virtue is invariably below the medium height, and that it is always simple and infantine. These women –'

'Are mine.'

'I see a haughty, proud, and wicked lady. She is tall and queenly. I remark that all proud and wicked women are tall and queenly. That woman –'

'Is mine,' said the phantom, wringing his hands.

'I see several things continually impending. I observe that whenever an accident, a murder, or death is about to happen, there is something in the furniture, in the locality, in the atmosphere, that foreshadows and suggests it years in advance. I cannot say that in real life I have noticed it, – the perception of this surprising fact belongs –'

'To me!' said the phantom. The Haunted Man continued, in a despairing tone: –

'I see the influence of this in the magazines and daily papers; I see weak imitators rise up and enfeeble the world with senseless formula. I am getting tired of it. It won't do, Charles! it won't do!' and the Haunted Man buried his head in his hands and groaned.

The Haunted Man started, and – woke. The bright sunshine streamed into the room. The air was sparkling with frost. He ran joyously to the window and opened it. A small boy saluted him with 'Merry Christmas.' The Haunted Man instantly gave him a Bank of England note. 'How much like Tiny Tim, Tom, and Bobby that boy looked, – bless my soul, what a genius this Dickens has!'

A knock at the door, and Boots entered.

'Consider your salary doubled instantly. Have you read *David Copperfield?*'

'Yezzur.'

'Your salary is quadrupled. What do you think of the *Old Curiosity Shop?*'

The man instantly burst into a torrent of tears, and then into a roar of laughter.

'Enough! Here are five thousand pounds. Open a porter-house, and call it, "Our Mutual Friend." Huzza! I feel so happy!' And the Haunted Man danced about the room.

And so, bathed in the light of that blessed sun, and yet glowing with the warmth of a good action, the Haunted Man, haunted no longer, save by those shapes which make the dreams of children beautiful, re-seated himself in his chair, and finished *Our Mutual Friend.*

From *Condensed Novels* by Bret Harte, 1899

Delia

to the tune of 'Frankie and Johnny'

Delia cursed Tony,
On a Saturday night,
Cursted him such a wicked curse
That he swore he'd take her life,
 Delia's gone,
 One more round,
 Delia's gone.

The first time he shot her,
Shot her in the side,
The second time he shot her,
She bowed her head and died. *(Chorus)*

They sent for the doctor,
He came dressed in black,
Done everything a doctor could do,
But he couldn't bring Delia back. *(Chorus)*

Monday he was 'rested,
Tuesday he was tried,
The jury found him guilty,
And the judge said, 'Ninety-nine.' *(Chorus)*

'Ninety-nine years in the prison,
Judge, that ain't no time,
I've got a brother in New Orleans
With nine hundred and ninety-nine.' *(Chorus)*

Now Tony he's in the jailhouse,
Drinkin' out a silver cup,
Delia she's in the graveyard,
Tryin' her best to get up. *(Chorus)*

'Jailer, O Jailer,
How can I sleep?
When all around my bedside,
My little Delia creeps.' *(Chorus)*

American folk song

The Key

The news had come that day that the squire was to be down next morning at Applewale; and not sorry was I, for I thought I was sure to be sent home again to my mother. And right glad was I, and I was thinkin' of a' at hame, and my sister, Janet, and the kitten and the pymag, and Trimmer the tike, and all the rest, and I got sa fidgetty, I couldn't sleep, and the clock struck twelve, and me wide awake, and the room as dark as pick. My back was turned to the door, and my eyes towards the wall opposite.

Well, it could na be a full quarter past twelve, when I sees a lightin' on the wall befoore me, as if something took fire behind, and the shadas o' the bed, and the chair, and my gown, that was hangin' from the wall, was dancin' up and down, on the ceilin' beams and the yak pannels; and I turns my head ower my shouther quick, thinkin' something must a gone a' fire.

And what sud I see, by Jen! but the likeness o' the ald beldame, bedizened out in her satins and velvets, on her dead body, simperin', wi' her eyes as wide as saucers, and her face like the fiend himself. 'Twas a red light that rose about her in a fuffin low, as if her dress round her feet was blazin'. She was drivin' on right for me, wi' her ald shrivelled hands crooked as if she was goin' to claw me. I could not stir, but she passed me straight by, wi' a blast o' cald air, and I sid her, at the wall, in the alcove as my aunt used to call it, which was a recess where the state

[169]

bed used to stand in ald times, wi' a door open wide, and her hands gropin' in at somethin' was there. I never sid that door befoore. And she turned round to me, like a thing on a pivot, flyrin' (grinning), and all at once the room was dark, and I standin' at the far side o' the bed; I don't know how I got there, and I found my tongue at last, and if I did na blare a yellock, rennin' down the gallery and almost pulled Mrs Wyvern's door, off t'hooks, and frightened her half out o' her wits.

Ye may guess I did na sleep that night; and wi' the first light, down wi' me to my aunt, as fast as my two legs cud carry me.

Well, my aunt did na frump or flite me, as I thought she would, but she held me by the hand, and looked hard in my face all the time. And she telt me not to be feared; and says she:

'Hed the appearance a key in its hand?'

'Yes,' says I, bringin' it to mind, 'a big key in a queer brass handle.'

'Stop a bit,' says she, lettin' go ma hand, and openin' the cupboard-door. 'Was it like this?' says she, takin' one out in her fingers and showing it to me, with a dark look in my face.

'That was it,' says I, quick enough.

'Are ye sure?' she says, turnin' it round.

'Sart,' says I, and I felt like I was gain' to faint when I sid it.

'Well, that will do, child,' says she, saftly thinkin', and she locked it up again.

'The squire himself will be here to-day, before twelve o'clock, and ye must tell him all about it.' . . .

Loth was I, and my heart in my mouth, and fast I held by my aunt's hand as I stept into that awsome room, and showed them both how she came and passed me by, and the spot where she stood, and where the door seemed to open.

There was an ald empty press against the wall then, and shoving it aside, sure enough there was the tracing of a door in the wainscot, and a keyhole stopped with wood, and planed across as smooth as the rest, and the joining of the door all stopped wi' putty the colour o' yak, and, but for the hinges that showed a bit when the press was shoved aside, ye would not consayt there was a door there at all.

'Ha!' says he, wi' a queer smile, 'this looks like it.'

It took some minutes wi' a small chisel and hammer to pick the bit o' wood out o' the keyhole. The key fitted, sure enough, and, wi' a strang twist and a lang skreeak, the boult went back and he pulled the door open.

There was another door inside, stranger than the first, but the lacks was gone, and it opened easy. Inside was a narrow floor and walls and vault o' brick; we could not see what was in it, for 'twas dark as pick.

When my aunt had lighted the candle the squire held it up and stept in.

My aunt stood on tiptoe tryin' to look over his shouther, and I did na see nout.

'Ha! ha!' says the squire, steppin' backward. 'What's that? Gi'ma the poker – quick!' says he to my aunt. And as she went to the hearth I peeps beside his arm, and I sid squat down in the far corner a monkey or a flayin' on the chest, or else the maist shrivelled up, wizzened ald wife that ever was sen on yearth.

'By Jen!' says my aunt, as, puttin' the poker in his hand, she keeked by his shouther, and sid the ill-favoured thing, 'hae a care sir, what ye're doin'. Back wi' ye, and shut to the door!'

But in place o' that he steps in saftly, wi' the poker pointed like a swoord, and he gies it a poke, and down it a' tumbles together, head and a', in a heap o' bayans and dust, little meyar an' a hatful.

'Twas the bayans o' a child; a' the rest went to dust at a touch. They said nout for a while, but he turns round the skull as it lay on the floor.

Young as I was I consayted I knew well enough what they was thinkin' on.

From 'Madam Crowl's Ghost' by Sheridan Le Fanu, 1870–1

'One need not be a Chamber'

One need not be a Chamber – to be Haunted –
One need not be a House –
The Brain has Corridors – surpassing
Material Place –

Far safer, of a Midnight Meeting
External Ghost
Than its interior Confronting –
That Cooler Host.

Far safer, through an Abbey gallop,
The Stones a'chase –
Than Unarmed, one's a'self encounter –
In lonesome Place –

Oneself behind ourself, concealed –
Should startle most –
Assassin hid in our Apartment
Be Horror's least.

The Body – borrows a Revolver –
He bolts the Door –
O'erlooking a superior spectre –
Or More –

Emily Dickinson, *c.*1863

Mr Jones

As she crossed the threshold, Lady Jane remembered the housekeeper's attempt to prevent her touching the contents of the desk.

Mrs Clemm's room, like herself, was neat, glossy and extremely cold. Only Mrs Clemm herself was no longer like Mrs Clemm. The red-apple glaze had barely faded from her cheeks, and not a lock was disarranged in the unnatural lustre of her false front; even her cap ribbons hung symmetrically along either cheek. But death had happened to her, and had made her into someone else. At first glance it was impossible to say if the unspeakable horror in her wide open eyes were only the reflection of that change, or of the agent by whom it had come. Lady Jane, shuddering, paused a moment while Stramer went up to the bed.

'Her hand is warm still – but no pulse.' He glanced about the room. 'A glass anywhere?' The cowering Georgiana took a hand glass from the neat chest of drawers, and Stramer held it over the housekeeper's drawn-back lip. . . .

'She's dead,' he pronounced.

'Oh, poor thing! But how –?' Lady Jane drew near, and was kneeling down, taking the inanimate hand in hers, when Stramer touched her on the arm, and then silently raised a finger of warning. Georgiana was crouching in the farther corner of the room, her face buried in her lifted arms.

'Look here,' Stramer whispered. He pointed to Mrs Clemm's throat, and Lady Jane, bending over, distinctly saw a circle of red marks on it – the marks of recent bruises. She looked again into the awful eyes.

'She's been strangled,' Stramer whispered.

Lady Jane, with a shiver of fear, drew down the housekeeper's lids. Georgiana, her face hidden, was still sobbing convulsively in the corner. There seemed, in the air of the cold orderly room, something that forbade wonderment and silenced conjecture. Lady Jane and Stramer stood and looked at each other without speaking. At length Stramer crossed over to Georgiana, and touched her on the shoulder. She appeared unaware of the touch, and he grasped her shoulder and shook it. 'Where is Mr Jones?' he asked.

The girl looked up, her face blurred and distorted with weeping, her eyes dilated as if with the vision of some latent terror. 'Oh, sir, she's not really dead, is she?'

Stramer repeated his question in a loud authoritative tone; and slowly she echoed it in a scarce-heard whisper. 'Mr Jones –?'

'Get up, my girl, and send him here to us at once, or tell us where to find him.'

Georgiana, moved by the old habit of obedience, struggled to her feet and stood unsteadily, her heaving shoulders braced against the wall. Stramer asked her sharply if she had not heard what he had said.

'Oh, poor thing, she's so upset –' Lady Jane intervened compassionately. 'Tell me, Georgiana: where shall we find Mr Jones?'

The girl turned to her with eyes as fixed as the dead woman's. 'You won't find him anywhere,' she slowly said.

'Why not?'

'Because he's not here.'

'Not here? Where is he, then?' Stramer broke in.

Georgiana did not seem to notice the interruption. She continued to stare at Lady Jane with Mrs Clemm's awful eyes. 'He's in his grave in the churchyard – these years and years he is. Long before ever I was born . . . my aunt hadn't ever seen him herself, not since she was a tiny child. . . . That's the terror of it . . . that's why she always had to do what he told her to . . . because you couldn't ever answer him back. . . .' Her horrified gaze turned from Lady Jane to the stony face and fast-glazing pupils of the dead woman. 'You hadn't ought to have meddled with his papers, my lady. . . . That's what he's punished her for. . . . When it came to those papers he wouldn't ever listen to human reason . . . he wouldn't. . . .' Then, flinging her arms above her head, Georgiana straightened herself to her full height before falling in a swoon at Stramer's feet.

From 'Mr Jones' by Edith Wharton, 1930

'Untranslatable'

HARRY: The sudden solitude in a crowded desert
In a thick smoke, many creatures moving
Without direction, for no direction
Leads anywhere but round and round in that vapour –
Without purpose, and without principle of conduct
In flickering intervals of light and darkness;
The partial anæsthesia of suffering without feeling

And partial observation of one's own automatism
While the slow stain sinks deeper through the skin
Tainting the flesh and discolouring the bone –
This is what matters, but it is unspeakable,
Untranslatable: I talk in general terms
Because the particular has no language. One thinks to escape.
By violence, but one is still alone
In an over-crowded desert, jostled by ghosts.
It was only reversing the senseless direction
For a momentary rest on the burning wheel
That cloudless night in the mid-Atlantic
When I pushed her over.

From *The Family Reunion* by T. S. Eliot, 1939

The Weeping Child

'Well, I have seen a ghost,' said Mrs Ingham, 'and it was the ghost of someone who is still alive.'

Then she got up and left them, putting down her knitting on a cane chair and walking off rather bent forward and clenching her rheumaticky hands. She was a big old woman with a large jaw and determined mouth, white hair screwed back anyhow, but eyes quite gentle. She visited her daughter in Jamaica – a lawyer's wife – in their beautiful great house in the mountains above Kingston harbour every other year at the end of January after the marmalade.

'I thought I heard the children,' she said coming back. She picked up her knitting and sat back in her chair. 'I was wrong. No. Now. It is a very short story and not I think usual. I saw the ghost of a weeping child. It was standing in the corner of a greenhouse in an old kitchen garden. It was a boy. Eight years old.'

'Oh, I'm sure this country is full of ghosts,' said the judge's wife comfortably.

'This was not Jamaica,' said Mrs Ingham, 'it was at home in Surrey. It was just outside Reigate. Last summer.'

'Ma,' said Miranda, 'are you all right?'

'It was on August the twentieth – a Wednesday – at three o'clock in the afternoon. It was the house of people I don't know. I had been told that the woman might lend the house for a Red Cross function and I had gone over to see if it would be suitable. When I got there I was given a cup of tea and was shown round and saw at once that the place would be most *un*suitable. There were imitation daffodils in a Ming vase and an indoor swimming pool. Very vulgar. No windows open and a fur sofa! I saw only the housekeeper who was a slut and kept a television set going – with the sound turned down – the whole time I was with her. All the time I talked she looked at it. She could hardly find her mouth with her cigarette.

'When I got up to go she said, "They said you'd want to see the gardens."

'"No thank you," I said.

'Then, when I got into the drive again I saw that the gardens were very much the best things there, and round the corner of a rose garden – beautifully kept – I thought I saw a kitchen garden wall. Now I am very fond of kitchen gardens and I said that I thought I would change my mind. "I will have a quick look about," I said and there was no need for her to accompany me.

'Well, round the end of the rose garden, things were not so promising. There was a stable block, very broken down. Empty loose boxes put to no use. But I walked on a little and found a gate in a red wall and through it a really excellent kitchen garden. An *excellent* place. Beautifully kept. Huge. I could see the gardener bending over some beans at the far end and the wall beyond him was covered in the most splendid peaches and the wall at right angles to it – to the peach wall – had one of the longest conservatories I have ever seen in a private house running along it. Long enough for – two or three hundred tomato plants, I dare say. But oh, very battered and unpainted, very broken. Inside there was an old stone path stretching away down it with moss in the cracks and a huge vine with a bulging trunk, running everywhere. Miles and miles of it. In all directions. Beautifully cared for. The numbers on the bunches had been pruned out marvellously. I walked the whole length of the greenhouse, looking up into the branches and the dozens and dozens of bunches – it was a little white grape – like so many lanterns. Glorious. It was hot and steamy and good manure on all the roots, and the smell of greenhouse – delicious – very strong.

'And so quiet. I was admiring the vine so much and it was so quiet and the air so heavy and still that I felt, well, really quite reverent. Like in a church. I walked all the way down the greenhouse and all the way back gazing up above my head.

'And then, when I was nearly back to the door again I heard a child crying and saw that there was a little boy standing near the tap in the corner. He was sobbing and weeping dreadfully. As if his heart was quite broken. I went up to him and talked to him and tried to stop and comfort him but he paid no attention. He was in leggings and a shirt and he had red hair. He had his fists in his eyes and just stood there beside the bright brass tap and the more I spoke to him the more he wept and turned away from me.

'So I went out and said to the gardener who was still down at the end of the gardens with the beans that there was a boy crying in the greenhouse and he said, "Oh aye. It's me."

'I begged his pardon.

'He said, "It's me, ma'am. I'm often there. People are often seeing me."

'But I said, this was a child. Not more than nine.

'He said, "Eight, ma'am. I was eight," and he got up off his haunches and eased his back and looked at me with that look Scotsmen have. A sandy, grizzly-haired man. Tall. Abrupt. He was about seventy years old. A straight sort of a man. And a bit of an old stick, I should say. He didn't mind whether I believed him or not.

'"I was wrongfully accused," he said, "for something I never did. I'm very often there." Then he got down on his haunches again and went on picking beans and flinging them in handfuls into a chip basket.

'I went off back to the greenhouse but the child was not there any more. The tap was there, perhaps not so bright – and the vine was just the same – the rough, pale, splintery trunk, the dark leaves above. The light seemed different, though, and it was not so quiet.'

'Go on,' said Stephen. 'Ma – do go on.'

'That is all,' said Mrs Ingham. 'That is the story.'

'But didn't you go back?' said Miranda. 'Go back and ask him more?'

'What more?'

'Well – what it was he'd done? Whether he'd done it?'

'Oh, he hadn't done it. I rather think he'd forgotten what it was all about. I had that feeling. He certainly hadn't done anything wrong.'

'How could you be sure?' asked Robert Shaw.

'Oh, the weeping,' she said, 'it was the weeping. It was not remorse or anger the weeping. It was – well, tremendous disappointment and bitterness and sorrow. A sort of' – she wrinkled her sensible forehead – 'it was a sort of essence of sorrow. Like a scent. A smell. Something very heavy and thick in the air.'

In the silence that followed she said, nodding round brightly, 'We ought to be so *careful* when we advise children. It's quite frightening what we do.'

'You never told me,' said her daughter, 'why ever didn't you tell me about it?' and she felt the usual dismal guilt confronting her mother's open face and with it an unusual violence and resentment. Ridiculously – her Jamaican friends looked at her in surprise – she thumped the chair arms. 'You might have *told* me that story. I should have been *told*. Why didn't you *write it* to me?'

'D'you know, I just can't say.' Her mother wound up her knitting and stuck the needles through the ball of wool. 'In a way I just seem to have remembered it.' Her voice, cool and self-reliant and thoughtful, left Miranda excluded.

'You might have *told* me.'

'But, dear, it seemed so – well, so ordinary at the time. Whatever time, of course –' and she gave her most sensible Queen's Guide smile, 'whatever time of course it was.'

From 'The Weeping Child' by Jane Gardam, 1975

'You sit and gnaw your nails'

You sit and gnaw your nails, and let your pipe out,
And listen to the silence: on the ceiling
There's one big, dizzy moth that bumps and flutters;
And in the breathless air outside the house
The garden waits for something that delays.
There must be crowds of ghosts among the trees, –
Not people killed in battle – they're in France –
But horrible shapes in shrouds – old men who died
Slow, natural deaths – old men with ugly souls,
Who wore their bodies out with nasty sins.

From 'Repression of War Experience' by Siegfried Sassoon, 1917

The man made of transplants

SEPTEMBEREMBEREMBEREMBEREMBER THE FIRST

I found myself with a pistol barrel in my mouth wondering why. I remember why now, I think. I have read this journal, and I think I remember thoughts of a few minutes ago. They were not my thoughts. But they are my memories.

This gun has killed. These hands pulled the trigger. This heart beat faster as the gun fired. These ears still ache from the explosions. These eyes wept in remorse. My mouth still tastes of vomit.

But I did not kill. Please, God, I did not kill.

I was killed. Mabey says so and I remember a mad face and a meatcleaver, coming from nowhere in the depths of a crowd of smiling, laughing, loving faces. I remember a moment of pain, and then

No. This I cannot

I can think of no reason to believe that this journal is a fraud.

I have looked in the mirror. I am the man I remembered myself to be.

[177]

3 SEPTEMBER

I have met with Hyman, Ron, Moral, Chaste, and Egan. The answers are clear. Such a great sin has never been committed, and yet the hearts of those who sinned were pure.

Surely the humble fishermen whose hearts' love had been torn from them did not sin in wishing him alive again. And in the wishing, neither did these disciples of God's Deliverance sin. But ours is a different age, and it was the genius of Egan and Chaste, the deft hands of Hyman, the force of will of Ron and Moral that have brought me back, not from the grave, for I never was there, but from where I was, and that is sin enough. . . . It is no jest that religion forbids all good things, and the stronger the forbidding, the better the thing forbidden. But the forbidding is only for a time. To own is forbidden, until the thing owned has been earned. To copulate is forbidden, until that copulation is locked within a family. And to die and to kill are forbidden, until God himself reaches down his hand and releases us from life. This I have taught them now. I see that it must be the cornerstone.

10 SEPTEMBER

They ask me, again and again, what is death like? What did I feel? What did I see?

I show them, but they see not. I tell them, but they hear not. If death were not desirable, it would not have been forbidden us. We are taught to fear it, and we are forbidden to seek those who have died, because if we knew, if we understood what lies within our reach, at the cost of a pill, a bullet, a blade, a breath, then in the moment we understood, this world would be unpopulated. We would leap into our graves like a lecher into his lady's bed.

But we do not know, and the fear is on us, and God in his mercy will deliver us from ourselves if we can school our passions.

Perhaps God will let me stand on a high hill and look out into the promised land before he lets me return to him. Then my people will mourn me. But I will go singing.

From 'Malpractice' by Orson Scott Card, 1977

Six

REVENGE

Thy pangs of anguish rip my cerecloth up;
And lo, the ghost of old Andrugio
Forsakes his coffin! Antonio, revenge!
I was empoisoned by Piero's hand;
Revenge my blood! – take spirit, gentle boy –
Revenge my blood!

JOHN MARSTON

There are spirits that are created for vengeance,
and in their fury they lay on grievous torments.

ECCLESIASTICUS

Tuwhakararo

Tuwhakararo, wild with pain and hampered by his tupuni, tried to rub his eyes; and the young man struck him on the head and killed him. The Ati Hapai, in a mood for sport, were delighted to see the tables turned so suddenly. They rushed in screaming and laughing, and seized Tuwhakararo's body and, remembering now what had been done to Kae, their chiefs had it cooked, and they ate his flesh.

Then they scraped his bones and hung them up in a basket beneath the ridgepole of Te Tihi o Manono. Thus was Kae avenged and Mairatea plunged in grief. For there in the meeting house of her husband's tribe she heard the bones of her own brother rattling in their basket. They seemed to be saying, 'Tauparoro, tauparoro,' (the name for playing mapara, or castanets), and Mairatea answered them: 'You rattle in vain, O bones of him who was devoured by the Ati Hapai. For who is there to take utu for him?'

The fact is, Tuwhakararo had died before having any sons who might avenge him.

From Maori Myths, collected by Anthony Alpers, 1964

'The Ghost of Thyestes'

Escaped from gloomy Pluto's murky realm
And leaving Tartara's deep pit I come,
All doubting which abode I hate the more;
That world I flee, but this I put to flight.
My soul shrinks back, my limbs do quake with fear.
I see my father's house – my brother's too!

*

Now, now, this house shall flow again with blood,
But this of Atreus' stock! Swords, axes, darts
I see, and that proud head with murderous stroke
Asunder cleft; now impious crimes are near,
Now treachery, slaughter, blood; the feast is spread.
The cause, Aegisthus, of thy shameful birth,
Is come at last. But why hangs down thy head
In shame? Why hesitates thy faltering hand
And sinks inactive? Why dost counsel take
Within thy heart, and turn away, and ask
Whether this deed become thee? Do but think

Upon thy mother; then wilt thou confess
It doth become thee well. But what drags out
In long delay this summer night's brief span
To winter's hours of darkness? And what cause
Prevents the stars from sinking in the sky?
The sun shrinks from my face. I must away,
That so he may bring back the light of day.
(*The* GHOST *vanishes.*)

From the *Agamemnon* of Seneca, first century AD,
translated by F. J. Miller

Signior Simile

ANTONIO: Blow hence these sapless jests. I tell you bloods
My spirit's heavy, and the juice of life
Creeps slowly through my stiffened arteries.
Last sleep my sense was steeped in horrid dreams:
Three parts of night were swallowed in the gulf
Of ravenous time when to my slumb'ring powers
Two meager ghosts made apparition.
The one's breast seemed fresh-paunched with bleeding wounds
Whose bubbling gore sprang in frighted eyes:
The other ghost assumed my father's shape;
Both cried, 'Revenge!' At which my trembling joints
(Icèd quite over with a frozed cold sweat)
Leaped forth the sheets. Three times I gasped at shades,
And thrice, deluded by erroneous sense,
I forced my thoughts make stand; when, lo, I oped
A large bay window, through which the night
Struck terror to my soul. The verge of heaven
Was ringed with flames and all the upper vault
Thick-laced with flakes of fire; in midst whereof
A blazing comet shot his threat'ning train
Just on my face. Viewing these prodigies,
I bowed my naked knee and pierced the star
With an outfacing eye, pronouncing thus:
Deus imperat astris. At which my nose straight bled!
Then doubted I my word, so slunk to bed.
BALURDO: Verily, Sir Geoffrey had a monstrous strange dream the last
night. For methought I dreamt I was asleep, and methought the
ground yawned and belked up the abominable ghost of a misshapen
Simile, with two ugly pages, the one called Master *Even-as*, going

before, and the other Mounser *Even-so*, following after, whilst
Signior Simile stalked most prodigiously in the midst. At which I
bewrayed the fearfulness of my nature, and – being ready to forsake
the fortress of my wit – start up, called for a clean shirt, eat a mess of
broth, and with that I awaked.

From *Antonio's Revenge* by John Marston, 1601

'Whither wilt thou lead me?'

HAMLET: Whither wilt thou lead me? speak; I'll go no further.
GHOST: Mark me.
HAMLET:　　　　　I will.
GHOST:　　　　　　　　My hour is almost come,.
　　When I to sulphurous and tormenting flames
　　Must render up myself.
HAMLET:　　　　　　　　Alas! poor ghost.
GHOST: Pity me not, but lend thy serious hearing
　　To what I shall unfold.
HAMLET:　　　　　　　　Speak; I am bound to hear.
GHOST: So art thou to revenge, when thou shalt hear.
HAMLET: What?
GHOST: I am thy father's spirit;
　　Doom'd for a certain term to walk the night,
　　And for the day confin'd to fast in fires,
　　Till the foul crimes done in my days of nature
　　Are burnt and purg'd away. But that I am forbid
　　To tell the secrets of my prison-house,
　　I could a tale unfold whose lightest word
　　Would harrow up thy soul, freeze thy young blood,
　　Make thy two eyes, like stars, start from their spheres,
　　Thy knotted and combined locks to part,
　　And each particular hair to stand an end,
　　Like quills upon the fretful porpentine:
　　But this eternal blazon must not be
　　To ears of flesh and blood. List, list, O list
　　If thou didst ever thy dear father love –
HAMLET: O God!
GHOST: Revenge his foul and most unnatural murder.
HAMLET: Murder!
GHOST: Murder most foul, as in the best it is;
　　But this most foul, strange, and unnatural.

HAMLET: Haste me to know 't, that I, with wings as swift
  As meditation or the thoughts of love,
  May sweep to my revenge.

From *Hamlet, Prince of Denmark* by William Shakespeare, 1603–4

The Ghost of SYLLA *rises*

Dost thou not feel me, Rome? not yet! is night
So heavy on thee, and my weight so light?
Can Sylla's ghost arise within thy walls,
Less threatening than an earthquake, the quick falls
Of thee and thine? Shake not the frighted heads
Of thy steep towers, or shrink to their first beds?
Or, as their ruin the large Tyber fills,
Make that swell up, and down thy seven proud hills?
What sleep ist his doth seize thee so like death,
And is not it? wake, feel her in my breath:
Behold, I come, sent from the Stygian sound,
As a dire vapour that had cleft the ground,
To ingender with the night, and blast the day;
Or like a pestilence that should display
Infection through the world: which thus I do. –

From *Catiline* by Ben Jonson, 1611

Comedy jeers at Tragedy

A Chorus too comes howling in,
And tels us of the worrying of a cat,
Then of a filthie whining ghost,
Lapt in some foule sheete, or leather pelch,
Comes skreaming like a pigge half stickt,
And cries *Vindicta*, revenge, revenge:
With that a little Rosen flasheth forth
Like smoke out of a Tobacco pipe, or a boyes squib.

From *A Warning for Faire Women*, anon., 1955

Dido

Dido shall come, in a black Sulph'ry flame;
When death has once dissolv'd her Mortal frame.
Shall smile to see the Traitor vainly weep,
Her angry Ghost arising from the Deep,
Shall haunt thee waking, and disturb thy Sleep

From *Virgil's Aeneis* by John Dryden, 1697

Ngoc Tam and Nhan Diep

Ngoc Tam, a modest farmer, had married Nhan Diep. The two young
people were poor but in excellent health, and they seemed destined to
enjoy the happiness of a simple rural life. The husband worked in the
paddy and cultivated a small field of mulberry trees, and the wife engaged in raising silkworms.

But Nhan Diep was a coquette at heart. She was lazy, and dreamed
of luxury and pleasures. She was also clever enough to hide her desires
and ambitions from her husband, whose love was genuine, but neither
demanding nor discerning. He supposed his wife to be content with her
lot and happy in her daily chores.

Ngoc Tam toiled diligently, hoping to ease their poverty and improve their station in life.

Suddenly Nhan Diep was carried away by death. Ngoc Tam was
plunged into such deep sorrow that he would not leave his wife's body
and opposed its burial.

One day, after having sold his possessions, he embarked in a sampan
with the coffin and sailed away.

One morning he found himself at the foot of a fragrant, green hill
which perfumed the countryside.

He went ashore and discovered a thousand rare flowers and orchards
of trees laden with the most varied kinds of fruit.

There he met an old man who supported himself with a bamboo
cane. His hair was white as cotton and his face wrinkled and sun-
burned, but under his blond eyelashes his eyes sparkled like those of a
young boy. By this last trait Ngoc Tam recognized the genie of medicine, who traveled throughout the world on his mountain, Thien Thai,
to teach his science to the men of the earth and to alleviate their ills.

Ngoc Tam threw himself at the genie's feet.

Then the genie spoke to him:

[184]

'Having learned of your virtues, Ngoc Tam, I have stopped mymountain on your route. If you wish, I will admit you to the company of my disciples.'

Ngoc Tam thanked him profusely but said that he desired only to live with his wife. He had never thought of any life other than the one he would lead with her, and he begged the genie to bring her back to life.

The genie looked at him with kindness mixed with pity and said:

'Why do you cling to this world of bitterness and gall? The rare joys of this life are only a snare. How foolish you were to entrust your destiny to a weak and inconstant being! I want to grant your wishes, but I fear that you will regret it later.'

Then, on the genie's order, Ngoc Tam opened the coffin; he cut the tip of his finger and let three drops of blood fall on Nhan Diep's body. The latter opened her eyes slowly, as if awakening from a deep sleep. Then her faculties quickly returned.

'Do not forget your obligations,' the genie said to her. 'Remember your husband's devotion. May you both be happy.'

On the voyage home Ngoc Tam rowed day and night, eager to reach his native land again. One evening he went ashore in a certain port to buy provisions.

During his absence a large ship came alongside the wharf, and the owner, a rich merchant, was struck by Nhan Diep's beauty. He entered into conversation with her and invited her to have refreshments aboard his vessel. As soon as she was aboard, he gave the order to cast off and sailed away.

Ngoc Tam searched an entire month for his wife before locating her aboard the merchant's vessel.

She answered his questions without the least hesitation, but had grown accustomed to her new life. It satisfied her completely and she refused to return home with him. Then for the first time, Ngoc Tam saw her in her true light. Suddenly he felt all love for her vanish, and he no longer desired her return.

'You are free,' he said to her. 'Only return to me the three drops of blood that I gave to bring you back to life. I do not want to leave the least trace of myself in you.'

Happy to be set free so cheaply, Nhan Diep took a knife and cut the tip of her finger. But, as soon as the blood began to flow, she turned pale and sank to the ground. An instant later she was dead.

Even so, the light-hearted frivolous woman could not resign herself to leave this world forever. She returned in the form of a small insect and followed Ngoc Tam relentlessly, in order to steal the three drops of blood from him, which would restore her to human life. Day and night she worried her former husband, buzzing around him incessantly, protesting her innocence, and begging his pardon. Later, she received the name of 'mosquito.' Unfortunately for us, her race has multiplied many times.

From *Vietnamese Legends*, translated by George F. Schultz, 1965

Mrs Archer's secret

The eyelids were lifted no more. Once I looked at Bertha as she watched the face of the dying one. She wore a rich *peignoir*, and her blond hair was half covered by a lace cap: in her attire she was, as always, an elegant woman, fit to figure in a picture of modern aristocratic life: but I asked myself how that face of hers could ever have seemed to me the face of a woman born of woman, with memories of childhood, capable of pain, needing to be fondled? The features at that moment seemed so preternaturally sharp, the eyes were so hard and eager – she looked like a cruel immortal, finding her spiritual feast in the agonies of a dying race. For across those hard features there came something like a flash when the last hour had been breathed out, and we all felt that the dark veil had completely fallen. What secret was there between Bertha and this woman? I turned my eyes from her with a horrible dread lest my insight should return, and I should be obliged to see what had been breeding about two unloving women's hearts. I felt that Bertha had been watching for the moment of death as the sealing of her secret: I thanked Heaven it could remain sealed for me.

Meunier said quietly, 'She is gone.' He then gave his arm to Bertha, and she submitted to be led out of the room.

I suppose it was at her order that two female attendants came into the room, and dismissed the younger one who had been present before. When they entered, Meunier had already opened the artery in the long thin neck that lay rigid on the pillow, and I dismissed them, ordering them to remain at a distance till we rang: the doctor, I said, had an operation to perform – he was not sure about the death. For the next twenty minutes I forgot everything but Meunier and the experiment in which he was so absorbed, that I think his senses would have been closed against all sounds or sights which had no relation to it. It was my task at first to keep up the artificial respiration in the body after the transfusion had been effected, but presently Meunier relieved me, and I could see the wondrous slow return of life; the breast began to heave, the inspirations became stronger, the eyelids quivered, and the soul seemed to have returned beneath them. The artificial respiration was withdrawn: still the breathing continued, and there was a movement of the lips.

Just then I heard the handle of the door moving: I suppose Bertha had heard from the women that they had been dismissed: probably a vague fear had arisen in her mind, for she entered with a look of alarm. She came to the foot of the bed and gave a stifled cry.

The dead woman's eyes were wide open, and met hers in full recognition – the recognition of hate. With a sudden strong effort, the hand that Bertha had thought for ever still was pointing towards her, and the haggard face moved. The gasping eager voice said:

'You mean to poison your husband ... the poison is in the black cabinet ... I got it for you ... you laughed at me, and told lies about me behind my back, to make me disgusting ... because you were jealous ... are you sorry ... now?'

The lips continued to murmur, but the sounds were no longer distinct. Soon there was no sound – only a slight movement: the flame had leaped out, and was being extinguished the faster. The wretched woman's heartstrings had been set to hatred and vengeance: the spirit of life had swept the chords for an instant, and was gone again for ever. Great God! Is this what it is to live again ... to wake up with our unstilled thirst upon us, with our unuttered curses rising to our lips, with our muscles ready to act out their half-committed sins?

Bertha stood pale at the foot of the bed, quivering and helpless, despairing of devices, like a cunning animal whose hiding-places are surrounded by swift-advancing flame. Even Meunier looked paralysed; life for that moment ceased to be a scientific problem to him. As for me, this scene seemed of one texture with the rest of my existence: horror was my familiar, and this new revelation was only like an old pain recurring with new circumstances.

From 'The Lifted Veil' by George Eliot, 1859

The Tomb-Legions

When Dr Herbert West disappeared a year ago, the Boston police questioned me closely. ... I was West's closest friend and only confidential assistant. We had met years before, in medical school, and from the first I had shared his terrible researches. He had slowly tried to perfect a solution which, injected into the veins of the newly deceased, would restore life; a labor demanding an abundance of fresh corpses and therefore involving the most unnatural actions. Still more shocking were products of some of the experiments – grisly masses of flesh that had been dead, but that West waked to a blind, brainless, nauseous animation. There were the usual results, for in order to reawaken the mind it was necessary to have specimens so absolutely fresh that no decay could possibly affect the delicate brain cells.

This need for very fresh corpses had been West's moral undoing. They were hard to get, and one awful day he had secured his specimen while it was still alive and vigorous. A struggle, a needle, and a powerful alkaloid had transformed it to a very fresh corpse, and the experiment had succeeded for a brief and memorable moment; but West had emerged with a soul calloused and seared, and a hardened eye which sometimes glanced with a kind of hideous and calculating appraisal at men of especially sensitive brain and especially vigorous physique. Toward the last I became acutely afraid of West, for he began to look at me that way. People did not seem to notice his glances, but they noticed my fear; and after his disappearance used that as a basis for some absurd suspicions.

West, in reality, was more afraid than I; for his abominable pursuits entailed a life of furtiveness and dread of every shadow. Partly it was the police he feared; but sometimes his nervousness was deeper and more nebulous, touching on certain indescribable things into which he had injected a morbid life, and from which he had not seen that life depart. He usually finished his experiments with a revolver, but a few times he had not been quick enough. There was that first specimen on whose rifled grave marks of clawing were later seen. There was also that Arkham professor's body which had done cannibal things before it had been captured and thrust unidentified into a madhouse cell at Sefton, where it beat the walls for sixteen years. Most of the other possibly surviving results were things less easy to speak of – for in later years West's scientific zeal had degenerated to an unhealthy and fantastic mania, and he had spent his chief skill in vitalizing not entire human bodies but isolated parts of bodies, or parts joined to organic matter other than human. It had become fiendishly disgusting by the time he disappeared; many of the experiments could not even be hinted at in print. The Great War, through which both of us served as surgeons, had intensified this side of West.

In saying that West's fear of his specimens was nebulous, I have in mind particularly its complex nature. Part of it came merely from knowing of the existence of such nameless monsters, while another part arose from apprehension of the bodily harm they might under certain circumstances do him. Their disappearance added horror to the situation – of them all West knew the whereabouts of only one, the pitiful asylum thing. Then there was a more subtle fear – a very fantastic sensation resulting from a curious experiment in the Canadian army in 1915. West, in the midst of a severe battle, had reanimated Major Sir Eric Moreland Clapham-Lee, DSO, a fellow-physician who knew about his experiments and could have duplicated them. The head had been removed, so that the possibilities of quasi-intelligent life in the trunk might be investigated. Just as the building was wiped out by a German shell, there had been a success. The trunk had moved intelligently; and, unbelievable to relate, we were both sickeningly sure that articulate sounds had come from the detached head as it lay in a shadowy corner of the laboratory. The shell had been merciful, in a way – but West could never feel as certain as he wished, that we two were the only survivors. He used to make shuddering conjectures about the possible actions of a headless physician with the power of re-animating the dead. . . .

The end of Herbert West began one evening in our joint study when he was dividing his curious glance between the newspaper and me. A strange headline item had struck at him from the crumpled pages, and a nameless titan claw had seemed to reach down through sixteen years. Something fearsome and incredible had happened at Sefton Asylum fifty miles away, stunning the neighborhood and baffling the police. In the small hours of the morning a body of silent men had entered the grounds and their leader had aroused the attendants. He was a menacing military figure who talked without moving his lips and whose voice seemed almost ventriloquially connected with an immense black case he carried. His expressionless face was handsome to the point of radiant beauty, but had shocked the superintendent when the hall light fell on it – for it was a wax face with eyes of painted glass. Some nameless accident had befallen this man. A larger man guided his steps; a repellent hulk whose bluish face seemed half eaten away by some unknown malady. The speaker had asked for the custody of the cannibal monster committed from Arkham sixteen years before; and upon being refused, gave a signal which precipitated a shocking riot. The fiends had beaten, trampled, and bitten every attendant who did not flee; killing four and finally succeeding in the liberation of the monster. Those victims who could recall the event without hysteria swore that the creatures had acted less like men than like unthinkable automata guided by the wax-faced leader. By the time help could be summoned, every trace of the men and of their mad charge had vanished.

From the hour of reading this item until midnight, West sat almost paralyzed. At midnight the doorbell rang, startling him fearfully. All the servants were asleep in the attic, so I answered the bell. As I have told the police, there was no wagon in the street; but only a group of strange-looking figures bearing a large square box which they deposited in the hallway after one of them had grunted in a highly unnatural voice, 'Express – prepaid.' They filed out of the house with a jerky tread, and as I watched them go I had an odd idea that they were turning toward the ancient cemetery on which the back of the house abutted. When I slammed the door after them West came downstairs and looked at the box. It was about two feet square, and bore West's correct name and present address. It also bore the inscription, 'From Eric Moreland Clapham-Lee, St Eloi, Flanders.' Six years before, in Flanders, a shelled hospital had fallen upon the headless reanimated trunk of Dr Clapham-Lee, and upon the detached head which – perhaps – had uttered articulate sounds.

West was not even excited now. His condition was more ghastly. Quickly he said, 'It's the finish – but let's incinerate – this.' We carried the thing down to the laboratory – listening. I do not remember many particulars – you can imagine my state of mind – but it is a vicious lie to say it was Herbert West's body which I put into the incinerator. We both inserted the whole unopened wooden box, closed the door, and started the electricity. Nor did any sound come from the box, after all.

It was West who first noticed the falling plaster on that part of the wall where the ancient tomb masonry had been covered up. I was going to run, but he stopped me. Then I saw a small black aperture, felt a ghoulish wind of ice, and smelled the charnel bowels of a putrescent earth. There was no sound, but just then the electric lights went out and I saw outlined against some phosphorescence of the nether world a horde of silent toiling things which only insanity – or worse – could create. Their outlines were human, semi-human, fractionally human, and not human at all – the horde was grotesquely heterogeneous. They were removing the stones quietly, one by one, from the centuried wall. And then, as the breach became large enough, they came out into the laboratory in single file; led by a stalking thing with a beautiful head made of wax. A sort of mad-eyed monstrosity behind the leader seized on Herbert West. West did not resist or utter a sound. Then they all sprang at him and tore him to pieces before my eyes, bearing the fragments away into that subterranean vault of fabulous abominations. West's head was carried off by the wax-headed leader, who wore a Canadian officer's uniform. As it disappeared I saw that the blue eyes behind the spectacles were hideously blazing with their first touch of frantic, visible emotion.

Servants found me unconscious in the morning. West was gone. The incinerator contained only unidentifiable ashes. Detectives have questioned me, but what can I say? The Sefton tragedy they will not connect with West; not that, nor the men with the box, whose existence they deny. I told them of the vault, and they pointed to the unbroken plaster wall and laughed. So I told them no more. They imply that I am either a madman or a murderer – probably I am mad. But I might not be mad if those accursed tomb-legions had not been so silent.

From 'Herbert West – Reanimator' by H. P. Lovecraft, 1934

The Witch of Coos

I stayed the night for shelter at a farm
Behind the mountain, with a mother and son,
Two old-believers. They did all the talking.

MOTHER: Folks think a witch who has familiar spirits
    She could call up to pass a winter evening,
    But won't, should be burned at the stake or something.
    Summoning spirits isn't 'Button, button,
    Who's got the button,' I would have them know.

SON: Mother can make a common table rear
    And kick with two legs like an army mule.

MOTHER: And when I've done it, what good have I done?
    Rather than tip a table for you, let me
    Tell you what Ralle the Sioux Control once told me.
    He said the dead had souls, but when I asked him
    How could that be – I thought the dead were souls,
    He broke my trance. Don't that make you suspicious
    That there's something the dead are keeping back?
    Yes, there's something the dead are keeping back.

SON: You wouldn't want to tell him what we have
    Up attic, mother?

MOTHER: Bones – a skeleton.

SON: But the headboard of mother's bed is pushed
    Against the attic door: the door is nailed.
    It's harmless. Mother hears it in the night
    Halting perplexed behind the barrier
    Of door and headboard. Where it wants to get
    Is back into the cellar where it came from.

MOTHER: We'll never let them, will we, son! We'll never!

SON: It left the cellar forty years ago
    And carried itself like a pile of dishes
    Up one flight from the cellar to the kitchen,
    Another from the kitchen to the bedroom,
    Another from the bedroom to the attic,
    Right past both father and mother, and neither stopped it.
    Father had gone upstairs; mother was downstairs.
    I was a baby: I don't know where I was.

MOTHER: The only fault my husband found with me –

I went to sleep before I went to bed,
Especially in winter when the bed
Might just as well be ice and the clothes snow.
The night the bones came up the cellar-stairs
Toffile had gone to bed alone and left me,
But left an open door to cool the room off
So as to sort of turn me out of it.
I was just coming to myself enough
To wonder where the cold was coming from,
When I heard Toffile upstairs in the bedroom
And thought I heard him downstairs in the cellar.
The board we had laid down to walk dry-shod on
When there was water in the cellar in spring
Struck the hard cellar bottom. And then someone
Began the stairs, two footsteps for each step,
The way a man with one leg and a crutch,
Or a little child, comes up. It wasn't Toffile:
It wasn't anyone who could be there.
The bulkhead double-doors were double-locked
And swollen tight and buried under snow.
The cellar windows were banked up with sawdust
And swollen tight and buried under snow.
It was the bones. I knew them – and good reason.
My first impulse was to get to the knob
And hold the door. But the bones didn't try
The door; they halted helpless on the landing,
Waiting for things to happen in their favor.
The faintest restless rustling ran all through them.
I never could have done the thing I did
If the wish hadn't been too strong in me
To see how they were mounted for this walk.
I had a vision of them put together
Not like a man, but like a chandelier.
So suddenly I flung the door wide on him.
A moment he stood balancing with emotion,
And all but lost himself. (A tongue of fire
Flashed out and licked along his upper teeth.
Smoke rolled inside the sockets of his eyes.)
Then he came at me with one hand outstretched,
The way he did in life once; but this time
I struck the hand off brittle on the floor,
And fell back from him on the floor myself.
The finger-pieces slid in all directions.
(Where did I see one of those pieces lately?

Hand me my button-box – it must be there.)
I sat up on the floor and shouted, 'Toffile,
It's coming up to you.' It had its choice
Of the door to the cellar or the hall.
It took the hall door for the novelty,
And set off briskly for so slow a thing,
Still going every which way in the joints, though,
So that it looked like lightning or a scribble,
From the slap I had just now given its hand.
I listened till it almost climbed the stairs
From the hall to the only finished bedroom,
Before I got up to do anything;
Then ran and shouted, 'Shut the bedroom door,
Toffile, for my sake!' 'Company?' he said,
'Don't make me get up; I'm too warm in bed.'
So lying forward weakly on the handrail
I pushed myself upstairs, and in the light
(The kitchen had been dark) I had to own
I could see nothing. 'Toffile, I don't see it.
It's with us in the room though. It's the bones.'
'What bones?' 'The cellar bones – out of the grave.'
That made him throw his bare legs out of bed
And sit up by me and take hold of me.
I wanted to put out the light and see
If I could see it, or else mow the room,
With our arms at the level of our knees,
And bring the chalk-pile down. 'I'll tell you what –
It's looking for another door to try.
The uncommonly deep snow had made him think
Of his old song, *The Wild Colonial Boy*,
He always used to sing along the tote-road.
He's after an open door to get out-doors.
Let's trap him with an open door up attic.'
Toffile agreed to that, and sure enough,
Almost the moment he was given an opening,
The steps began to climb the attic stairs.
I heard them. Toffile didn't seem to hear them.
'Quick!' I slammed to the door and held the knob.
'Toffile, get nails.' I made him nail the door shut
And push the headboard of the bed against it.
Then we asked was there anything
Up attic that we'd ever want again.
The attic was less to us than the cellar.
If the bones liked the attic, let them have it.

Let them stay in the attic. When they sometimes
Come down the stairs at night and stand perplexed
Behind the door and headboard of the bed,
Brushing their chalky skull with chalky fingers,
With sounds like the dry rattling of a shutter,
That's what I sit up in the dark to say –
To no one any more since Toffile died.
Let them stay in the attic since they went there.
I promised Toffile to be cruel to them
For helping them be cruel once to him.

SON: We think they had a grave down in the cellar.

MOTHER: We know they had a grave down in the cellar.

SON: We never could find out whose bones they were.

MOTHER: Yes, we could too, son. Tell the truth for once.
They were a man's his father killed for me.
I mean a man he killed instead of me.
The least I could do was to help dig their grave.
We were about it one night in the cellar.
Son knows the story: but 'twas not for him
To tell the truth, suppose the time had come.
Son looks surprised to see me end a lie
We'd kept all these years between ourselves
So as to have it ready for outsiders.
But tonight I don't care enough to lie –
I don't remember why I ever cared.
Toffile, if he were here, I don't believe
Could tell you why he ever cared himself. . . .

She hadn't found the finger-bone she wanted
Among the buttons poured out in her lap.
I verified the name next morning: Toffile.
The rural letter-box said Toffile Lajway.

Robert Frost, 1923

Hand in Glove

Jasmine Lodge was favourably set on a residential, prettily-wooded hillside in the south of Ireland, overlooking a river and, still better, the roofs of a lively garrison town. Around 1904, which was the flowering period of the Miss Trevors, girls could not have had a more auspicious home – the neighbourhood spun merrily round the military. Ethel and Elsie, a spirited pair, garnered the full advantage – no ball, hop, picnic, lawn tennis, croquet or boating party was complete without them; in winter, though they could not afford to hunt, they trimly bicycled to all meets, and on frosty evenings, with their guitars, set off to *soirées*, snug inside their cab in their fur-tipped capes.

They possessed an aunt, a Mrs Varley de Grey, *née* Elysia Trevor, a formerly notable local belle, who, drawn back again in her widowhood to what had been the scene of her early triumphs, occupied a back bedroom in Jasmine Lodge. Mrs Varley de Grey had had no luck: her splashing match, in its time the talk of two kingdoms, had ended up in disaster – the well-born captain in a cavalry regiment having gone so far as to blow out his brains in India, leaving behind him nothing but her and debts. Mrs Varley de Grey had returned from India with nothing but seven large trunks crammed with recent finery; and she also had been impaired by shock. This had taken place while Ethel and Elsie, whose father had married late, were still unborn – so it was that, for as long as the girls recalled, their aunt had been the sole drawback to Jasmine Lodge. Their parents had orphaned them, somewhat thoughtlessly, by simultaneously dying of scarlet fever when Ethel was just out and Elsie soon to be – they were therefore left lacking a chaperone and, with their gift for putting everything to some use, propped the aunt up in order that she might play that role. Only when her peculiarities became too marked did they feel it necessary to withdraw her: by that time, however, all the surrounding ladies could be said to compete for the honour of taking into society the sought-after Miss Trevors. From then on, no more was seen or heard of Mrs Varley de Grey. ('Oh, just a trifle unwell, but nothing much!') She remained upstairs, at the back; when the girls were giving one of their little parties, or a couple of officers came to call, the key of her room would be turned in the outer lock. . . .

They wore their clothes well. 'A pin on either of those two would look smart!' declared other girls. All that they were short of was evening gloves – they had two pairs each, which they had been compelled to buy. *What* could have become of Mrs Varley de Grey's presumably sumptuous numbers of this item, they were unable to fathom, and it was too bad. Had gloves been overlooked in her rush from India? – or, were they here, in that *one* trunk the Trevors could not get at? All other locks had yielded to pulls or pickings, or the sisters found keys to fit them, or they had used the toolbox; but this last stronghold defied them. In that sad little soiled silk sack, always on her person, Mrs Varley de Grey, they became convinced, hoarded the operative keys, along with some frippery rings and brooches – all true emeralds, pearls and diamonds having been long ago, as they knew, sold. Such contrariety on their aunt's part irked them – meanwhile, gaieties bore hard on their existing gloves. Last thing at nights when they came in, last thing in the evenings before they would manfully dab away at the fingertips. So, it must be admitted that a long whiff of benzine pursued them as they whirled round the ballroom floor. . . .

Ethel's decision took place late one spring. She set her cap, in a manner worthy of her, at the second son of an English marquess. Lord Fred had come on a visit, for the fishing, to a mansion some miles down the river from Jasmine Lodge. She conjured up all her fascinations. But was something further needed, to do the trick?

It was now that she began to frequent her aunt.

'You don't think you'll kill her, Ethel?' the out-of-it Elsie asked. 'Forever sitting on top of her, as you now do. Can it be healthy, egging here on to talk? What's this attraction, all of a sudden? – whatever's this which has sprung up between you two? She and you are becoming quite hand-in-glove.'

Elsie merely remarked this, and soon forgot: she had her own fish to fry. It was Ethel who had cause to recall the words – for, the afternoon of the very day they were spoken, Aunt Elysia whizzed off on another track, screamed for what was impossible and, upon being thwarted, went into a seizure unknown before. The worst of it was, at the outset her mind cleared – she pushed her shawl back, reared up her unkempt grey head and looked at Ethel, unblinkingly studied Ethel, with a lucid accumulation of years of hate. 'You fool of a gawk,' she said, and with such contempt! 'Coming running to me to know how to trap a man. Could *you* learn, if it was from Venus herself? Wait till I show you beauty. – Bring down those trunks!'

'Oh, Auntie.'

'Bring them down, I say. I'm about to dress myself up.'

'Oh, but I cannot; they're heavy; I'm single-handed.'

'Heavy? – they came here heavy. But there've been rats in the attic. – I saw you, swishing downstairs in my *eau-de-nil*!'

'Oh, you dreamed that!'

'Through the crack of the door. – Let me up, then. Let us go where they are, and look – we shall soon see!' Aunt Elysia threw back the bedclothes and began to get up. 'Let's take a look,' she said, 'at the rats' work.' She set out to totter towards the door.

'Oh, but you're not fit!' Ethel prtested.

'And when did a doctor say so?' There was a swaying: Ethel caught her in time and, not gently, lugged her back to the bed – and Ethel's mind the whole of this time was whirling, for tonight was the night upon which all hung. Lord Fred's last local appearance was to be, like his first, at a ball: tomorrow he left for London. So it must be tonight, at this ball, or never! How was it that Ethel felt so strangely, wildly confident of the outcome? It was time to begin on her coiffure, lay out her dress. Oh, tonight she would shine as never before! She flung back the bedclothes over the helpless form, heard a clock strike, and hastily turned to go.

'I will be quits with you,' said the voice behind her.

Ethel, in a kimono, hair half down, was in her own room, in front of the open glove-drawer, when Elsie came in – home from a tennis party. Elsie acted oddly – she went at once to the drawer and buried her nose in it. 'Oh my goodness,' she said, 'it's all too true, and it's awful!'

'What is?' Ethel carelessly asked.

'Ethel dear, would you face it out if I were to tell you a certain rumour I heard today at the party as to Lord Fred?'

Ethel turned from her sister, took up the heated tongs and applied more crimps to her natural curliness. She said: 'Certainly; spit it out.'

'Since childhood, he's recoiled from the breath of benzine. He wilts away when it enters the very room!'

'Who says that's so?'

'He confided it to his hostess, who is now spitefully putting it around the country.'

Ethel bit her lip and put down the tongs, while Elsie sorrowfully concluded, 'And your gloves stink, Ethel, as I'm sure do mine.' Elsie then thought it wiser to slip away.

In a minute more, however, she was back, and this time, with still more peculiar air, she demanded: 'In what state did you leave Auntie? She was sounding so very quiet that I peeped in, and *I* don't care for the looks of her now at all!' Ethel swore, but consented to take a look. She stayed in there in the back room, with Elsie biting her thumb-nail outside the door, for what seemed an ominous length of time; when she did emerge, she looked greenish, but held her head high. The sisters' eyes met. Ethel said, stonily, 'Dozing.'

'You're certain she's *not* . . . ? She *couldn't* ever be – you know?'

'Dozing, I tell you.' Ethel stared Elsie out.

'If she *was* gone,' quavered the frailer sister, 'just think of it – why, we'd never get to the ball! And a ball that everything hangs on,' she ended, with a scared but conspiratorial glance at Ethel.

'Reassure yourself. Didn't you hear me say?'

As she spoke, Ethel, chiefly from habit, locked her late Aunt's door on the outside. The act caused a sort of secret jingle to be heard from inside her fist, and Elsie asked: 'What's that you've got hold of, now?'

'Just a few little keys and trinkets she made me keep,' replied Ethel, disclosing the small bag she had found where she'd looked for it, under the dead one's pillow. 'Scurry on now, Elsie, or you'll never be dressed. Care to make use of my tongs, while they're so splendidly hot?'

Alone at last, Ethel drew in a breath, and, with a gesture of resolution, re-tied her kimono-sash tightly over her corset. She took the key from the bag and regarded it, murmuring, 'Providential!' then gave a glance upward, towards where the attics were. The late spring sun had set, but an apricot afterglow, not unlike the light cast by a Chinese lantern, crept through the upper storey of Jasmine Lodge. The cessation of all those rustlings, tappings, whimpers and moans from inside Mrs Varley de Grey's room had set up an unfamiliar, somewhat unnerving hush. Not till a whiff of singeing hair announced that Elsie was well employed did Ethel set out on the quest which held all her hopes. Success was imperative – she *must* have gloves. Gloves, gloves . . .

Soundlessly, she set foot on the attic stairs.

Under the skylight she had to suppress a shriek, for a rat – yes, of all things! – leaped at her out of an empty hatbox: and the rodent gave her a wink before it darted away. Now Ethel and Elsie knew for a certain fact that there never *had* been rats in Jasmine Lodge. However, she continued to steel her nerves, and to push her way to the one inviolate trunk.

All Mrs Varley de Grey's other Indian luggage gaped and yawned at Ethel, void, showing its linings, on end or toppling, forming a barricade around the object of her search. She pushed, pitched and pulled, scowling as the dust flew into her hair. But the last trunk, when it came into view and reach, still had something select and bridal about it: on top, the initials E. V. de G. stared out, quite luminous in a frightening way – for indeed how dusky the attic was! Shadows not only multiplied in the corners but seemed to finger their way up the sloping roof. Silence pierced up through the floor from that room below – and, worst, Ethel had the sensation of being watched by that pair of fixed eyes she had not stayed to close. She glanced this way, that way, backward over her shoulder. But, Lord Fred was at stake! – she knelt down and got to work with the key.

This trunk had two neat brass locks, one left, one right, along the front of the lid. Ethel, after fumbling, opened the first – then, so great was her hurry to know what might be within that she could not wait but slipped her hand in under the lifted corner. She pulled out one pricelessly lacy tip of what must be a bride-veil, and gave a quick laugh – must not this be an omen? She pulled again, but the stuff resisted, almost as though it were being grasped from inside the trunk – she let go, and either her eyes deceived her or the lace began to be drawn back slowly, in again, inch by inch. What was odder was that the spotless finger tip of a white kid glove appeared for a moment, as though exploring its way out, then withdrew.

Ethel's heart stood still – but she turned to the other lock. Was a giddy attack overcoming her? – for, as she gazed, the entire lid of the trunk seemed to bulge upward, heave and strain so that the E. V. de G. upon it rippled.

Untouched by the key in her trembling hand, the second lock tore itself open.

She recoiled, while the lid slowly rose – of its own accord.

She should have fled. But oh, how she craved what lay there exposed! – layer upon layer, wrapped in transparent paper, of elbow-length magnolia-pure white gloves, bedded on the inert folds of the veil. 'Lord Fred,' thought Ethel, 'now you're within my grasp!'

That was her last thought, nor was the grasp to be hers. Down on her knees again, breathless with lust and joy, Ethel flung herself forward on to that sea of kid, scrabbling and seizing. The glove she had seen before was now, however, readier for its purpose. At first it merely pounced after Ethel's fingers, as though making mock of their greedy course; but the hand within it was all the time filling out . . . With one snowy flash through the dusk, the glove clutched Ethel's front hair, tangled itself in her black curls and dragged her head down. She began to choke among the sachets and tissue – then the glove let go, hurled her back, and made its leap at her throat.

It was a marvel that anything so dainty should be so strong. So great, so convulsive was the swell of the force that, during the strangling of Ethel, the seams of the glove split.

In any case, the glove would have been too small for her.

The shrieks of Elsie, upon the attic threshold, began only when all other sounds had died down . . . The ultimate spark of the once-famous cleverness of the Miss Trevors appeared in Elsie's extrication of herself from this awkward mess – for, who was to credit how Ethel came by her end? The sisters' reputation for warmth of heart was to stand the survivor in good stead – for, could those affections nursed in Jasmine Lodge, extending so freely even to the unwell aunt, have culminated in Elsie's setting on Ethel? No. In the end, the matter was hushed up – which is to say, is still talked about even now. Ethel Trevor and Mrs Varley de Grey were interred in the same grave, as everyone understood that they would have wished. What conversation took place under the earth one does not know.

Elizabeth Bowen, 1952

Seven
NASTY SHOCKS

'Do you believe in ghosts?'
'No, but I am afraid of them.'

attrib. MADAME DU DEFFAND

Nothing satisfies us on Christmas Eve but to hear each
other tell authentic anecdotes about spectres. It is a
genial, festive season, and we love to muse upon graves,
and dead bodies, and murder, and blood.

JEROME K. JEROME

'This ol' fella'

This ol' fella he was goin' bird huntin'. He got out in the graveyard, an' had a open grave dug. Covey of quail flew up an' he shot, an' it kicked him over in the grave an' knocked him cold.

This night, though, a drunk man was comin' through there – he was really loaded. He heard somebody hollerin', 'It's cold down here. It's cold down here.'

That ol' drunk man he got on his knees an' looked over in 'ere an' he says, 'Hell, well no wonder; you done kicked all the dirt off of you!'

Woodrow Turner, in 'A Joke Session by Deer Hunters in Middle Georgia',
collected by Nan Gilmer Lang, 1967

The Yao Kuei

A virtuous man, travelling with his wife and family, stopped at an inn a large section of which was locked up and disused because it was haunted by a Yao Kuei. The traveller offered to stay up all night and destroy the ghost, and sitting fearlessly sword in hand, at about midnight, was confronted by a venerable old gentleman with a long white beard. The armed man rose to his feet, accused the newcomer of being an evil demon and made ready to slay him. The old man smiled and explained that he was not a Kuei, but the guardian spirit of the district, and had called in person to thank the traveller for his kindness – 'Your arrival has disposed of the Yao Kuei ... but should they return before morning, have at them with your sword!' The old gentleman departed and the traveller remained on guard. Soon, a strange black-faced creature entered the room – he struck off its head. Later he had the same experience with a white-faced creature; and so it continued at intervals till cock-crow, when he called the people of the inn to witness his victory. Each brought a lantern and the haunted room was soon filled with light. The walls were splashed and the floor streaming with blood, and there in a heap lay the decapitated corpses of the traveller's wife, children, and servants. 'The Yao Kuei has tricked me!' he cried, and fell dead.

Chinese folk tale, in *A Survey of the Occult* by John Franklyn, 1935

The Ride on the Gravestone

Late one evening a certain artisan happened to be returning home from a jovial feast in a distant village. There met him on the way an old friend, one who had been dead some ten years.

'Good health to you!' said the dead man.

'I wish you good health!' replied the reveller, and straightway forgot that his acquaintance had ever so long ago bidden the world farewell.

'Let's go to my house. We'll quaff a cup or two once more.'

'Come along. On such a happy occasion as this meeting of ours, we may as well have a drink.'

They arrived at a dwelling and there they drank and revelled.

'Now then, good-bye! It's time for me to go home,' said the artisan.

'Stay a bit. Where do you want to go now? Spend the night here with me.'

'No, brother! don't ask me; it cannot be. I've business to do to-morrow, so I must get home as early as possible.'

'Well, good-bye! but why should you walk? Better get on my horse; it will carry you home quickly.'

'Thanks! let's have it.'

He got on its back, and was carried off – just as a whirlwind flies! All of a sudden a cock crew. It was awful! All around were graves, and the rider found he had a gravestone under him!

Russian folk tale, collected by Afanasief, 1863,
translated by W. R. S. Ralston, 1873

In which Socrates make a miraculous recovery . . .

I fell into a cold sweat, and my heart trembled with feare, insomuch that the bed over me did likewise rattle and shake. Then spake Panthia unto Meroe and said, Sister let us by and by teare him in pieces, or tye him by the members, and so cut them off. Then Meroe (being so named because she was a Taverner, and loved wel good wines) answered, Nay rather let him live, and bury the corps of this poore wretch in some hole of the earth; and therewithall shee turned the head of Socrates on the other side, and thrust her sword up to the hilts into the left part of his necke, and received the bloud that gushed out, into a pot, that no drop thereof fell beside: which things I saw with myne owne eyes, and as I thinke to the intent she might alter nothing that pertained to sacrifice, which she accustomed to make, she thrust her hand downe into the intrals of his body, and searching about, at length brought forth the heart of my miserable companion Socrates, who having his throat cut in such sort, yeelded out a dolefull cry and gave up the ghost. Then Panthia stopped the wide wound of his throat with the Sponge, and said, O Sponge sprung and made of the sea, beware that thou passe not by running River. This being sayd, the one of them moved and turned up my bed, and then they strid over mee, and clapped their buttocks upon my face, and all bepissed mee till I was wringing wet. When this was ended they went their wayes, and the doores closed fast, the posts stood in their old places, and the lockes and bolts were shut againe. But I that lay upon the ground like one without soule, naked and cold, and wringing wet with pisse, like to one that were more than halfe dead, yet reviving my selfe, and appointed as I thought for the Gallowes, began to say, Alasse what shall become of me to morrow, when my companion shall be found murthered here in the chamber?

Whereupon Socrates as waking out of a sleepe, did rise up first and sayd, It is not without cause that strangers do speake evill of all such Hostlers, for this Caitife in his comming in, and with his crying out, I thinke under a colour to steale away somthing, hath waked me out of a sound sleepe. Then I rose up joyfull with a merry countenance, saying, Behold good Hostler, my friend, my companion and my brother, whom thou didst falsly affirme to be slaine by mee this night. And therewithall I embraced my friend Socrates and kissed him: but hee smelling the stinke of the pisse wherewith those Hagges had embrued me, thrust me away and sayd, Clense thy selfe from this filthy odour, and then he began gently to enquire, how that noysome sent hapned unto mee. But I finely feigning and colouring the matter for the time, did breake off his talk, and tooke him by the hand and sayd, Why tarry we? Why lose wee the pleasure of this faire morning? Let us goe, and so I tooke up my packet, and payed the charges of the house and departed: and we had not gone a mile out of the Towne but it was broad day, and then I diligently looked upon Socrates throat, to see if I could espy the place where Meroe thrust in her sword: but when I could not perceive any such thing, I thought with my selfe, What a mad man am I, that being overcome with wine yester night, have dreamed such terrible things? Behold, I see Socrates is sound, safe, and in health. Where is his wound? where is the Sponge? Where is his great and new cut? And then I spake to him and sayd, Verily it is not without occasion, that Physitians of experience do affirme, That such as fill their gorges abundantly with meat and drinke, shall dreame of dire and horrible sights: for I my selfe, not tempering my appetite yester night from the pots of wine, did seeme to see this night strange and cruel visions, that even yet I think my self sprinkled and wet with human blood: whereunto Socrates laughing made answer and said, Nay, thou art not wet with the blood of men, but thou art imbrued with stinking pisse; and verily I my self dreamed this night that my throat was cut, and that I felt the paine of the wound, and that my heart was pulled out of my belly, and the remembrance thereof makes me now to feare, for my knees do so tremble that I can scarce goe any further, and therefore I would faine eat somewhat to strengthen and revive my spirits. Then said I, Behold here thy breakfast, and therwithall I opened my script that hanged upon my shoulder, and gave him bread and cheese, and we sate downe under a great Plane tree, and I eat part with him; and while I beheld him eating greedily, I perceived that he waxed meigre and pale, and that his lively colour faded away, insomuch that beeing in great fear, and remembring those terrible furies of whom I lately dreamed, the first morsell of bread that I put in my mouth (which was but very small) did so sticke in my jawes, that I could neither swallow it downe, nor yet yeeld it up, and moreover the small time of our being together increased my feare, and what is hee that seeing his companion die in the high-way before his face, would not greatly lament and bee sorry? But when that Socrates had eaten sufficiently he waxed very thirsty, for indeed he had well nigh devoured all a whole Cheese: and behold evill fortune! there was behinde the Plane tree a pleasant running water as cleere as Crystal, and I sayd unto him, Come hither Socrates to this water and drinke thy fill. And then he rose and came to the River, and kneeled downe upon the side of the banke to drinke, but he had scarce touched the water with his lips when as behold the wound of his throat opened wide, and the Sponge suddenly fell into the water, and after issued out a little remnant of bloud, and his body being then without life, had fallen into the river, had not I caught him by the leg and so pulled him up. And after that I had lamented a good space the death of my wretched companion, I buried him in the Sands there by the river.

From *The Golden Ass*, second century AD, translated by William Aldington, as
The First Book of Lucius Apuleius, 1566

The youth who could not shiver

A father had two sons. The eldest was prudent and clever, and able to do everything. The younger was dull, unable to understand or learn, and people who saw him said that he would prove a burden to his father. When anything was required, it was always the elder who was called upon; yet if his father asked him late, or in the night, to fetch something, and the way lay through the churchyard or some lonely spot, he would reply, 'Oh no, father! I cannot go there, it makes me shiver;' for he was afraid. In the winter evenings likewise, when people sat by the fire and told stories which made the hair stand on end, the listeners would sometimes exclaim, 'It makes me shiver.' The youngest sat in a corner and listened with the others, but could never comprehend what they meant: 'They are always saying, "I shiver, I shiver:" *I* never shiver; that is a thing I do not understand.'

One day his father said to him, 'Listen, you in the corner, you are tall and strong, and must learn something that will earn you your bread. See how your brother works; but everything is thrown away on you.' 'Yes, father,' replied he, 'I am quite ready to learn something, and if it could be managed I should like to learn to shiver, for I understand nothing at all about it.' The eldest son laughed when he heard this, saying to himself, 'What a simpleton my brother is; he will never do anything.' The father sighed and said, 'You may learn to shiver, but that will never enable you to earn your bread, my son.'

[After several adventures, but no shivering, the youth tells an innkeeper of his quest.]
He left the host no peace until the latter had related to him, that not far from the inn was an enchanted castle, and any one passing three nights there could not fail to understand what shivering was. The king had promised his daughter for a wife to any one brave enough to venture to do this, and she was the most beautiful princess the sun ever shone upon. Besides this, great treasures were hidden in the castle, watched over by evil spirits. This treasure would then be set free, and would be riches enough for a poor man. Many had already undertaken to watch three nights in the enchanted castle, and had entered for that purpose, but not one had ever returned.

[On the first and second nights, he encounters spectral cats and dogs, a moving bed, old men who play bowls with skulls, but still he cannot shiver.]
'Shiver!' said the youth; 'I was never more merry in my life. Oh, if I could only shiver!'

The next night he seated himself again upon his bench, and was repeating to himself in a melancholy tone, 'Oh! if I could only shiver!' when six tall men entered, carrying a coffin between them. Upon seeing what they carried, 'This is certainly my cousin,' said he, 'who died a day or two ago;' so he beckoned, saying at the same time, 'Come, cousin; come!' The men then placed the coffin on the ground, and he, going nearer, took off the lid, and saw that a dead man lay within. He felt his face, but it was cold as ice. 'Wait!' he cried, 'I will warm you a little.' So, going to the fire, he warmed his own hands, and then placed them on the dead man's face, which remained as cold as ever. Then taking the dead man out, he placed him by the fire, rubbing in vain his limbs in order to restore circulation to the blood. He then thought of another way, and placing him on the bed, covered him up, and lay down himself beside the body. After a while the dead man became warm, and began to stir. Then the youth said, 'Now, cousin, have I not warmed you at last?' But the dead man sat up and said, 'I will strangle you!' 'What!' returned the other, 'is this your gratitude? You shall go back instantly into your coffin.' So he lifted him up, cast him in the coffin, and shut the lid down; then the six men appeared, raised the coffin, and bore it away. 'If I stay all my life here,' said the youth, 'I shall never shiver.'

At this moment a huge man entered, of most hideous aspect; he was old, and had a long white beard. 'Mortal!' he cried to the young man, 'soon shalt thou learn to shiver, for thou shalt die.' 'Not so fast,' said the other, 'if I am to die you must have my consent first.' But the monster said, with a grim smile, 'I do not think that at all necessary; I can easily kill you.' 'Softly, softly,' said the youth; 'I am as strong as you, perhaps stronger.' 'That we shall soon see,' replied the old man; 'if you prove stronger than I, you shall go free; come, let us try.' The old man conducted the youth through a dark passage to a smith's fire or forge, seized an axe, and with one blow struck one of the anvils into the ground. 'I can do better than that,' said the other, and went towards the other anvil; the old man placed himself near to observe what was taking place, and his white beard hung down. Then seizing an axe, with one blow the youth split the anvil, and fastened the old man's beard at the same moment in the cleft. 'Now I have you fast,' said he, 'and you shall die.' Taking up an iron rod, he struck him several blows, until he shrieked out, begging him to cease, and he would make him rich for the rest of his days. The youth then set free his axe, and gave the old man his liberty. The latter led him back to the castle, and showed him a cellar where there were three chests full of gold. 'Take these,' said he; 'one is for the poor, one for the king, and the third for you.' At that moment the clock struck twelve, the ghost vanished, and the youth found himself in pitch darkness. 'I will soon find my way out, however,' said he; and he groped about till he found himself in the old chamber, where he slept peacefully by his fire until the morning. The king did not fail to appear, with the old question. 'I know nothing more about shivering,' said the youth, 'but I have seen my cousin, and an old man with a beard came, who showed me plenty of gold in the cellar, but said not a word about shivering.' Then the king took him by the hand, and said, 'You have delivered the castle from the evil spirits, and you shall marry my daughter.' 'That is all very pleasant,' returned the other, 'but shall I never be able to learn to shiver?' The gold was now brought up, and the marriage celebrated; but although the young king was very happy with his bride, he continually repeated the old refrain, 'Oh, if I could shiver!' This at last began to annoy his wife; but her waiting woman said, 'With your permission, I will soon find a way to teach him to shiver.' She went to the brook which ran through the garden, and got a tub full of gudgeons. At night, when the young king had retired to rest,

the queen withdrew the covering, and threw the entire contents of the
tub over him, so the little fish splashed about all over him, which made
him wake up with a start, exclaiming, 'Wife, what makes me shiver so?
Now I know what it means to shiver.'

From *Grimm's Fairy Tales*, 1812–15; anonymous translation

'Every suggestion that horror could inspire . . . '

'Heaven nor hell shall impede my designs,' said Manfred, advancing
again to seize the princess. At that instant the portrait of his grandfather, which hung over the bench where they had been sitting, uttered
a deep sigh, and heaved its breast. Isabella, whose back was turned to
the picture, saw not the motion, nor whence the sound came but
started, and said:

'Hark, my lord! what sound was that?' and at the same time made
towards the door. Manfred, distracted between the flight of Isabella,
who had now reached the stairs, and yet unable to keep his eyes from
the picture, which began to move, had, however, advanced some steps
after her, still looking backwards on the portrait, when he saw it quit its
panel, and descend on the floor with a grave and melancholy air.

'Do I dream?' cried Manfred, returning; 'or are the devils themselves
in league against me? Speak, infernal spectre! or, if thou art my grand-
sire, why dost thou, too, conspire against thy wretched descendant,
who too dearly pays for –' Ere he could finish the sentence, the vision
sighed again, and made a sign to Manfred to follow him.

'Lead on!' cried Manfred: 'I will follow thee to the gulf of perdition.'
The spectre marched sedately, but dejected, to the end of the gallery,
and turned into a chamber on the right hand. Manfred accompanied
him a little distance, full of anxiety and horror, but resolved. As he
would have entered the chamber, the door was clapped to with
violence by an invisible hand. The prince, collecting courage from this
delay, would have forcibly burst open the door with his foot, but found
that it resisted his utmost efforts.

'Since hell will not satisfy my curiosity,' said Manfred, 'I will use the
human means in my power for preserving my race; Isabella shall not
escape me.'

That lady, whose resolution had given way to terror the moment she
had quitted Manfred, continued her flight to the bottom of the principal
staircase. There she stopped, not knowing whither to direct her steps,
nor how to escape from the impetuosity of the prince. . . .

An awful silence reigned throughout those subterraneous regions, except now and then some blasts of wind that shook the doors she had passed, and which, grating on the rusty hinges, were re-echoed through that long labyrinth of darkness. Every murmur struck her with new terror; yet more she dreaded to hear the wrathful voice of Manfred urging his domestics to pursue her. She trod as softly as impatience would give her leave, – yet frequently stopped, and listened to hear if she was followed. In one of those moments she thought she heard a sigh. She shuddered, and recoiled a few paces. In a moment she thought she heard the step of some person. Her blood curdled; she concluded it was Manfred. Every suggestion that horror could inspire rushed into her mind.

From *The Castle of Otranto* by Horace Walpole, 1764

The Ghosts' High Noon

CHORUS OF FAMILY PORTRAITS
Painted emblems of a race,
    All accurst in days of yore,
Each from his accustomed place
    Steps into the world once more!

(The Pictures step from their frames and march round the stage.)

SIR RODERIC: When the night wind howls in the chimney cowls, and the bat in the moonlight flies,
And inky clouds, like funeral shrouds, sail over the midnight skies –
When the footpads quail at the night-bird's wail, and black dogs bay at the moon,
Then is the spectres' holiday – then is the ghosts' high-noon!
CHORUS: Ha! ha!
            Then is the ghosts' high-noon!

From *Ruddigore* by W. S. Gilbert, 1887

Dr Johnson's Ghost

(On Boswell's Journal of a Tour to the Hebrides)

'Twas at the solemn hour of night,
　When men and spirits meet,
That Johnson, huge majestic sprite,
　Repaired to Boswell's feet.

His face was like the full-orbed moon
　Wrapped in a threatening cloud,
That bodes the tempest bursting soon,
　And winds that bluster loud.

Terrific was his angry look,
　His pendent eyebrows frowned;
Thrice in his hand he waved a book,
　Then dashed it on the ground.

'Behold,' he cried, 'perfidious man,
　This object of my rage:
Bethink thee of the sordid plan
　That formed this venal page.

'Was it to make this base record
　That you my friendship sought;
Thus to retain each vagrant word,
　Each undigested thought?

'Dar'st thou pretend that, meaning praise,
　Thou seek'st to raise my name,
When all thy babbling pen betrays
　But gives me churlish fame?

'Do readers in these annals trace
　The man that's wise and good?
No! – rather one of savage race,
　Illiberal, fierce and rude.

'A traveller, whose discontent
　No kindness can appease;
Who finds for spleen perpetual vent
　In all he hears and sees

'One whose ingratitude displays
  The most ungracious guest;
Who hospitality repays
  With bitter, biting jest.

'Ah! would, as o'er the hills we sped,
  And climbed the sterile rocks,
Some vengeful stone had struck thee dead,
  Or steeple, spared by Knox!

'Thy adulation now I see,
  And all its schemes unfold:
Thy avarice, Boswell, cherished me
  To turn me into gold.

'So keepers guard the beasts they show,
  And for their wants provide;
Attend their steps where'er they go,
  And travel by their side.

'O! were it not that, deep and low,
  Beyond thy reach I'm laid,
Rapacious Boswell had ere now
  Johnson a mummy made.'

He ceased, and stalked from Boswell's sight
  With fierce indignant mien,
Scornful as Ajax' sullen sprite
  By sage Ulysses seen.

Dead paleness Boswell's cheek o'erspread,
  His limbs with horror shook;
With trembling haste he left his bed,
  And burnt his fatal book.

And thrice he called on Johnson's name.
  Forgiveness to implore!
Then thrice repeated – 'injured fame!'
  And word – wrote never more.

Elizabeth Moody, 1786

Adelgunda and the Clock

Cyprian stood up; and, as was his habit when his mind was occupied, and he needed a little time to arrange his words, he walked several times up and down the room. Presently he sat down, and began:–

'You may remember that some little time ago, just before the last campaign, I was paying a visit to Colonel von P— at his country house. The colonel was a good-tempered, jovial man, and his wife quietness and simpleness personified. At the time I speak of, the son was away with the army, so that the family circle consisted, besides the colonel and his lady, of two daughters and an elderly French lady who was trying to persuade herself that she was fulfilling the duties of a governess – though the young ladies appeared to be beyond the period of being "governed". The elder of the two daughters was a most lively and cheerful girl, vivacious even to ungovernability; not without plenty of brains, but so constituted that she could not go five yards without cutting at least three entrechats. She sprang in the same fashion in her conversation and everything that she did, restlessly from one thing to another. I myself have seen her within the space of five minutes work at needlework, read, draw, sing, dance, or cry about her poor cousin who was killed in battle and then while the tears were still in her eyes burst into a splendid infectious burst of laughter when the French-woman spilled the contents of her snuffbox over the pug. The pug began to sneeze frightfully, and the old lady cried, "Ah, che fatalità! Ah carino! Poverino!" (She always spoke to the dog in Italian because he was born in Padua.) Moreover, this young lady was the loveliest blonde ever seen, and for all her odd caprices, full of the utmost charm, goodness, kindliness and attractiveness, so that whether she wanted to or not she exerted the most irresistible charm over everyone.

'Her younger sister was the greatest possible contrast to her (her name was Adelgunda). I try in vain to find words in which to express to you the extraordinary impression which this girl produced upon me when I first saw her. Picture to yourselves the most exquisite figure, and the most marvellously beautiful face; but her cheeks and lips wear a deathly pallor, and she moves gently, softly, slowly, with measured steps; and then, when you hear a low-toned word from her scarcely opened lips you feel a sort of shudder of spectral awe. Of course I soon got over this eerie feeling, and, when I managed to get her to emerge from her deep self-absorbed condition and converse, I was obliged to admit that the strangeness, the eeriness, was only external; and by no means came from within. In the little she said she displayed a delicate womanliness, a clear head, and a kindly disposition. She had not a trace of over-excitability, though her melancholy smile, and her glance, heavy as if with tears, seemed to speak of some morbid bodily condition producing a hostile influence on her mental state. It struck me as very strange that the whole family, not excepting the French lady, seemed to get into a state of anxiety as soon as anyone began to talk to this girl, and tried to interrupt the conversation, often breaking into it in a very forced manner. But the most extraordinary thing of all was that, as soon as it was eight o'clock in the evening, the young lady was reminded, first by the French lady and then by her mother, sister, and father, that it was time to go to her room, just as little children are sent to bed so that they will not overtire themselves. The French lady went with her, so that neither of them ever appeared at supper, which was at nine o'clock. The lady of the house, probably noticing my surprise at those proceedings, threw out (by way of preventing indiscreet inquiries) a sort of sketchy statement to the effect that Adelgunda was in very poor health, that, particularly about nine in the evening, she was liable to feverish attacks, and that the doctors had ordered her to have complete rest at that time. I saw there must be more in the affair than this, though I could not imagine what it might be; and it was only today that I ascertained the terrible truth, and discovered what the events were which have wrecked the peace of that happy circle in the most frightful manner.

'Adelgunda was at one time the most blooming, vigorous, cheerful creature to be seen. Her fourteenth birthday came, and a number of her friends and companions had been invited to spend it with her. They were all sitting in a circle in the shrubbery, laughing and amusing themselves, taking little heed that the evening was getting darker and darker, for the soft July breeze was blowing refreshingly, and they were just beginning thoroughly to enjoy themselves. In the magic twilight they set about all sorts of dances, pretending to be elves and woodland sprites. Adelgunda cried, "Listen, children! I shall go and appear to you as the White Lady whom our gardener used to tell us about so often while he was alive. But you must come to the bottom of the garden, where the old ruins are." She wrapped her white shawl round her, and went lightly dancing down the leafy path, the girls following her, in full tide of laughter and fun. But Adelgunda had scarcely reached the old crumbling arches, when she suddenly stopped, and stood as if paralyzed in every limb. The castle clock struck nine.

'"Look, look!" cried she, in a hollow voice of the deepest terror. "Don't you see it? the figure – close before me – stretching her hand out at me. Don't you see her?"

'The children saw nothing whatever; but terror came upon them, and they all ran away, except one, more courageous than the rest, who hastened up to Adelgunda, and was going to take her in her arms. But Adelgunda, turning pale as death, fell to the ground. At the screams of

the other girl everybody came hastening from the castle, and Adelgunda was carried in. At last she recovered from her faint, and,
trembling all over, told them that as soon as she reached the ruins she
saw an airy form, as if shrouded in mist, stretching its hand out towards
her. Of course everyone ascribed this vision to some deceptiveness of
the twilight; and Adelgunda recovered from her alarm so completely
that night that no further evil consequences were anticipated, and the
whole affair was supposed to be at an end. However, it turned out altogether otherwise. The next evening, when the clock struck nine,
Adelgunda sprang up, in the midst of the people about her, and cried,
"There she is! there she is. Don't you see her – just before me?"

'Since that unlucky evening, Adelgunda declared that as soon as the
clock struck nine, the figure stood before her, remaining visible for
several seconds, although no one but herself could see anything of it, or
trace by any psychic sensation the proximity of an unknown spiritual
principle. So that poor Adelgunda was thought to be out of her mind;
and, in a strange perversion of feeling, the family were ashamed of this
condition of hers. I have told you already how she was dealt with in
consequence. There was, of course, no lack of doctors, or of plans of
treatment for ridding the poor soul of the *idée fixe*, as people were
pleased to term the apparition which she said she saw. But nothing had
any effect; and she implored, with tears, to be left in peace, inasmuch as
the form which in its vague, uncertain traits had nothing terrible or
alarming about it no longer caused her any fear; although for a time
after seeing it she felt as if her inner being and all her thoughts and
ideas were turned out from her, and were hovering, bodiless, outside of
her. At last the colonel made the acquaintance of a celebrated doctor
who had the reputation of being specially clever in the treatment of the
mentally afflicted. When this doctor heard Adelgunda's story he
laughed aloud, and said nothing could be easier than to cure a condition
of the kind, which resulted solely from an overexcited imagination. The
idea of the appearing of the spectre was so intimately associated with
the striking of nine o'clock that the mind could not dissociate them. So
that all that was necessary was to effect this separation by external
means. About this there would be no difficulty, as it was only necessary
to deceive the patient as to the time, and let nine o'clock pass without
her being aware of it. If the apparition did not then appear, she would
be convinced herself that it was an illusion; and measures to give tone
to the general system would be all that would then be necessary to
complete the cure.

'This unfortunate advice was taken. One night all the clocks at the
castle were put back an hour – the hollow, booming tower clock included – so that, when Adelgunda awoke in the morning, although she
did not know it, she was really an hour wrong in her time. When evening came, the family were assembled, as usual, in a cheerful corner

room; no stranger was present, and the mother constrained herself to talk about all sorts of cheerful subjects. The colonel began (as was his habit, when in specially good humour) to carry on an encounter of wit with the old French lady, in which Augusta, the older of the daughters, aided and abetted him. Everybody was laughing, and more full of enjoyment than ever. The clock on the wall struck eight (although it was really nine o'clock) and Adelgunda fell back in her chair, pale as death. Her work dropped from her hands; she rose, with a face of horror, stared before her into the empty part of the room, and murmured, in a hollow voice, "What! an hour early! Don't you see it? Don't you see it? Right before me!"

'Everyone rose up in alarm. But as none of them saw the smallest vestige of anything, the colonel cried, "Calm yourself, Adelgunda, there is nothing there! It is a vision of your brain, only your imagination. We see nothing, nothing whatever; and if there really were a figure close to you we should see it as well as you! Calm yourself."

'"Oh God!" cried Adelgunda, "they think I am out of my mind. See! it is stretching out its long arm, it is making signs to me!"

'And, as though she were acting under the influence of another, without exercise of her own will, with eyes fixed and staring, she put her hand back behind her, took up a plate which chanced to be on the table, held it out before her into vacancy, and let it go.

'The plate did not drop, but floated about among the persons present, and then settled gently on the table. Augusta and her mother fainted; and these fainting fits were succeeded by violent nervous fever. The colonel forced himself to retain his self-control, but the profound impression which this extraordinary occurrence made on him was evident in his agitated and disturbed condition.

'The French lady had fallen on her knees and prayed in silence with her face turned to the floor, and both she and Adelgunda remained free from evil consequences. The mother very soon died. Augusta survived the fever; but it would have been better had she died. She who, when I first saw her, was an embodiment of vigorous, magnificent youthful happiness, is now hopelessly insane, and that in a form which seems to me the most terrible and gruesome of all the forms of *idée fixe* ever heard of. For she thinks she is the invisible phantom which haunts Adelgunda; and therefore she avoids everyone, or, at all events, refrains from speaking, or moving if anybody is present. She scarce dares to breathe, because she firmly believes that if she betrays her presence in any way everyone will die. Doors are opened for her, and her food is set down, she slinks in and out, eats in secret, and so forth. Can a more painful condition be imagined?

'The colonel, in his pain and despair, followed the colours to the next campaign, and fell in the victorious engagement at W—. It is remarkable, most remarkable that since then Adelgunda has never seen the phantom. She nurses her sister with the utmost care, and the French lady helps her. Only this very day Sylvester told me that the uncle of these poor girls is here, taking the advice of our celebrated R—, as to the means of cure to be tried in Augusta's case. God grant that the cure may succeed, improbable as it seems.'

When Cyprian finished, the friends all kept silence, looking meditatively before them.

From 'Automata' by E. T. A. Hoffman, 1814–15, translated from the German
by Mrs Alexander Ewing

The Mail

I jumped forward, waved my hat, and shouted. The mail came down at full speed, and passed me. For a moment I feared that I had not been seen or heard, but it was only for a moment. The coachman pulled up; the guard, muffled to the eyes in capes and comforters, and apparently sound asleep in the rumble, neither answered my hail nor made the slightest effort to dismount; the outside passenger did not even turn his head. I opened the door for myself, and looked in. There were but three travellers inside, so I stepped in, shut the door, slipped into the vacant corner, and congratulated myself on my good fortune.

The atmosphere of the coach seemed, if possible, colder than that of the outer air, and was pervaded by a singularly damp and disagreeable smell. I looked round at my fellow-passengers. They were all three, men, and all silent. They did not seem to be asleep, but each leaned back in his corner of the vehicle, as if absorbed in his own reflections. I attempted to open a conversation.

'How intensely cold it is tonight,' I said, addressing my opposite neighbour.

He lifted his head, looked at me, but made no reply.

'The winter,' I added, 'seems to have begun in earnest.'

Although the corner in which he sat was so dim that I could distinguish none of his features very clearly, I saw that his eyes were still turned full upon me. And yet he answered never a word.

At any other time I should have felt, and perhaps expressed, some annoyance, but at the moment I felt too ill to do either. The icy coldness of the night air had struck a chill to my very marrow, and the strange smell inside the coach was affecting me with an intolerable nausea. I shivered from head to foot, and, turning to my left-hand neighbour, asked if he had any objection to an open window?

He neither spoke nor stirred.

[216]

I repeated the question somewhat more loudly, but with the same result. Then I lost patience, and let the sash down. As I did so the leather strap broke in my hand, and I observed that the glass was covered with a thick coat of mildew, the accumulation, apparently, of years. My attention being thus drawn to the condition of the coach, I examined it more narrowly, and saw by the uncertain light of the outer lamps that it was in the last stage of dilapidation. Every part of it was not only out of repair, but in a condition of decay. The sashes splintered at a touch. The leather fittings were crusted over with mould, and literally rotting from the woodwork. The floor was almost breaking away beneath my feet. The whole machine, in short, was foul with damp, and had evidently been dragged from some outhouse in which it had been mouldering away for years, to do another day or two of duty on the road.

I turned to the third passenger, whom I had not yet addressed, and hazarded one more remark.

'This coach,' I said, 'is in a deplorable condition. The regular mail, I suppose, is under repair?'

He moved his head slowly, and looked me in the face, without speaking a word. I shall never forget that look while I live. I turned cold at heart under it. I turn cold at heart even now when I recall it. His eyes glowed with a fiery unnatural lustre. His face was livid as the face of a corpse. His bloodless lips were drawn back as if in the agony of death, and showed the gleaming teeth between.

The words that I was about to utter died upon my lips, and a strange horror – a dreadful horror – came upon me. My sight had by this time become used to the gloom of the coach, and I could see with tolerable distinctness. I turned to my opposite neighbour. He, too, was looking at me, with the same startling pallor in his face, and the same stony glitter in his eyes. I passed my hand across my brow. I turned to the passenger on the seat beside my own, and saw – oh Heaven! how shall I describe what I saw? I saw that he was no living man – that none of them were living men, like myself! A pale phosphorescent light – the light of putrefaction – played upon their awful faces; upon their hair, dank with the dews of the grave; upon their clothes, earth-stained and dropping to pieces; upon their hands, which were as the hands of corpses long buried. Only their eyes, their terrible eyes, were living; and those eyes were all turned menacingly upon me!

A shriek of terror, a wild unintelligible cry for help and mercy, burst from my lips as I flung myself against the door, and strove in vain to open it.

In that single instant, brief and vivid as a landscape beheld in the flash of summer lightning, I saw the moon shining down through a rift of stormy cloud – the ghastly sign-post rearing its warning finger by the wayside – the broken parapet – the plunging horses – the black gulf below. Then, the coach reeled like a ship at sea. Then, came a mighty crash – a sense of crushing pain – and then, darkness.

From 'The Phantom Coach' by Amelia B. Edwards, 1864

The Frontier

Simpson, for the first time, hesitated; then, ashamed of his alarm and indecision, took a few hurried steps ahead; the next instant stopped dead in his tracks. Immediately in front of him all signs of the trail ceased; both tracks came to an abrupt end. On all sides, for a hundred yards or more, he searched in vain for the least indication of their continuance. There was – nothing.

The trees were very thick just there, big trees all of them, spruce, cedar, hemlock; there was no underbrush. He stood, looking about him, all distraught; bereft of any power of judgment. Then he set to work to search again, and again, and yet again, but always with the same result: *nothing*. The feet that printed the surface of the snow thus far had now, apparently, left the ground!

And it was in that moment of distress and confusion that the whip of terror laid its most nicely calculated lash about his heart. It dropped with deadly effect upon the sorest spot of all, completely unnerving him. He had been secretly dreading all the time that it would come – and come it did.

Far overhead, muted by great height and distance, strangely thinned and wailing, he heard the crying voice of Défago, the guide.

The sound dropped upon him out of that still, wintry sky with an effect of dismay and terror unsurpassed. The rifle fell to his feet. He stood motionless an instant, listening as it were with his whole body, then staggered back against the nearest tree for support, disorganised hopelessly in mind and spirit. To him, in that moment, it seemed the most shattering and dislocating experience he had ever known, so that his heart emptied itself of all feeling whatsoever as by a sudden draught.

'Oh! oh! This fiery height! Oh, my feet of fire! My burning feet of fire...!' ran in far, beseeching accents of indescribable appeal this voice of anguish down the sky. Once it called – then silence through all the listening wilderness of trees.

And Simpson, scarcely knowing what he did, presently found himself running wildly to and fro, searching, calling, tripping over roots and boulders, and flinging himself in a frenzy of undirected pursuit after the Caller. Behind the screen of memory and emotion with which experience veils events, he plunged, distracted and half-deranged, picking up false lights like a ship at sea, terror in his eyes and heart and soul. For the Panic of the Wilderness had called to him in that far voice – the Power of untamed Distance – the Enticement of the Desolation that destroys. He knew in that moment all the pains of someone hopelessly and irretrievably lost, suffering the lust and travail of a soul in the final Loneliness. A vision of Défago, eternally hunted, driven and pursued across the skiey vastness of those ancient forests fled like a flame across the dark ruin of his thoughts. . . .

It seemed ages before he could find anything in the chaos of his disorganised sensations to which he could anchor himself steady for a moment, and think. . . . The cry was not repeated; his own hoarse calling brought no response; the inscrutable forces of the Wild had summoned their victim beyond recall – and held him fast.

From 'The Wendigo' by Algernon Blackwood, 1914

The Ghost That Jim Saw

Why, as to that, said the engineer,
Ghosts ain't things we are apt to fear;
Spirits don't fool with levers much,
And throttle-valves don't take to such;
　　And as for Jim,
　　What happened to him
Was one half fact, and t' other half whim!

Running one night on the line, he saw
A house – as plain as the moral law –
Just by the moonlit bank, and thence
Came a drunken man with no more sense
　　Than to drop on the rail
　　Flat as a flail,
As Jim drove by with the midnight mail.

Down went the patents – steam reversed.
Too late! for there came a 'thud', Jim cursed
As the fireman, there in the cab with him,
Kinder stared in the face of Jim,
　　And says, 'What now?'
　　Says Jim, 'What now!
I've just run over a man, – that's how!'

[219]

The fireman stared at Jim. They ran
Back, but they never found house nor man, –
Nary a shadow within a mile.
Jim turned pale, but he tried to smile,
   Then on he tore
   Ten mile or more,
In quicker time than he'd made afore.

Would you believe it! the very next night
Up rose that house in the moonlight white,
Out comes the chap and drops as before,
Down goes the brake and the rest encore;
   And so, in fact,
   Each night that act
Occurred, till folks swore Jim was cracked.

Humph! let me see; it's a year now, 'most,
That I met Jim, East, and says, 'How's your ghost?'
'Gone,' says Jim; 'and more, it's plain
That ghost don't trouble me again.
   I thought I shook
   That ghost when I took
A place on an Eastern line, – but look!

'What should I meet, the first trip out,
But the very house we talked about,
And the selfsame man! "Well," says I, "I guess
It's time to stop this 'yer foolishness."
   So I crammed on steam,
   When there came a scream
From my fireman, that jest broke my dream:

'"You've killed somebody!" Says I, "Not much!
I've been thar often, and thar ain't no such,
And now I'll prove it!" Back we ran,
And – darn my skin! – but thar *was* a man
   On the rail, dead,
   Smashed in the head! –
Now I call that meanness!' That's all Jim said.

Bret Harte, *c.*1870

'New Bedford'

A ghost that haunted a family in New Bedford was even less desirable, at least in the opinion of those outside the family, for, occasionally, when anyone called at the house, the ghost and not the servant answered the door and slapped the face of the caller soundly.

From *Family Ghosts* by Elliot O'Donnell, 1933

Someone in the Room: 1

How long that first sleep lasted, she never knew. She could only remember, in the after-time, that she woke instantly.

Every faculty and perception in her passed the boundary line between insensibility and consciousness, so to speak, at a leap. Without knowing why, she sat up suddenly in the bed, listening for she knew not what. Her head was in a whirl; her heart beat furiously, without any assignable cause. But one trivial event had happened during the interval while she had been asleep. The night-light had gone out; and the room, as a matter of course, was in total darkness.

She felt for the match-box, and paused after finding it. A vague sense of confusion was still in her mind. She was in no hurry to light the match. The pause in the darkness was, for the moment, agreeable to her.

In the quieter flow of her thoughts during this interval, she could ask herself the natural question: – What cause had awakened her so suddenly, and had so strangely shaken her nerves? Had it been the influence of a dream? She had not dreamed at all – or, to speak more correctly, she had no waking remembrance of having dreamed. The mystery was beyond her fathoming: the darkness began to oppress her. She struck the match on the box, and lit her candle.

As the welcome light diffused itself over the room, she turned from the table and looked towards the other side of the bed.

In the moment when she turned, the chill of a sudden terror gripped her round the heart, as with the clasp of an icy hand.

She was not alone in her room!

There – in the chair at the bedside – there, suddenly revealed under the flow of light from the candle, was the figure of a woman, reclining. Her head lay back over the chair. Her face, turned up to the ceiling, had the eyes closed as if she were wrapped in a deep sleep.

The shock of the discovery held Agnes speechless and helpless. Her first conscious action, when she was in some degree mistress of herself again, was to lean over the bed, and to look closer at the woman who had so incomprehensibly stolen into her room in the dead of night. One glance was enough: she started back with a cry of amazement. The person in the chair was no other than the widow of the dead Montbarry – the woman who had warned her that they were to meet again, and that the place might be Venice!

Her courage returned to her, stung into action by the natural sense of indignation which the presence of the Countess provoked.

'Wake up!' she called out. 'How dare you come here? How did you get in? Leave the room – or I will call for help!'

She raised her voice at the last words. It produced no effect. Leaning farther over the bed, she boldly took the Countess by the shoulder and shook her. Not even this effort succeeded in rousing the sleeping woman. She still lay back in the chair, possessed by a torpor like the torpor of death – insensible to sound, insensible to touch. Was she really sleeping? Or had she fainted?

Agnes looked closer at her. She had not fainted. Her breathing was audible, rising and falling in deep heavy gasps. At intervals she ground her teeth savagely. Beads of perspiration stood thickly on her forehead. Her clenched hands rose and fell slowly from time to time on her lap. Was she in the agony of a dream? or was she spiritually conscious of something hidden in the room?

The doubt involved in that last question was unendurable. Agnes determined to rouse the servants who kept watch in the hotel at night.

The bell-handle was fixed to the wall, on the side of the bed by which the table stood.

She raised herself from the crouching position which she had assumed in looking close at the Countess; and, turning towards the other side of the bed, stretched out her hand to the bell. At the same instant, she stopped and looked upward. Her hand fell helplessly at her side. She shuddered, and sank back on the pillow.

What had she seen?

She had seen another intruder in her room.

Midway between her face and the ceiling, there hovered a human head – severed at the neck, like a head struck from the body by the guillotine.

Nothing visible, nothing audible, had given her any intelligible warning of its appearance. Silently and suddenly, the head had taken its place above her. No supernatural change had passed over the room, or was perceptible in it now. The dumbly-tortured figure in the chair; the broad window opposite the foot of the bed, with the black night beyond it; the candle burning on the table – these, and all other objects in the room, remained unaltered. One object more, unutterably horrid, had been added to the rest. That was the only change – no more, no less.

By the yellow candlelight she saw the head distinctly, hovering in mid-air above her. She looked at it steadfastly, spell-bound by the terror that held her.

The flesh of the face was gone. The shrivelled skin was darkened in hue, like the skin of an Egyptian mummy – except at the neck. There it was of a lighter colour; there it showed spots and splashes of the hue of that brown spot on the ceiling, which the child's fanciful terror had distorted into the likeness of a spot of blood. Thin remains of a discoloured moustache and whiskers, hanging over the upper lip, and over the hollows where the cheeks had once been, made the head just recognisable as the head of a man. Over all the features death and time had done their obliterating work. The eyelids were closed. The hair on the skull, discoloured like the hair on the face, had been burnt away in places. The bluish lips, parted in a fixed grin, showed the double row of teeth. By slow degrees, the hovering head (perfectly still when she first saw it) began to descend towards Agnes as she lay beneath. By slow degrees, that strange doubly-blended odour, which the Commissioners had discovered in the vaults of the old palace – which had sickened Francis Westwick in the bed-chamber of the new hotel – spread its fetid exhalations over the room. Downward and downward the hideous apparition made its slow progress, until it stopped close over Agnes – stopped, and turned slowly, so that the face of it confronted the upturned face of the woman in the chair.

There was a pause. Then, a supernatural movement disturbed the rigid repose of the dead face.

The closed eyelids opened slowly. The eyes revealed themselves, bright with the glassy film of death – and fixed their dreadful look on the woman in the chair.

Agnes saw that look; saw the eyelids of the living woman open slowly like the eyelids of the dead; saw her rise, as if in obedience to some silent command – and saw no more.

Her next conscious impression was of the sunlight pouring in at the window; of the friendly presence of Lady Montbarry at the bedside; and of the children's wondering faces peeping in at the door.

From *The Haunted Hotel* by Wilkie Collins, 1879

Someone in the Room: 2

He woke up, and the room was dark, the light off, and he felt a little sick. Turning in bed to find comfort for his body, he remembered that he had been in the middle of a crisis of fear. He looked about him in the dark, and saw again the dawn on the curtains. Then he heard a chink by the washstand, several feet nearer to his bed than the grandfather chair. He was not alone; the thing was still in the room.

By the faint light from the curtains he could just see that his visitor was by the washstand. There was a gentle clinking of china and a sound of water, and dimly he could see a woman standing.

'Undressing,' he said to himself, 'washing.'

His gorge rose at the thought that came to him. Was it possible that the woman was coming to bed?

It was that thought that had driven him with a wild rush from the room, and sent him marching for a second time up and down his grey and dewy lawns.

'And now,' thought Mr Templeton as he stood in the neat bedroom in the afternoon light and looked around him, 'Hettie's got to believe in the unfaithful or the supernatural.'

He crossed to the grandfather chair, and taking it in his two hands was about to push it on to the landing. But he paused. 'I'll leave it where it is to-night,' he thought, 'and go to bed as usual. For both our sakes I must find out something more about all this.'

Spending the rest of the afternoon out of doors, he played golf after tea, and eating a very light dinner he went to bed. His head ached badly from lack of sleep, but he was pleased to notice that his heart beat steadily. He took a couple of aspirin tablets to ease his head, and with a light novel settled himself down in bed to read and watch. Hettie would arrive at half-past twelve, and the butler was waiting up to let her in. Sandwiches, nicely covered from the air, were placed ready for her on a tray in the corner of the bedroom.

It was now eleven. He had an hour and a half to wait. 'She may come at any time,' he said (thinking of his visitor). He had turned the grandfather chair towards him, so that he could see the seat.

Quarter of an hour went by, and his head throbbed so violently that he put the book on his knees and altered the lights, turned out the brilliant reading lamp, and switched on the light which illumined the large face of the clock over the mantelpiece, so that he sat in shadow. Five minutes later he was asleep.

He lay with his face buried in the pillow, the pain still drumming in his head, aware of his headache even at the bottom of his sleep. Dimly he heard his wife arrive, and murmured a hope to himself that she would not wake him. A slight movement rustled around him as she entered the room and undressed, but his pain was so bad that he could not bring himself to give a sign of life, and soon, while he clung to his half sleep, he felt the bedclothes gently lifted and heard her slip in beside him.

Feeling chilly he drew his blanket closer round him. It was as though a draught was blowing about him in the bed, dispelling the mists of sleep and bringing him to himself. He felt a touch of remorse at his lack of welcome, and putting out his hand he sought his wife's beneath the sheet. Finding her wrist his fingers closed round it. She too was cold, strange, icy, and from her stillness and silence she appeared to be asleep.

'A cold drive from the station,' he thought, and held her wrist to warm it as he dozed again. 'She is positively chilling the bed,' he murmured to himself.

He was awakened by a roar beneath the window and the sweep of a light across the wall of the room. With amazement he heard the bolts shoot back across the front door. On the illuminated face of the clock over the fireplace he saw the hands standing at twenty-seven minutes past twelve. Then Mr Templeton, still gripping the wrist beside him, heard his wife's clear voice in the hall below.

From 'The Amorous Ghost' by Enid Bagnold, 1926

Someone in the Room: 3

It was dark when she opened her eyes. The pain in her head had woken her up. The digital clock on the dresser said ten thirty. Thirst, terrible thirst, and the glass by the bed was empty. *Someone else was in the room.*

She turned over on her back. Light through the thin white curtains. Yes, there. A child, a little girl. She was sitting in the chair against the wall.

Jesse could just see the outline clearly – the long yellow hair, the puff-sleeved dress, the dangling legs that didn't touch the floor. She tried to focus. Child . . . not possible. Apparition. No. Something occupying space. Something malevolent. Menace – And the child was looking at her.

Claudia.

She scrambled out of the bed, half falling, the bag in her arms still as she backed up against the wall. The little girl got up. There was the clear sound of her feet on the carpet. The sense of menace seemed to grow stronger. The child moved into the light from the window as she came towards Jesse, and the light struck her blue eyes, her rounded cheeks, her soft naked little arms.

Jesse screamed. Clutching the bag against her, she rushed blindly in the direction of the door. She clawed at the lock and chain, afraid to look over her shoulder. The screams were coming out of her uncontrollably. Someone was calling from the other side, and finally she had the door open and she was stumbling out into the hallway.

People surrounded her; but they couldn't stop her from getting away from the room. But then someone was helping her up because apparently she'd fallen again. Someone else had gotten a chair. She cried, trying to be quiet, yet unable to stop it, and she held the bag with the doll and the diary in both hands.

From *The Queen of the Damned* by Anne Rice, 1988

Thirty horse-power

She was a writing medium. This is what she wrote:

... I remember so well walking down the platform and looking at the illuminated clock at the end which told me that it was half-past eleven. I remember also my wondering whether I could get home before midnight. Then I remember the big motor, with its glaring head-lights and glitter of polished brass, waiting for me outside. It was my new thirty-horse-power Robur, which had only been delivered that day. I remember also asking Perkins, my chauffeur, how she had gone, and his saying that he thought she was excellent.

'I'll try her myself,' said I, and I climbed into the driver's seat....

We were just over the brow of this hill, where the grade is steepest, when the trouble began. I had been on the top speed, and wanted to get her on the free; but she stuck between gears, and I had to get her back on the top again. By this time she was going at a great rate, so I clapped on both brakes, and one after the other Perkins and I threw our bodies across, and then the next instant, going at fifty miles an hour, my right front wheel struck full on the right-hand pillar of my own gate. I heard the crash. I was conscious of flying through the air, and then – and then – !

When I became aware of my own existence once more I was among some brushwood in the shadow of the oaks upon the lodge side of the drive. A man was standing beside me. I imagined at first that it was Perkins, but when I looked again I saw that it was Stanley, a man whom I had known at college some years before, and for whom I had a really genuine affection. There was always something peculiarly sympathetic to me in Stanley's personality; and I was proud to think that I had some similar influence upon him. At the present moment I was surprised to see him, but I was like a man in a dream, giddy and shaken and quite prepared to take things as I found them without questioning them.

'What a smash!' I said. 'Good Lord, what an awful smash!'

He nodded his head, and even in the gloom I could see that he was smiling the gentle, wistful smile which I connected with him.

I was quite unable to move. Indeed, I had not any desire to try to move. But my senses were exceedingly alert. I saw the wreck of the motor lit up by the moving lanterns. I saw the little group of people and heard the hushed voices. There were the lodge-keeper and his wife, and one or two more. They were taking no notice of me, but were very busy round the car. Then suddenly I heard a cry of pain.

'The weight is on him. Lift it easy,' cried a voice.

'It's only my leg!' said another one, which I recognized as Perkins's. 'Where's master?' he cried.

'Here I am,' I answered, but they did not seem to hear me. They were all bending over something which lay in front of the car.

Stanley laid his hand upon my shoulder, and his touch was inexpressibly soothing. I felt light and happy, in spite of all.

'No pain, of course?' said he.

'None,' said I.

'There never is,' said he.

And then suddenly a wave of amazement passed over me. Stanley! Stanley! Why, Stanley had surely died of enteric at Bloemfontein in the Boer War!

'Stanley!' I cried, and the words seemed to choke my throat – 'Stanley, you are dead.'

He looked at me with the same old gentle, wistful smile.

'So are you,' he answered.

From 'How It Happened' by Sir Arthur Conan Doyle, 1918

Killing Time

Darkness crept in through my ear like oil. Someone was trying to break up the frozen globe of the earth with a massive hammer. The hammer struck the earth precisely eight times. But the earth failed to break up. It only cracked a little.

Eight o'clock, eight at night.

I woke with a shake of the head. My body was numb, my head ached. Had someone put me in a cocktail shaker with cracked ice and like a madman shaken me up?

There's nothing worse than waking up in total darkness. It's like having to go back and live life all over from the beginning. When I first opened my eyes, it was as if I were living someone else's life. After an extremely long time, this began to match up with my own life. A curious overlap this, my own life as someone else's. It was improbable that such a person as myself could even be living.

I went to the kitchen sink and splashed water on my face, then drank down a couple of glasses quickly. The water was cold as ice, but still my face was burning hot. I sat back down on the sofa amid the darkness and silence and began gradually to gather up the pieces of my life. I couldn't manage to grasp too much, but at least it was my life. Slowly I returned to myself. It's hard to explain what it is to get there, and it'd undoubtedly try your interest.

I had the feeling that someone was watching me, but I didn't pay it any mind. It's a feeling you get when you're all alone in a big room.

I thought about cells. Like my ex-wife had said, ultimately every last cell of you is lost. Lost even to yourself. I pressed the palm of my hand against my cheek. The face my hand felt in the dark wasn't my own, I didn't think. It was the face of another that had taken the shape of my face. But I couldn't remember the details. Everything – names, sensations, places – dissolved and was swallowed into the darkness.

In the dark the clock struck eight-thirty. The snow had stopped, but thick clouds still covered the sky. No light anywhere. For a long time, I lay buried in the sofa, fingers in my mouth. I couldn't see my hand. The heater was off, so the room was cold. Curled up under the blanket, I stared blankly out. I was crouching in the bottom of a deep well.

Time. Particles of darkness configured mysterious patterns on my retina. Patterns that degenerated without a sound, only to be replaced by new patterns. Darkness but darkness alone was shifting, like mercury in motionless space.

I put a stop to my thoughts and let time pass. Let time carry me along. Carry me to where a new darkness was configuring yet newer patterns.

The clock struck nine. As the ninth chime faded away, silence slipped in to fill its place.

'May I say my piece?' said the Rat.

'Fine by me,' said I.

'Fine by me,' said I.

'I came an hour earlier than the appointed time,' said the Rat apologetically.

'That's okay. As you can see, I wasn't doing anything.'

The Rat laughed quietly. He was behind me. Almost as if we were back-to-back.

'Seems like the old days,' said the Rat.

'I guess we can never get down to a good honest talk unless we've got time on our hands,' I said.

'It sure seems that way.' The Rat smiled.

Even in absolute lacquer-black darkness, seated back-to-back, I could tell he was smiling. You can tell a lot just by the tiniest change in the air. We used to be friends. So long ago, though, I could hardly remember when.

'Didn't someone once say, "A friend to kill time is a friend sublime"?'

'That was you who said that, no?'

'Sixth sense, sharp as ever. Right you are.'

I sighed. 'But this time around, with all this happening, my sixth sense has been way off. So far off it's embarrassing. And despite the number of hints you all have been giving me.'

'Can't be helped. You did better than most.'

We fell silent. The Rat seemed to be looking at his hand.

'I really made you go through a lot, didn't I?' said the Rat. 'I was a real pain. But it was the only way. There wasn't another soul I could depend on. Like I wrote in those letters.'

'That's what I want to ask you about. Because I can't accept everything just like that.'

'Of course not,' said the Rat, 'not without my setting the record straight. But before that, let's have a beer.'

The Rat stopped me before I could stand up.

'I'll get it,' said the Rat. 'This is my house, after all.'

I heard the Rat walk his regular path to the kitchen in total darkness and take an armful of beer out of the refrigerator, me opening and closing my eyes the whole while. The darkness of the room was only a bit different from the darkness of my eyes shut.

The Rat returned with his beer, which he set on the table. I felt around for a can, removed the pull ring, and drank half.

'It hardly seems like beer if you can't see it,' I said.

'You have to forgive me, but it has to be dark.'

We said nothing while we drank. . . .

'What happened after that is difficult to talk about,' said the Rat.

The Rat took his second empty can and squeezed a dent into it.

'Maybe you could ask me questions? You already know pretty much what there is to know, right?'

'Okay, but if it makes no difference to you, let's not start at the beginning.'

'Fire away.'

'You're already dead, aren't you?'

I don't know how long it took the Rat to reply. Could have been a few seconds, could have been . . . It was a long silence. My mouth was all dry inside.

'That's right,' said the Rat finally. 'I'm dead.'

From *A Wild Sheep Chase* by Haruki Murakami, 1982; translated from the Japanese by Alfred Birnbaum

Mary's Ghost

A PATHETIC BALLAD

1
'Twas in the middle of the night,
  To sleep young William tried,
When Mary's ghost came stealing in,
  And stood at his bed-side.

2
O William dear! O William dear!
  My rest eternal ceases;
Alas! my everlasting peace
  Is broken into pieces.

3
I thought the last of all my cares
  Would end with my last minute;
But tho' I went to my long home,
  I didn't stay long in it.

4
The body-snatchers they have come,
  And made a snatch at me;
It's very hard them kind of men
  Won't let a body be!

5
You thought that I was buried deep
  Quite decent like and chary,
But from her grave in Mary-bone
  They've come and boned your Mary.

6
The arm that used to take your arm
  Is took to Dr Vyse;
And both my legs are gone to walk
  The hospital at Guy's.

7
I vow'd that you should have my hand,
  But fate gives us denial;
You'll find it there, at Dr Bell's,
  In spirits and a phial.

8
As for my feet, the little feet
  You used to call so pretty,
There's one, I know, in Bedford Row,
  The t'other's in the city.

9
I can't tell where my head is gone,
  But Doctor Carpue can:
As for my trunk, it's all pack'd up
  To go by Pickford's van.

10
I wish you'd go to Mr P.
  And save me such a ride;
I don't half like the outside place,
  They've took for my inside.

11
The cock it crows – I must begone!
  My William we must part!
But I'll be yours in death, altho'
  Sir Astley has my heart.

12
Don't go to weep upon my grave,
  And think that there I be;
They haven't left an atom there
  Of my anatomie.

Thomas Hood, 1827

Eight

THINGS THAT GO BUMP

From ghoulies and ghosties and
long-leggetty beasties and things
that go bump in the night,
Good Lord, deliver us . . .

SCOTTISH PRAYER

The Cauld Lad o' Hilton

Wae's me, wae's me,
The acorn's not yet
Fallen from the tree
That's to grow the wood,
That's to make the cradle,
That's to rock the bairn,
That's to grow a man,
That's to lay me.

Poem by a Poltergeist: TRADITIONAL

'A lamentable noise'

Many vse at this day to serch and sifte, euery corner of the house before they go to bed, y they may sleep more soundly: & yet neuerthelesse, they heare some scrying out, and making a lamentable noise. &c.

It hath many times chaunced, that those of the house haue verily thought, that some body hath ouerthrowne the pots, platters, tables and trenchers, and tumbled them downe the stayres: but after it waxed day, they haue found all things orderly set in their places againe.

It is reported, that some spirits haue throwne the dore of from the hookes, and haue troubled and set all things in the house out of order, neuer setting them in their due place againe, and that they haue maruellously disquieted men with rumbling and making a great noise.

Sometimes there is heard a great noise in Abbeis, and in other solitarie places, as if it were coupers hooping and stopping vp wine vessels, or some other handicraftes men occupied about their labour, when it is most certayn, that all in the house are gone to bed, and haue betaken themselues to rest.

When houses are in building, the neighbours many times heare the carpenters, masons, and other artificers handling all things in such sorte, as if they were busily labouring in the day time. And this straunge wonder is ioyfully receiued as a sure token of good lucke.

There be some which iudge it commeth to passe naturally, that we suppose we heare these things in the nighte, which we heard before in the day time. Which question I leaue to be discussed of better learned than my selfe.

From *Of Ghostes and Spirits Walkyng by Nyghte*, 1512, anon. translation
from *De Spectris* by Louis Lavater, 1570

'In the time of Bishop Hugh'

We read in the History of the Bishops of Mans, that in the time of Bishop Hugh, who lived in 1135, they heard, in the house of Provost Nicholas, a spirit, who alarmed the neighbours and those who lived in the house, by uproar and frightful noises, as if he had thrown enormous stones against the walls, with a force which shook the roof, walls, and ceilings; he transported the dishes and the plates from one place to another, without their seeing the hand which moved them. This genius lighted a candle, though very far from the fire. Sometimes, when the meat was placed on the table, he would scatter bran, ashes, or soot, to prevent them from touching any of it. Amica, the wife of the Provost

Nicholas, having prepared some thread to be made into cloth, the spirit twisted and ravelled it in such a way, that all who saw it could not sufficiently admire the manner in which it was done.

Priests were called in, who sprinkled holy water every where, and desired all those who were there to make the sign of the cross. Towards the first and second night, they heard as it were the voice of a young girl, who, with sighs that seemed drawn from the bottom of her heart, said in a lamentable and sobbing voice, that her name was Garnier; and addressing itself to the provost, said, 'Alas! whence do I come? from what distant country, through how many storms, dangers, through snow, cold, fire, and bad weather, have I arrived at this place! I have not received power to harm any one – but prepare yourselves with the sign of the cross against a band of evil spirits, who are here only to do you harm; have a mass of the Holy Ghost said for me, and a mass for those defunct; and you, my dear sister-in-law, give some clothes to the poor, for me.'

They asked this spirit several questions on things past and to come, to which it replied very pertinently; it explained even the salvation and damnation of several persons; but it would not enter into any argument, nor yet into conference with learned men, who were sent by the Bishop of Mans; this last circumstance is very remarkable, and casts some suspicion on this apparition.

From *The Phantom World* by Augustine Calmet, 1746, translated by the
Rev. H. Christmas

A Visit to the Drummer of Tedworth

About this time I went to the House, on purpose, to enquire the Truth of those Passages, of which there was so loud a report. It had ceased from its Drumming and ruder Noises before I came thither, but most of the more remarkable Circumstances before related, were confirmed to me there, by several of the Neighbours together, who had been present at them. At this time it used to haunt the Children, and that as soon as they were laid. They went to Bed that Night I was there, about 8 of the Clock, when a Maid servant coming down from them, told us it was come. The Neighbours that were there, and two Ministers who had seen and heard divers times, went away, but Mr *Mompesson* and I, and a Gentleman that came with me, went up. I heard a strange scratching as I went up the Stairs, and when we came into the Room, I perceived it was just behind the bolster of the Childrens Bed, and seemed to be against the Tick. It was as loud a scratching, as one with long Nails could make upon a Bolster. There were little modest Girls in the Bed, between 7 and 8 Years old, as I guest. I saw their Hands out of the Cloaths, and they could not contribute to the Noise that was behind their Heads; they had been used to it, and had still some body or other in the Chamber with them, and therefore seemed not to be much affrighted. I standing at the Bed's head, thrust my Hand behind the Bolster, directing it to the place whence the Noise seem'd to come, whereupon the Noise ceased there, and was heard in another part of the Bed; but when I had taken out my Hand it returned, and was heard in the same place as before. I had been told that it would imitate Noises, and made trial by scratching several times upon the Sheet, as 5 and 7 and 10, which it followed and still stop'd at my Number. I search'd under and behind the Bed, turned up the Cloaths to the Bed-cords, grasp'd the Bolster, sounded the Wall behind, and made all the search that possibly I could to find if there were any Trick, Contrivance, or common Cause of it; the like did my Friend, but we could discover nothing. So that I was then verily persuaded, and am so still, that the Noise was made by some *Daemon* or *Spirit*. After it had scratch'd about half an Hour or more, it went into the midst of the Bed under the Children, and there seem'd to pant like a Dog out of Breath very loudly. I put my Hand upon the place, and felt the Bed bearing up against it, as if something within had thrust it up. I grasp'd the Feathers, to feel if any living thing were in it. I look'd under and every where about, to see if there were any Dog or Cat, or any such Creature in the Room, and so we all did, but found nothing. The motion it caused by this panting was so strong, that it shook the Room and Windows very sensibly. It continued thus more than half an Hour, while my Friend and I stayed in the Room, and as long after, as we were told.

From *Saducismus Triumphatus* by Joseph Glanvill, 1681

The Daemon of Spraiton

The next day the young man was riding home to his Masters house, accompanyed by a Servant of the Gentle womans near *Totness*, and near about the time of their entrance (or a little before they came) into the Parish of *Spraiton*, there appeared to be upon the horse behind the young man, the resemblance of the *second wife* of the old Gentleman. This Daemon often threw the young man off his horse, and cast him with such violence to the ground, as was great astonishment, not only to the Gentlewomans Servant (with him) but to divers others, who were spectators of the frightful action, the ground resounding with great noise, by reason of the incredible force, with which he was cast upon it.

At divers other times he hath been in danger to be strangled with Cravats, and Handkerchiefs, that he hath worn about his Neck, which have been drawn so close, that with the sudden violence he hath near been choaked, and hardly escaped death.

The Spectre hath shewed great offence at the Perriwigs which the young man used to wear, for they are often torn from his head after a very strange manner, one, that he esteemed above the rest, he put in a small box, and that box he placed in another, which he set against the wall of his Chamber, placing a Joint-stool, with other weight, a top of it; but in short time the boxes were broken in sunder, and the Perriwig rended into many small parts and tatters: Another time, lying in his Masters Chamber, with his Perriwig on his Head, to secure it from danger, within a little time it was torn from him, and reduced into very small fragments. At another time one of his Shoe-strings was observed (without the assistance of any hand) to come of its own accord out of his shoe, and fling itself to the other side of the Room; the other was crawling after it, but a Maid espying that, with her hand drew it out, and it strangely *clasp'd*, and *curl'd* about her hand like a living *Eel*, or *Serpent*; this is testified by a Lady of considerable Quality, too great for exception, who was an Eye-witness. The same Lady shewed Mr *C.* one of the young mans Gloves, which was torn in his pocket, whilst she was by; which is so dexterously tatter'd, and so artificially torn, that it is conceived a Cutler could not have contrived an Instrument, to have laid it abroad so accurately, and all this done in the pocket, in the compass of one minute.

The Female Ghost comes with a great deal of violence, and an impetuous Temper, as if disgusted for the performance of what the other Spectre enjoined, and this seems the more probable, if we consider how quickly she gets behind the young man, after he had answered the desires of the other Ghost; she permits him not to go home in quiet, but seizes him as soon as he comes within the verge of the Parish: by which it looks as if these Spirits were tyed to some limits, or bounds, that they cannot pass. . . . The whole Narrative of that She-Dæmon abounds with a great deal of Malice, and a great many ludicrous passages; but doubtless (were it not for the restraining power of the Almighty) the Comical part would soon end in dreadful Tragedy.

From *Pandæmonium* by Richard Bovet, 1684

Old Jeffrey

John Wesley's 'Summary of the Phenomena' at Epworth Rectory in 1716:

1. Presently after any noise was heard the wind commonly rose, and whistled very loud round the house, and increased with it.

2. The signal was given, which my father likens to the turning round of a windmill when the wind changes; Mr. Hoole (Rector of Haxey) to the planing of deal boards; my sister, to the swift winding up of a jack. It commonly began at the corner of the top of the nursery.

3. Before it came into any room the latches were frequently lifted up, the windows clattered, and whatever iron or brass was about the chamber rung and jarred exceedingly.

4. When it was in any room, let them make what noise they would, as they sometimes did on purpose, its dead, hollow note would be closely heard above them all.

5. It constantly knocked while the prayers for the king and prince were repeating, and was plainly heard by all in the room but my father, and sometimes by him, as were also the thundering knocks at the *amen*.

6. The sound very often seemed in the air in the middle of a room, nor could they ever make any such themselves by any contrivance.

7. Though it seemed to rattle down the pewter, to clap the doors, draw the curtains, kick the man's shoes up and down, etc., yet it never moved anything except the latches, otherwise than making it tremble; unless once, when it threw open the nursery door.

8. The mastiff, though he barked violently at it the first day he came, yet whenever it came after that, nay, sometimes before the family perceived it, he ran whining, or quite silent, to shelter himself behind some of the company.

9. It never came by day till my mother ordered the horn to be blown.

10. After that time scarce any one would go from one room into another but the latch of the room they went to was lifted up before they touched it.

11. It never came once into my father's study till he talked to it sharply, called it *deaf and dumb devil*, and bid it cease to disturb the innocent children, and come to him in his study if it had anything to say to him.

12. From the time of my mother desiring it not to disturb her from five to six, it was never heard in her chamber from five till she came downstairs, nor at any other time when she was employed in devotion.

13. Whether our clock went right or wrong, it always came as near as could be guessed when by the night it wanted a quarter of ten.

From *The Records of Samuel Wesley. Collected and Described by John Wesley, c.*1771

'She could not help trembling . . .'

The men having withdrawn, the lady seated herself at the dressing table, and having opened her portmantau to take out some linen for the ensuing day, she burst into tears on viewing the small quantity of necessaries she possessed; she cast a retrospection on her past calamities, they made her shudder; she looked forward to the future, all was dark and gloomy; she wrung her hands. 'What will become of me, unhappy as I am, where can I fly? who will receive a poor unfortunate, without family or friends? The little money I have will be soon exhausted, and what it is to be the fate of poor Albert, who has left all to follow me!' Overcome with sorrow, she wept aloud. When, turning her eyes to the window, she saw a light glide by from the opposite wing, which her room fronted, and which Bertha had informed her was particularly haunted. At first she thought it was imagination; she arose and placed her candle in the chimney; curiosity suspended sorrow – she returned and seated herself at the window, and very soon after she saw a faint glimmering light pass a second time; exceedingly surprised, but not terrified, she continued in her situation: she saw nothing further. She at length determined to go to rest, but with an intention to visit every part of the house the following day. She got into bed, but could not sleep. About twelve o'clock she heard plainly a clanking of chains, which was followed by two or three heavy groans; she started up and listened, it was presently repeated, and seemed to die away by gentle degrees; soon after she heard a violent noise, like two or three doors clapping to with great force. Though unaccustomed to fear, she could not help trembling. She felt some inclination to call up Joseph, she then recollected Albert was in the next room; she knocked at the wainscot and called Albert! No answer was made. She got out of bed, and throwing on a loose gown, took her candle, and, opening the door of the next apartment, went up to the bed; she saw he was buried under the clothes. 'Albert,' said she, 'do not be afraid, 'tis your mistress with a light;' he then ventured to raise himself, and though but little inclined to mirth, she could not refrain from smiling at the fright he was in; the drops of perspiration ran down his face, his eyes were starting, and he was incapable of speaking for some time. 'Pray, Albert,' said his lady, 'have you heard any particular noise?' 'Noise,' repeated he. 'O Lord! all the ghosts have been here together to frighten me.' 'Here – where,' asked she, 'in this room?' 'I believe so,' he replied; 'in this or the next I am sure they were; there was a score or two in chains, then there were groans and cries: but pray, madam, leave the candle a minute at the door, I will throw on my clothes and get down into the kitchen and never come up stairs again.' . . .

She conceived there must be some mystery which, on the following day, if her health permitted, she resolved, if possible, to explore.

From *The Castle of Wolfenbach* by Eliza Parsons, 1793

The racketing spectre

'About eight o'clock in the evening a fresh scene began; the first thing that happened, was a whole row of pewter dishes, except one, fell from off a shelf to the middle of the floor, rolled about a little while, then settled; and, what is almost beyond belief, as soon as they were quiet, turned upside down; they were then put on the dresser, and went through the same a second time; next fell a whole row of pewter plates from off the second shelf over the dresser to the ground, and being taken up and put on the dresser one in another, they were thrown down again.

'The next thing was two eggs that were upon one of the pewter shelves; one of them flew off, crossed the kitchen, struck a cat on the head, and then broke in pieces. . . .

'The next thing that followed was a mustard pot, that jumped out of a closet, and was broken. A single cup that stood upon the table (almost the only thing remaining) jumped up, flew across the kitchen, ringing like a bell, and then was dashed to pieces against the dresser. A candlestick that stood on the chimney-shelf flew across the kitchen to the parlour door, at about fifteen feet distance. A tea-kettle, under the dresser, was thrown out about two feet; another kettle that stood at one end of the range, was thrown against the iron that is fixed to prevent children falling into the fire. A tumbler with rum-and-water in it that stood upon a waiter upon a table in the parlour, jumped about ten feet, and was broken. The table then fell down, and along with it a silver tankard belonging to Mrs Golding, the waiter, in which stood the tumbler, and a candlestick. A case bottle then flew to pieces.

'The next circumstance was a ham that hung in one side of the kitchen chimney; it raised itself from the hook and fell down to the ground. Some time after, another ham that hung on the other side of the chimney, likewise underwent the same fate. Then a flitch of bacon, which hung up in the same chimney, fell down.

'All the family were eye-witnesses to these circumstances, as well as other persons, some of whom were so alarmed and shocked, that they could not bear to stay, and were happy in getting away, though the unhappy family were left in the midst of their distresses. Most of the genteel families around were continually sending to inquire after them,and whether all was over or not. Is it not surprising that some among them had not the inclination and resolution to try to unravel this most intricate affair, at a time when it would have been in their power to have done so?'

From *The Nightside of Nature* by Catharine Crowe, 1849

Tietjens is uneasy

In the very short pauses of thunder I tried to sleep, but it seemed that some one wanted me very urgently. He, whoever he was, was trying to call me by name, but his voice was no more than a husky whisper. The thunder ceased, and Tietjens went into the garden and howled at the low moon. Somebody tried to open my door, walked about and about through the house, and stood breathing heavily in the verandahs, and just when I was falling asleep I fancied that I heard a wild hammering and clamouring above my head or on the door.

I ran into Strickland's room and asked him whether he was ill, and had been calling for me. He was lying on his bed half dressed, a pipe in his mouth. 'I thought you'd come,' he said. 'Have I been walking round the house recently?'

I explained that he had been tramping in the dining-room and the smoking-room and two or three other places; and he laughed and told me to go back to bed. I went back to bed and slept till the morning, but through all my mixed dreams I was sure I was doing some one an injustice in not attending to his wants. What those wants were I could not tell; but a fluttering, whispering, bolt-fumbling, lurking, loitering Someone was reproaching me for my slackness, and, half awake, I heard the howling of Tietjens in the garden and the threshing of the rain.

I lived in that house for two days. Strickland went to his office daily, leaving me alone for eight or ten hours with Tietjens for my only companion. As long as the full light lasted I was comfortable, and so was Tietjens; but in the twilight she and I moved into the back verandah and cuddled each other for company. We were alone in the house, but none the less it was much too fully occupied by a tenant with whom I did not wish to interfere. I never saw him, but I could see the curtains between the rooms quivering where he had just passed through; I could hear the chairs creaking as the bamboos sprung under a weight that had just quitted them; and I could feel when I went to get a book from the dining-room that somebody was waiting in the shadows of the front verandah till I should have gone away. Tietjens made the twilight more interesting by glaring into the darkened rooms with every hair erect, and following the motions of something that I could not see. She never entered the rooms, but her eyes moved interestedly: that was quite sufficient. Only when my servant came to trim the lamps and make all light and habitable she would come in with me and spend her time sitting on her haunches, watching an invisible extra man as he moved about behind my shoulder. Dogs are cheerful companions.

I explained to Strickland, gently as might be, that I would go over to the Club and find for myself quarters there.

From 'The Return of Imray' by Rudyard Kipling, 1900

Annie

'I know what you say about ghosts is quite true. We 'ad one to our cottage. Oh, yes! We come down to cottage arter it were empty, like, and I got Vicar to come and bless cottage. You see, it did belong to old Annie Luker, and she wasn't well liked. Everybody said she 'ad dark dealings; could turn 'erself into a rabbit. Well, arter she died, there weren't no one as 'ud go near. But my 'usband 'e was a clever man, bit too clever, if you ask me, 'e say, "We'll go to cottage." So us took it.

'Folk in village didn't like it very much, and they come and say to me, "Does 'ee know 'twas Annie Luker's cottage?"

'I says, "Yes, I'll get Vicar to come and bless it."

'So we did, and we went there, me and my 'usband, and our daughter Mary. Well, us 'ad been there about three months, when all of a sudden, one night, I 'ears a girt bang. I sits up in bed, and I listens, and someone come in! I could 'ear 'en downstairs. I nudges 'usband, see.

'"Bob," I says, "wake up, will 'ee? What be it?"

'Well, we sat up in bed, and then we could 'ear someone coming upstairs – bump, bump, and kerflop, kerflop.

'"Usband, 'e got proper cross, an 'e calls out, "Mary, what be 'ee about? Coming in this time o' night!"

'Then us 'eard our Mary, from 'er bedroom next to ours, by the passage-way, and she say, "Dad, oh! Dad, I've been 'ome hours. Whatever is it?" And then 'er goes under blankets, like I did.

'My 'usband, 'e listened, and then we 'eard 'en again, thump, thump, kerflop, kerflop coming along up the stairs towards our door, and all of a sudden, my 'usband – 'oo nothing much worried 'im – 'e say, "Oh! 'Tis old Annie Luker!" And 'e come under blankets too.

'Well, sometimes she'd come and sometimes she 'ouldn't. Never see 'er but 'ear 'er, yes. And then, my 'usband, 'e was took ill, and not long ago 'e died. 'Aven't 'eard Annie since. Folks say she knew what she wanted, and she come for 'im.'

Collected in Somerset in 1963, for Folktales of England
by K. M. Briggs and Ruth L. Tongue

'We four'

By now she had led us into the kitchen at the back of the house, and there she and my mother stood together on the coconut mat in front of the range and clung together in a curiously calm yet passionate embrace. I was very much puzzled by their imprudence. Surely the person who had thrown the poker through the window and overturned the wardrobe, or whatever it was, must still be in the house, and presumably at large. I was thinking that it was extraordinary of them to take no precautions for their defence, but to stand there crying and vulnerable, when a movement outside the window caught my eye. A few yards from the house there was a clothesline, on which there were hanging four dishcloths. Three heavy iron saucepans sailed through the air, hit the dishcloths, and fell on the ground. Evidently they had taken to the air without due preparation, for their lids were scattered on the ground below them. I put down the poker, for I realised the nature of the violence raging through this house.

'Is this what you call a poltergeist?' I asked Mamma. We had read about them in books by Andrew Lang.

'Yes, Rose,' said Mamma, her voice quivering with indignation, 'you see I am right, supernatural things are horrible.'

I was a little frightened, but not much; and I tried to remain imperturbable, because I assumed that the supernatural took this coarse form in Constance's house because she lived among common people, and I had no desire to be impolite by drawing attention to her circumstances.

'If you are old-fashioned enough to eat soup in the middle of the day,' said Constance, 'I have still some of the turkey broth, and I was thinking of frying some Christmas pudding, and there are tangerines.

Oh, my dear, it has been so dreadful. There is a thing called the Society of Psychical Research – oh, watch the dresser, it's starting again.'

Out in the pantry, a jug fell off a shelf and was smashed to pieces on the floor. Through the open door we were showered with small pieces of coal. Outside a tattoo was banged on the side of a saucepan, louder and louder, so that for the time being it was useless to talk.

When the din had died away my mother breathed indignantly, looking about her with a curled lip. 'The lowest of the low.'

'The dregs,' agreed Constance, 'but this Society, it made everything so much worse. They seemed to think poor Rosamund had something to do with it. They followed her about as if she were a pickpocket, they questioned me about her as if she were a bad child, though it happens just as much when she is not in the house or anywhere near it, and though the wretched things are harder on her than on anyone else, they drag the clothes off her bed at night.'

'It is always terribly hard on the children,' sighed Mamma.

'Well, it was hard on us,' said Constance calmly, 'and we are here.'

My mother made a tragic gesture. But Constance ignored it and continued. 'The trouble is to arrange for her to have friends. You are lucky in having four, they can find company among themselves. But as Rosamund is the only one she must find friends outside and she could have done it if these people had not come bothering us, for she can keep her own secrets, but now everyone knows.' Her eyes moved from my mother to me and were benignant. 'But now you have come, Rose, she has at least one friend. Go out and fetch her. She is in the garden.'

'Do I have to go out past the clothes-line?' I asked.

She looked out of the window and saw what I meant. A large cooking pot had sailed through the air just as the saucepans had done.

'My preserving pan, which I packed away in the attic for the winter!' she said primly, as if it were a housemaid's fault that it had taken this journey through space. 'Come with me, I will show you the other way out.' She took me into the dining-room, which looked as if a lunatic had been laying about him with a hatchet, and opened the French windows, which gave on to a neatly-kept strip of garden running down to a railway cutting. At the very end were some hutches, and by these was kneeling a little girl of my sort of age. . . .

There was a golden heaviness about her face, to look on it was like watching honey drop slowly from a spoon.

'There's one thing,' said Rosamund, coming to a halt. 'They never hurt us. They just break things and spoil things, so that we have to spend our lives mending and washing.' Thus she managed to say 'Don't be afraid,' without making it plain that she had noticed I was afraid, as for the last few moments, finding I had a mob of spectral monsters between my Mamma and me, I certainly had been, though not to the degree that an adult would have been. That was Rosamund's way, I was to find.

So we went in by the back door, and before we reached the kitchen heard the din that possessed it. Mamma and Constance were sitting at the table, their faces contorted as by neuralgic pain, while a flour-dredger, a tin-tray, and a spikey cloud of kitchen cutlery were thrown into the room through the other door, forks striking spoons, knives clashing on knives. But as soon as Rosamund and I entered the kitchen all this possessed ironmongery suddenly became quiet. Each fork, each spoon, knife, the flour-dredger and the tray, wavered slowly downwards and softly took the ground, after the meditative fashion of falling leaves. There they lay and stirred no more, nor were ever to stir again in all the known history of that house. To drive out the evil presence it had been needed simply that we four should be in a room together, nothing more.

We ate in the kitchen, because all the other rooms were even more disordered. It was a very good meal, for all the Christmas things were still about. While I was eating my turkey soup I noticed that a packet of table salt on the mantelpiece had been overturned and was soberly voiding its contents in a thin white trickle which spread out into a fine spray as it reached the hearthstone below. I exclaimed in wonder, but without apprehension. There was nothing violent or malicious about the staid little flow, and so did Rosamund, but though our mothers looked sharply in the direction of my pointing finger, they looked away again at once. Rosamund and I thought they had not seen the salt and tried to direct their attention to it, but they kept their eyes on the table-cloth and asked us questions about our schools. It may be that they knew more than we did, that in setting the salt to pour out quietly on the hearthstone the defeated presence had performed a rite which was sad for them, and that, therefore, it was ungenerous for us, the victors, to spy on them. I can never be sure.

From *The Fountain Overflows* by Rebecca West, 1956

Nine

FAKES AND MISTAKES

The town it long has been in pain
   About the phantom in Cock Lane
To find it out they strove in vain
   Not one thing they neglected:
They searched the bed and room compleat,
   To see if man was any cheat,
While little miss that looks so sweet,
   Was not the least suspected.

            BROADSIDE BALLAD

A father comes home

PHILOLACHES: Whatever shall I do? My father will arrive and find me drunk, the house full of guests and women. It's a nice time to be asking myself what to do, with my father at the door – as bad as digging a well when your throat's parched with thirst. . . .

TRANIO: Never say die. I'll see you're all right. Look, what do you say if I fix it so that when your father arrives, he won't come in – what's more, he'll run for his life in the opposite direction? Only you others must get inside, and get all this stuff cleared away, as quick as you can.

[Later]

(THEOPROPIDES *goes up to the door, is surprised to find it locked.*)

THEOPROPIDES: What's the meaning of this? The door bolted and barred, in the daytime? I'll have to knock. . . . Is anybody there? . . . Will someone open this door?

(*He continues to hammer at the door;* TRANIO *approaches, as if just arrived from a distance.*)

TRANIO: Who can that be, outside our house?

THEOPROPIDES *(seeing him)*: It's Tranio. My servant Tranio! . . .

TRANIO: Fly, sir, fly, I beseech you; avoid this house! Come away, come away, over here. (*He drags him as far away as possible.*) You're sure you touched the door?

THEOPROPIDES: How do you think I could knock at the door without touching it?

TRANIO: Alas, you have surely caused the death –

THEOPROPIDES: Whose death?

TRANIO: Of all your house. . . .

THEOPROPIDES: For the love of all the gods, tell me what this is about. . . .

TRANIO: A horrible crime has been committed.

THEOPROPIDES: What crime? What are you talking about?

TRANIO: A crime. A horrible crime. An old and ancient crime.

THEOPROPIDES: An ancient crime?

TRANIO: So it seems, according to what we have found out.

THEOPROPIDES: Well, *what* crime, and who did it? Out with it.

TRANIO: A host took his guest by the throat and murdered him; the very man, I suppose, who sold you this house.

THEOPROPIDES: Murdered his guest?

TRANIO: And robbed his guest; and buried his guest; here in this very house.

THEOPROPIDES: How did you get on the track of this terrible occurrence?

TRANIO: I'll tell you. It was like this. One evening your son happened to be dining out. As soon as he got home, we all went to bed. We all went to sleep. There was a light burning which I had accidentally forgotten to put out. Suddenly he let out a terrible cry.

THEOPROPIDES: Who did? My son?

TRANIO: Don't interrupt, please. Just listen. He said the dead man had appeared to him in his sleep.

THEOPROPIDES: In his sleep? Really?

TRANIO: Yes, really. Listen. The dead man, so your son says, spoke to him as follows –

THEOPROPIDES: In his sleep?

TRANIO: He couldn't very well speak to him awake, could he, since he was killed sixty years ago? Really, sometimes you are so dense –

THEOPROPIDES: All right, all right, I won't say a word. Go on.

TRANIO: And this is what the dead man said, to your son, in his sleep: 'I am a stranger from over the seas; my name is Diapontius. But here I dwell; here is my appointed habitation. For Hades will not grant me leave to cross the waters of Acheron, since I was untimely slain. I trusted and was deceived. My host slew me in this house, and in this house he buried me, without rite or ceremony, secretly, in this very house, the villain; and he did it for my money. You must go hence, for this house is a house of abomination, a domicile of sin.' That is what the ghost said. As for the ghostly manifestations that have been going on here, it would take more than a year to describe them all.
(A noise issues from the house.)

THEOPROPIDES: Hark, what was that?

TRANIO: Oh my goodness, what was it?

THEOPROPIDES: Someone at the door!

TRANIO: The ghost walks!

THEOPROPIDES: My blood is frozen! The dead are coming to drag me to Acheron! . . . Hercules, come to my aid! . . . *(He hurries off.)*

TRANIO: And mine . . . to get this old man properly twisted today. Look down, oh great immortal gods, upon my wonderful wickedness!

Mostellaria (or *The Ghost*) by Plautus, *c.*200 BC, translated by E. F. Watling

'The artificial sort'

Various ways have been proposed by the learned for the laying of ghosts. Those of the artificial sort are easily quieted. Thus when a fryer, personating an apparition, haunted the chambers of the last Emperor Josephus, the present King Augustus, then at the Imperial Court, flung him out of the window and laid him effectually.

From *The Gentleman's Magazine*, 1732

Cock Lane

On the night of the 1st of February, many gentlemen, eminent for their rank and character, were, by the invitation of the Reverend Mr Aldrich, of Clerkenwell, assembled at his house, for the examination of the noises supposed to be made by a departed spirit, for the detection of some enormous crime.

'About ten at night the gentlemen met in the chamber in which the girl, supposed to be disturbed by a spirit, had, with proper caution, been put to bed by several ladies. They sat rather more than an hour, and, hearing nothing, went downstairs, when they interrogated the father of the girl, who denied, in the strongest terms, any knowledge or belief of fraud.

'The supposed spirit had before publicly promised, by an affirmative knock, that it would attend one of the gentlemen into the vault under the church of St John, Clerkenwell, where the body is deposited, and give a token of her presence there by a knock upon her coffin; it was therefore determined to make this trial of the existence or veracity of the supposed spirit.

'While they were inquiring and deliberating, they were summoned into the girl's chamber by some ladies who were near her bed, and who had heard knocks and scratches. When the gentlemen entered, the girl declared that she felt the spirit like a mouse upon her back, and was required to hold her hands out of bed. From that time, though the spirit was very solemnly required to manifest its existence by appearance, by impression on the hand or body of any present, by scratches, knocks, or any other agency, no evidence of any preternatural power was exhibited.

'The spirit was then very seriously advertised that the person to whom the promise was made of striking the coffin was then about to visit the vault, and that the performance of the promise was then claimed. The company at one o'clock went into the church, and the gentleman to whom the promise was made went with another into the vault. The spirit was solemnly required to perform its promise, but nothing more than silence ensued: the person supposed to be accused by the spirit then went down with several others, but no effect was perceived. Upon their return they examined the girl, but could draw no confession from her. Between two and three she desired and was permitted to go home with her father.

'It is, therefore, the opinion of the whole assembly, that the child has some art of making or counterfeiting a particular noise, and that there is no agency of any higher cause.'

A report by Samuel Johnson in *The Gentleman's Magazine*, 1762

Don Juan

Lord Henry, who had now discuss'd his chocolate,
 Also the muffin whereof he complain'd,
Said, Juan had not got his usual look elate,
 At which he marvell'd, since it had not rain'd;
Then ask'd her Grace what news were of the duke of late?
 Her Grace replied, *his* Grace was rather pain'd
With some slight, light, hereditary twinges
Of gout, which rusts aristocratic hinges.

Then Henry turn'd to Juan, and address'd
 A few words of condolence on his state:
'You look,' quoth he, 'as if you had had your rest
 Broken in upon by the Black Friar of late.'
'What Friar?' said Juan; and he did his best
 To put the question with an air sedate,
Or careless; but the effort was not valid
To hinder him from growing still more pallid.

'Oh! have you never heard of the Black Friar?
 The spirit of these walls?' – 'In truth not I.'
'Why Fame – but Fame you know's sometimes a liar –
 Tells an odd story, of which by and by:
Whether with time the spectre has grown shyer,
 Or that our sires had a more gifted eye
For such sights, though the tale is half believed,
The Friar of late has not been oft perceived.'

*

The night was as before: he was undrest,
 Saving his night-gown, which is an undress;
Completely *sans culotte*, and without vest;
 In short, he hardly could be clothed with less:
But apprehensive of his spectral guest,
 He sate with feelings awkward to express
(By those who have not had such visitations),
Expectant of the ghost's fresh operations.

And not in vain he listen'd; – Hush! what's that?
 I see – I see – Ah, no! – 'tis not – yet 'tis –
Ye powers! it is the – the – the – Pooh! the cat!
 The devil may take that stealthy pace of his!
So like a spiritual pit-a-pat,

Or tiptoe of an amatory Miss,
Gliding the first time to a *rendezvous*,
And dreading the chaste echoes of her shoe.

Again – what is't? The wind! No, no, – this time
    It is the sable Friar as before,
With awful footsteps regular as rhyme,
    Or (as rhymes may be in these days) much more.
Again through shadows of the night sublime,
    When deep sleep fell on men, and the world wore
The starry darkness round her like a girdle
Spangled with gems – the monk made his blood curdle.

A noise like to wet fingers drawn on glass,
    Which sets the teeth on edge; and a slight clatter
Like showers which on the midnight gusts will pass,
    Sounding like very supernatural water,
Came over Juan's ear, which throbb'd, alas!
    For immaterialism's a serious matter;
So that even those whose faith is the most great
In souls immortal, shun them *tête-à-tête*.

Were his eyes open? – Yes! and his mouth too.
    Surprise has this effect – to make one dumb,
Yet leave the gate which eloquence slips through
    As wide, as if a long speech were to come.
Nigh and more nigh the awful echoes drew,
    Tremendous to a mortal tympanum:
His eyes were open, and (as was before
Stated) his mouth. What open'd next? – the door.

It open'd with a most infernal creak,
    Like that of hell. 'Lasciate ogni speranza
Voi ch' entrate!' The hinge seem'd to speak,
    Dreadful as Dante's rima, or this stanza:
Or – but all words upon such themes are weak;
    A single shade's sufficient to entrance a
Hero – for what is substance to a spirit?
Or how is't *matter* trembles to come near it?

The door flew wide, not swiftly, – but, as fly
    The sea-gulls, with a steady, sober flight –
And then swung back; nor close – but stood awry,
    Half letting in long shadows on the light,
Which still in Juan's candlesticks burn'd high,

For he had two, both tolerably bright,
And in the doorway, darkening darkness stood
The sable Friar in his solemn hood.

Don Juan shook, as erst he had been shaken
    The night before; but being sick of shaking,
He first inclined to think he had been mistaken;
    And then to be ashamed of such mistaking;
His own internal ghost began to awaken
    Within him, and to quell his corporal quaking –
Hinting that soul and body on the whole
Were odds against a disembodied soul.

And then his dread grew wrath, and his wrath fierce,
    And he arose, advanced – the shade retreated;
But Juan, eager now, the truth to pierce,
    Followed, his veins no longer cold, but heated,
Resolved to thrust the mystery *carte* and *tierce*,
    At whatsoever risk of being defeated:
The ghost stopp'd, menaced, then retired, until
He reach'd the ancient wall, then stood stone still.

Juan put forth one arm – Eternal powers!
    It touch'd no soul, nor body, but the wall,
On which the moonbeams fell in silvery showers,
    Chequer'd with all the tracery of the hall:
He shudder'd, as no doubt the bravest cowers
    When he can't tell what 'tis that doth appal.
How odd, a single hobgoblin's nonentity
Should cause more fear than a whole host's identity!

But still the shade remain'd: the blue eyes glared,
    And rather variably for stony death;
Yet one thing rather good the grave had spared,
    The ghost had a remarkably sweet breath:
A straggling curl show'd he had been fairhair'd;
    A red lip, with two rows of pearls beneath,
Gleam'd forth, as through the casement's ivy shroud
The moon peep'd, just escaped from a grey cloud.

And Juan, puzzled, but still curious, thrust
    His other arm forth – Wonder upon wonder!
It press'd upon a hard but glowing bust,
    Which beat as if there was a warm heart under.
He found, as people on most trials must,

That he had made at first a silly blunder,
And that in his confusion he had caught
Only the wall, instead of what he sought.

The ghost, if ghost it were, seem'd a sweet soul
    As ever lurk'd beneath a holy hood:
A dimpled chin, a neck of ivory, stole
    Forth into something much like flesh and blood;
Back fell the sable frock and dreary cowl,
    And they reveal'd – alas! that e'er they should!
In full, voluptuous, but *not o'er*grown bulk,
The phantom of her frolic Grace – FitzFulke!

*

Our Hero was, in Canto the Sixteenth,
    Left in a tender moonlight situation,
Such as enables Man to show his strength
    Moral or physical: on this occasion
Whether his virtue triumphed – or, at length,
    His vice – for he was of a kindling nation –
Is more than I shall venture to describe; –
Unless some Beauty with a kiss should bribe.

I leave the thing a problem, like all things: –
    The morning came – and breakfast, tea and toast,
Of which most men partake, but no one sings.
    The company whose birth, wealth, worth, have cost
My trembling Lyre already several strings,
    Assembled with our hostess, and mine host;
The guests dropped in – the last but one, Her Grace,
The latest, Juan, with his virgin face.

Which best it is to encounter – Ghost, or none,
    'Twere difficult to say – but Juan looked
As if he had combated with more than one,
    Being wan and worn, with eyes that hardly brooked
The light, that through the Gothic windows shone:
    Her Grace, too, had a sort of air rebuked –
Seemed pale and shivered, as if she had kept
A vigil, or dreamt rather more than slept.

From *Don Juan* by Lord Byron, 1819–24

Ichabod's ride

Just as this moment a plashy tramp by the side of the bridge caught the sensitive ear of Ichabod. In the dark shadow of the grove, on the margin of the brook, he beheld something huge, misshapen, black, and towering. It stirred not, but seemed gathered up in the gloom, like some gigantic monster ready to spring upon the traveller.

The hair of the affrighted pedagogue rose upon his head with terror. What was to be done? To turn and fly was now too late; and besides, what chance was there of escaping ghost or goblin, if such it was, which could ride upon the wings of the wind? Summoning up, therefore, a show of courage, he demanded in stammering accents – 'Who are you?' He received no reply. He repeated his demand in a still more agitated voice. Still there was no answer. Once more he cudgelled the sides of the inflexible Gunpowder, and, shutting his eyes, broke forth with involuntary fervour into a psalm tune. Just then the shadowy object of alarm put itself in motion, and, with a scramble and a bound, stood at once in the middle of the road. Though the night was dark and dismal, yet the form of the unknown might now in some degree be ascertained. He appeared to be a horseman of large dimensions, and mounted on a black horse of powerful frame. He made no offer of molestation or sociability, but kept aloof on one side of the road, jogging along on the blind side of old Gunpowder, who had now got over his fright and waywardness.

Ichabod, who had no relish for this strange midnight companion, and bethought himself of the adventure of Brom Bones with the Galloping Hessian, now quickened his steed, in hopes of leaving him behind. The stranger, however, quickened his horse to an equal pace. Ichabod pulled up, and fell into a walk, thinking to lag behind – the other did the same. His heart began to sink within him; he endeavoured to resume his psalm tune, but his parched tongue clove to the roof of his mouth, and he could not utter a stave. There was something in the moody and dogged silence of this pertinacious companion, that was mysterious and appalling. It was soon fearfully accounted for. On mounting a rising ground, which brought the figure of his fellow-traveller in relief against the sky, gigantic in height, and muffled in a cloak, Ichabod was horror-struck, on perceiving that he was headless! – but his horror was still more increased, on observing that the head, which should have rested on his shoulders, was carried before him on the pommel of the saddle: his terror rose to desperation; he rained a shower of kicks and blows upon Gunpowder, hoping, by a sudden movement, to give his companion the slip – but the spectre started full jump with him. Away then they dashed, through thick and thin; stones flying, and sparks flashing, at every bound. Ichabod's flimsy garments fluttered in the air, as he stretched his long lank body away over his horse's head in the eagerness of his flight.

They had now reached the road which turns off to Sleepy Hollow; but Gunpowder, who seemed possessed with a demon, instead of keeping up it, made an opposite turn, and plunged headlong downhill to the left. This road leads through a sandy hollow, shaded by trees for about a quarter of a mile, where it crosses the bridge famous in goblin story, and just beyond swells the green knoll on which stands the white-washed church. . . .

He saw the walls of the church dimly glaring under the trees beyond. He recollected the place where Brom Bones' ghostly competitor had disappeared. 'If I can but reach that bridge,' thought Ichabod, 'I am safe.' Just then he heard the black steed panting and blowing close behind him; he even fancied that he felt his hot breath. Another convulsive kick in the ribs, and old Gunpowder sprang upon the bridge; he thundered over the resounding planks; he gained the opposite side; and now Ichabod cast a look behind to see if his pursuer should vanish, according to rule, in a flash of fire and brimstone. Just then he saw the goblin rising in his stirrups, and in the very act of hurling his head at him. Ichabod endeavoured to dodge the horrible missile, but too late. It encountered his cranium with a tremendous crash – he was tumbled headlong into the dust, and Gunpowder, the black steed, and the goblin rider, passed by like a whirlwind.

The next morning the old horse was found without his saddle, and with the bridle under his feet, soberly cropping the grass at his master's gate. Ichabod did not make his appearance at breakfast – dinner-hour came, but no Ichabod. The boys assembled at the school-house, and strolled idly about the banks of the brook; but no schoolmaster. Hans Van Ripper now began to feel some uneasiness about the fate of poor Ichabod, and his saddle. An inquiry was set on foot, and after diligent investigation they came upon his traces. In one part of the road leading to the church was found the saddle trampled in the dirt; the tracks of horses' hoofs deeply dented in the road, and evidently at furious speed, were traced to the bridge, beyond which, on the bank of a broad part of the brook, where the water ran deep and black, was found the hat of the unfortunate Ichabod, and close beside it a shattered pumpkin.

The brook was searched, but the body of the schoolmaster was not to be discovered. Hans Van Ripper, as executor of his estate, examined the bundle which contained all his worldly effects. . . .

The stories of Brouwer, of Bones, and a whole budget of others, were called to mind; and when they had diligently considered them all, and compared them with the symptoms of the present case, they shook their heads, and came to the conclusion that Ichabod had been carried off by the galloping Hessian. As he was a bachelor, and in nobody's debt, nobody troubled his head any more about him: the school was removed to a different quarter of the hollow, and another pedagogue reigned in his stead.

It is true, an old farmer, who had been down to New York on a visit several years after, and from whom this account of the ghostly adventure was received, brought home the intelligence that Ichabod Crane was still alive; that he had left the neighbourhood, partly through fear of the goblin and Hans Van Ripper, and partly in mortification at having been suddenly dismissed by the heiress; that he had changed his quarters to a distant part of the country; had kept school and studied law at the same time; had been admitted to the bar, turned politician, electioneered, written for the newspapers, and finally had been made a justice of the Ten Pound Court. Brom Bones too, who shortly after his rival's disappearance conducted the blooming Katrina in triumph to the altar, was observed to look exceedingly knowing whenever the story of Ichabod was related, and always burst into a hearty laugh at the mention of the pumpkin; which led some to suspect that he knew more about the matter than he chose to tell.

The old country wives, however, who are the best judges of these matters, maintain to this day that Ichabod was spirited away by supernatural means; and it is a favourite story often told about the neighbourhood round the winter evening fire. The bridge became more than ever an object of superstitious awe, and that may be the reason why the road has been altered of late years, so as to approach the church by the border of the mill-pond. The school-house being deserted, soon fell to decay, and was reported to be haunted by the ghost of the unfortunate pedagogue; and the plough-boy, loitering homeward of a still summer evening, has often fancied his voice at a distance, chanting a melancholy psalm tune among the tranquil solitudes of Sleepy Hollow.

From 'The Legend of Sleepy Hollow' by Washington Irving, 1819–20

The Robber

At this time especially, such robberies were carried on after a strange and frightful fashion on Strellin heath at Gützkow; but by God's help it all came to light just as I journeyed thither with my man-servant to the fair, and I will here tell how it happened. Some months before a man had been broken on the wheel at Gützkow, because, being tempted of

Satan, he murdered a travelling workman. The man, however, straightway began to walk after so fearful a fashion, that in the evening and night-season he sprang down from the wheel in his gallows' dress whenever a cart passed by the gallows, which stands hard by the road to Wolgast, and jumped up behind the people, who in horror and dismay flogged on their horses, and thereby made a great rattling on the log embankment which leads beside the gallows into a little wood called the Kraulin. And it was a strange thing that on the same night the travellers were almost always robbed or murdered on Strellin heath. Hereupon the magistrates had the man taken down from the wheel and buried under the gallows, in hopes of laying his ghost. But it went on just as before, sitting at night snow-white on the wheel, so that none durst any longer travel the road to Wolgast. Until at last it happened that, at the time of the above-named fair, young Rüdiger von Nienkerken of Mellenthin, in Usedom, who had been studying at Wittenberg and elsewhere, and was now on his way home, came this road by night with his carriage. Just before, at the inn, I myself had tried to persuade him to stop the night at Gützkow on account of the ghost, and to go on his journey with me next morning, but he would not. Now as soon as this young lord drove along the road, he also espied the apparition sitting on the wheel, and scarcely had he passed the gallows when the ghost jumped down and ran after him. The driver was horribly afraid, and lashed on the horses, as everybody else had done before, and they, taking fright, galloped away over the log-road with a marvellous clatter. Meanwhile, however, the young nobleman saw by the light of the moon how that the apparition flattened a ball of horse-dung whereon it trod, and straightway felt sure within himself that it was no ghost. Whereupon he called to the driver to stop; and as the man would not hearken to him, he sprang out of the carriage, drew his rapier, and hastened to attack the ghost. When the ghost saw this he would have turned and fled, but the young nobleman gave him such a blow on the head with his fist that he fell upon the ground with a loud wailing. *Summa*: the young lord, having called back his driver, dragged the ghost into the town again, where he turned out to be a shoemaker called Schwelm.

From *The Amber Witch* by William Meinhold, 1841–2; translated from the German by Lady Duff Gordon

Mr Sludge, the Medium

Now, don't, sir! Don't expose me! Just this once!
This was the first and only time, I'll swear, –

Look at me, – see, I kneel, – the only time,
I swear, I ever cheated, – yes, by the soul
Of Her who hears – (your sainted mother, sir!)
All, except this last accident, was truth –
This little kind of slip! – and even this,
It was your own wine, sir, the good champagne,
(I took it for Catawba, you're so kind)
Which put the folly in my head!
                            'Get up?'
You still inflict on me that terrible face?
You show no mercy? – Not for Her dear sake,
The sainted spirit's, whose soft breath even now
Blows on my cheek – (don't you feel something, sir?)
You'll tell?
                Go tell, then! Who the devil cares
What such a rowdy chooses to . . .
                            Aie – aie – aie!
Please, sir! your thumbs are through my windpipe, sir!
Ch – ch!
            Well, sir, I hope you've done it now!
Oh Lord! I little thought, sir, yesterday,
When your departed mother spoke those words
Of peace through me, and moved you, sir, so much,
You gave me – (very kind it was of you)
These shirt-studs – (better take them back again,
Please, sir) – yes, little did I think so soon
A trifle of trick, all through a glass too much
Of his own champagne, would change my best of friends
Into an angry gentleman!

From 'Mr Sludge, the Medium' in *Dramatis Personae* by Robert Browning, 1865

A ghost meets his match

For a moment he paused there, the wind blowing his long grey locks about his head, and twisting into grotesque and fantastic folds the nameless horror of the dead man's shroud. Then the clock struck the quarter, and he felt the time was come. He chuckled to himself, and turned the corner; but no sooner had he done so, than, with a piteous wail of terror, he fell back, and hid his blanched face in his long, bony hands. Right in front of him was standing a horrible spectre, motionless as a carven image, and monstrous as a madman's dream! Its head was bald and burnished; its face round, and fat, and white; and hideous laughter seemed to have writhed its features into an eternal grin. From the eyes streamed rays of scarlet light, the mouth was a wide well of fire, and a hideous garment, like to his own, swathed with its silent snows the Titan form. On its breast was a placard with strange writing in antique characters, some scroll of shame it seemed, some record of wild sins, some awful calendar of crime, and, with its right hand, it bore aloft a falchion of gleaming steel.

Never having seen a ghost before, he naturally was terribly frightened, and, after a second hasty glance at the awful phantom, he fled back to his room, tripping up in his long winding-sheet as he sped down the corridor, and finally dropping the rusty dagger into the Minister's jack-boots, where it was found in the morning by the butler. Once in the privacy of his own apartment, he flung himself down on a small pallet-bed, and hid his face under the clothes. After a time, however, the brave old Canterville spirit asserted itself, and he determined to go and speak to the other ghost as soon as it was daylight. Accordingly, just as the dawn was touching the hills with silver, he returned towards the spot where he had first laid eyes on the grisly phantom, feeling that, after all, two ghosts were better than one, and that, by the aid of his new friend, he might safely grapple with the twins. On reaching the spot, however, a terrible sight met his gaze. Something had evidently happened to the spectre, for the light had entirely faded from its hollow eyes, the gleaming falchion had fallen from its hand, and it was leaning up against the wall in a strained and uncomfortable attitude. He rushed forward and seized it in his arms, when, to his horror, the head slipped off and rolled on the floor, the body assumed a recumbent posture, and he found himself clasping a white dimity bed-curtain, with a sweeping-brush, a kitchen cleaver, and a hollow turnip lying at his feet! Unable to understand this curious transformation, he clutched the placard with feverish haste, and there, in the grey morning light, he read these fearful words:–

> ## ÞE OTIS GHOSTE.
> ### Þe onlie True and Originale Spook.
> ### Beware of Þe Imitationes.
> ### All others are Counterfeite.

The whole thing flashed across him. He had been tricked, foiled, and outwitted! The old Canterville look came into his eyes; he ground his toothless gums together; and, raising his withered hands high above his head, swore, according to the picturesque phraseology of the antique school, that when Chanticleer had sounded twice his merry horn, deeds of blood would be wrought, and Murder walk abroad with silent feet.

Hardly had he finished this awful oath when, from the red-tiled roof of a distant homestead, a cock crew. He laughed a long, low, bitter laugh, and waited. Hour after hour he waited, but the cock, for some strange reason, did not crow again. Finally, at half-past seven, the arrival of the housemaids made him give up his fearful vigil, and he stalked back to his room, thinking of his vain hope and baffled purpose. There he consulted several books of ancient chivalry, of which he was exceedingly fond, and found that, on every occasion on which his oath had been used, Chanticleer had always crowed a second time. 'Perdition seize the naughty fowl,' he muttered, 'I have seen the day when, with my stout spear, I would have run him through the gorge, and made him crow for me an 'twere in death!' He then retired to a comfortable lead coffin, and stayed there till evening.

From 'The Canterville Ghost' by Oscar Wilde, 1887

The Night the Ghost Got In

'No sign o' nuthin',' said the cop who had first spoken to mother. 'This guy,' he explained to the others, jerking a thumb at me, 'was nekked. The lady seems historical.' They all nodded, but said nothing; just looked at me. In the small silence we all heard a creaking in the attic. Grandfather was turning over in bed. 'What's 'at?' snapped Joe. Five or six cops sprang for the attic door before I could intervene or explain. I realized that it would be bad if they burst in on grandfather unannounced, or even announced. He was going through a phase in which he believed that General Meade's men, under steady hammering by Stonewall Jackson, were beginning to retreat and even desert.

When I got to the attic, things were pretty confused. Grandfather had evidently jumped to the conclusion that the police were deserters from Meade's army, trying to hide away in his attic. He bounded out of bed wearing a long flannel nightgown over long woolen underwear, a nightcap, and a leather jacket around his chest. The cops must have realized at once that the indignant white-haired old man belonged in the house, but they had no chance to say so. 'Back, ye cowardly dogs!' roared grandfather. 'Back t' the lines, ye goddam lily-livered cattle!' With that, he fetched the officer who found the zither a flat-handed smack alongside his head that sent him sprawling. The others beat a retreat, but not fast enough; grandfather grabbed Zither's gun from its holster and let fly. The report seemed to crack the rafters; smoke filled the attic. A cop cursed and shot his hand to his shoulder. Somehow, we all finally got downstairs again and locked the door against the old gentleman. He fired once or twice more in the darkness and then went back to bed. 'That was grandfather,' I explained to Joe, out of breath. 'He thinks you're deserters.' 'I'll say he does,' said Joe.

The cops were reluctant to leave without getting their hands on somebody besides grandfather; the night had been distinctly a defeat for them. Furthermore, they obviously didn't like the 'layout'; something looked – and I can see their viewpoint – phony. They began to poke into things again. A reporter, a thin-faced, wispy man, came up to me. I had put on one of mother's blouses, not being able to find anything else. The reporter looked at me with mingled suspicion and interest. 'Just what the hell is the real lowdown here, Bud?' he asked. I decided to be frank with him. 'We had ghosts,' I said. He gazed at me a long time as if I were a slot machine into which he had, without results, dropped a nickel. Then he walked away. The cops followed him, the one grandfather shot holding his now-bandaged arm, cursing and blaspheming. 'I'm gonna get my gun back from that old bird,' said the zither-cop. 'Yeh,' said Joe. 'You – and who else?' I told them I would bring it to the station house the next day.

'What was the matter with that one policeman?' mother asked, after they had gone. 'Grandfather shot him,' I said. 'What for?' she demanded. I told her he was a deserter. 'Of all things!' said mother. 'He was such a nice-looking young man.'

Grandfather was fresh as a daisy and full of jokes at breakfast next morning. We thought at first he had forgotten all about what had happened, but he hadn't. Over his third cup of coffee, he glared at Herman and me. 'What was the idee of all them cops tarryhootin' round the house last night?' he demanded. He had us there.

From *My Life and Hard Times* by James Thurber, 1933

One Little Adventure

I happened to glance at my hands the other day and noticed they were yellow. Conclusion: I am growing old (though I claim that I am not yet too old to dream). Further conclusion: I should set about writing my memoirs. Be assured that such a book would be remarkable, for to the extraordinary adventures which have been my lot there is no end. (Nor will there be.) Here is one little adventure that will give you some idea. Many years ago a Dublin friend asked me to spend an evening with him. Assuming that the man was interested in philosophy and knew that immutable truth can sometimes be acquired through the kinesis of disputation, I consented. How wrong I was may be judged from the fact that my friend arrived at the rendezvous in a taxi and whisked me away to a licensed premises in the vicinity of Lucan. Here I was induced to consume a large measure of intoxicating whiskey. My friend would not hear of another drink in the same place, drawing my attention by nudges to a very sinister-looking character who was drinking stout in the shadows some distance from us. He was a tall cadaverous person, dressed wholly in black, with a face of deathly grey. We left and drove many miles to the village of Stepaside, where a further drink was ordered. Scarcely to the lip had it been applied when both of us noticed – with what feelings I dare not describe – the same tall creature in black, residing in a distant shadow and apparently drinking the same glass of stout. We finished our own drinks quickly and left at once, taking in this case the Enniskerry road and entering a hostelry in the purlieus of that village. Here more drinks were ordered but had hardly appeared on the counter when, to the horror of myself and friend, the sinister stranger was discerned some distance away, still patiently dealing with his stout. We swallowed our drinks raw and hurried out. My friend was now thoroughly scared, and could not be dissuaded from making for the far-away hamlet of Celbridge; his idea was that, while another drink was absolutely essential, it was equally essential to put as many miles as possible between ourselves and the sinister presence we had just left. Need I say what happened? We noticed with relief that the public house we entered in Celbridge was deserted, but as our eyes became more accustomed to the poor light, *we saw him again*: he was standing in the gloom, a more terrible apparition than ever before, ever more menacing with each meeting. My friend had purchased a bottle of whiskey and was now dealing with the stuff in large gulps. I saw at once that a crisis had been reached and that desperate action was called for.

'No matter where we go,' I said, 'this being will be there unless we can now assert a superior will and confound evil machinations that are on foot. I do not know whence comes this apparition, but certainly of this world it is not. It is my intention to challenge him.'

My friend gazed at me in horror, made some gesture of remonstrance, but apparently could not speak. My own mind was made up. It was me or this diabolical adversary: there could be no evading the clash of wills, only one of us could survive. I finished my drink with an assurance I was far from feeling and marched straight up to the presence. A nearer sight of him almost stopped the action of my heart; here undoubtedly was no man but some spectral emanation from the tomb, the undead come on some task of inhuman vengeance.

'I do not like the look of you,' I said, somewhat lamely.

'I don't think so much of you either,' the thing replied; the voice was cracked, low and terrible.

'I demand to know,' I said sternly, 'why you persist in following myself and my friend everywhere we go.'

'I cannot go home until you first go home,' the thing replied. There was an ominous undertone in this that almost paralysed me.

'Why not?' I managed to say.

'Because I am the – taxi-driver!'

Out of such strange incidents is woven the pattern of what I am pleased to call my life.

Myles na Gopaleen (Flann O'Brien), from *The Best of Myles*, 1968

Finn

'Yeah?' The voice, barely more than a whisper, seemed to come from nowhere in particular.

'I told you already,' Sally said.

'I don't jive.'

'I wanna talk to him,' she said, her voice hard and careful.

'He's dead.'

'I know that.'

A silence followed, and Kumiko heard a sound that might have been the wind, a cold, grit-laden wind scouring the curve of the geodesics far above them.

'He's not here,' the voice said, and seemed to recede. 'Round the corner, half a block, left into the alley.'

Kumiko would remember the alley always: dark brick slick with damp, hooded ventilators trailing black streamers of congealed dust, a yellow bulb in a cage of corroded alloy, the low growth of empty bottles that sprouted at the base of either wall, the man-sized nests of crumpled fax and white foam packing-segments, and the sound of Sally's bootheels.

Past the bulb's dim glow was darkness, though a reflected gleam on wet brick showed a final wall, cul-de-sac, and Kumiko hesitated, frightened by a sudden stir of echo, a scurrying, the steady dripping of water . . .

Sally raised her hand. A tight beam of very bright light framed a sharp circle of paint-scrawled brick, then smoothly descended.

Descended until it found the thing at the base of the wall, dull metal, an upright rounded fixture that Kumiko mistook for another ventilator.

Near its base were the stubs of white candles, a flat plastic flask filled with a clear liquid, an assortment of cigarette packets, a scattering of loose cigarettes, and an elaborate, multi-armed figure drawn in what appeared to be white powdered chalk.

Sally stepped forward, the beam held steady, and Kumiko saw that the armored thing was bolted into the brickwork with massive rivets. 'Finn?'

A rapid flicker of pink light from a horizontal slot.

'Hey, Finn, man . . .' An uncharacteristic hesitation in her voice . . .

'Moll.' A grating quality, as if through a broken speaker. . . .

Sally lowered the light; it fell on the candles, the flask, the damp gray cigarettes, the white symbol with its feathery arms.

'Help yourself to the offerings,' said the voice. 'That's half a liter of Moskovskaya there. The hoodoo mark's flour. Tough luck; the high-rollers draw 'em in cocaine.'

'Jesus,' Sally said, an odd distance in her voice, squatting down, 'I don't believe this.'

Kumiko watched as she picked up the flask and sniffed at the contents.

'Drink it. It's good shit. Fuckin' better be. Nobody short-counts the oracle, not if they know what's good for 'em.'

'Finn,' Sally said, then tilted the flask and swallowed, wiping her mouth with the back of her hand, 'you gotta be crazy . . .'

'I should be so lucky. A rig like this, I'm pushing it to have a little imagination, let alone crazy.'

Kumiko moved closer, then squatted beside Sally.

'It's a construct, a personality job?' Sally put the flask of vodka down and stirred the damp flour with the tip of a white fingernail.

'Sure. You seen 'em before. Real-time memory if I wanna, wired into c-space if I wanna. Got this oracle gig to keep my hand in, you know?' The thing made a strange sound: laughter. 'Got love troubles? Got a bad woman don't understand you?' The laugh-noise again, like peals of static. 'Actually I'm more into business advice. It's the local kids leave the goodies. Adds to the mystique, kinda. And once in a while I get a sceptic, some asshole figures he'll help himself to the take.' A scarlet hairline flashed from the slit and a bottle exploded somewhere to Kumiko's right. Static laughter. 'So what brings you this way, Moll?'

Watching the hypnotic sweep of the scanning pink ember, Kumiko had some idea of what it was that Sally spoke with. There were similar things in her father's study, four of them, black lacquered cubes arranged along a low shelf of pine. Above each cube hung a formal portrait. The portraits were monochrome photographs of men in dark suits and ties, four very sober gentlemen whose lapels were decorated with small metal emblems of the kind her father sometimes wore.

Though her mother had told her that the cubes contained ghosts, the ghosts of her father's evil ancestors, Kumiko found them more fascinating than frightening. If they did contain ghosts, she reasoned, they would be quite small, as the cubes themselves were scarcely large enough to contain a child's head.

Her father sometimes meditated before the cubes, kneeling on the bare tatami in an attitude that connoted profound respect. She had seen him in this position many times, but she was ten before she heard him address the cubes. And one had answered. The question had meant nothing to her, the answer less, but the calm tone of the ghost's reply had frozen her where she crouched, behind a door of paper, and her father had laughed to find her there; rather than scolding her, he'd explained that the cubes housed the recorded personalities of former executives, corporate directors. Their souls, she'd asked. No, he'd said, and smiled, then added that the distinction was a subtle one. 'They are not conscious. They respond, when questioned, in a manner approximating the response of the subject. If they are ghosts, then holograms are ghosts.'

After Sally's lecture on the history and hierarchy of the Yakuza, in the robata bar in Earl's Court, Kumiko had decided that each of the men in the photographs, the subjects of the personality-recordings, had been an *oyabun*.

The thing in the armored housing, she reasoned, was of a similar nature, though perhaps more complex, just as Colin was a more complex version of the Michelin guide her father's secretaries had carried on her Shinjuki shopping expeditions. Finn, Sally called it, and it was evident that this had been a friend or associate of hers.

But did it wake, Kumiko wondered, when the alley was empty? Did its laser vision scan the silent fall of midnight snow?

From *Mona Lisa Overdrive* by William Gibson, 1989

'Now you're talking'

BUT I ASSURE YOU, YOU ARE NOT DEAD. TAKE IT FROM ME.

The duke giggled. He had found a sheet from somewhere and had draped it over himself, and was sidling along some of the castle's more deserted corridors. Sometimes he would go 'whoo-oo' in a low voice.

This worried Death. He was used to people claiming that they were *not* dead, because death always came as a shock and a lot of people had some trouble getting over it. But people claiming that they were dead with every breath in their body was a new and unsettling experience.

'I shall jump out on people,' said the duke dreamily. 'I shall rattle my bones all night. I shall perch on the roof and foretell a death in the house –'

THAT'S BANSHEES.

'I shall if I want,' said the duke, with a trace of earlier determination. 'And I shall float through walls, and knock on tables, and drip ectoplasm on anyone I don't like. Ha. Ha.'

IT WON'T WORK. LIVING PEOPLE AREN'T ALLOWED TO BE GHOSTS. I'M SORRY.

The duke made an unsuccessful attempt to float through a wall, gave up, and opened a door out on to a crumbling section of the battlements. The storm had died away a bit, and a thin rind of moon lurked behind the clouds like a ticket tout for eternity.

Death stalked through the wall behind him.

'Well, then,' said the duke, 'if I'm *not* dead, why are you here?'

He jumped up on to the wall and flapped his sheet.

WAITING.

'Wait forever, bone face!' said the duke triumphantly. 'I shall hover in the twilight world, I shall find some chains to shake, I shall –'

He stepped backwards, lost his balance, landed heavily on the wall and slid. For a moment the remnant of his right hand scrabbled ineffectually at the stonework, and then it vanished.

Death is obviously potentially everywhere at the same time, and in one sense it is no more true to say that he was on the battlements, picking vaguely at non-existent particles of glowing metal on the edge of his scythe blade, than that he was waist-deep in the foaming, rock-toothed waters in the depths of Lancre gorge, his calcareous gaze sweeping downwards and stopping abruptly at a point where the torrent ran a few treacherous inches over a bed of angular pebbles.

After a while the duke sat up, transparent in the phosphorescent waves.

'I shall haunt their corridors,' he said, 'and whisper under the doors on still nights.' His voice grew fainter, almost lost in the ceaseless roar of the river. 'I shall make basket chairs creak most alarmingly, just you wait and see.'

Death grinned at him.

NOW YOU'RE TALKING.

It started to rain.

From *Wyrd Sisters* by Terry Pratchett, 1988

Ten

SOLDIERS AND SAILORS

And I saw askant the armies,
I saw as in noiseless dreams hundreds of battle-flags,
Borne through the smoke of the battles and pierc'd with missiles I saw
    them,
And carried hither and yon through the smoke, and torn and bloody,
And at last but a few shreds left on the staffs, (and all in silence,)
And the staffs all splinter'd and broken.

I saw battle-corpses, myriads of them,
And the white skeletons of young men, I saw them,
I saw the debris and debris of all the slain soldiers of the war,
But I saw they were not as was thought,
They themselves were fully at rest, they suffer'd not,
The living remain'd and suffer'd, the mother suffered,
And the wife and the child and the musing comrade suffer'd,
And the armies that remain'd suffer'd.

WALT WHITMAN

Marathon

It was at this point of Attica that the barbarians landed, and were beaten in battle, and lost some of their ships as they were putting off to sea. In the plain is the grave of the Athenians, and over it are tombstones with the names of the fallen arranged according to tribes. There is another grave for the Boeotians of Plataea and the slaves; for slaves fought then for the first time. There is a separate tomb of Miltiades, son of Cimon. He died subsequently, after he had failed to capture Paros, and had been put on his trial for it by the Athenians. Here every night you may hear horses neighing and men fighting. To go on purpose to see the sight never brought good to any man; but with him who unwittingly lights upon it by accident the spirits are not angry.

From *Pausanias's Description of Greece* (c.AD 160), translated by J. G. Frazer

Strange Meeting

It seemed that out of battle I escaped
Down some profound dull tunnel, long since scooped
Through granites which titanic wars had groined.
Yet also there encumbered sleepers groaned,
Too fast in thought or death to be bestirred.
Then, as I probed them, one sprang up, and stared
With piteous recognition in fixed eyes,
Lifting distressful hands as if to bless.
And by his smile, I knew that sullen hall,
By his dead smile, I knew we stood in Hell.
With a thousand pains that vision's face was grained;
Yet no blood reached there from the upper ground,
And no guns thumped, or down the flues made moan.
'Strange friend,' I said, 'here is no cause to mourn.'
'None,' said the other, 'save the undone years,
The hopelessness. Whatever hope is yours,
Was my life also; I went hunting wild
After the wildest beauty in the world,
Which lies not calm in eyes, or braided hair,
But mocks the steady running of the hour,
And if it grieves, grieves richlier than here.
For of my glee might many men have laughed,
And of my weeping something had been left,

Which must die now. I mean the truth untold,
The pity of war, the pity war distilled.
Now men will go content with what we spoiled,
Or, discontent, boil bloody, and be spilled.
They will be swift with swiftness of the tigress.
None will break ranks, though nations trek from progress.
Courage was mine, and I had mystery,
Wisdom was mine, and I had mastery:
To miss the march of this retreating world
Into vain citadels that are not walled.
Then, when much blood had clogged their chariot-wheels,
I would go up and wash them from sweet wells,
Even with truths that lie too deep for taint.
I would have poured my spirit without stint
But not through wounds; not on the cess of war.
Foreheads of men have bled where no wounds were.
I am the enemy you killed, my friend.
I knew you in this dark: for so you frowned
Yesterday through me as you jabbed and killed.
I parried; but my hands were loath and cold.
Let us sleep now. . . .'

Wilfred Owen, 1918

Family Ghosts

The strings' excitement, the applauding drum,
Are but the initiating ceremony
That out of cloud the ancestral face may come,

And never hear their subaltern mockery,
Graffiti-writers, moss-grown with whimsies,
Loquacious when the watercourse is dry.

It is your face I see, and morning's praise
Of you is ghost's approval of the choice,
Filtered through roots of the effacing grass.

Fear, taking me aside, would give advice
'To conquer her, the visible enemy,
It is enough to turn away the eyes.'

Yet there's no peace in the assaulted city,
But speeches at the corners, hope for news,
Outside the watchfires of a stronger army.

And all emotions to expression come,
Recovering the archaic imagery:
This longing for assurance takes the form

Of a hawk's vertical stooping from the sky;
These tears, salt for a disobedient dream,
The lunatic agitation of the sea;

While this despair with hardened eyeballs cries
'A Golden Age, a Silver ... rather this,
Massive and taciturn years, the Age of Ice'.

W. H. Auden, c.1928

Patroclus

When lo! the shade, before his closing eyes,
Of sad Patroclus rose, or seem'd to rise:
In the same robe he living wore, he came:
In stature, voice, and pleasing look, the same.
The form familiar hover'd o'er his head,
'And sleeps Achilles? (thus the phantom said:)
Sleeps my Achilles, his Patroclus dead?
Living, I seem'd his dearest, tenderest care,
But now forgot, I wander in the air.
Let my pale corse the rites of burial know,
And give me entrance in the realms below:
Till then the spirit finds no resting-place,
But here and there the unbodied spectres chase
The vagrant dead around the dark abode,
Forbid to cross the irremeable flood.
Now give thy hand; for to the farther shore
When once we pass, the soul returns no more:
When once the last funereal flames ascend,
No more shall meet Achilles and his friend;
No more our thoughts to those we loved make known;
Or quit the dearest, to converse alone.
Me fate has sever'd from the sons of earth,
The fate fore-doom'd that waited from my birth:
Thee too it waits; before the Trojan wall

Even great and godlike thou art doom'd to fall.
Hear then; and as in fate and love we join,
Ah suffer that my bones may rest with thine!
Together have we lived; together bred,
One house received us, and one table fed;
That golden urn, thy goddess-mother gave,
May mix our ashes in one common grave.'

From The Odyssey, translated by Alexander Pope, 1725–6

The Scalped Men

Men slain and scalped in battle are regarded as not truly dead; they
become magic beings, dwelling in caves or haunting the wilds, for
shame prevents them from returning to their own people. Their heads
are bloody and their bodies mutilated, as left by their enemies, and
address one another by names descriptive of the patches of hair still left
upon their heads – 'One-Hair, Forehead-Hair, Hair-Back-of-the-Head,
all of you come!'

A man had lost wife and son, and in his bereavement was wandering
over the prairies in quest of death. He was met by the Scalped Men of
his tribe, and these, taking pity upon him, implored Tirawa to return
the dead to the land of the living. The request was granted with certain
restrictions – dead and living were to encamp for four days, side by
side, without speaking to one another; the bereaved father might speak
to his son, but might not touch him. The tribesfolk assembled in camp;
they beheld a huge dust approaching; the spirits of their departed
friends passed before them. But when the father saw his son among the
dead, he seized hold of him and hugged him, and in his heart he said, 'I
will not let you go!' The people shrieked; the dead disappeared; and
death has continued upon earth.

Pawnee legend, from North American Mythology by H. B. Alexander, 1916

Masses

When the battle was over,
And the fighter was dead, a man came toward him
And said to him: 'Do not die; I love you so!'
But the corpse, it was sad! went on dying.

And two came near, and told him again and again:
'Do not leave us! Courage! Return to life!'
But the corpse, it was sad! went on dying.

Twenty arrived, a hundred, a thousand, five hundred thousand,
Shouting: 'So much love, and it can do nothing against death!'
But the corpse, it was sad! went on dying.

Millions of persons stood around him,
All speaking the same thing: 'Stay here, brother!'
But the corpse, it was sad! went on dying.

Then all the men on the earth
Stood around him; the corpse looked at them sadly, deeply moved;

He sat up slowly,
Put his arms around the first man; started to walk . . .

From *España, Aparta De Me Este Caliz* by César Vallejo, 1938,
translated from the Spanish by Robert Bly

'The Ghost Dance was spreading like a prairie fire'

In the Drying Grass Moon (October 9, 1890), about a year after the
breaking up of the Great Reservation, a Minneconjou from the
Cheyenne River agency came to Standing Rock to visit Sitting Bull.
His name was Kicking Bear, and he brought news of the Paiute Messiah, Wovoka, who had founded the religion of the Ghost Dance.
Kicking Bear and his brother-in-law, Short Bull, had returned from a
long journey beyond the Shining Mountains in search of the Messiah.
Hearing of this pilgrimage, Sitting Bull had sent for Kicking Bear in
order to learn more about the Ghost Dance.

Kicking Bear told Sitting Bull of how a voice had commanded him to
go forth and meet the ghosts of Indians who were to return and inhabit
the earth. On the cars of the Iron Horse he and Short Bull and nine
other Sioux had traveled far toward the place where the sun sets,
traveled until the railroad stopped. There they were met by two Indians
they had never seen before, but who greeted them as brothers and gave
them meat and bread. They supplied the pilgrims with horses and they

rode for four suns until they came to a camp of Fish Eaters (Paiutes) near Pyramid Lake in Nevada.

The Fish Eaters told the visitors that Christ had returned to earth again. Christ must have sent for them to come there, Kicking Bear said: it was foreordained. To see the Messiah they had to make another journey to the agency at Walker Lake.

For two days Kicking Bear and his friends waited at Walker Lake with hundreds of other Indians speaking in dozens of different tongues. These Indians had come from many reservations to see the Messiah.

Just before sundown on the third day the Christ appeared, and the Indians made a big fire to throw light on him. Kicking Bear had always thought that Christ was a white man like the missionaries, but this man looked like an Indian. After a while he rose and spoke to the waiting crowd. 'I have sent for you and am glad to see you,' he said. 'I am going to talk to you after a while about your relatives who are dead and gone. My children, I want you to listen to all I have to say to you. I will teach you how to dance a dance, and I want you to dance it. Get ready for your dance, and when the dance is over, I will talk to you.' Then he commenced to dance, everybody joining in, the Christ singing while they danced. They danced the Dance of the Ghosts until late at night, when the Messiah told them they had danced enough.

Next morning, Kicking Bear and the others went up close to the Messiah to see if he had the scars of crucifixion which the missionaries on the reservations had told them about. There was a scar on his wrist and one on his face, but they could not see his feet, because he was wearing moccasins. Throughout the day he talked to them. In the beginning, he said, God made the earth, and then sent the Christ to earth to teach the people, but white men had treated him badly, leaving scars on his body, and so he had gone back to heaven. Now he had returned to earth as an Indian, and he was to renew everything as it used to be and make it better.

In the next springtime, when the grass was knee high, the earth would be covered with new soil which would bury all the white men, and new land would be covered with sweet grass and running water and trees. Great herds of buffalo and wild horses would come back. The Indians who danced the Ghost Dance would be taken up in the air and suspended there while a wave of new earth was passing, and then they would be set down among the ghosts of their ancestors on the new earth, where only Indians would live.

After a few days at Walker Lake, Kicking Bear and his friends learned how to dance the Ghost Dance, and then they mounted their horses to return to the railroad. As they rode along, the Messiah flew above them in the air, teaching them songs for the new dance. At the railroad, he left them, telling them to return to their people and teach what they had learned. When the next winter was passed, he would bring the ghosts of their fathers to meet them in the new resurrection.

After returning to Dakota, Kicking Bear had started the new dance at Cheyenne River, Short Bull had brought it to Rosebud, and others were introducing it at Pine Ridge. Big Foot's band of Minneconjous, Kicking Bear said, was made up mostly of women who had lost husbands or other male relatives in fights with Long Hair and Three Stars and Bear Coat; they danced until they fainted, because they wanted to bring their dead warriors back.

Sitting Bull listened to all that Kicking Bear had to relate about the Messiah and the Ghost Dance. He did not believe it was possible for dead men to return and live again, but his people had heard of the Messiah and were fearful he would pass them by and let them disappear when the new resurrection came, unless they joined in the dancing. Sitting Bull had no objections to his people dancing the Ghost Dance, but he had heard that agents at some reservations were bringing soldiers in to stop the ceremonies. He did not want soldiers coming in to frighten and perhaps shoot their guns at his people. Kicking Bear replied that if the Indians wore the sacred garments of the Messiah – Ghost Shirts painted with magic symbols – no harm could come to them. Not even the bullets of the Bluecoats' guns could penetrate a Ghost Shirt.

With some skepticism, Sitting Bull invited Kicking Bear to remain with his band at Standing Rock and teach them the Dance of the Ghosts. This was in the Moon of Falling Leaves, and across the West on almost every Indian reservation the Ghost Dance was spreading like a prairie fire under a high wind.

From *Bury My Heart at Wounded Knee* by Dee Brown, 1971

'The Gray Champion'

The people had been drawing nearer and nearer, and drinking in the words of their champion, who spoke in accents long disused, like one unaccustomed to converse, except with the dead of many years ago. But his voice stirred their souls. They confronted the soldiers, not wholly without arms, and ready to convert the very stones of the street into deadly weapons. Sir Edmund Andros looked at the old man; then he cast his hard and cruel eye over the multitude, and beheld them burning with that lurid wrath, so difficult to kindle or to quench; and again he fixed his gaze on the aged form, which stood obscurely in an open space, where neither friend nor foe had thrust himself. What were his thoughts, he uttered no word which might discover. But whether the oppressor were overawed by the Gray Champion's look, or perceived his peril in the threatening attitude of the people, it is certain that he gave back, and ordered his soldiers to commence a slow and guarded retreat. Before another sunset, the Governor, and all that rode so proudly with him, were prisoners, and long ere it was known that James had abdicated, King William was proclaimed throughout New England.

But where was the Gray Champion? Some reported, that when the troops had gone from King Street, and the people were thronging tumultuously in their rear, Bradstreet, the aged Governor, was seen to embrace a form more aged than his own. Others soberly affirmed, that while they marveled at the venerable grandeur of his aspect, the old man had faded from their eyes, melting slowly into the hues of twilight, till, where he stood, there was an empty space. But all agreed, that the hoary shape was gone. The men of that generation watched for his reappearance, in sunshine and in twilight, but never saw him more, nor knew when his funeral passed, nor where his gravestone was.

And who was the Gray Champion? Perhaps his name might be found in the records of that stern Court of Justice, which passed a sentence, too mighty for the age, but glorious in all after times, for its humbling lesson to the monarch and its high example to the subject. I have heard, that, whenever the descendants of the Puritans are to show the spirit of their sires, the old man appears again. When eighty years had passed, he walked once more in King Street. Five years later, in the twilight of an April morning, he stood on the green, beside the meeting house, at Lexington, where now the obelisk of granite, with a slab of slate inlaid, commemorates the first fallen of the Revolution. And when our fathers were toiling at the breastwork on Bunker's Hill, all through that night the old warrior walked his rounds. Long, long may it be, ere he comes again! His hour is one of darkness, and adversity, and peril. But should domestic tyranny oppress us, or the invader's step pollute our soil, still may the Gray Champion come; for he is the type of New England's hereditary spirit: and his shadowy march, on the eve of danger, must ever be the pledge, that New England's sons will vindicate their ancestry.

Nathaniel Hawthorne, Twice Told Tales, 1835

Banshees

There are many recorded accounts of banshee hauntings abroad. Genuine banshees are said to have been heard, often, immediately prior to battles both on Irish soil and abroad. McAnnaly [in *Irish Wonders*] writes: 'Before the Battle of the Boyne, banshees were heard singing in the air over the Irish camp, the truth of the prophecy being verified by the death-roll of the next morning'; and there are recorded instances of banshee demonstrations to Irish soldiers in Spain, during the Peninsular War; in Belgium, the night before Waterloo; and in South Africa, during the Boer War. There is a tradition that a banshee was heard by my direct ancestor James O'Donnell and his brother Daniel, when they were fighting under their cousin, Patrick Sarsfield, Earl of Lucan, in the Irish Brigade, in Flanders, during the Marlborough Campaign.

From *Family Ghosts* by Elliot O'Donnell, 1933

The Two Grenadiers

Grant me one boon, dear brother:
when I now die
take my body to France with you
and bury me in French earth.

My cross of honour on its red riband
you must lay on my heart;
put my musket in my hand
and gird my sword to my side.

So, like a sentry, I will lie in my grave,
and I will silently listen out
until one day I hear the roar of cannon
and the trot of neighing horses.

Then my Emperor will ride over my grave,
many swords will clash and glitter;
then I will rise, armed, from my grave
to protect the Emperor!

From 'The Two Grenadiers' by Heinrich Heine, 1827; translated from the German by S. S. Prawer

The Song of Soldiers

As I sat musing by the frozen dyke,
There was one man marching with a bright steel pike,

Marching in the dayshine like a ghost came he,
And behind me was the moaning and the murmur of the sea.

As I sat musing, 'twas not one but ten –
Rank on rank of ghostly soldiers marching o'er the fen,
Marching in the misty air they showed in dreams to me,
And behind me was the shouting and the shattering of the sea.

As I sat musing, 'twas a host in dark array,
With their horses and their cannon wheeling onward to the fray,
Moving like a shadow to the fate the brave must dree,
And behind me roared the drums, rang the trumpets of the sea.

Walter de la Mare, 1930

Edgehill

Edge-Hill, in the very confines of Warwickshire, neere unto Keynton
in Northamptonshire, a place, as appeares by the sequele, destined for
civill warres and battells; as where King John fought a battell with his
Barons, and where, in defence of the Kingdomes lawes and libertie, was
fought a bloody conflict betweene his Majesties and the Parliaments
forces; at this Edge-Hill, in the very place where the battell was
strucken, have since, and doth appeare, strange and portentuous Apparitions of two jarring and contrary Armies, as I shall in order deliver, it
being certified by the men of most credit in those parts, as, William
Wood, Esquire, Samuel Marshall, Minister, and others, on Saturday,
which was in Christmas time, as if the Saviour of the world, who died
to redeem mankinde, had beene angry that so much Christian blood
was there spilt, and so had permitted those infernall Armies to appeare
where the corporeall Armies had shed so much blood: – between
twelve and one o'clock of the morning was heard by some sheepherds,
and other countrey-men, and travellers, first the sound of drummes afar
off, and the noyse of souldiers, as it were, giving out their last groanes;
at which they were much amazed, and amazed stood still, till it seemed,
by the neereness of the noyse, to approach them; at which too much
affrighted, they sought to withdraw as fast as possibly they could; but
then, on the sudden, whilest they were in these cogitations, appeared in
the ayre the same incorporeall souldiers that made those clamours, and
immediately, with Ensignes display'd, Drummes beating, Musquets
going off, Cannons discharged, Horses neyghing, which also to these
men were visible, the alarum, or entrance to this game of death was
strucke up, one Army, which gave the first charge, having the King's

colours, and the other the Parliaments, in their head or front of the battells, and so pell mell to it they went; the battell that appeared to the
Kings forces seeming at first to have the best, but afterwards to be put
into apparent rout; but till two or three in the morning, in equall scale
continued this dreadfull fight, the clattering of Armes, noyse of
Cannons, cries of souldiers, so amazing and terrifying the poore men,
that they could not believe they were mortall, or give credit to their
eares and eyes; runne away they durst not, for feare of being made a
prey to these infernall souldiers, and so they, with much feare and
affright, stayed to behold the successe of the businesse, which at last
suited to this effect: after some three houres fight, that Army which
carryed the Kings colours withdrew, or rather appeared to flie; the
other remaining, as it were, masters of the field, stayed a good space
triumphing, and expressing all the signes of joy and conquest, and then,
with all their Drummes, Trumpets, Ordnance, and Souldiers, vanished;
the poore men glad they were gone, that had so long staid them there
against their wils, made with all haste to Keinton, and there knocking
up Mr Wood, a Justice of Peace, who called up his neighbour, Mr Marshall, the Minister, they gave them an account of the whole passage,
and averred it upon their oaths to be true. . . .

What this doth portend, God only knoweth, and time perhaps will
discover; but doubtlessly it is a signe of his wrath against this Land, for
these civill wars, which He in his good time finish, and send a sudden
peace between his Majestie and Parliament.

From *Memorials of John Hampden*, (1594–1643), edited by Lord Nugent, 1832

Kipling watches army manoeuvres at Frensham Ponds at Aldershot, in the hot summer of 1913

Many of the officers had been juniors in the Boer War, known to
Gwynne, one of the guests, and some to me. When the sham fight was
developing, the day turned blue-hazy, the sky lowered, and the heat
struck like the Karroo, as one scuttled among the heaths, listening to
the uncontrolled clang of the musketry fire. It came over me that anything might be afoot in such weather, pom-poms for instance, half
heard on a flank, or the glint of a helio through a cloud-drift. In short I
conceived the whole pressure of our dead of the Boer War flickering
and re-forming as the horizon flickered in the heat; the galloping feet of
a single horse, and a voice once well-known that passed chanting
ribaldry along the flank of a crack battalion. ('But Winnie is one of the
lost – poor dear!' was that song, if any remember it or its Singer in

1900–1901.) In an interval, while we lay on the grass, I told Gwynne what was in my head; and some officers also listened. The finale was to be manoeuvres abandoned and a hurried calling-off of all arms by badly frightened Commandants – the men themselves sweating with terror though they knew not why.

From 'Something of Myself' by Rudyard Kipling, 1937

An Army of Ghosts

The distant gun-fire had crashed and rumbled all night, muffled and terrific with immense flashes, like waves of some tumult of water rolling along the horizon. Now there came an interval of silence in which I heard a horse neigh, shrill and scared and lonely. Then the procession of the returning troops began. The camp-fires were burning low when the grinding jolting column lumbered back. The field guns came first, with nodding men sitting stiffly on weary horses, followed by wagons and limbers and field-kitchens. After this rumble of wheels came the infantry, shambling, limping, straggling and out of step. If anyone spoke it was only a muttered word, and the mounted officers rode as if asleep. The men had carried their emergency water in petrol-cans, against which bayonets made a hollow clink; except for the shuffling of feet, this was the only sound. Thus, with an almost spectral appearance, the lurching brown figures flitted past with slung rifles and heads bent forward under basin-helmets. Moonlight and dawn began to mingle, and I could see the barley swaying indolently against the sky. A train groaned along the riverside, sending up a cloud of whitish fiery smoke against the gloom of the trees. The Flintshire Fusiliers were a long time arriving. On the hill behind us the kite balloon swayed slowly upward with straining ropes, its looming bulbous body reflecting the first pallor of daybreak. Then, as if answering our expectancy, a remote skirling of bagpipes began, and the Gordon Highlanders hobbled in. But we had been sitting at the crossroads nearly six hours, and faces were recognizable, when Dottrell hailed our leading Company.

Soon they had dispersed and settled down on the hillside, and were asleep in the daylight which made everything seem ordinary. None the less I had seen something that night which overawed me. It was all in the day's work – an exhausted Division returning from the Somme Offensive – but for me it was as though I had watched an army of ghosts. It was as though I had seen the War as it might be envisioned by the mind of some epic poet a hundred years hence.

From *Memoirs of an Infantry Officer* by Siegfried Sassoon, 1930

Septimus in the Park

He had only to open his eyes; but a weight was on them; a fear. He strained; he pushed; he looked; he saw Regent's Park before him. Long streamers of sunlight fawned at his feet. The trees waved, brandished. We welcome, the world seemed to say; we accept; we create. Beauty, the world seemed to say. And as if to prove it (scientifically) wherever he looked, at the houses, at the railings, at the antelopes stretching over the palings, beauty sprang instantly. To watch a leaf quivering in the rush of air was an exquisite joy. Up in the sky swallows swooping, swerving, flinging themselves in and out, round and round, yet always with perfect control as if elastics held them; and the flies rising and falling; and the sun spotting now this leaf, now that, in mockery, dazzling it with soft gold in pure good temper; and now and again some chime (it might be a motor horn) tinkling divinely on the grass stalks – all of this, calm and reasonable as it was, made out of ordinary things as it was, was the truth now; beauty, that was the truth now. Beauty was everywhere.

'It is time,' said Rezia.

The word 'time' split its husk; poured its riches over him; and from his lips fell like shells, like shavings from a plane, without his making them, hard, white, imperishable, words, and flew to attach themselves to their places in an ode to Time; an immortal ode to Time. He sang. Evans answered from behind the tree. The dead were in Thessaly, Evans sang, among the orchids. There they waited till the War was over, and now the dead, now Evans himself –

'For God's sake don't come!' Septimus cried out. For he could not look upon the dead.

But the branches parted. A man in grey was actually walking towards them. It was Evans! But no mud was on him; no wounds; he was not changed. I must tell the whole world, Septimus cried, raising his hand (as the dead man in the grey suit came nearer), raising his hand like some colossal figure who has lamented the fate of man for ages in the desert alone with his hands pressed to his forehead, furrows of despair on his cheeks, and now sees light on the desert's edge which broadens and strikes the iron-black figure (and Septimus half rose from his chair), and with legions of men prostrate behind him he, the giant mourner, receives for one moment on his face the whole –

'But I am so unhappy, Septimus,' said Rezia, trying to make him sit down.

The millions lamented; for ages they had sorrowed. He would turn round, he would tell them in a few moments, only a few moments more, of this relief, of this joy, of this astonishing revelation –

'The time, Septimus,' Rezia repeated. 'What is the time?'

He was talking, he was starting, this man must notice him. He was looking at them.

'I will tell you the time,' said Septimus, very slowly, very drowsily, smiling mysteriously at the dead man in the grey suit. As he sat smiling, the quarter struck – the quarter to twelve.

From *Mrs Dalloway* by Virginia Woolf, 1925

To a Conscript of 1940

Qui n'a pas une fois désespéré de l'honneur, ne sera jamais un héros.
Georges Bernanos

A soldier passed me in the freshly fallen snow,
His footsteps muffled, his face unearthly grey;
And my heart gave a sudden leap
As I gazed on a ghost of five-and-twenty years ago.

I shouted Halt! and my voice had the old accustom'd ring
And he obeyed it as it was obeyed
In the shrouded days when I too was one
Of an army of young men marching

Into the unknown. He turned towards me and I said:
'I am one of those who went before you
Five-and-twenty years ago: one of the many who never returned,
Of the many who returned and yet were dead.

We went where you are going, into the rain and the mud;
We fought as you will fight
With death and darkness and despair;
We gave what you will give – our brains and our blood.

We think we gave in vain. The world was not renewed.
There was hope in the homestead and anger in the streets,
But the old world was restored and we returned
To the dreary field and workshop, and the immemorial feud

Of rich and poor. Our victory was our defeat.
Power was retained where power had been misused
And youth was left to sweep away
The ashes that the fires had strewn beneath our feet.

But one thing we learned: there is no glory in the dead
Until the soldier wears a badge of tarnish'd braid;
There are heroes who have heard the rally and have seen
The glitter of a garland round their head.

Theirs is the hollow victory. They are deceived.
But you, my brother and my ghost, if you can go
Knowing that there is no reward, no certain use
In all your sacrifice, then honour is reprieved.

To fight without hope is to fight with grace,
The self reconstructed, the false heart repaired.'
Then I turned with a smile, and he answered my salute
As he stood against the fretted hedge, which was like white lace.

Herbert Read, 1940

High Street, Edinburgh

Here's where to make a winter fire of stories
And burn dead heroes to keep your shinbones warm,
Bracing the door against the jackboot storm
With an old king or two, stuffing the glories
Of rancid martyrs with their flesh on fire
Into the broken pane that looks beyond Fife
Where Alexander died and a vain desire,
Hatched in Macbeth, sat whittling at his life.

Across this gulf where skeins of duck once clattered
Round the black Rock and now a tall ghost wails
Over a shuddering train, how many tales
Have come from the hungry North of armies shattered,
An ill cause won, a useless battle lost,
A head rolled like an apple on the ground;
And Spanish warships staggering west and tossed
On frothing skerries; and a king come to be crowned.

Look out into this brown November night
That smells of herrings from the Forth and frost;
The voices humming in the air have crossed
More than the Grampians; East and West unite,
In dragonish swirlings over the city park,

Their tales of deaths and treacheries, and where
A tall dissolving ghost shrieks in the dark
Old history greets you with a Bedlam stare.

He talks more tongues than English now. He fetches
The unimagined corners of the world
To ride this smoky sky, and in the curled
Autumnal fog his phantoms move. He stretches
His frozen arm across three continents
To blur this window. Look out from it. Look out
From your November. Tombs and monuments
Pile in the air and invisible armies shout.

Norman MacCaig, 1955

The restless Heiké

More than seven hundred years ago, at Dan-no-ura, in the Straits of
Shimonoséki, was fought the last battle of the long contest between the
Heiké, or Taira clan, and the Genji, or Minamoto clan. There the Heiké
perished utterly, with their women and children, and their infant
emperor likewise – now remembered as Antoku Tennō. And that sea
and shore have been haunted for seven hundred years. . . . Elsewhere I
told you about the strange crabs found there, called Heiké crabs, which
have human faces on their backs, and are said to be the spirits of Heiké
warriors. But there are many strange things to be seen and heard along
that coast. On dark nights thousands of ghostly fires hover about the
beach, or flit above the waves, – pale lights which the fishermen call
Oni-bi, or demon-fires; and, whenever the winds are up, a sound of
great shouting comes from that sea, like a clamor of battle.

In former years the Heiké were much more restless than they now
are. They would rise about ships passing in the night, and try to sink
them; and at all times they would watch for swimmers, to pull them
down. It was in order to appease those dead that the Buddhist temple,
Amidaji, was built at Akamagaséki. A cemetery also was made close
by, near the beach; and within it were set up monuments inscribed with
the names of the drowned emperor and of his great vassals; and Buddhist services were regularly performed there, on behalf of the spirits of
them. After the temple had been built, and the tombs erected, the Heiké
gave less trouble than before; but they continued to do queer things at
intervals, – proving that they had not found the perfect peace.

From 'The Story of Mimi–Nashi–Hoichi' in *Kwaidun* by Lafcadio Hearn, 1904

On the evening of the day that Thorkel and his men were drowned, Gudrun happened to go to the church at Helgafell after the rest of the household had gone to bed. And as she passed through the lich-gate she saw a ghost standing in front of her. The ghost leaned down towards her and said, 'Grave news, Gudrun!'

Gudrun replied, 'Then be quiet about it, wretch!'

Gudrun went on towards the church, as she had intended, and when she reached the church she thought she saw Thorkel and his men returned home and standing in front of the church. She saw that sea-water was streaming from their clothes. Gudrun did not speak to them, and went into the church and stayed there as long as she thought fit. Then she went back to the house, for she thought that Thorkel and his men would have gone there. But when she came inside there was no one there. And now Gudrun was greatly disturbed by everything that had happened.

On Good Friday, Gudrun sent men to get news of Thorkel's movements, some in along the coast, and some out to the islands. By then the flotsam had drifted far and wide about the islands and to both shores of the fjord. On the Saturday before Easter, people heard the news and thought it very grave, for Thorkel had been a great chieftain. Thorkel was forty-eight years old when he was drowned, and that was four years before King Olaf the Saint fell.

Gudrun was deeply affected by Thorkel's death, but bore it with great fortitude.

From the Laxdaela Saga, c.1245,
translated by Magnus Magnusson and Herman Pálsson

Admiral Hosier's Ghost

As, near Porto-Bello lying
  On the gently swelling flood,
At midnight with streamers flying
  Our triumphant navy rode;
There, while Vernon sat all glorious
  From the Spaniards' late defeat,
And his crews with shouts victorious
  Drank success to England's fleet;

On a sudden, shrilly sounding,
   Hideous yells and shrieks were heard;
Then, each heart with fear confounding,
   A sad troop of ghosts appeared,
All in dreary hammocks shrouded,
   Which for winding-sheets they wore,
And, with looks by sorrow clouded,
   Frowning on that hostile shore.

On them gleamed the moon's wan lustre,
   When the shade of Hosier brave
His pale bands was seen to muster,
   Rising from their watery grave;
O'er the glimm'ring wave he hied him,
   Where the Burford reared her sail,
With three thousand ghosts beside him,
   And in groans did Vernon hail.

'Heed, Oh heed our fatal story!
   I am Hosier's injured ghost.
You, who now have purchased glory
   At this place where I was lost,
Though in Porto-Bello's ruin
   You now triumph, free from fears,
When you think on our undoing,
   You will mix your joy with tears!

*

'Unrepining at thy glory,
   Thy successful arms we hail;
But remember our sad story,
   And let Hosier's wrongs prevail.
After this proud foe subduing,
   When your patriot friends you see,
Think on vengeance for my ruin,
   And for England shamed in me.'

Richard Glover, 1740

'A troop of spirits blest'

Oh sleep! it is a gentle thing,
Beloved from pole to pole!

To Mary Queen the praise be given!
She sent the gentle sleep from Heaven,
That slid into my soul.

The silly buckets on the deck,
That had so long remained,
I dreamt that they were filled with dew;
And when I awoke, it rained.

My lips were wet, my throat was cold,
My garments all were dank;
Sure I had drunken in my dreams,
And still my body drank.

I moved, and could not feel my limbs:
I was so light – almost
I thought that I had died in sleep,
And was a blessèd ghost.

And soon I heard a roaring wind:
It did not come anear;
But with its sound it shook the sails,
That were so thin and sere.

The upper air burst into life!
And a hundred fire-flags sheen,
To and fro they were hurried about!
And to and fro, and in and out,
The wan stars danced between.

And the coming wind did roar more loud,
And the sails did sigh like sedge;
And the rain poured down from one black cloud;
The Moon was at its edge.

The thick black cloud was cleft, and still
The Moon was at its side:
Like waters shot from some high crag,
The lightning fell with never a jag,
A river steep and wide.

The loud wind never reached the ship,
Yet now the ship moved on!
Beneath the lightning and the Moon
The dead men gave a groan.

They groaned, they stirred, they all uprose,
Nor spake, nor moved their eyes;
It had been strange, even in a dream,
To have seen those dead men rise.

The helmsman steered, the ship moved on;
Yet never a breeze up-blew;
The mariners all 'gan work the ropes,
Where they were wont to do;
They raised their limbs like lifeless tools –
We were a ghastly crew.

The body of my brother's son
Stood by me, knee to knee:
The body and I pulled at one rope,
But he said nought to me.

'I fear thee, ancient Mariner!'
Be calm, thou Wedding-Guest!
'Twas not those souls that fled in pain,
Which to their corses came again,
But a troop of spirits blest.'

From *The Rime of the Ancient Mariner* by Samuel Taylor Coleridge, 1798

'Some never-to-be-imparted secret'

With every knot of way the ship made, the swelling of the black stupendous seas became more dismally appalling. At times we gasped for breath at an elevation beyond the albatross – at times became dizzy with the velocity of our descent into some watery hell, where the air grew stagnant, and no sound disturbed the slumbers of the kraken.

We were at the bottom of one of these abysses, when a quick scream from my companion broke fearfully upon the night. 'See! see!' cried he, shrieking in my ears. 'Almighty God! see! see!' As he spoke I became aware of a dull sullen glare of red light which streamed down the sides of the vast chasm where we lay, and threw a fitful brilliancy upon our deck. Casting my eyes upwards, I beheld a spectacle which froze the current of my blood. At a terrific height directly above us, and upon the very verge of the precipitous descent, hovered a gigantic ship, of perhaps four thousand tons. Although upreared upon the summit of a wave more than a hundred times her own altitude, her apparent size still exceeded that of any ship of the line or East Indiaman in existence.

Her huge hull was of a deep dingy black, unrelieved by any of the customary carvings of a ship. A single row of brass cannon protruded from her open ports, and dashed from the polished surfaces the fires of innumerable battle-lanterns which swung to and fro about her rigging. But what mainly inspired us with horror and astonishment, was that she bore up under a press of sail in the very teeth of that supernatural sea, and of that ungovernable hurricane. When we first discovered her, her bows were alone to be seen, as she rose slowly from the dim and horrible gulf beyond her. For a moment of intense terror she paused upon the giddy pinnacle as if in contemplation of her own sublimity, then trembled, and tottered, and – came down.

The ship and all in it are imbued with the spirit of Eld. The crew glide to and fro like the ghosts of buried centuries, their eyes have an eager and uneasy meaning; and when their figures fall athwart my path in the wild glare of the battle-lanterns, I feel as I have never felt before, although I have been all my life a dealer in antiquities, and have imbibed the shadows of fallen columns at Balbec, and Tadmor, and Persepolis, until my very soul has become a ruin. . . .

When I look around me, I feel ashamed of my former apprehension. If I trembled at the blast which has hitherto attended us, shall I not stand aghast at a warring of wind and ocean, to convey any idea of which, the words tornado and simoon are trivial and ineffective? All in the immediate vicinity of the ship is the blackness of eternal night, and a chaos of foamless water; but, about a league on either side of us, may be seen, indistinctly and at intervals, stupendous ramparts of ice, towering away into the desolate sky, and looking like the walls of the universe. . . .

As I imagined, the ship proves to be in a current – if that appellation can properly be given to a tide which, howling and shrieking by the white ice, thunders on to the southward with a velocity like the headlong dashing of a cataract. . . .

To conceive the horror of my sensations is, I presume, utterly impossible; yet a curiosity to penetrate the mysteries of these awful regions predominates even over my despair, and will reconcile me to the most hideous aspect of death. It is evident that we are hurrying onward to some exciting knowledge – some never-to-be-imparted secret, whose attainment is destruction. Perhaps this current leads us to the southern pole itself. It must be confessed that a supposition apparently so wild has every probability in its favour. . . .

The crew pace the deck with unquiet and tremulous step; but there is upon their countenance and expression more of the eagerness of hope than the apathy of despair.

In the meantime the wind is still in our poop, and, as we carry a crowd of canvas, the ship is at times lifted bodily from out the sea! Oh, horror upon horror! – the ice opens suddenly to the right, and to the left, and we are whirling dizzily, in immense concentric circles, round and round the borders of a gigantic amphitheatre, the summit of whose walls is lost in the darkness and the distance. But little time will be left me to ponder upon my destiny! The circles rapidly grow small – we are plunging madly within the grasp of the whirlpool – and amid a roaring, and bellowing, and thundering of ocean and tempest, the ship is quivering – oh God! and – going down!

From 'MS Found in a Bottle' by Edgar Allan Poe, 1831

Doomed

From a shealing of turf and straw, within the pitch of a bar from the spot where we stood, came out an old woman bent with age, and leaning on a crutch. 'I heard the voice of that lad Andrew Lammie; can the chield be drowning, that he skirls sae uncannilie?' said the old woman, seating herself on the ground, and looking earnestly at the water. 'Ou ay,' she continued, 'he's doomed, he's doomed; heart and hand can never save him; boats, ropes, and man's strength and wit, all vain! vain! he's doomed, he's doomed!'

By this time I had thrown myself into the shallop, followed reluctantly by Richard Faulder, over whose courage and kindness of heart superstition had great power; and with one push from the shore, and some exertion in sculling, we came within a quoit-cast of the unfortunate fisherman. He stayed not to profit by our aid; for when he perceived us near, he uttered a piercing shriek of joy, and bounded towards us through the agitated element the full length of an oar. I saw him for a second on the surface of the water; but the eddying current sucked him down; and all I ever beheld of him again was his hand held above the flood, and clutching in agony at some imaginary aid. I sat gazing in horror on the vacant sea before us: but a breathing time before, a human being, full of youth, and strength, and hope, was there; his cries were still ringing in my ears, and echoing in the woods; and now nothing was seen or heard save the turbulent expanse of water, and the sound of its chafing on the shores. We pushed back our shallop, and resumed our station on the cliff beside the old mariner and his descendant.

'Wherefore sought ye to peril your own lives fruitlessly?' said Mark, 'in attempting to save the doomed. Whoso touches those infernal ships, never survives to tell the tale. Woe to the man who is found nigh them at midnight when the tide has subsided, and they arise in their former beauty, with forecastle, and deck, and sail, and pennon, and shroud! Then is seen the streaming of lights along the water from their cabin windows, and then is heard the sound of mirth and the clamour of tongues, and the infernal whoop and halloo, and song, ringing far and wide. Woe to the man who comes nigh them!'

To all this my Allanbay companion listened with a breathless attention. I felt something touched with a superstition to which I partly believed I had seen one victim offered up; and I inquired of the old mariner, 'How and when came these haunted ships there? To me they seem but the melancholy relics of some unhappy voyagers, and much more likely to warn people to shun destruction, than entice and delude them to it.'

'And so,' said the old man with a smile, which had more of sorrow in it than of mirth; 'and so, young man, these black and shattered hulks seem to the eye of the multitude. But things are not what they seem; that water, a kind and convenient servant to the wants of man, which seems so smooth, and so dimpling, and so gentle, has swallowed up a human soul even now; and the place which it covers, so fair and so level, is a faithless quicksand, out of which none escape. Things are otherwise than they seem. Had you lived as long as I have had the sorrow to live; had you seen the storms, and braved the perils, and endured the distresses which have befallen me; had you sat gazing out on the dreary ocean at midnight on a haunted coast; had you seen comrade after comrade, brother after brother, and son after son, swept away by the merciless ocean from your very side; had you seen the shapes of friends, doomed to the wave and the quicksand, appearing to you in the dreams and visions of the night, – then would your mind have been prepared for crediting the maritime legends of mariners; and the two haunted Danish ships would have had their terrors for you, as they have for all who sojourn on this coast.

'Of the time and the cause of their destruction,' continued the old man, 'I know nothing certain: they have stood as you have seen them for uncounted time; and while all other ships wrecked on this unhappy coast have gone to pieces, and rotted, and sunk away in a few years, these two haunted hulks have neither sunk in the quicksand, nor has a single spar or board been displaced. Maritime legend says, that two ships of Denmark having had permission, for a time, to work deeds of darkness and dolour on the deep, were at last condemned to the whirl-pool and the sunken rock, and were wrecked in this bonnie bay, as a sign to seamen to be gentle and devout. The night when they were lost was a harvest evening of uncommon mildness and beauty; the sun had newly set; the moon came brighter and brighter out; and the reapers, laying their sickles at the root of the standing corn, stood on rock and bank, looking at the increasing magnitude of the waters, for sea and land were visible from Saint Bees to Barnhourie. The sails of two vessels were soon seen bent for the Scottish coast; and with a speed outrunning the swiftest ship, they approached the dangerous quicksands and headland of Borran Point. On the deck of the foremost ship not a living soul was seen, or shape, unless something in darkness and form resembling a human shadow could be called a shape, which flitted from extremity to extremity of the ship, with the appearance of trimming the sails, and directing the vessel's course. But the decks of its companion were crowded with human shapes; the captain, and mate, and sailor, and cabin boy, all seemed there; and from them the sound of mirth and minstrelsy echoed over land and water. The coast which they skirted along was one of extreme danger; and the reapers shouted to warn them to beware of sandbank and rock; but of this friendly counsel no notice was taken, except that a large and famished dog, which sat on the prow, answered every shout with a long, loud, and melancholy howl.'

From 'The Haunted Ships' by Alan Cunningham (1784–1842)

The Flying Dutchman

A confused noise was heard among the seamen, who were collected together, and, looking in the direction of the vessel's quarter, 'A ship! no – Yes, it is!' was repeated more than once.

'They think they see a ship,' said Schriften, coming on the poop. 'He! he!'

'Where?'

'There in the gloom!' said the pilot, pointing to the darkest quarter in the horizon, for the sun had set.

The captain, Hillebrant, and Philip directed their eyes to the quarter pointed out, and thought they could perceive something like a vessel. Gradually the gloom seemed to clear away, and a lambent pale blaze to light up that part of the horizon. Not a breath of wind was on the water – the sea was like a mirror – more and more distinct did the vessel appear, till her hull, masts, and yards were clearly visible. They looked and rubbed their eyes to help their vision, for scarcely could they believe that which they did see. In the centre of the pale light, which extended about fifteen degrees above the horizon, there was indeed a large ship about three miles distant; but although it was a perfect calm, she was to all appearance buffeting in a violent gale, plunging and lifting over a surface that was smooth as glass, now careening to her bearings, then recovering herself. Her topsails and mainsail were furled, and the yards pointed to the wind; she had no sail set, but a close-reefed foresail, a storm staysail, and trysail abaft. She made little way through the water, but apparently neared them fast, driven down by the force of the gale. Each minute she was plainer to the view. At last she was seen to wear, and in so doing, before she was brought to the wind on the other tack, she was so close to them that they could distinguish the men on board: they could see the foaming water as it was hurled from her bows; hear the shrill whistle of the boatswain's pipes, the creaking of the ship's timbers, and the complaining of her masts: and then the gloom gradually rose, and in a few seconds she had totally disappeared!

'God in heaven!' exclaimed Mynheer Kloots.

Philip felt a hand upon his shoulder, and the cold darted through his whole frame. He turned round and met the one eye of Schriften, who screamed in his ear:

'PHILIP VANDERDECKEN – That's the *Flying Dutchman*!'

From *The Phantom Ship* by Captain Frederick Marryat (1839)

The Dead Ship of Harpswell

What flecks the outer grey beyond
    The sundown's golden trail?
The white flash of a sea-bird's wing,
    Or gleam of slanting sail?
Let young eyes watch from Neck and Point,
    And sea-worn elders pray, –
The ghost of what was once a ship
    Is sailing up the bay!

From grey sea-fog, from icy drift,
    From peril and from pain,
The home-bound fisher greets thy lights,
    O hundred-harboured Maine!
But many a keel shall seaward turn,
    And many a sail outstand,
When, tall and white, the Dead Ship looms
    Again the dusk of land.

She rounds the headland's bristling pines;
    She threads the isle-set bay;
No spur of breeze can speed her on,
    Nor ebb of tide delay.

Old men still walk the Isle of Orr
  Who tell her date and name,
Old shipwrights sit in Freeport yards
  Who hewed her oaken frame.

What weary doom of baffled quest,
  Thou sad sea-ghost, is thine?
What makes thee in the haunts of home
  A wonder and a sign?
No foot is on thy silent deck,
  Upon thy helm no hand;
No ripple hath the soundless wind
  That smites thee from the land!

For never comes the ship to port,
  Howe'er the breeze may be;
Just when she nears the waiting shore
  She drifts again to sea.
No tack of sail, nor turn of helm,
  Nor sheer of veering side;
Stern-fore she drives to sea and night,
  Against the wind and tide.

In vain o'er Harpswell Neck the star
  Of evening guides her in;
In vain for her the lamps are lit
  Within thy tower, Seguin!
In vain the harbour-boat shall hail,
  In vain the pilot call;
No hand shall reef her spectral sail,
  Or let her anchor fall.

Shake, brown old wives, with dreary joy,
  Your gray-head hints of ill,
And, over sick-beds whispering low,
  Your prophecies fulfil.
Some home amid yon birchen trees
  Shall drape its door with woe;
And slowly where the Dead Ship sails
  The burial boat shall row!

From Wolf Neck and from Flying Point,
  From island and from main,
From sheltered cove and tided creek,
  Shall glide the funeral train.

The dead-boat with the bearers four,
　　The mourners at her stern, –
And one shall go the silent way
　　Who shall no more return!

And men shall sigh, and women weep,
　　Whose dear ones pale and pine,
And sadly over sunset seas
　　Await the ghostly sign.
They know not that its sails are filled
　　By pity's tender breath,
Nor see the Angel at the helm
　　Who steers the Ship of Death!

John Greeley Whittier, 1867

'Old Peter'

A naval officer visited a friend in the country. Several men were sitting round the smoking-room fire when he arrived, and a fox-terrier was with them. Presently the heavy, shambling footsteps of an old dog, and the metallic shaking sound of his collar, were heard coming up stairs.

'Here's old Peter!' said his visitor.

'*Peter's dead!*' whispered his owner.

The sounds passed through the closed door, heard by all; they pattered into the room; the fox-terrier bristled up, growled, and pursued a viewless object across the carpet; from the hearth-rug sounded a shake, a jingle of a collar and the settling weight of a body collapsing into repose.

This pleasing anecdote rests on what is called *nautical evidence*, which, for reasons inexplicable to me, was (in these matters) distrusted by Sir Walter Scott.

From The Book of Dreams and Ghosts by Andrew Lang, 1897

'Dying first'

When Bill Burtenshaw left the sea and got married he lost sight of Silas altogether, and the on'y thing he 'ad to remind him of 'im was a piece o' paper which they 'ad both signed with their blood, promising that the fust one that died would appear to the other. Bill agreed to it one evenin' when he didn't know what he was doing, and for years arterwards 'e used to get the cold creeps down 'is back when he thought of

Silas dying fust. And the idea of dying fust 'imself gave 'im cold creeps all over. . . .

Bill got worse as he got older, and even made away with the furniture to get drink with. And then he used to tell 'is missis that he was drove to the pub because his 'ome was so uncomfortable.

Just at the time things was at their worst, Silas Winch, who 'appened to be ashore and 'ad got Bill's address from a pal, called to see 'im. . . . 'A better 'usband, when he's sober, you couldn't wish to see,' she ses, wiping her eyes agin. 'Well, I s'pose I can stay and see 'im?' ses Silas. 'Me and 'im used to be great pals at one time, and many's the good turn I've done him. Wot time'll he be 'ome?'

'Any time after twelve,' ses Mrs Burtenshaw; 'but you'd better not be here then. You see, 'im being in that condition, he might think you was your own ghost come according to promise and be frightened out of 'is life. He's often talked about it.'

Silas Winch scratched his head and looked at 'er thoughtful-like.

'Why shouldn't he mistake me for a ghost?' he ses at last; 'the shock might do 'im good. And, if you come to that, why shouldn't I pretend to be my own ghost and warn 'im off the drink?'

It was past twelve when a couple o' pals brought him 'ome, and, arter offering to fight all six of 'em, one arter the other, Bill hit the wall for getting in 'is way, and tumbled upstairs to bed. In less than ten minutes 'e was fast asleep, and pore Mrs Burtenshaw, arter trying her best to keep awake, fell asleep too.

She was woke up suddenly by a noise that froze the marrer in 'er bones – the most 'artrending groan she 'ad ever heard in 'er life; and, raising her 'ead, she saw Silas Winch standing at the foot of the bed. He 'ad done his face and hands over with wot is called loominous paint, his cap was pushed at the back of his 'ead, and wet wisps of 'air was hanging over his eyes. For a moment Mrs Burtenshaw's 'art stood still, and then Silas let off another groan that put her on edge all over. It was a groan that seemed to come from nothing a'most until it spread into a roar that made the room tremble and rattled the jug in the washstand basin. It shook everything in the room but Bill, and he went on sleeping like an infant. Silas did two more groans, and then 'e leaned over the foot o' the bed and stared at Bill, as though 'e couldn't believe his eyesight.

'Try a squeaky one,' said Mrs Burtenshaw.

Silas tried five squeaky ones, and then he 'ad a fit o' coughing that would ha' woke the dead, as they say, but it didn't wake Bill.

'Now some more deep ones,' ses Mrs Burtenshaw, in a w'isper.

Silas licked his lips – forgetting the paint – and tried the deep ones agin.

[295]

'Now mix 'em a bit,' ses Mrs Burtenshaw.

Silas stared at her. 'Look 'ere,' he ses, very short, 'do you think I'm a fog-horn, or wot?'

He stood there sulky for a moment, and then 'e invented a noise that nothing living could miss hearing; even Bill couldn't. He moved in 'is sleep, and arter Silas 'ad done it twice more he turned and spoke to 'is missis about it. 'D'ye hear?' he ses; 'stop it. Stop it at once.'

Mrs Burtenshaw pretended to be asleep, and Bill was just going to turn over agin when Silas let off another groan. It was on'y a little one this time, but Bill sat up as though he 'ad been shot, and he no sooner caught sight of Silas standing there than 'e gave a dreadful 'owl and, rolling over, wropped 'imself up in all the bed-clothes 'e could lay his 'ands on. Then Mrs Burtenshaw gave a 'owl and tried to get some of 'em back; but Bill, thinking it was the ghost, only held on tighter than ever.

'BILL,' ses Silas Winch, in an awful voice.

Bill gave a kick, and tried to bore a hole through the bed.

'Bill,' ses Silas agin, 'why don't you answer me? I've come all the way from the bottom of the Pacific Ocean to see you, and this is all I get for it. Haven't you got anything to say to me?'

'Good-bye,' ses Bill, in a voice all smothered with the bed-clothes.

Silas Winch groaned agin, and Bill, as the shock 'ad made a'most sober, trembled all over.

'The moment I died,' ses Silas, 'I thought of my promise towards you. "Bill's expecting me," I ses, and, instead of staying in comfort at the bottom of the sea, I kicked off the body of the cabin-boy wot was clinging round my leg, and 'ere I am.' . . .

'We was always pals, Bill, you and me,' ses Silas; 'many a v'y'ge 'ave we had together, mate, and now I'm a-laying at the bottom of the Pacific Ocean, and you are snug and 'appy in your own warm bed. I 'ad to come to see you, according to promise, and, over and above that, since I was drownded my eyes 'ave been opened. Bill, you're drinking yourself to death!'

'I – I – didn't know it,' ses Bill, shaking all over. 'I'll knock it – off a bit, and – thank you – for – w – w – warning me. G – g – good-bye.'

'You'll knock it off altogether,' ses Silas Winch, in a awful voice. 'You're not to touch another drop of beer, wine, or spirits as long as you live. D'ye hear me?'

'Not – not as medicine?' ses Bill, holding the clothes up a bit so as to be more distinct.

'Not as anything,' ses Silas; 'not even over Christmas pudding.'

From 'Keeping Up Appearances' in *Sailor's Knots* by W. W. Jacobs, 1909

The Quivering Ship

'The minutes passed slowly and then, abruptly I saw something new. There were grey things floating in the air about the ship which were so vague and attenuated that at first I could not be sure that I saw anything, but in a while there could be no doubt that they were there.

'They began to show plainer in the constant glare of the quiet lightning and growing darker and darker they increased visibly in size. They appeared to be but a few feet above the level of the sea and they began to assume humped shapes.

'For quite half an hour, which seemed indefinitely longer, I watched those strange humps like little hills of blackness floating just above the surface of the water and moving round and round the vessel with a slow, everlasting circling that produced on my eyes the feeling that it was all a dream.

'It was later still that I discovered still another thing. Each of those great vague mounds had begun to oscillate as it circled round about us. I was conscious at the same time that there was communicated to the vessel the beginning of a similar oscillating movement, so very slight at first that I could scarcely be sure she so much as moved.

'The movement of the ship grew with a steady oscillation, the bows lifting first and then the stern, as if she were pivoted amid-ships. This ceased and she settled down to a level keel with a series of queer jerks as if her weight were being slowly lowered again to the buoying of the water.

'Suddenly there came a cessation of the extraordinary lightning and we were in an absolute blackness with only the pale sickly glow of the Electric Pentacle above us and the faint buzz of the apparatus seeming far away in the night. Can you picture it all? The five of us there, tense and watchful and wondering what was going to happen.

'The thing began gently – a little jerk upward of the starboard side of the vessel, then a second jerk, then a third and the whole ship was canted distinctly to port. It continued in a kind of slow rhythmic tilting with curious timed pauses between the jerks and suddenly, you know, I saw that we were in absolute danger, for the vessel was being capsized by some enormous Force in the utter silence and blackness of that night.

'My God, mister, stop it!' came the captain's voice, quick and very hoarse. 'She'll be gone in a moment! She'll be gone!'

From 'The Haunted Jarvee' in *Carnacki the Ghost Finder*
by William Hope Hodgson, 1910

The Yachts

contend in a sea which the land partly encloses
shielding them from the too heavy blows
of an ungoverned ocean which when it chooses

tortures the biggest hulls, the best man knows
to pit against it beatings, and sinks them pitilessly.
Mothlike in mists, scintillant in the minute

brilliance of cloudless days, with broad bellying sails
they glide to the wind tossing green water
from their sharp prows while over them the crew crawls

ant like, solicitously grooming them, releasing,
making fast as they turn, lean far over and having
caught the wind again, side by side, head for the mark.

In a well guarded arena of open water surrounded by
lesser and greater craft which, sycophant, lumbering
and flitting follow them, they appear youthful, rare

as the light of a happy eye, live with the grace
of all that in the mind is feckless, free and
naturally to be desired. Now the sea which holds them

is moody, lapping their glossy sides, as if feeling
for some slightest flaw but fails completely.
Today no race. Then the wind comes again. The yachts

move, jockeying for a start, the signal is set and they
are off. Now the waves strike at them but they are too
well made, they slip through, though they take in canvas.

Arms with hands grasping seek to clutch at the prows.
Bodies thrown recklessly in the way are cut aside.
It is a sea of faces about them in agony, in despair

until the horror of the race dawns staggering the mind,
the whole sea become an entanglement of watery bodies
lost to the world bearing what they cannot hold. Broken,

beaten, desolate, reaching from the dead to be taken up
they cry out, failing, failing! their cries rising
in waves still as the skillful yachts pass over.

William Carlos Williams, 1935

Supreme Death

Fishing on a wide river from a boat
A corpse was caught, her black hair like a huge weed,
The hook stuck in a black shroud strangely marked.

There were others. Hundreds gathered round the boat,
Some turning, their white faces like pillows.
I lost my oars, and the river quickened.

On the towpath, men in their hundreds
Ran with the tide, singing, and pushing,
When they felt like it, some poor fool into the river.

Death, the best of all mysteries, layer
After layer is peeled off your secrecy
Until all that is left is an inexplicable ooze.

Too late, it is myself.
Too late, my heart is a beautiful top.
Too late, all the dead in the river are my friends.

Douglas Dunn, 1972

Eleven

DEADSTOWN

Hell from beneath is moved to meet thee at thy coming; it stirreth
up the dead for thee, even all the chief ones of the earth; it hath
raised up from their thrones all the kings of the nations.
All they shall speak and say unto thee, Art thou also become weak
as we? art thou become like unto us?
Thy pomp is brought down to the grave, and the noise of thy viols:
the worm is spread under thee, and the worms cover thee.

ISAIAH XIV

Ye realms, yet unreveal'd to human sight,
Ye Gods, who rule the Regions of the Night,
Ye gliding Ghosts, permit me to relate
The mystick Wonders of your silent state.

JOHN DRYDEN

Fourmillant cité, cité pleine des rêves
Ou le spectre, an plein jour, racrocche le passant!

CHARLES BAUDELAIRE

Enkidu rescues the pukku

'If only I had left the *pukku* in the carpenter's house today!*
I would have left the carpenter's wife like the mother who bore
me,
I would have left the carpenter's daughter like my little sister.
Today the *pukku* fell into the Earth
And my *mekkû* fell into the Earth.'
Enkidu asked Gilgamesh,
'My lord, what did you weep for, and your heart grow sad?
I shall bring up the *pukku* from the Earth today,
I shall bring up the *mekkû* from the Earth.'

Gilgamesh said to Enkidu,
'If you go down to the Earth,
You must follow my instructions.
You must not put on a clean garment,
For they will recognize that you are a stranger.
You must not be anointed with perfumed oil from an ointment
jar,
For they will gather around you at the smell of it.
You must not toss a throw-stick into the Earth,
For those who are hit by the throw-stick will encircle you.
You must not raise a club in your hands,
For ghosts will flit around you.
You must not put shoes on your feet
Lest you make a noise in the Earth.
You must not kiss the wife you love,
You must not hit the wife you hate,
You must not kiss the son you love,
You must not hit the son you hate,
For the Earth's outcry will seize you.
She who sleeps and sleeps, the mother of Ninazu who sleeps –
Her pure shoulders are not covered with a garment,
Her breasts are not pendulous like an ointment jar in a *šappatu-*
basin.'

He did not follow his lord's instructions.
He put on a clean garment,
So they recognized that he was a stranger.
He was anointed with perfumed oil from an ointment jar
So they gathered around him at the smell of it.
He tossed a throw-stick into the Earth,
So those who were hit by the throw-stick encircled him.

He raised a club in his hands,
So ghosts flitted around him.
He put shoes on his feet,
He made a noise in the Earth.
He kissed the wife he loved,
He hit the wife he hated,
He kissed the son he loved,
He hit the son he hated,
And the Earth's outcry did seize him.
She who sleeps and sleeps, the mother of Ninazu who sleeps –
Her pure shoulders were not covered with a garment,
Her breasts were not pendulous like an ointment jar in a *šikkatu-*
   basin.
When Enkidu tried to go up again out of the Earth,
Namtar did not seize him, nor did Asakku seize him: the Earth
   seized him.
The croucher, Ukur the merciless, did not seize him: the Earth
   seized him.
He did not fall in a fight among males: the Earth seized him.
Then the son of Ninsun went and wept for his servant Enkidu.
He went off on his own to Ekur, Ellil's temple. . . .

Father Ea answered him,
He spoke to the warrior Ukur,
   'Warlike young man Ukur
   You must open up a hole in the Earth now,
   So that the spirit of Enkidu can come out of the Earth like a
   gust of wind.
   And return to his brother Gilgamesh.'
The warlike young man Ukur
Opened up a hole in the Earth then,
And the spirit of Enkidu came out of the Earth like a gust of wind.
They hugged and kissed,
They discussed, they agonized.
   'Tell me, my friend, tell me, my friend,
   Tell me Earth's conditions that you found!'
   'I can't tell you, my friend, I can't tell you!
   If I tell you Earth's conditions that I found,
   You must sit and weep!
   I would sit and weep!
   Your wife whom you touched, and your heart was glad,
   Vermin eat like an old garment.
   Your son whom you touched, and your heart was glad,
   Sits in a crevice full of dust.
   "Woe" she said, and grovelled in the dust.

[303]

"Woe" he said, and grovelled in the dust.
I saw the father of one whom you once saw
Covered
He weeps bitterly over it.
I saw the father of two whom you once saw
He eats bread sitting on two bricks
I saw the father of three whom you once saw
He drinks water from a waterskin
I saw the father of four whom you once saw
His heart is glad with a team of four!
I saw the father of five whom you once saw:
Like a first-rate scribe he is open-handed,
Enters the palace as a matter of course.

I saw him, whom you saw die a sudden death:
He lies in bed and drinks pure water.
I saw him, whom you saw killed in battle:
His father and mother honour him and his wife weeps over
him.
I saw him, whose corpse you saw abandoned in the open
country:
His ghost does not sleep in the Earth.

I saw him whom you saw, whose ghost has nobody to supply
it:
He feeds on dregs from dishes, and bits of bread that lie abandoned in the streets.'

* *pukku* and *mekkû* – ritual drum and drumstick

From *Gilgamesh*, Tablet XII; translated by Stephanie Dalley

'Like mist sitting'

They are sitting about in the camp, among the branches, along
the back of the camp:
Sitting in rows in the camp, in the shade of paperbark trees:
Sitting in rows, like new white spreading clouds:
In the shade of paperbark trees, they are sitting resting like
clouds.
People of the clouds, living there like mist, like mist sitting, rest-
ing with arms on knees.

[304]

In toward the shade, in the Lily Place, the shade of the paper-
barks.
Sitting there in rows, those Wonguri-Mandjigai people, paper-
barks along like a cloud.
Living on cycad nut bread, sitting there with white-stained
fingers,
Sitting in there resting, those people of the Sandfly clan . . .
Sitting there like mist, at that Place of the Dugong . . . and of the
Dugong's Entrails . . .
Sitting resting there in the Place of the Dugong . . .
In that Place of the Moonlight Clay-pan, and at the Place of the
Dugong . . .
There at that Dugong Place they are sitting along in rows.

From the ancient Australian Wonguri-Mandjigai oral song cycle
of the Moon-Bone, translated by Ronald M. Berndt

The message of Er

'I shall tell you,' I said, 'a story, not of Alcinous, but of a valiant man,
Er, son of Armenius, of the race of Pamphylia. Once upon a time he fell
in battle. On the tenth day they took up the dead, who were now stinking, but his body was found fresh. They took him home, and were
going to bury him when on the twelfth day he came to life as he was
lying on the pyre. When he had revived, he told them what he had seen
yonder. His soul, he said, departed from him, and journeyed along with
a great company, until they arrived at a certain ghostly place where
there were two openings in the earth side by side, and opposite them
and above two openings in the heaven. In the middle sat judges. These,
when they had given their judgment, ordered the just to take the road
to the right, which led upward through heaven, first binding tablets on
them in front signifying their judgments. The unjust they ordered to
take the road to the left, which led downward. They also had tablets
signifying all that they had done bound on their backs. When it came to
his turn they told him that it was laid upon him to be a messenger to
men concerning the things that were there, and they ordered him to
listen to and look at everything in the place. . . .

'Now the souls, when they came thither, had to go at once to Lachesis.
Then a prophet first marshalled them in order, and then taking lots and
patterns of lives from the lap of Lachesis, mounted upon a high pulpit
and spoke: "The word of the daughter of Necessity, maid Lachesis.
Souls of a day, here beginneth another circle that bears the mortal race

to death. The angel will not cast lots for you, but you shall choose your angel. Let him whose lot falls first have first choice of a life to which he shall be bound by Necessity. But virtue has no master, and as a man honours or despises her, so will he have more of her or less. The responsibility is on him that chooseth. There is none on God.”

‘So saying, the prophet cast the lots to all, and each man took up the lot that fell beside him, except Er. Him the prophet forbade. And as each took it up he knew what order in the lot he had obtained. And after this the prophet laid on the ground before them the patterns of lives, many more patterns than there were persons present. Now there were patterns of all kinds. There were lives of all living creatures, and with them all human lives. Among them were tyrannies, some lasting, others destroyed in mid course and ending in poverty and exile and beggary. There were lives of famous men also, some famed for their comeliness and beauty, or for their strength and prowess, others for their lineage and the virtues of their ancestors; similarly there were lives of unknown men; and also the lives of women. But there was no determination of soul, because of necessity the soul becomes different according as she chooses a different life. All other things were mixed with each other, and with wealth and poverty; some with disease and some with health, and there were also mean conditions of these things. And it is here, it seems, my dear Glaucon, that man’s greatest danger lies; and for those reasons we must give all heed that each of us, putting aside all other learning, may search after and study this alone, if in any way he may be able to learn and discover who will give him capacity and knowledge to discern the good and the evil in life, and always and everywhere to choose the better according to his ability.

‘And when all the souls had chosen their lives they went unto Lachesis in the order of their choosing. And she gave each the angel he had chosen to be a guard throughout his life and to accomplish his choice. The angel first led the soul towards Clotho, passing it under her hand and under the sweep of the whirling spindle, so ratifying the fate which the man had chosen in his turn. He touched the spindle, and then led the soul on to where Atropos was spinning, so that the threads might be made unalterable. Thence the man went without turning under the throne of Necessity, and after coming out on the other side he first waited for the others to pass through, and then all proceeded through terrible burning heat to the plain of Lethe where grew no plants nor any trees. At last they encamped at evening by the river of Forgetfulness, whose water no pitcher may hold. All had to drink a certain measure of this water, but those who were not preserved by wisdom drank more than the measure. Each as he drank it forgot everything. Then they went to sleep, and it was midnight; there was thunder and an earthquake, and at once they were carried up from thence along different ways to their birth, shooting like stars. But he himself had been forbidden to drink of the water. When or how he returned to the body he did not know, but he suddenly opened his eyes and saw it was morning and he was lying on the pyre.

From Plato's *Republic*, fourth century BC; translated by A. D. Lindsay

Acheron

They passe the bitter waves of Acheron,
Where many soules sit *w*ailing *w*oefully,
And come to *fi*ery *fl*ood of *Ph*legeton,
Whereas the damned ghosts in torments fry,
And with *s*harp, *s*hrilling *s*hrieks doth bootlesse cry . . .

Edmund Spenser, *The Faerie Queene*, 1589–96

'Obscure they went'

Obscure they went thro dreery Shades, that led
Along the waste Dominions of the dead:
Thus wander Travellers in Woods by Night,
By the Moon's doubtful, and malignant Light:
When *Jove* in dusky Clouds involves the Skies;
And the faint Crescent shoots by fits before their Eyes.

From *Virgil's Aeneis* by John Dryden, 1697

The Poet's Vision

But in her Temple's last recess inclos'd,
On Dulness' lap th' Anointed head repos'd.
Him close she curtains round with Vapours blue,
And soft besprinkles with Cimmerian dew.
Then raptures high the seat of Sense o'erflow,
Which only heads refin'd from Reason know.
Hence, from the straw where Bedlam's Prophet nods,
He hears loud Oracles, and talks with Gods:
Hence the Fool's Paradise, the Statesman's Scheme,
The air-built Castle, and the golden Dream,
The Maid's romantic wish, the Chemist's flame,
And Poet's vision of eternal Fame.

And now, on Fancy's easy wing convey'd,
The King descending, views th' Elysian Shade.
A slip-shod Sibyl led his steps along,
In lofty madness meditating song;
Her tresses staring from Poetic dreams,
And never wash'd, but in Castalia's streams.
Taylor, their better Charon, lends an oar,
(Once swan of Thames, tho' now he sings no more.)
Benlowes, propitious still to blockheads, bows;
And Shadwell nods the Poppy on his brows.
Here, in a dusky vale where Lethe rolls,
Old Bavius sits, to dip poetic souls,
And blunt the sense, and fit it for a skull
Of solid proof, impenetrably dull:
Instant, when dipt, away they wing their flight,
Where Brown and Mears unbar the gates of Light,
Demand new bodies, and in Calf's array,
Rush to the world, impatient for the day.
Millions and millions on these banks he views,
Thick as the stars of night, or morning dews,
As thick as bees o'er vernal blossoms fly,
As thick as eggs at Ward in Pillory.

From *The Dunciad* by Alexander Pope, 1743

Don Juan in Hell

When, having reached the subterranean wave,
Don Juan paid his passage from the shore,
Proud as Antisthenes, a surly knave
With vengeful arms laid hold of either oar.

With hanging breasts between their mantles showing
Sad women, writhing under the black sky,
Made, as they went, the sound of cattle lowing
As from a votive herd that's led to die.

Sganarelle for his wages seemed to linger,
And laughter; while to the dead assembled there,
Don Luis pointed out with trembling finger
The son who dared to flout his silver hair.

Chilled in her crêpe, the chaste and thin Elvira,
Standing up close to her perfidious spouse,
Seemed to be pleading from her old admirer
For that which thrilled his first, unbroken vows.

A great stone man in armour leaped aboard;
Seizing the helm, the coal-black wave he cleft.
But the calm hero, leaning on his sword,
Had eyes for nothing but the wake they left.

From *Les Fleurs du Mal* by Charles Baudelaire, 1857 translated by Roy Campbell

Hauntings

In the grey tumult of these after-years
    Oft silence falls; the incessant wranglers part;
And less-than-echoes of remembered tears
    Hush all the loud confusion of the heart;
And a shade, through the toss'd ranks of mirth and crying,
    Hungers, and pains, and each dull passionate mood, –
Quite lost, and all but all forgot, undying,
    Comes back the ecstasy of your quietude.

So a poor ghost, beside his misty streams,
Is haunted by strange doubts, evasive dreams,
    Hints of a pre-Lethean life, of men,
Stars, rocks, and flesh, things unintelligible,
    And light on waving grass, he knows not when,
And feet that ran, but where, he cannot tell.

                                        Rupert Brooke, 1914

Sonnet

When you to Acheron's ugly water come,
Where darkness is and formless mourners brood,
And down the shelves of that distasteful flood
Survey the human rank in order dumb.
When the pale dead go forward, tortured more
By nothingness and longing than by fire,
Which bear their hands in suppliance with desire,
With stretched desire for the ulterior shore.

Then go before them like a royal ghost
And tread like Egypt or like Carthage crowned;
Because in your Mortality the most
Of all we may inherit has been found –
    Children for memory: the Faith for pride;
    Good land to leave: and young Love satisfied.

Hilaire Belloc, *Sonnets and Verses*, 1923

Ghosts and Fairies

It is especially dangerous to be out late on the last night of November, for it is the closing scene of the revels – the last night when the dead have leave to dance on the hill with the fairies, and after that they must all go back to their graves and lie in the chill, cold earth, without music or wine till the next November comes round, when they all spring up again in their shrouds and rush out into the moonlight with mad laughter.

One November night, a woman of Shark Island, coming home late at the hour of the dead, grew tired and sat down to rest, when presently a young man came up and talked to her.

'Wait a bit,' he said, 'and you will see the most beautiful dancing you ever looked on there by the side of the hill.'

And she looked at him steadily. He was very pale, and seemed sad.

'Why are you so sad?' she asked, 'and as pale as if you were dead?'

'Look well at me,' he answered. 'Do you not know me?'

'Yes, I know you now,' she said. 'You are young Brien that was drowned last year when out fishing. What are you here for?'

'Look,' he said, 'at the side of the hill and you will see why I am here.'

And she looked, and saw a great company dancing to sweet music; and amongst them were all the dead who had died as long as she could remember – men, women, and children, all in white, and their faces were pale as the moonlight.

'Now,' said the young man, 'run for your life; for if once the fairies bring you into the dance you will never be able to leave them any more.'

But while they were talking, the fairies came up and danced round her in a circle, joining their hands. And she fell to the ground in a faint, and knew no more till she woke up in the morning in her own bed at home. And they all saw that her face was pale as the dead, and they knew that she had got the fairy-stroke. So the herb doctor was sent for, and every measure tried to save her, but without avail, for just as the moon rose that night, soft, low music was heard round the house, and when they looked at the woman she was dead.

'The Dance of the Dead', from *Ancient Legends of Ireland* by Lady Wilde, 1887

Steenie claims his rent receipt

'Stephen,' said Sir John, still in the same soft, sleekit tone of voice – 'Stephen Stevenson, or Steenson, ye are down here for a year's rent behind the hand, due at last term.'

STEPHEN: 'Please your honour, Sir John, I paid it to your father.'

SIR JOHN: 'Ye took a receipt then, doubtless, Stephen, and can produce it?'

STEPHEN: 'Indeed I hadna time, an it like your honour; for nae sooner had I set down the siller, and just as his honour Sir Robert, that's gaen, drew it till him to count it, and write out the receipt, he was ta'en wi' the pains that removed him.'

'That was unlucky,' said Sir John, after a pause. . . .

'Somewhere the money must be, if there is a word of truth in your story,' said Sir John; 'I ask where you think it is, and demand a correct answer.'

'In hell, if you *will* have my thoughts of it,' said my gudesire, driven to extremity – 'in hell! with your father, his jackanape, and his silver whistle.'

On he rode, little caring where. It was a dark night turned, and the trees made it yet darker, and he let the beast take its ain road through the wood; when, all of a sudden, from tired and wearied that it was before, the nag began to spring, and flee, and stend, that my gudesire could hardly keep the saddle; upon the whilk, a horseman, suddenly riding up beside him, said, 'That's a mettle beast of yours, freend; will you sell him?' So saying, he touched the horse's neck with his riding-wand, and it fell into its auld heigh-ho of a stumbling trot. 'But his spunk's soon out of him, I think,' continued the stranger, 'and that is like mony a man's courage, that thinks he wad do great things till he come to the proof.'

My gudesire scarce listened to this, but spurred his horse, with 'Gude e'en to you, freend.'

But it's like the stranger was ane that doesna lightly yield his point; for, ride as Steenie liked, he was aye beside him at the selfsame pace. At last my gudesire, Steenie Steenson, grew half angry, and, to say the truth, half feared.

'What is it that ye want with me, freend?' he said. 'If ye be a robber, I have nae money; if ye be a leal man, wanting company, I have nae heart to mirth or speaking; and if ye want to ken the road, I scarce ken it mysell.'

'If you will tell me your grief,' said the stranger, 'I am one that, though I have been sair misca'd in the world, am the only hand for helping my freends.'

So my gudesire, to ease his ain heart, mair than from any hope of help, told him the story from beginning to end.

'It's a hard pinch,' said the stranger; 'but I think I can help you.'

'If you could lend the money, sir, and take a lang day – I ken nae other help on earth,' said my gudesire.

'But there may be some under the earth,' said the stranger. 'Come, I'll be frank wi' you; I could lend you the money on bond, but you would maybe scruple my terms. Now, I can tell you that your auld laird is disturbed in his grave by your curses, and the wailing of your family, and if ye daur venture to go to see him, he will give you the receipt.'

My gudesire's hair stood on end at this proposal, but he thought his companion might be some humorsome chield that was trying to frighten him, and might end with lending him the money. Besides, he was bauld wi' brandy, and desperate wi' distress; and he said he had courage to go to the gate of hell, and a step farther, for that receipt.

The stranger laughed.

Weel, they rode on through the thickest of the wood, when, all of a sudden, the horse stopped at the door of a great house; and, but that he knew the place was ten miles off, my father would have thought he was at Redgauntlet Castle. They rode into the outer courtyard, through the muckle faulding yetts, and aneath the auld portcullis; and the whole front of the house was lighted, and there were pipes and fiddles, and as much dancing and deray within as used to be in Sir Robert's house at Pace and Yule, and such high seasons. They lap off, and my gudesire, as seemed to him, fastened his horse to the very ring he had tied him to that morning, when he gaed to wait on the young Sir John.

'God!' said my gudesire, 'if Sir Robert's death be but a dream!'

He knocked at the ha' door just as he was wont, and his auld acquaintance, Dougal MacCallum, just after his wont, too, came to open the door, and said, 'Piper Steenie, are ye there, lad? Sir Robert has been crying for you.'

My gudesire was like a man in a dream; he looked for the stranger, but he was gane for the time. At last he just tried to say, 'Ha! Dougal Driveower, are ye living? I thought ye had been dead.'

'Never fash yoursell wi' me,' said Dougal, 'but look to yoursell; and see ye tak naething frae onybody here, neither meat, drink, or siller, except just the receipt that is your ain.'

So saying, he led the way out through halls and trances that were weel kenn'd to my gudesire, and into the auld oak parlour; and there was as much singing of profane sangs, and birling of red wine, and speaking blasphemy and sculduddry, as had ever been in Redgauntlet Castle when it was at the blythest.

But, Lord take us in keeping! what a set of ghastly revellers they were that sat round that table! . . .

Sir Robert Redgauntlet, in the midst of a' this fearful riot, cried, wi' a voice like thunder, on Steenie Piper to come to the board-head where he was sitting, his legs stretched out before him, and swathed up with flannel, with his holster pistols aside him, while the great broadsword rested upon his chair, just as my gudesire had seen him the last time upon earth – the very cushion for the jackanape was close to him, but the creature itsell was not there; it wasna its hour, it's likely; for he heard them say as he came forward, 'Is not the major come yet?' And another answered, 'The jackanape will be here betimes the morn.' And when my gudesire came forward, Sir Robert, or his ghaist, or the deevil in his likeness, said, 'Weel, piper, hae ye settled wi' my son for the year's rent?'

With much ado my father gat breath to say that Sir John would not settle without his honour's receipt.

'Ye shall hae that for a tune of the pipe, Steenie,' said the appearance of Sir Robert. 'Play us up, "Weel hoddled, Luckie."'

Now this was a tune my gudesire learned frae a warlock, that heard it when they were worshipping Satan at their meetings, and my gudesire had sometimes played it at the ranting suppers in Redgauntlet Castle, but never very willingly; and now he grew cauld at the very name of it, and said, for excuse, he hadna his pipes wi' him.

'MacCallum, ye limb of Beelzebub,' said the fearfu' Sir Robert, 'bring Steenie the pipes that I am keeping for him!'

MacCallum brought a pair of pipes might have served the piper of Donald of the Isles. But he gave my gudesire a nudge as he offered them; and looking secretly and closely, Steenie saw that the chanter was of steel, and heated to a white heat; so he had fair warning not to trust his fingers with it. So he excused himself again, and said he was faint and frightened, and had not wind aneugh to fill the bag.

'Then ye maun eat and drink, Steenie,' said the figure; 'for we do little else here; and it's ill speaking between a fou man and a fasting.'

Now these were the very words that the bloody Earl of Douglas said to keep the king's messenger in hand, while he cut the head off MacLellan of Bombie, at the Threave Castle, and that put Steenie mair and mair on his guard. So he spoke up like a man, and said he came neither to eat, or drink, or make minstrelsy, but simply for his ain – to ken what was come o' the money he had paid, and to get a discharge for it;

and he was so stout-hearted by this time, that he charged Sir Robert for conscience' sake (he had no power to say the holy name), and as he hoped for peace and rest, to spread no snares for him, but just to give him his ain.

The appearance gnashed its teeth and laughed, but it took from a large pocket-book the receipt, and handed it to Steenie. 'There is your receipt, ye pitiful cur; and for the money, my dog-whelp of a son may go look for it in the Cat's Cradle.'

My gudesire uttered mony thanks, and was about to retire when Sir Robert roared aloud, 'Stop though, thou sack-doudling son of a whore! I am not done with thee. HERE we do nothing for nothing; and you must return on this very day twelvemonth to pay your master the homage that you owe me for my protection.'

My father's tongue was loosed of a suddenty, and he said aloud, 'I refer mysell to God's pleasure, and not to yours.'

He had no sooner uttered the word than all was dark around him, and he sunk on the earth with such a sudden shock, that he lost both breath and sense.

How lang Steenie lay there, he could not tell; but when he came to himsell, he was lying in the auld kirkyard of Redgauntlet parochine, just at the door of the family aisle, and the scutcheon of the auld knight, Sir Robert, hanging over his head. There was a deep morning fog on grass and gravestane around him, and his horse was feeding quietly beside the minister's twa cows. Steenie would have thought the whole was a dream, but he had the receipt in his hand, fairly written and signed by the auld laird; only the last letters of his name were a little disorderly, written like one seized with sudden pain.

From 'Wandering Willie's Tale' in *Redgauntlet* by Sir Walter Scott, 1824

Under the hill

And sometimes nurse told me tales that she had heard from her great-grandmother, who was very old, and lived in a cottage on the mountain all alone. . . . She told me one very strange story about the hill, and I trembled when I remembered it. She said that people always went there in summer, when it was very hot, and they had to dance a good deal. It would be all dark at first, and there were trees there, which made it much darker, and people would come, one by one, from all directions, by a secret path which nobody else knew, and two persons would keep the gate, and every one as they came up had to give a very curious sign, which nurse showed me as well as she could, but she said she couldn't show me properly. And all kinds of people would come; there would be gentle folks and village folks, and some old people and boys and girls, and quite small children, who sat and watched. And it would all be dark as they came in, except in one corner where some one was burning something that smelt strong and sweet, and made them laugh, and there one would see a glaring of coals, and the smoke mounting up red. So they would all come in, and when the last had come there was no door any more, so that no one else could get in, even if they knew there was anything beyond. And once a gentleman who was a stranger and had ridden a long way, lost his path at night, and his horse took him into the very middle of the wild country, where everything was upside down, and there were dreadful marshes and great stones everywhere, and holes underfoot, and the trees looked like gibbet-posts, because they had great black arms that stretched out across the way. And this strange gentleman was very frightened, and his horse began to shiver all over, and at last it stopped and wouldn't go any farther, and the gentleman got down and tried to lead the horse, but it wouldn't move, and it was all covered with a sweat, like death. So the gentleman went on all alone, going farther and farther into the wild country, till at last he came to a dark place, where he heard shouting and singing and crying, like nothing he had ever heard before. It all sounded quite close to him, but he couldn't get in, and so he began to call, and while he was calling, something came behind him, and in a minute his mouth and arms and legs were all bound up, and he fell into a swoon. And when he came to himself, he was lying by the roadside, just where he had first lost his way, under a blasted oak with a black trunk, and his horse was tied beside him. So he rode on to the town and told the people there what had happened, and some of them were amazed; but others knew. So when once everybody had come, there was no door at all for anybody else to pass in by. And when they were all inside, round in a ring, touching each other, some one began to sing in the darkness, and some one else would make a noise like thunder with a thing they had on purpose, and on still nights people would hear the thundering noise far, far away beyond the wild land, and some of them, who thought they knew what it was, used to make a sign on their breasts when they woke up in their beds at dead of night and heard that terrible deep noise, like thunder on the mountains. And the noise and the singing would go on and on for a long time, and the people who were in a ring swayed a little to and fro; and the song was in an old, old language that nobody knows now, and the tune was queer. Nurse said her great-grandmother had known some one who remembered a little of it.

From 'The White People' by Arthur Machen, 1899

The seven brothers

Seven brothers were hunting and drying the meat of the pigs which they had killed, but a man appeared who stole the food and made away with it, the brother who had been left on guard being unable to stop him. When the turn of the youngest came, he succeeded in spearing the robber in the back, but the culprit ran off and disappeared with the spear still sticking in him. Now the spear belonged to the boys' grandfather, who, angry at its loss, demanded that they find it and return it. The brothers, therefore, went to a great hole in the earth, from which, they had discovered, the robber usually emerged. Taking a long vine, the others lowered the eldest, but he, soon terrified at the darkness, demanded to be hauled up again; and thus it went with all six older brothers, only the youngest being brave enough to reach the bottom. Once arrived, he found himself in the underworld and there soon discovered a town. Asking if he might come in, he was refused admittance on the ground that the chief was suffering from a great spear with which he had been wounded, and which was still embedded in his back. The young hero thereupon declared that he could cure the sufferer and was accordingly admitted to the chief's house; but when he was alone with the patient, he killed him, pulled out the spear, and hastened to regain the place where he had been let down. On the way he met seven beautiful maidens who wished to accompany him to the upper world, and so all were pulled up together by the brothers stationed above, and each of them then took one of the girls for his wife.

Folk tale from the Celebes Islands, told by R. B. Dixon,
in *Oceanic Mythology*, 1916

The last gift of Yama to Sâvitrî

With that the gloomy God fitted his noose,
And forced forth from the Prince the soul of him –
Subtile, a thumb in length – which being reft,
Breath stayed, blood stopped, his body's grace was gone,
And all life's warmth to stony coldness turned.
Then, binding it, the Silent Presence bore
Satyavan's soul away toward the South.

But Sâvitrî the Princess followed him;
Being so bold in wifely purity,

So holy by her love: and so upheld,
She followed him.

                    Presently Yama turned.
'Go back,' quoth he; 'pay him the funeral dues.
Enough, O Sâvitrî! is wrought for love;
Go back! too far already hast thou come.'

Then Sâvitrî made answer: 'I must go
Where my lord goes, or where my lord is borne;
Nought other is my duty. Nay, I think,
By reason of my vows, my services
Done to the Gurus, and my faultless love,
Grant but thy grace, I shall unhindered go. . . .

                    *

But, sweeter than before, the Princess sang:–

       'In paths of peace and virtue
       Always the good remain;
       And sorrow shall not stay with them,
       Nor long access of pain;
       At meeting or at parting
       Joys to their bosom strike;
       For good to good is friendly,
       And virtue loves her like.
       The great sun goes his journey
       By their strong truth impelled;
       By their pure lives and penances
       Is earth itself upheld;
       Of all which live or shall live
       Upon its hill and fields,
       Pure hearts are the "protectors,"
       For virtue saves and shields.
       Never are noble spirits
       Poor while their like survive;
       True love has gems to render,
       And virtue wealth to give.
       Never is lost or wasted
       The goodness of the good;
       Never against a mercy,
       Against a right, it stood;
       And seeing this, that virtue
       Is always friend to all,
       The virtuous and true-hearted,
       Men their "protectors" call.'

'Line for line, Princess! as thou sangest so,'
Quoth Yama, 'all that lovely praise of good,
Grateful to hallowed minds, lofty in sound,
And couched in dulcet numbers – word by word –
Dearer thou grew'st to me. O thou great heart,
Perfect and firm! ask any boon from me, –
Ask an incomparable boon!'

She cried
Swiftly, no longer stayed: 'Not heaven I crave,
Nor heavenly joys, nor bliss incomparable,
Hard to be granted even by thee; but *him*,
My sweet lord's life, without which I am dead;
Give me that gift of gifts! I will not take
Aught less without him, – not one boon, – no praise,
No splendors, no rewards, – not even those sons
Whom thou didst promise. Ah, thou wilt not, now,
Bear hence the father of them, and my hope!
Make thy free word good; give me Satyavan
Alive once more.'

And thereupon the God –
The Lord of Justice, high Vaivaswata –
Loosened the noose and freed the Prince's soul,
And gave it to the lady, saying this,
With eyes grown tender: 'See, thou sweetest queen
Of women, brightest jewel of thy kind!
Here is thy husband. He shall live and reign
Side by side with thee, – saved by thee, – in peace,
And fame, and wealth, and health, many long years;
For pious sacrifices world-renowned.
Boys shalt thou bear to him, as I did grant, –
Kshatriya kings, fathers of kings to be,
Sustainers of thy line. Also, thy sire
Shall see his name upheld by sons of sons,
Like the immortals, valiant, Mâlavas.'

These gifts the awful Yama gave, and went
Unto his place; but Sâvitrî – made glad,
Having her husband's soul – sped to the glade
Where his corse lay. She saw it there, and ran,
And, sitting on the earth, lifted its head,
And lulled it on her lap full tenderly.
Thereat warm life returned: the white lips moved;

The fixed eyes brightened, gazed, and gazed again;
As when one starts from sleep and sees a face –
The well-belovèd's – grow clear, and, smiling, wakes,
So Satyavan. 'Long have I slumbered, Dear,'
He sighed, 'why didst thou not arouse me? Where
Is gone that gloomy man that haled at me?'

Answered the Princess: 'Long, indeed, thy sleep,
Dear Lord, and deep; for he that haled at thee
Was Yama, God of Death; but he is gone;
And thou, being rested and awake, rise now,
If thou canst rise; for, look, the night is near!'

From the *Mahābhārata*, *c.*500 BC, translated by Sir Edwin Arnold

Hirotari's journey

Fujiwara Hirotari died suddenly while recuperating in a mountain temple from a severe illness. His family were summoned and preparations were made for his funeral. But on the third day he came back to life and told them the following story.

'Two men came for me wearing armour over their crimson garments and carrying swords and spears in their hands. They struck me on the back and hurried me away, saying that I was to appear at once before the king of hell. The road ended at a deep river, black as ink and dismal to look upon, with a row of trees to mark the ford. The messenger in front warned me to follow close behind him as we waded across, and thus we reached the other side safely. Ahead stood a lofty tower, many stories high and dazzlingly bright. One of the messengers ran inside and said, "He is here." "Bring him inside then," came a voice from within. I went inside and a voice from behind a screen asked, "Do you recognise the person behind you?" I looked behind me and saw my wife, who had died in childbirth some three years before. "Yes," I replied, "it is my wife".

'"It is at her request that we summoned you," they said. "Of the six years that she must suffer here, she has already endured three. Those three remaining years she wishes to pass with you, because it was with your child that she died."'

Hirotari went on to tell how he offered to rescue her from further torture by copying and reciting the Lotus Sutra. 'If he will do as he says,' his wife declared, 'I will forgive him and let him go home.' The pact sealed, Hirotari was just passing out of the gate of the tower, when he thought to ask the name of the being who had summoned him there.

'My name is Emma Ō,' the personage replied, 'but in your country they call me the Bodhisattva Jizō.' With these words he touched Hirotari on the forehead and told him that the mark he had received would preserve him from disaster. Thereupon Hirotari came to life again, realising that the judge of hell and the saviour from its torments were one and the same person.

From the *Nihon Ryōiki*, eleventh century Japan, summarised by Carmen Blacker

Dido among the lovers

Not far from thence, the mournful Fields appear;
So call'd, from Lovers that inhabit there.
The Souls, whom that unhappy Flame invades,
In secret Solitude, and Myrtle Shades,
Make endless Moans, and pining with Desire,
Lament too late, their unextinguish'd Fire.
Here *Procris*, *Eryphile* here, he found
Baring her Breast, yet bleeding with the Wound
Made by her Son. He saw *Pasiphae* there,
With *Phædra's* Ghost, a foul incestuous pair;
There *Laodamia*, with *Evadne*, moves:
Unhappy both; but loyal in their Loves.
Cæneus, a Woman once, and once a Man;
But ending in the Sex she first began.
Not far from these *Phœnician Dido* stood;
Fresh from her Wound, her Bosom bath'd in Blood.
Whom, when the *Trojan* Heroe hardly knew,
Obscure in Shades, and with a doubtful view,
(Doubtful as he who sees thro' dusky Night,
Or thinks he sees the Moon's uncertain Light:)
With Tears he first approach'd the sullen Shade;
And, as his Love inspir'd him, thus he said.
Unhappy Queen! then is the common breath
Of Rumour true, in your reported Death,
And I, alas, the Cause! By Heav'n, I vow,
And all the Pow'rs that rule the Realms below,
Unwilling I forsook your friendly State:
Commanded by the Gods, and forc'd by Fate.
Those Gods, that Fate, whose unresisted Might
Have sent me to these Regions, void of Light,
Thro' the vast Empire of eternal Night.

Nor dar'd I to presume, that, press'd with Grief,
My Flight should urge you to this dire Relief.
Stay, stay your Steps, and listen to my Vows:
'Tis the last Interview that Fate allows!
In vain he thus attempts her Mind to move,
With Tears and Pray'rs, and late repenting Love.
Disdainfully she look'd; then turning round,
But fix'd her Eyes unmov'd upon the Ground.
And, what he says, and swears, regards no more
Than the deaf Rocks, when the loud Billows roar.
But whirl'd away, to shun his hateful sight,
Hid in the Forest, and the Shades of Night.
Then sought *Sicheus*, thro' the shady Grove,
Who answer'd all her Cares, and equal'd all her Love.
  Some pious Tears the pitying Heroe paid;
  And follow'd with his Eyes the flitting Shade.
  Then took the forward Way, by Fate ordain'd, . . .

From *Virgil's Aeneis* by John Dryden, 1697

Orpheus, Eurydice, Hermes

That was the strange unfathomed mine of souls.
And they, like silent veins of silver ore,
were winding through its darkness. Between roots
welled up the blood that flows on to mankind,
like blocks of heavy porphyry in the darkness.
Else there was nothing red.

But there were rocks
and ghostly forests. Bridges over voidness
and that immense, grey, unreflecting pool
that hung above its so far distant bed
like a grey rainy sky above a landscape.
And between meadows, soft and full of patience,
appeared the pale strip of the single pathway
like a long line of linen laid to bleach.

And on this single pathway they approached.

In front the slender man in the blue mantle,
gazing in dumb impatience straight before him.

His steps devoured the way in mighty chunks
they did not pause to chew; his hands were hanging,
heavy and clenched, out of the falling folds,
no longer conscious of the lightsome lyre,
the lyre which had grown into his left
like twines of rose into a branch of olive.
It seemed as though his senses were divided:
for, while his sight ran like a dog before him,
turned round, came back, and stood, time and again,
distant and waiting, at the path's next turn,
his hearing lagged behind him like a smell.
It seemed to him at times as though it stretched
back to the progress of those other two
who should be following up this whole ascent.
Then once more there was nothing else behind him
but his climb's echo and his mantle's wind.
He, though, assured himself they still were coming;
said it aloud and heard it die away.
They still were coming, only they were two
that trod with fearful lightness. If he durst
but once look back (if only looking back
were not undoing of this whole enterprise
still to be done), he could not fail to see them,
the two light-footers, following him in silence:

The god of faring and of distant message,
the travelling-hood over his shining eyes,
the slender wand held out before his body,
the wings around his ankles lightly beating,
and in his left hand, as entrusted, *her*.

She, so belov'd, that from a single lyre
more mourning rose than from all women-mourners, –
that a whole world of mourning rose, wherein
all things were once more present: wood and vale
and road and hamlet, field and stream and beast, –
and that around this world of mourning turned,
even as around the other earth, a sun
and a whole silent heaven full of stars,
a heaven of mourning with disfigured stars: –
she, so beloved.

But hand in hand now with that god she walked,
her paces circumscribed by lengthy shroudings,

uncertain, gentle, and without impatience.
Wrapt in herself, like one whose time is near,
she thought not of the man who went before them,
nor of the road ascending into life.
Wrapt in herself she wandered. And her deadness
was filling her like fullness.
Full as a fruit with sweetness and with darkness
was she with her great death, which was so new
that for the time she could take nothing in.

She had attained a new virginity
and was intangible; her sex had closed
like a young flower at the approach of evening,
and her pale hands had grown so disaccustomed
to being a wife, that even the slim god's
endlessly gentle contact as he led her
disturbed her like a too great intimacy.

Even now she was no longer that blonde woman
who'd sometimes echoed in the poet's poems,
no longer the broad couch's scent and island,
nor yonder man's possession any longer.

She was already loosened like long hair,
and given far and wide like fallen rain,
and dealt out like a manifold supply.

She was already root.

And when abruptly,
the god had halted her and, with an anguished
outcry, outspoke the words: He has turned round! –
she took in nothing, and said softly: Who?

But in the distance, dark in the bright exit,
someone or other stood, whose countenance
was indistinguishable. Stood and saw
how, on a strip of pathway between meadows,
with sorrow in his look, the god of message
turned silently to go behind the figure
already going back by that same pathway,
its paces circumscribed by lengthy shroudings,
uncertain, gentle, and without impatience.

Rainer Maria Rilke, 1904, translated by J. B. Leishman

The Underground

There we were in the vaulted tunnel running,
You in your going-away coat speeding ahead
And me, me then like a fleet god gaining
Upon you before you turned to a reed

Or some new white flower japped with crimson
As the coat flapped wild and button after button
Sprang off and fell in a trail
Between the Underground and the Albert Hall.

Honeymooning, mooning around, late for the Proms.
Our echoes die in that corridor and now
I come as Hansel came on the moonlit stones
Retracing the path back, lifting the buttons

To end up in a draughty lamplit station
After the trains have gone, the wet track
Bared and tensed as I am, all attention
For your step following and damned if I look back.

Seamus Heaney, 1984

How Epistemon, who had his Head cut off, was finely healed by Panurge, and of the Newes which he brought from the Devils, and of the damned People in Hell

This Gigantal victory being ended, Pantagruel withdrew himself to the place of the flaggons, and called for Panurge and the rest, who came unto him safe and sound, except Eusthenes, whom one of the Giants had scratched a little in the face, whilest he was about the cutting of his throat, and Epistemon, who appeared not at all: whereat Pantagruel was so aggrieved, that he would have killed himself: but Panurge said unto him, Nay, Sir, stay a while, and we will search for him amongst the dead, and finde out the truth of all: thus as they went seeking after him, they found him stark dead, with his head between his armes all bloody. Then Eusthenes cried out, Ah cruel death! hast thou taken from me the perfectest amongst men? At which words Pantagruel rose up with the greatest grief that ever any man did see, and said to Panurge, Ha, my friend, the prophecy of your two glasses, and the javelin staffe, was a great deal too deceitful, but Panurge answered. My dear bullies all, weep not one drop more, for he being yet all hot, I will make him as sound as ever he was; in saying this, he took the head, and held it warme fore-gainst his Codpiece, that the winde might not enter into it, Eusthenes and Carpalin carried the body to the place where they had banqueted, not out of any hope that ever he would recover, but that Pantagruel might see it.

Nevertheless Panurge gave him very good comfort, saying, If I do not heale him, I will be content to lose my head (which is a fooles wager), leave off therefore crying, and help me. Then cleansed he his neck very well with pure white wine, and after that, took his head, and into it synapised some powder of diamerdis, which he alwayes carried about him in one of his bags. Afterwards, he anointed it with I know not what ointment, and set it on very just, veine against veine, sinew against sinew, and spondyle against spondyle, that he might not be wry-necked, (for such people he mortally hated) this done, he gave it round about some fifteen or sixteen stitches with a needle, that it might not fall off again, then on all sides, and every where he put a little oint-ment on it, which he called resuscitative.

Suddenly Epistemon began to breath, then opened his eyes, yawned, sneezed, and afterwards let a great household fart; whereupon Panurge said, Now certainly he is healed, and therefore gave him to drink a large full glasse of strong white wine, with a sugred toast. In this fashion was Epistemon finely healed, only that he was somewhat hoarse for above three weeks together, and had a dry cough of which he could not be rid, but by the force of continual drinking: and now he began to speak, and said, that he had seen the divel, had spoken with Lucifer familiarly, and had been very merry in hell, and in the Elysian fields, affirming very seriously before them all, that the devils were boone companions, and merry fellowes: but in respect of the damned, he said he was very sorry that Panurge had so soon called him back into this world again; for (said he) I took wonderful delight to see them: How so? said Pantagruel: because they do not use them there (said Epistemon) so badly as you think they do: their estate and con-dition of living is but only changed after a very strange manner; for I saw Alexander the great there, amending and patching on clowts upon old breeches and stockins, whereby he got but a very poor living.

Xerxes was a Cryer of mustard.
Romulus, a Salter and patcher of patines.
Numa, a nailsmith.
Tarquin, a Porter.
Piso, a clownish swaine.
Sylla, a Ferrie-man.

Cyrus, a Cowheard.
Themistocles, a glasse-maker.
Epaminondas, a maker of Mirrours or Looking-glasses.
Brutus and Cassius, Surveyors or Measurers of land.
Demosthenes, a Vine-dresser.
Cicero, a fire-kindler.
Fabius, a threader of beads.
Artaxerxes, a rope-maker.
Æneas, a Miller.
Achilles was a scauld-pated maker of hay-bundles.
Agamemnon, a lick-box.
Ulysses, a hay-mower.
Nestor, a Deer-keeper or Forrester.
Darius a Gold-finder, or Jakes-farmer.
Ancus Martius, a ship-trimmer.
Camillus, a foot-post.
Marcellus, a sheller of beans.
Drusus, a taker of money at the doors of play-houses.
Scipio Africanus, a Crier of Lee in a wooden slipper.
Asdrubal, a Lanterne-maker.
Hannibal, a Kettlemaker and seller of eggeshels.
Priamus, a seller of old clouts.
Lancelot of the lake was a flayer of dead horses.

All the Knights of the round Table were poore day-labourers, employed to rowe over the rivers of Cocytus, Phlegeton, Styx, Acheron and Lethe, when my Lords, the devils had a minde to recreate themselves upon the water, as in the like occasion are hired the boatmen at Lions, the gondeleers of Venice, and oares at London; but with this difference, that these poor Knights have only for their fare a bob or flirt on the nose, and in the evening a morsel of course mouldie bread.

From *Gargantua and Pantagruel*, 1532–4, by François Rabelais, translated from the French by Sir Thomas Urquhart, 1653

In which the Author is Privy to a Literary Dispute

I then observed Shakespeare standing between Betterton and Booth, and deciding a difference between those two great actors, concerning the placing an accent in one of his lines: this was disputed on both sides with a warmth, which surprised me in Elysium, till I discovered by intuition that every soul retained its principal characteristic, being, indeed, its very essence. The line was that celebrated one in Othello:
Put out the light, and then put out the light,
according to Betterton. Mr Booth contended to have it thus:

Put out the light, and then put out THE *light,*
I could not help offering my conjecture on this occasion, and suggested
it might perhaps be:
Put out the light, and then put out THY *light,*
Another hinted a reading very sophisticated in my opinion,
Put out the light, and then put out THEE *light,*
making light to be the vocative case. Another would have altered the
last word, and read,
Put out thy light, and then put out thy sight.
But Betterton said, if the text was to be disturbed, he saw no reason
why a word might not be changed as well as a letter, and instead of
'put out thy light,' you may read, 'put out thy eyes.' At last it was
agreed on all sides, to refer the matter to the decision of Shakespeare
himself, who delivered his sentiments as follows: 'Faith, gentlemen, it
is so long since I wrote the line I have forgot my meaning.'

From *A Journey from this World to the Next* by Henry Fielding, 1743

'Thick orchestration'

'Harry,' I said, 'what are you doing there?'

'Nothing,' said he in the mirror, 'I am only waiting. I am waiting for
death.'

'Where is death then?'

'Coming,' said the other. And I heard from the empty spaces within
the theater the sound of music, a beautiful and awful music, that music
from *Don Giovanni* that heralds the approach of the guest of stone. With
an awful and an iron clang it rang through the ghostly house, coming
from the other world, from the immortals.

'Mozart,' I thought, and with the word conjured up the most beloved
and the most exalted picture that my inner life contained.

At that, there rang out behind me a peal of laughter, a clear and ice-
cold laughter out of a world unknown to men, a world beyond all
suffering, and born of divine humor. I turned about, frozen through
with the blessing of this laughter, and there came Mozart. He passed by
me laughing as he went and, strolling quietly on, he opened the door of
one of the boxes and went in. Eagerly I followed the god of my youth,
the object, all my life long, of love and veneration. The music rang on.
Mozart was leaning over the front of the box. Of the theater nothing
was to be seen. Darkness filled the boundless space.

'You see,' said Mozart, 'it goes all right without the saxophone –

though to be sure, I shouldn't wish to tread on the toes of that famous instrument.'

'Where are we?' I asked.

'We are in the last act of *Don Giovanni*. Leporello is on his knees. A superb scene, and the music is fine too. There is a lot in it, certainly, that's very human, but you can hear the other world in it – the laughter, eh?'

'It is the last great music ever written,' said I with the pomposity of a schoolmaster. 'Certainly, there was Schubert to come. Hugo Wolf also, and I must not forget the poor, lovely Chopin either. You frown, Maestro? Oh, yes, Beethoven – he is wonderful too. But all that – beautiful as it may be – has something rhapsodical about it, something of disintegration. A work of such plenitude and power as *Don Giovanni* has never since arisen among men.'

'Don't overstrain yourself,' laughed Mozart, in frightful mockery. 'You're a musician yourself, I perceive. Well, I have given up the trade and retired to take my ease. It is only for amusement that I look on at the business now and then.'

He raised his hands as though he were conducting, and a moon, or some pale constellation, rose somewhere. I looked over the edge of the box into immeasurable depths of space. Mist and clouds floated there. Mountains and seashores glimmered, and beneath us extended worldwide a desert plain. On this plain we saw an old gentleman of a worthy aspect, with a long beard, who drearily led a large following of some ten thousand men in black. He had a melancholy and hopeless air; and Mozart said:

'Look, there's Brahms. He is striving for redemption, but it will take him all his time.'

I realized that the thousands of men in black were the players of all those notes and parts in his scores which according to divine judgment were superfluous.

'Too thickly orchestrated, too much material wasted,' Mozart said with a nod.

And thereupon we saw Richard Wagner marching at the head of a host just as vast, and felt the pressure of those thousands as they clung and closed upon him. Him, too, we watched as he dragged himself along with slow and sad step.

'In my young days,' I remarked sadly, 'these two musicians passed as the most extreme contrasts conceivable.'

Mozart laughed.

'Yes, that is always the way. Such contrasts, seen from a little distance, always tend to show their increasing similarity. Thick orchestration was in any case neither Wagner's nor Brahms' personal failing. It was a fault of their time.'

'What? And have they got to pay for it so dearly?' I cried in protest.

'Naturally. The law must take its course. Until they have paid the debt of their time it cannot be known whether anything personal to themselves is left over to stand to their credit.'

'But they can't either of them help it!'

'Of course not. They cannot help it either that Adam ate the apple. But they have to pay for it all the same.'

'But that is frightful.'

'Certainly. Life is always frightful. We cannot help it and we are responsible all the same. One's born and at once one is guilty. You must have had a remarkable sort of religious education if you did not know that.'

From Steppenwolf by Hermann Hesse, 1927, translated by
Joseph Mileck and Horst Franz

I and my palm-wine tapster in the Deads' Town

When it was 8 o'clock in the morning, then we entered the town and asked for my palm-wine tapster whom I was looking for from my town when he died, but the deads asked for his name and I told him that he was called 'BAITY' before he died, but now I could not definitely know his present name as he had died.

When I told them his name and said that he had died in my town, they did not say anything but stayed looking at us. When it was about five minutes that they were looking at us like that, one of them asked us from where did we come? I replied that we were coming from my town, then he said where. I told him that it was very far away to this town and he asked again were the people in that town alives or deads? I replied that the whole of us in that town had never died. When he heard that from me, he told us to go back to my town where there were only alives living, he said that it was forbidden for alives to come to the Deads' Town. . . .

Then he went back to the house of my tapster and told him that two alives were waiting for him. After a few minutes, my palm-wine tapster came, but immediately he saw us, he thought that I had died before coming there, so he gave the sign of deads to us, but we were unable to reply to him, because we never died, and at the same time that he reached us, he knew that we could not live with them in the town as we could not reply to his signal, then before we started any conversation, he built a small house there for us. . . .

After that we started conversation which went thus – I told him that after he had died, I wanted to die with him and follow him to this

Deads' Town because of the palm-wine that he was tapping for me and nobody could tap it for me like him, but I could not die. . . . So one day, I thought what I could do, then I thought within myself that I should find him (palm-wine tapster) wherever he might be and tell him to follow me to my father's town and begin to tap palm-wine for me as usual.

So after I had related how the story went to him, he did not talk a single word, but he went back to the town, and after a while, he brought about twenty kegs of palm-wine for me, then I started to drink it. After that he started his own story: – He said that after he had died in my town, he went to a certain place, which anybody who just died must go to first, because a person who just died could not come here (Deads' Town) directly. He said that when he reached there, he spent two years in training and after he had qualified as a full dead man, then he came to this Deads' Town and was living with deads and he said that he could not say what happened to him before he died in my town. But when he said so, I told him that he fell down from a palm-tree on a Sunday evening when he was tapping palm-wine and we buried him at the foot of the very palm-tree on which he fell.

Then he said that if that should be the case, he overdrank on that day.

After that, he said that he came back to my house on the very night that he fell and died at the farm and looked at everyone of us, but we did not see him, and he was talking to us, but we did not answer, then he went away. He told us that both white and black deads were living in the Deads' Town, not a single alive was there at all. Because everything that they were doing there was incorrect to alives and everything that all alives were doing was incorrect to deads too.

He said that did I not see that both dead persons and their domestic animals of this town were walking backwards? Then I answered 'Yes.' Then he told me that he could not follow me back to my town again, because a dead man could not live with alives and their characteristics would not be the same and said that he would give me anything that I liked in the Deads' Town. When he said so, I thought over what had happened to us in the bush, then I was very sorry for my wife and myself and I was then unable to drink the palm-wine which he gave me at that moment. Even I myself knew already that deads could not live with alives, because I had watched their doings and they did not correspond with ours at all. When it was five o'clock in the evening, he went to his house and brought food for us again and he went back after three hours. But when he came back early in the morning, he brought another 50 kegs of palm-wine which I drank first of all that morning. But when I thought that he would not follow us to my town, and again, my wife was pressing me too much to leave there very early, when he came, I told him that we should leave here tomorrow morning, then he gave me an 'EGG'. He told me to keep it as safely as gold and said that if I reached my town, I should keep it inside my box and said that the use of the egg was to give me anything that I wanted in this world and if I wanted to use it, I must put it in a big bowl of water, then I would mention the name of anything that I wanted. After he gave me the egg we left there on the third day after we arrived there and he showed us another shorter road and it was a really road, not a bush as before.

Now we started our journey from the Deads' Town directly to my home town which I had left for many years. As we were going on this road, we met over a thousand deads who were just going to the Deads' Town and if they saw us coming towards them on that road, they would branch into the bush and come back to the road at our back. Whenever they saw us, they would be making bad noise which showed us that they hated us and also were very annoyed to see alives. These deads were not talking to one another at all, even they were not talking plain words except murmuring. They always seemed as if they were mourning, their eyes would be very wild and brown and everyone of them wore white clothes without a single stain.

From *The Palm-Wine Drinkard* by Amos Tutuola, 1952

Crouch End

There were phone directories stacked under the table – phone directories and something else, phone-directory-shaped, that wasn't a phone directory. I bent down and pulled it out by its spine. It *was* a phone directory. *North London Book of the Dead*, ran the title; and then underneath: *A–Z*. The cover was the usual yellow flimsy card and there was also the usual vaguely arty line drawing – in this instance of Kensal Green Cemetery. I started to leaf through the pages.

'So, you're not here five minutes and you want to use the phone,' said Mother coming back in from the kitchenette.

'What's this, Mother?' I held up the directory.

'Oh that. Well, I guess you might call it a kind of religious text.' She giggled unnervingly.

'Mother, don't you think it's about time you came clean with me about all of this?'

We sat down at the table (similar melamine finish, similar blue, flower-patterned tablecloth) with the *North London Book of the Dead* in between us.

'Well, it's like this,' began Mother. 'When you die you go and live in another part of London. And that's it.'

'Whaddya mean, that's it?' I could already see all sorts of difficulties with this radical new view of death, even if I was sitting inside an example of it. 'Whaddya mean, that's it? Who decides which part of London? How is it that no one's ever heard of this before? How come people don't notice all the dead people clogging up the transport system? What about paying bills? What about this phone book? You can't tell me this lists all the people who have ever died in North London, it isn't thick enough. And what about the dead estate agents, who do they work for? A Supreme Estate Agent? And why Crouch End? You hate Crouch End.'

'It could have been worse, some dead people live in Wanstead.'

From 'The North London Book of the Dead' by Will Self, 1991

My Church in Spittle-fields

And it came into my Mind on reading this Account that this was the Site of the Mysteries, as Mirabilis had once related them to me: here the Boy who is to be Sacrificed is confin'd to the Chamber beneath the Earth and a large Stone rolled across its Face; here he sits in Darknesse for seven dayes and seven nights, by which time he is presum'd to have been led past the Gates of Death, and then on the eighth Day his Corse is led out of the Cave with much rejoycing: that Chamber is known itself as a Holy Place, which is inshrined to the Lord of Death. Thus when I spoke to Walter of our new Sepulture, or Enclosure, my Thoughts were buryed far beneath: my own House under Ground will be dark indeed, and a true Labyrinth for those who may be placed there. It will not be so empty as Kott's Hole neither: there are no Grave-stones nor Vaults there but it is beside the Pitte, now quite over-laid and forgotten, where my Parents had been discharg'd and so many Hundred (I should say Thousand) Corses also. It is a vast Mound of Death and Nastinesse, and my Church will take great Profit from it: this Mirabilis once describ'd to me, *viz* a Corn when it dies and rots in the Ground, it springs again and lives, so, *said he,* when there are many Persons dead, only being buryed and laid in the Earth, there is an Assembling of Powers. If I put my Ear to the Ground I hear them lie promiscuously one with another, and their small voices echo in my Church: they are my Pillars and my Foundation.

From *Hawksmoor* by Peter Ackroyd, 1983

'Beati mundo corde'

As when his earliest shaft of light assails
   The city where his Maker shed His blood,
   When Ebro lies beneath the lifted Scales.

And noontide scorches down on Ganges' flood,
   So rode the sun; thus day was nightward winging
   When there before us God's glad angel stood.

He on the bank, across the flames, stood singing
   Beati mundo corde, with a sound
   More than all earthly music sweet and ringing.

Then: 'Holy souls, there's no way on or round
   But through the bite of fire; in, then, and come!
   Nor be you deaf to what is sung beyond.'

As we approached him, thus his words struck home;
   And it was so with me when this I heard
   Even as with one who's carried to the tomb.

I leaned across my clasped hands, staring hard
   Into the fire, picturing vividly
   Sights I had seen, of bodies burned and charred.

Then both my friendly escorts turned to me,
   And Virgil spoke and said: 'My son, though here
   There may be torment, death there cannot be.

Remember, O remember! and if clear
   From harm I brought thee, even on Geryon's back,
   What shall I now, with God so much more near?

Rest thou assured that though this fiery track
   Should lap thee while a thousand years went by
   Thy head should not be singed nor one hair lack;

And if thou think that I deceive thee, why,
   Prove it – go close, hold out a little bit
   Of thy skirt's hem in thine own hand, and try.

Have done with fear henceforth, have done with it –
   Turn and go safe.' And there was I, for all
My conscience smote me, budging ne'er a whit. . . .

[333]

While from yon side sweet singing showed us how
To go, and led us, by the listening held,
Forth where the road lifts to the mountain's brow.

From Dante Alighieri, *Purgatorio*, c.1310–20; translated from the Italian by
Dorothy L. Sayers

'In Spirit and in Truth'

'We are nearly there,' said the boy. 'They are asleep. Shall I call? They will be so pleased to see you, for I have prepared them.'

Mr Bons moaned. They moved over the lunar rainbow, which ever and ever broke away behind their wheels. How still the night was! Who would be sentry at the Gate?

'I am coming,' he shouted, again forgetting the hundred resolutions. 'I am returning – I, the boy.'

'The boy is returning,' cried a voice to other voices, who repeated, 'The boy is returning.'

'I am bringing Mr Bons with me.'

Silence.

'I should have said Mr Bons is bringing me with him.'

Profound silence.

'Who stands sentry?'

'Achilles.'

And on the rocky causeway, close to the springing of the rainbow bridge, he saw a young man who carried a wonderful shield.

'Mr Bons, it is Achilles, armed.'

'I want to go back,' said Mr Bons.

The last fragment of the rainbow melted, the wheels sang upon the living rock, the door of the omnibus burst open. Out leapt the boy – he could not resist – and sprang to meet the warrior, who, stooping suddenly, caught him on his shield.

'Achilles!' he cried, 'let me get down, for I am ignorant and vulgar, and I must wait for that Mr Bons of whom I told you yesterday.'

But Achilles raised him aloft. He crouched on the wonderful shield, on heroes and burning cities, on vineyards graven in gold, on every dear passion, every joy, on the entire image of the Mountain that he had discovered, encircled, like it, with an everlasting stream. 'No, no,' he protested, 'I am not worthy. It is Mr Bons who must be up here.'

But Mr Bons was whimpering, and Achilles trumpeted and cried, 'Stand upright upon my shield!'

'Sir, I did not mean to stand! Something made me stand. Sir, why do you delay? Here is only the great Achilles, who you knew.'

Mr Bons screamed, 'I see no one. I see nothing. I want to go back.' Then he cried to the driver, 'Save me! Let me stop in your chariot. I have honoured you. I have quoted you. I have bound you in vellum. Take me back to my world.'

The driver replied, 'I am the means and not the end. I am the food and not the life. Stand by yourself, as that boy has stood, I cannot save you. For poetry is a spirit; and they that would worship it must worship in spirit and in truth.'

Mr Bons – he could not resist – crawled out of the beautiful omnibus. His face appeared, gaping horribly. His hands followed, one gripping the step, the other beating the air. Now his shoulders emerged, his chest, his stomach. With a shriek of 'I see London,' he fell – fell against the hard, moon-lit rock, fell into it as if it were water, fell through it, vanished, and was seen by the boy no more.

'Where have you fallen to, Mr Bons? Here is a procession arriving to honour you with music and torches. Here come the men and women whose names you know. The mountain is awake, the river is awake, over the race-course the sea is awaking those dolphins, and it is all for you. They want you —'

There was the touch of fresh leaves on his forehead. Some one had crowned him.

$$TE\Lambda o\Sigma$$

.   .   .   .   .

From the *Kingston Gazette, Surbiton Times,*
and *Raynes Park Observer.*

The body of Mr Septimus Bons has been found in a shockingly mutilated condition in the vicinity of the Bermondsey gas-works. The deceased's pockets contained a sovereign-purse, a silver cigar-case, a bijou pronouncing dictionary, and a couple of omnibus tickets. The unfortunate gentleman had apparently been hurled from a considerable height. Foul play is suspected, and a thorough investigation is pending by the authorities.

From 'The Celestial Omnibus' by E. M. Forster, 1911

Twelve

HARBINGERS

By the marriage-bed of their lords, 'tis said,
He flits on the bridal eve;
And 'tis held as faith, to their bed of death
He comes – but not to grieve.

When an heir is born, he is heard to mourn,
And when aught is to befall
That ancient line, in the pale moonshine,
He walks from hall to hall.

LORD BYRON

Augustine and Jerome

S. Augustine, in his Epistle (cv) addressed to S. Cyril, Bishop of Jerusalem, relates how at the very hour that S. Jerome who lay sick in the little city of Bethlehem, breathed forth his soul into the hands of God, he was himself at Hippo (of which city he was Bishop) and meditating deeply upon the blessedness of those who are in Paradise inasmuch as S. Severus, the disciple of S. Martin, had instantly besought him to treat of these matters. Taking pen and paper holy Augustine set himself to indite an epistle to S. Jerome in order to inquire of him concerning these high and mysterious things of God, well knowing that there was no living man who could better discourse of them than the learned doĉtor of Bethlehem. For, indeed, what S. Jerome did not know, there was no mortal man who knew. S. Augustine had already commenced his letter with the customary salutation when his room was filled with the most heavenly fragrance and all was aureoled in dazzling light. (Now it was about the hour of Compline.) The sweet odour and the exceeding glory so ravished the senses of S. Augustine that he fell into an ecstasy. Then from the very heart of this unearthly radiance there came a voice which said: *Augustine, what seekest thou to know? Canst thou pour the ocean into a little vessel? Or canst thou grasp the wide world in one hand? Canst thou stay the spheres in their celestial race? Can thine eyes see what never mortal eye hath seen, and thine ear hear what ear of man hath never heard? Canst thou understand what the mind of mortal man may not know? What end hath the infinite? How shall a man measure that which hath neither bound nor bourn? It is easier far to pour the ocean into a little vessel, to grassp the orb of the world in one hand, to stay the spheres in their course, than it is for a man to skill even dimly and afar the glory of those souls who are in Paradise with God unless thou hast tasted of that glory and hast been made a partaker in it, even as I am tasting and am made a partaker.* The words died away, and S. Augustine asked: *Who art thou, radiant with light, who speakest thus with me?* The voice replied: *I am Jerome, unto whom thou writest.*

From *A Treatise of Ghosts* by Father Noël Taillepied, 1588,
translated by M. Summers

'Let the candle burn'

Also a certain one of the same handmaids of God, being taken with the said disease and now brought to her last point, began suddenly about midnight to cry out to them that attended her, desiring them to put out the candle that was there burning: and when she ofttimes called and so desired them, and yet none of them would do as she bade them: 'I know,' put she in at the last, 'that ye think me thus to speak as if I were not in my right mind; but now at this time know ye that it is not so: for I tell you truly that I see this house filled with so great a light that that candle of yours seemeth to me altogether dim.' And when none of them did even yet answer unto these sayings of hers nor follow her bidding: 'Well,' quoth she again, 'let that candle burn as long as ye list; but yet know ye well that the same is not my light: for my light is to come to me when the morning beginneth.' And she began to tell that a certain man of God appeared unto her, which had died the same year, and said to her, that when the morning light drew near, she should depart hence to the everlasting light. The truth of which vision was proved by the speedy death of the maiden about the break of day.

From Bede's *Ecclesiastical History*, c.731 AD,
translated from the Latin by J. E. King

Sigrid and Thorstein

Early in the winter, disease broke out at the farm. The overseer of the farm, an unpopular man called Gardi, was the first to be taken ill, and die. In a short time many others had caught the disease, and died one after another. Then Thorstein Eiriksson and Sigrid, the wife of his namesake, fell ill.

One evening Sigrid wanted to go outside to the privy that was opposite the main door. Gudrid went with her. While they were outside, facing the door, Sigrid cried out, 'Oh!'

Gudrid said, 'We are being very careless; you should not have come out into the cold. We must hurry back inside.'

'I am not going in now,' said Sigrid, 'for all the dead are lined up before the door. I can see your husband Thorstein amongst them, and I can also see myself there. What a horrible sight!'

But it passed off, and she said, 'I cannot see them now.'

The dead overseer, who had seemed to her to be trying to flog the others with a whip, had also vanished. The women went back inside.

Sigrid was dead by the morning, and a coffin was made for her.

That same day some men went out fishing, and Thorstein of Lysufjord accompanied them down to the landing-place; and at dusk he went down again to see to the catch. Then Thorstein Eiriksson sent a message to him asking him to come back at once because there was trouble at home and Sigrid's corpse was trying to rise and get into bed with him. When he returned, she had reached the edge of Thorstein Eiriksson's bed; his namesake seized hold of her and drove an axe into her breast.

Thorstein Eiriksson died at nightfall.

From *Eirik's Saga*, mid-thirteenth century; translated from the Icelandic by
Magnus Magnusson and Hermann Pálsson

Ben Jonson's son

When the King came in England, at that tyme the pest was in London,
he being in the Country at S‍ʳ Robert Cottons house with old Cambden,
he saw in a vision his eldest sone then a child and at London, appear
unto him with ye Mark of a bloodie crosse on his forehead as if it had
been cutted with a suord, at which amazed he prayed unto God, & in
ye morning he came to Mr Cambdens chamber to tell him, who persuaded him it was but ane apprehension of his fantasie at which he
sould not be disjected in ye mean tyme comes your letters from his wife
of ye death of that Boy in ye plague. He appeared to him he said of a
manlie shape & of that Grouth that he thinks he shall be at the resurrection.

Ben Jonson; *Conversations with William Drummond of Hawthornden*, 1619

Mrs Donne

At this time of Mr Donne's, and his wife's living in Sir Robert Drury's
house in Drury-Lane, the Lord Haye was by King James sent upon a
glorious embassy, to the then French King Henry the IV and Sir Robert
put on a sudden resolution to accompany him to the French Court, and
to be present at his audience there. And Sir Robert put on as sudden a
resolution, to subject Mr Donne to be his companion in that journey;
and this desire was suddenly made known to his wife, who was then
with child, and otherwise under so dangerous a habit of body, as to her
health, that she protested an unwillingness to allow him any absence
from her; saying her divining soul boded her some ill in his absence,
and therefore desired him not to leave her. This made Mr Donne lay
aside all thoughts of his journey, and really to resolve against it. But Sir
Robert became restless in his persuasions for it, and Mr Donne was so
generous as to think he had sold his liberty, when he had received so
many charitable kindnesses from him, and told his wife so; who, therefore, with an unwilling willingness, did give a faint consent to the
journey, which was proposed to be but for two months: within a few
days after this resolve, the Ambassador, Sir Robert, and Mr Donne, left
London, and were the twelfth day got safe to Paris. Two days after
their arrival there, Mr Donne was left alone in the room, where Sir

Robert and he, with some others, had dined: to this place Sir Robert returned within half an hour, and as he left, so he found Mr Donne alone, but in such an extacy, and so altered as to his looks, as amazed Sir Robert to behold him, insomuch as he earnestly desired Mr Donne to declare what had befallen him in the short time of his absence? to which Mr Donne was not able to make a present answer, but after a long and perplexed pause, said, 'I have seen a dreadful vision since I saw you: I have seen my dear wife pass twice by me through this room, with her hair hanging about her shoulders, and a dead child in her arms; this I have seen since I saw you.' To which Sir Robert replied, 'Sure Sir, you have slept since I saw you, and this is the result of some melancholy dream, which I desire you to forget, for you are now awake.' To which Mr Donne's reply was, 'I cannot be surer that I now live, than that I have not slept since I saw you, and am sure that at her second appearing, she stopt and lookt at me in the face and vanished.' – Rest and sleep had not altered Mr Donne's opinion the next day, for he then affirmed this vision with a more deliberate, and so confirmed a confidence, that he inclined Sir Robert to a faint belief, that the vision was true. It is truly said, that desire and doubt have no rest, and it proved so with Sir Robert, for he immediately sent a servant to Drury-House, with a charge to hasten back and bring him word whether Mrs Donne were alive? and if alive, in what condition she was as to her health. The twelfth day the messenger returned with this account – that he found and left Mrs Donne very sad, sick in her bed, and that, after a long and dangerous labour, she had been delivered of a dead child: and upon examination, the abortion proved to be the same day, and about the very hour, that Mr Donne affirmed he saw her pass by him in his chamber.

From *The Life of John Donne* by Isaak Walton, 1640

'In 1763 . . .'

We talked of belief in ghosts. He said, 'Sir, I make a distinction between what a man may experience by the mere strength of his imagination, and what imagination cannot possibly produce. Thus, suppose I should think that I saw a form, and heard a voice cry, "Johnson, you are a very wicked fellow, and unless you repent you will certainly be punished;" my own unworthiness is so deeply impressed upon my mind that I might *imagine* I thus saw and heard, and therefore I should not believe that an external communication had been made to me. But if a form should appear, and a voice should tell me that a particular man had died at a particular place, and a particular hour, a fact which I had no apprehension of, nor any means of knowing, and this fact, with all its circumstances, should afterwards be unquestionably proved, I should, in that case, be persuaded that I had supernatural intelligence imparted to me.'

From *The Life of Dr Johnson* by James Boswell, 1791

Robert Blake

Early in 1787 Robert fell ill, and during the last fortnight William nursed him without taking rest by day or night, until, at the moment of death, he saw his brother's soul rise through the ceiling 'clapping its hands for joy'; whereupon he went to bed and slept for three days and nights. Robert was buried in Bunhill Fields on February 11. The register says: 'Feb. 11, 1787. Mr Robert Blake from Golden Square in a grave, 13/6.' But his spiritual presence was never to leave the mind of William Blake, who in 1800 we find writing to Hayley: 'Thirteen years ago I lost a brother, and with his spirit I converse daily and hourly in the spirit, and see him in remembrance, in the regions of my imagination. I hear his advice, and even now write from his dictate.' It was Robert whom he saw in a dream, not long after his death, telling him the method by which he was to engrave his poems and designs. The spiritual forms of William and of Robert, in almost exact parallel, are engraved on separate pages of the Prophetic Book of *Milton*.

From *William Blake* by Arthur Symons, 1907

Bílá paní – The White Lady

In some noble families, living mainly in southern Bohemian castles, the harbinger of death was a vision of the White Lady. Whenever she appeared, the family could expect some unusual event, sad or happy: a death, a wedding, or a birth. She always appeared in white, a sedate, shapely lady, wearing a widow's veil. Whenever she foretold a sad happening, she was said to wear black gloves. Sometimes she could be seen at high noon, but mostly she appeared at night.

She showed special concern for the noble families of Hradec and Rožmberk, to whom she had been related during her lifetime. In the year 1539 a son was born in Krumlov in southern Bohemia, to Sir Jošt of Rožmberk. The child, named Petr Vok, was the last male member of the ancient family. He was well cared for by his nurses, but he had another conscientious and kindly guardian: the White Lady. She appeared every night, when everybody in the castle slept. Even though the doors and windows of the child's bedroom were locked, suddenly, there she was, in the very centre of the chamber, lighting it up as though by moonbeams. She would stand by the cradle, move back its curtains, and gaze lovingly at the infant, the last member of the house of Rožmberk, while the nursemaids slept. If the child whimpered, she would lift him up in her arms, rock him, smile at him, and comfort him, until he quieted down again. Then tenderly putting him back in the cradle, she would disappear as suddenly as she had come.

Once, however, the nurse in charge awakened and saw the vision rocking the baby. Recognizing the White Lady, she froze with terror, and could neither move nor call out. She watched anxiously to see that no harm came to the child. After the visitor's disappearance, she woke the other nurse and told her what she had seen, and they looked their charge over carefully. But he slept on, rosy and quiet, and did not awaken until morning. He was in perfect health and remained so all day. The following night, after the child fell asleep, the two women waited in expectation of what would happen. They sat down near the cradle as usual, but did not close their eyes, watching the doors and windows, trembling at every chance sound. Suddenly, on the stroke of midnight, the room grew lighter, and there, in the glow, stood the White Lady.

She moved to the cradle, looked in, and at the child's first cry she nestled him in her arms and soon rocked him to sleep again. After she put him down in his cradle, she disappeared as before, and the nurses, bewildered, did not know how or where she had gone. The child, blooming with health, slept on peacefully. The terrified women relaxed somewhat, but were too excited to get any rest that night. On the next night, the White Lady appeared again, tended the child, and was gone. This time the nurses were able to go to sleep at once. And when the apparition continued to come and care for the baby night after night, the nurses stopped watching for her and rested through the night. They trusted her and no longer feared her.

But once it happened that one of the nurses fell ill and was replaced by another. When the new nursemaid happened to glimpse the White Lady that night, she trembled with fright. When she told her fellow-nurse about it in the morning, she was advised to forget it, get her sleep, and let the White Lady do her work. But the new nursemaid felt that this would be wrong. She did not trust the ghost and felt that she would be held responsible if her charge came to any harm. That night she stayed awake, anxiously waiting for midnight. The 'White Lady' came as usual, made for the cradle, and as soon as the baby whimpered, she picked him up to comfort him. No sooner had she done so, however, than the new nursemaid leapt to her feet and faced the vision like a mother hen about to protect her chick from harm. Forcibly, she took the child away from the White Lady, who did not resist, but stood there motionless and stern. Gazing at the daring nurse, she said:

'Woman, do you know what you are doing? I am this child's kinswoman and have every right to hold him. But you shall see me here no more!'

With these words, the vision went to the wall, made the sign of the cross, the wall opened for her, and she was gone. The bright glow disappeared, and the chamber became dark. The nursemaid, shaking like a leaf, could hardly make it to the cradle to put her charge down. After that, she never beheld the White Lady again, nor did the other nurses. The ghost never came back to care for young Petr.

Time passed, and the child grew to manhood. Having heard more than once how his ghostly kinswoman had cared for him and how she had disappeared in the wall, the idea came to him to investigate where she had gone, so he had that place in the wall of his old nursery torn down. When the bricks were removed, the workers found a big treasure, which had been put there by his ancestors. Petr Vok was glad to get it, and felt grateful to the White Lady who had shown him the way to so much gold and so many precious stones.

From *Old Czech Legends* by Alois Jirásek, 1894; translated from the Czech by
Marie Holeček

Tom O'r Nant

Many strange adventures occurred to Tom in South Wales, but those which befell him whilst officiating as a turnpike-keeper were certainly the most extraordinary. If what he says be true, as of course it is – for who shall presume to doubt Tom O' the Dingle's veracity? – whosoever fills the office of turnpike-keeper in Wild Wales should be a person of very considerable nerve.

'We were in the habit of seeing,' says Tom, 'plenty of passengers going through the gate without paying toll; I mean such things as are called phantoms or illusions – sometimes there were hearses and mourning coaches, sometimes funeral processions on foot, the whole to be seen as distinctly as anything could be seen, especially at nighttime. I saw myself on a certain night a hearse go through the gate whilst it was shut; I saw the horses and the harness, the postillion, and the coachman, and the tufts of hair such as are seen on the tops of hearses, and I saw the wheels scattering the stones in the road, just as other wheels would have done. Then I saw a funeral of the same character, for all the world like a real funeral; there was the bier and the black drapery. I have seen more than one. If a young man was to be buried there would be a white sheet, or something that looked like one – and sometimes I have seen a flaring candle going past.

'Once a traveller passing through the gate called out to me: "Look! yonder is a corpse candle coming through the fields beside the highway." So we paid attention to it as it moved, making apparently towards the church from the other side. Sometimes it would be quite near the road, another time some way into the fields. And sure enough after the lapse of a little time a body was brought by exactly the same route by which the candle had come, owing to the proper road being blocked up with snow.

'Another time there happened a great wonder connected with an old man of Carmarthen, who was in the habit of carrying fish to Brecon, Menny, and Monmouth, and returning with the poorer kind of Gloucester cheese: my people knew he was on the road and had made ready for him, the weather being dreadful, wind blowing and snow drifting. Well, in the middle of the night, my daughters heard the voice of the old man at the gate, and their mother called to them to open it quick, and invite the old man to come in to the fire! One of the girls got up forthwith, but when she went out there was nobody to be seen. On the morrow, lo and behold! the body of the old man was brought past on a couch, he having perished in the snow on the mountain of Tre'r Castell. Now this is the truth of the matter.'

From *Wild Wales* by George Borrow, 1862

'What is she?'

'Upon this, I looked around – and there she was! There at my shoulder, almost touching me with her clothes, gazing at me with her horrible little eyes, displaying the gloomy cavern of her mouth, fanning herself in a mocking manner, as if to make fun of my childish alarm.

'I passed from dread to the most furious anger, to savage and desperate rage. I dashed at the heavy old creature. I flung her against the wall. I put my hand to her throat. I felt of her face, her breast, the straggling locks of her gray hair until I was thoroughly convinced that she was a human being – a woman.

[345]

'Meanwhile she had uttered a howl which was hoarse and piercing at the same time. It seemed false and feigned to me, like the hypocritical expression of a fear which she did not really feel. Immediately afterwards she exclaimed, making believe to cry, though she was not crying, but looking at me with her hyena eyes:

'"Why have you picked a quarrel with me?"

'This remark increased my fright and weakened my wrath.

'"Then you remember," I cried, "that you have seen me somewhere else."

'"I should say so, my dear," she replied, mockingly. "Saint Eugene's night, in Jardines Street, three years ago."

'My very marrow was chilled.

'"But who are you?" I asked, without letting go of her. "Why do you follow me? What business have you with me?"

'"I am a poor weak woman," she answered, with a devilish leer. "You hate me, and you are afraid of me without any reason. If not, tell me, good sir, why you were so frightened the first time you saw me."

'"Because I have loathed you ever since I was born. Because you are the evil spirit of my life."

'"It seems, then, that you have known me for a long time. Well, look, my son, so have I known you."

'"You have known me? How long?"

'"Since before you were born! And when I saw you pass by me, three years ago, I said to myself, *that's the one.*"

'When I entered my house I met Colonel Falcón, who had just come to tell me that my Joaquina, my betrothed, all my hope and happiness and joy on earth, had died the day before in Santa Agueda. The unfortunate father had telegraphed Falcón to tell me – me, who should have divined it an hour before, when I met the evil spirit of my life! Don't you understand, now, that I must kill that born enemy of my happiness, that vile old hag, who is the living mockery of my destiny?

'But why do I say kill? Is she a woman? Is she a human being? Why have I had a presentiment of her ever since I was born? Why did she recognize me when she first saw me? Why do I never see her except when some great calamity has befallen me? Is she Satan? Is she Death? Is she Life? Is she Antichrist? Who is she? What is she?'

From 'The Tall Woman' by Pedro Antonio de Alarcón, (1833–91), translated from the Spanish by Rollo Ogden

'Dripping with water'

A lady, with whose family I am acquainted, had a son abroad. One night she was lying in bed, with a door open which led into an adjoining room, where there was a fire. She had not been to sleep, when she saw her son cross this adjoining room and approach the fire, over which he leant, as if very cold. She saw that he was shivering and dripping wet. She immediately exclaimed, 'That's my G.!' The figure turned its face round, looked at her sadly, and disappeared. That same night the young man was drowned.

Mr P., the American manager, in one of his voyages to England, being in bed, one night, between sleeping and waking, was disturbed by somebody coming into his cabin, dripping with water. He concluded that the person had fallen overboard, and asked him why he came there to disturb him, when there were plenty of other places for him to go to? The man muttered something indistinctly, and Mr P. then perceived that it was his own brother. This roused him completely, and feeling quite certain that somebody had been there, he got out of bed to feel if the carpet was wet on the spot where his brother stood. It was not, however; and when he questioned his shipmates, the following morning, they assured him that nobody had been overboard, nor had anybody been in his cabin. Upon this, he noted down the date and the particulars of the event, and, on his arrival at Liverpool, sent the paper sealed, to a friend in London, desiring it might not be opened till he wrote again. The Indian post, in due time, brought the intelligence that on that night Mr P.'s brother was drowned.

From *The Nightside of Nature* by Catharine Crowe, 1848

The Ghost's Walk

Mrs Rouncewell can trust to the discretion of her two young hearers, and may tell *them* how the terrace came to have that ghostly name. She seats herself in a large chair by the fast-darkening window, and tells them:

'In the wicked days, my dears, of King Charles the First – I mean, of course, in the wicked days of the rebels who leagued themselves against that excellent King – Sir Morbury Dedlock was the owner of Chesney Wold. Whether there was any account of a ghost in the family before those days, I can't say. I should think it very likely indeed.'

Mrs Rouncewell holds this opinion, because she considers that a family of such antiquity and importance has a right to a ghost. She regards a ghost as one of the privileges of the upper classes; a genteel distinction to which the common people have no claim.

'Sir Morbury Dedlock,' says Mrs Rouncewell, 'was, I have no occasion to say, on the side of the blessed martyr. But it *is* supposed that his Lady, who had none of the family blood in her veins, favoured the bad cause. It is said that she had relations among King Charles's enemies; that she was in correspondence with them; and that she gave them information. When any of the country gentlemen who followed His Majesty's cause met here, it is said that my Lady was always nearer to the door of their council-room than they supposed. Do you hear a sound like a footstep passing along the terrace, Watt?'

Rosa draws nearer to the housekeeper.

'I hear the rain-drip on the stones,' replies the young man, 'and I hear a curious echo – I suppose an echo – which is very like a halting step.'

The housekeeper gravely nods and continues:

'Partly on account of this division between them, and partly on other accounts, Sir Morbury and his Lady led a troubled life. She was a lady of a haughty temper. They were not well suited to each other in age or character, and they had no children to moderate between them. After her favourite brother, a young gentleman, was killed in the civil wars (by Sir Morbury's near kinsman), her feeling was so violent that she hated the race into which she had married. When the Dedlocks were about to ride out from Chesney Wold in the King's cause, she is supposed to have more than once stolen down into the stables in the dead of night, and lamed their horses: and the story is, that once, at such an hour, her husband saw her gliding down the stairs and followed her into the stall where his own favourite horse stood. There he seized her by the wrist; and in a struggle or in a fall, or through the horse being frightened and lashing out, she was lamed in the hip, and from that hour began to pine away.'

The housekeeper has dropped her voice to a little more than a whisper.

'She had been a lady of a handsome figure and a noble carriage. She never complained of the change; she never spoke to any one of being crippled, or of being in pain; but, day by day, she tried to walk upon the terrace; and with the help of the stone balustrade, went up and down, up and down, up and down, in sun and shadow, with greater difficulty every day. At last, one afternoon, her husband (to whom she had never, on any persuasion, opened her lips since that night), standing at the great south window, saw her drop upon the pavement. He hastened down to raise her, but she repulsed him as he bent over her, and looking at him fixedly and coldly, said "I will die here where I have walked. And I will walk here, though I am in my grave. I will walk here, until the pride of this house is humbled. And when calamity, or when disgrace is coming to it, let the Dedlocks listen for my step!"'

Watt looks at Rosa. Rosa in the deepening gloom looks down upon the ground, half frightened and half shy.

'There and then she died. And from those days,' says Mrs Rouncewell, 'the name has come down – The Ghost's Walk. If the tread is an echo, it is an echo that is only heard after dark, and is often unheard for a long while together. But it comes back, from time to time; and so sure as there is sickness or death in the family, it will be heard then.'

'– And disgrace, grandmother –' says Watt.

'Disgrace never comes to Chesney Wold,' returns the housekeeper.

Her grandson apologises, with 'True. True.'

'That is the story. Whatever the sound is, it is a worrying sound,' says Mrs Rouncewell, getting up from her chair, 'and what is to be noticed in it, is, that it *must be heard*. My Lady, who is afraid of nothing, admits that when it is there, it must be heard. You cannot shut it out. Watt, there is a tall French clock behind you (placed there, a purpose) that has a loud beat when it is in motion, and can play music. You understand how those things are managed?'

'Pretty well, grandmother, I think.'

'Set it a-going.'

Watt sets it a-going – music and all.

'Now, come hither,' says the housekeeper. 'Hither, child, towards my Lady's pillow. I am not sure that it is dark enough yet, but listen! Can you hear the sound upon the terrace, through the music, and the beat and everything?'

'I certainly can!'

'So my Lady says.'

From *Bleak House* by Charles Dickens, 1853

Grover Station

'It must have been about three o'clock in the morning that I was awakened by the crying of the dog, a whimper low, continuous and pitiful, and indescribably human. While I was blinking my eyes in an effort to get thoroughly awake, I heard another sound, the grating sound of chalk on a wooden black board, or of a soft pencil on a slate. I turned my head to the right, and saw a man standing with his back to me, chalking something on the bulletin board. At a glance I recognised the broad, high shoulders and the handsome head of my friend. Yet there was that about the figure which kept me from calling his name or from moving a muscle where I lay. He finished his writing and dropped the chalk, and I distinctly heard its click as it fell. He made a gesture as

[349]

though he were dusting his fingers, and then turned facing me, holding his left hand in front of his mouth. I saw him clearly in the soft light of the station lamp. He wore his dress clothes, and began moving towards the door silently as a shadow in his black stocking feet. There was about his movements an indescribable stiffness, as though his limbs had been frozen. His face was chalky white, his hair seemed damp and was plastered down close about his temples. His eyes were colourless jellies, dull as lead, and staring straight before him. When he reached the door, he lowered the hand he held before his mouth to lift the latch. His face was turned squarely towards me, and the lower jaw had fallen and was set rigidly upon his collar, the mouth was wide open and was *stuffed full of white cotton*! Then I knew it was a dead man's face I looked upon.

'The door opened, and that stiff black figure in stockings walked as noiselessly as a cat out into the night. I think I went quite mad then. I dimly remember that I rushed out upon the siding and ran up and down screaming, "Larry, Larry!" until the wind seemed to echo my call. The stars were out in myriads, and the snow glistened in their light, but I could see nothing but the wide, white plain, not even a dark shadow anywhere. When at last I found myself back in the station, I saw Duke lying before the door and dropped on my knees beside him, calling him by name. But Duke was past calling back. Master and dog had gone together, and I dragged him into the corner and covered his face, for his eyes were colourless and soft, like the eyes of that horrible face, once so beloved.

'The black board? O, I didn't forget that. I had chalked the time of the accommodation on it the night before, from sheer force of habit, for it isn't customary to mark the time of trains in unimportant stations like Grover. My writing had been rubbed out by a moist hand, for I could see the finger marks clearly, and in place of it was written in blue chalk simply,

C.B. & Q. 26387

'I sat there drinking brandy and muttering to myself before that black board until those blue letters danced up and down, like magic lantern pictures when you jiggle the slides. I drank until the sweat poured off me like rain and my teeth chattered, and I turned sick at the stomach. At last an idea flashed upon me. I snatched the way bill off the hook. The car of wool that had left Grover for Boston the night before was numbered 26387.

'I must have got through the rest of the night somehow, for when the sun came up red and angry over the white plains, the section boss found me sitting by the stove, the lamp burning full blaze, the brandy bottle empty beside me, and with but one idea in my head, that box car

26387 must be stopped and opened as soon as possible, and that some-how it would explain.

'I figured that we could easily catch it in Omaha, and wired the freight agent there to go through it carefully and report anything unusual. That night I got a wire from the agent stating that the body of a man had been found under a woolsack at one end of the car with a fan and an invitation to the inaugural ball at Cheyenne in the pocket of his dress coat.'

From 'The Affair at Grover Station' by Willa Cather, 1900

Aunt Férula

Everyone who witnessed the moment agrees that it was almost eight o'clock at night when Férula appeared without the slightest warning. They all saw her in her starched blouse, with her rings of keys at her waist and her old maid's bun, exactly as they had always seen her in the house. She entered the dining room just as Esteban was beginning to carve the roast, and they recognized her immediately, even though it had been six years since they last saw her, and she looked very pale and a great deal older. It was a Saturday and the twins, Jaime and Nicolás, had come home from school for the weekend, so they too were at the table. Their testimony is very important, because they were the only members of the family who lived completely removed from the three-legged table, protected from magic and spiritualism by their rigid English boarding school. First they felt a sudden draft in the dining room and Clara ordered the windows shut because she thought it was the wind. Then they heard the tinkling of the keys and the door burst open and Férula appeared, silent and with a distant expression on her face, at the exact same moment that Nana came in from the kitchen carrying the salad platter. Esteban Trueba stopped with the carving knife and fork suspended in midair, paralyzed with surprise, and the three children cried, 'Aunt Férula!' almost in unison. Blanca managed to rise to her feet to greet her, but Clara, who was seated beside her, reached out her hand and held her back. Clara was actually the only one to realize on first glance what was going on, despite the fact that nothing in her sister-in-law's appearance in any way betrayed her state. Férula stopped three feet from the table, looked at everyone with her empty, indifferent eyes, and advanced toward Clara, who stood up but made no effort to go any closer, and only closing her eyes and breath-ing rapidly as if she were about to have one of her asthma attacks. Férula approached her, put a hand on each shoulder, and kissed her on the forehead. All that could be heard in the dining room was Clara's labored breathing and the metallic clang of the keys at Férula's waist. After kissing her sister-in-law, Férula walked around her and went out the way she had come in, closing the door gently behind her. The family sat frozen in the dining room, as if they were in the middle of a nightmare. Suddenly Nana began to shake so hard that the salad spoons fell off the platter. The sound of the silver as it hit the floor made everybody jump. Clara opened her eyes. She was still having difficulty breathing, and tears were running down her cheeks and neck, staining her blouse.

'Férula is dead,' she announced.

From *The House of the Spirits* by Isabel Allende, 1985

The Fore-runner

I opened my eyes and found a heavy form over me. I fought to get out from under the form. I couldn't breathe. Then I heard harsh laughter in my ears and smelt rotting teeth and I struggled fiercely and threw the form off.

'You have sweet blood,' the form said in the dark.

I lit a candle. Dad was snoring on his three-legged chair. The beggar-woman had gone. I went and looked outside. The compound was empty. Up in the sky, I saw a star falling. I went back in and woke dad up.

'The woman has gone,' I said.

'What woman?'

'The beggarwoman.'

He turned his head away. Then, craning his neck towards me, he said:

'You mean Helen?'

'No,' I said. 'The old woman.'

'There wasn't an old woman. Go to sleep,' he said in an exasperated voice. I left him alone. I sat on the floor with my back against the wall. I heard the house breathing. Dad lifted his head suddenly and asked:

'Has your mother returned?'

'No.'

He went back to sleep again. I stayed up, watching the room, till dawn broke. All through that time I was struck by how free our air had become. Madame Koto's presence did not enter our nightspace. The strange wind didn't battle with dad's spirit. I heard the birds of sunlight singing when I fell asleep.

From *Songs of Enchantment* by Ben Okri, 1993

Thirteen

KINFOLK

Where art thou, my beloved Son . . .?

I look for ghosts; but none will force
Their way to me: 'tis falsely said
That there was ever intercouse
Between the living and the dead;
For, surely, then I should have sight
Of him I wait for day and night,
With love and longings infinite.

WILLIAM WORDSWORTH

If the apparitions of the souls of the dead were things in
nature and of their own choice, there would be few
persons who would not come back to visit the things or
the persons which have been dear to them during this
life. St. Augustine says it of his mother, St. Monica, who
had so tender and constant an affection for him,
and who, while she lived, followed him and
sought him by sea and land.

AUGUSTINE CALMET

Sometimes she studies sepia-dark photographs
from the 1940s – her mother
and grandmother doing farm-chores.

Theirs was never the good life
but occasionally she envies them
their slow days.

Were they to catch her up,
she would feel their reproaches rising
over her, like steam on her dark glasses.

KATHLEEN GALLAGHER

'A voice was heard in Ramah'

Thus saith the LORD: A voice was heard in Ramah, lamentation, *and* bitter weeping: Rahel weeping for her children refused to be comforted for her children, because they *were* not.

Thus saith the LORD: Refrain thy voice from weeping, and thine eyes from tears; for thy work shall be rewarded, saith the LORD; and they shall come again from the land of the enemy.

And there is hope in thine end, saith the LORD, that thy children shall come again to their own border.

Jeremiah, xxxi

Fade away

A mother's magic charm to protect her sleeping child,
sixteenth century BC:

Fade away!
he-ghost of the darkness,
sneaking in, nose behind him
looking backwards like a deadman,
fail in your mission!

Fade away!
she-ghost of the darkness,
sneaking in, nose behind her,
looking backwards like a deadwoman,
fail in your mission!

Have you come to kiss this child?
I won't let you kiss him!
Have you come to silence him?
I won't let you make him silent!
Have you come to hurt him?
I won't let you hurt him!
Have you come to take him?
I won't let you take him away from me!

I've made a charm against you
from clover – you can't get past that;
from onions – an unguent of pain for you;
from honey – sweet for the living, but bitter to the dead;

from eggs of the *abdju*-fish;
from the jawbone of the *meret*-fish;
from the backbone of a perch!

Adapted from the translation by John A. Wilson in *The Supplement to the ANET*

The woman who married a spirit

The Klickitat buried their dead on islands of the river, and it was here that the body of a young chief was carried. But neither his soul, on the isle of the dead, nor the mind of his beloved, who was with her people, could forget one another, and so he came to her in a vision and called her to him. At night her father took her in a canoe to the isle and left her with the dead. There she was conducted to the dance-house of the spirits, and found her lover more beautiful and strong than ever he was upon earth. When the sun rose, however, she awoke with horror to find herself surrounded by the hideous remains of the dead, while her body was clasped by the skeleton arm of her lover. Screaming she ran to the water's edge and paddled across the river to her home. But she was not allowed to remain, for the fear of the departed was now upon the tribe; and again she was sent back, and once more passed a night of happiness with the dead. In the course of time a child was born to her, more beautiful than any mortal. The grandmother was summoned, but was told that she must not look upon the child till after the tenth day; unable to restrain her curiosity, she stole a look at the sleeping babe, whereupon it died. Thenceforth, the spirit-people decreed, the dead should nevermore return, nor hold intercourse with the living.

Shahapatian story from *North American Mythology* by H. B. Alexander, 1916

'My grandfather'

As a schoolgirl ... I was in the habit of discussing my school problems with my grandfather, an old man with silky white hair and a little white goatee-beard, whom I adored. He was very well educated, and highly intelligent, and delighted in discussing with me the subjects I was studying in preparation for University entrance. When he died, I was about 18, and I was desolate.

About six months after his death, I had another big problem to resolve, and no-one to talk it over with. During that week once at about 3 a.m., my grandfather came through the outside wall of my bedroom, in a luminous circle of grey light, his head and shoulders clearly visible – and talked to me . . . Next day, I found I could understand my problem, and could proceed with my work. I told my mother about the happening, and she advised me to say nothing to anybody.

My 'grandfather' came again some months later when I again needed his help – but he has never come again since.

Quoted in *Apparitions* by Celia Green and Charles McCreery, 1975

Duppy Get Her

A man and woman have crept out of the cane field. They stand right at the edge of the bank of the canal. To look at the woman is to see an older Lilly. The man is all grey. The woman wears a plaid dress gathered at the waist, and her feet are without shoes. Her husband wears rubber shoes and stained khaki pants turned up at the ankles. His faded shirt is partially unbuttoned, his arm is around his wife's waist. They exude a gentleness like the petals of roses. The woman uses her index finger to beckon to Lilly. Jumping as if pulled from her seat, Lilly bounds toward the man and woman by the cane field beyond the canal and beyond the barbed wire fence. She scrambles over Beatrice's feet.

Beatrice yells, 'Lilly, Lilly, weh yuh a guh? Lilly! Is mad? Yuh mad? Min yuh fall down hurt yuhself. Lilly! Gal, weh yuh a guh?'

Richard runs after Lilly.

Beatrice repeats, 'Lilly, gal, wha get inna yuh?'

Lilly: 'Yuh rass-cloth, leabe me alone. Yuh nuh ear me granny a call me?' She points to what appears to be the canal.

They all stare, seeing no one, hearing nothing. Lilly is close to the fence, running, tearing off her clothes. . . .

The woman in the cane field beckons to Lilly, cajoling: 'Lilly, me picknie, come kiss yuh granny and granpa; yuh nuh long fi see we?'

Lilly, strident, gesticulates wildly like a man cheated out of his paycheck. She calls, 'Yes, Granny, me a come, me long fi see yuh.'

Beatrice and Richard struggle with Lilly. Their fright and confusion are as loud as Lilly's screams, Richard tries to rough her up but she merely bucks him off. Beatrice's jaws work, sweat forms on her forehead, and her fleshy arms flail about, comical.

Again, she tries to reason with Lilly: 'Lilly, gal, memba me and you did help dress Granny fah er funeral? Memba, memba, Lilly, how we did cry til we eye swell big? Granny dead. She nah call yuh.'

'Granny nuh dead; see, she stan deh wid Granpa. Oonuh let me guh.' At this, Lilly spits at Beatrice and Richard and frees herself from their hold.

She rushes toward the cane field like a man afire in search of water. Richard seizes her, but she now has the strength of many persons; he hollers for Errol and Basil. Lilly rips off her blouse and brassière, and her ample breasts flap about. Richard remembers the taste of her milk, only last night. More hands take hold of her; she bites, scratches and kicks. Miss Maud from next door, hearing the commotion, runs to her fence to learn all about it.

'Leh me guh, leh me guh! Yuh nuh see me granny a call me? Leh me guh.'

Richard: 'Lilly, shet yuh mout. Min Miss Edward ear yuh an yuh loose yuh wuk. Nuhbody nah call yuh.'

'Miss Edward bumbu-hole – Miss Edward rasscloth. Oonuh leave me alone mek me guh tuh me granny and granpa.'

Beatrice scolds: 'Lilly, gal, shet yuh mout. How yuh can speak suh bout Miss Edward? Gal, shet yuh mout for yuh loose yuh wuk.'

'Oonuh rass-cloth, oonuh bumbu-hole, oonuh leabe me alone – mek me guh to me granny.' . . .

The four find it difficult to hold Lilly. She kicks, bucks and tears at her remaining clothes. The evening sings:

> Steal away, steal away, duppy get yuh.
> Steal away . . . duppy get yuh . . .

It is generally agreed that Lilly must be returned to her place of birth – that for whatever reason, her dead grandparents don't want her where she is. Mrs Edwards is consulted and a car is summoned. Kicking and frothing at the mouth, Lilly is forced into the back of the car, Richard to her right and Basil to her left. Beatrice sits up front with the driver armed with Miss Maud's flask of potion. The car pulls off, leaving a trail of dust.

Mrs Edwards returns to her house; she fumbles inside her medicine cabinet and comes up with a brown vial, the contents of which she sprinkles at each doorway and window and in all four corners of every room. Then she goes back to her rocking chair, her hands folded in her lap, her eyes searching the grey sky.

Upon returning from taking Lilly home, Beatrice reports that Lilly calmed gradually as she approached her place of birth. In fact, by the time she got home, she was reasonable enough to request from her mother a cup of water sweetened with condensed milk. After drinking the milk, Lilly hugged her mother and they both cried; no one had to restrain her thereafter. Nothing needed to be explained to Lilly's mother, who had been expecting them all day. It appeared she had had a dream from her dead mother the night before.

Prior to this incident, Lilly always claimed that she saw duppies in Mrs Edwards's house and around the estate in general. Since no one else professed such powers, there was no way to verify her claim. Many came to her when they wanted to ask for protection from those in the other world. Often, when they were in Lilly's presence, they asserted that they felt their heads rise and swell to twice their size, but again, since this was only a feeling and nothing visible, nothing could be proven. There were others who wanted to be able to see duppies like Lilly and asked her how they could obtain such powers. Lilly's recommendations were the following: 'Rub dog matta inna yuh eye or visit a graveyard wen de clock strike twelve midnight. Once dere, put yuh head between yuh legs, spit, then get up an walk, not lookin back. Afta dat, yuh will see duppy all de time.'

It is not known if anyone ever followed Lilly's advice, although two women who went to see Lilly had taken to visiting the graveyard daily and were now in the habit of talking to themselves.

From 'Duppy Get Her' by Opal Palmer Adisa, 1986

The Wife of Usher's Well

There lived a wife at Usher's Well,
    And a wealthy wife was she;
She had three stout and stalwart sons
    And sent them over the sea.

They had not been a week from her,
    A week but barely ane,
When word came to the carlin wife
    That her three sons were gane.

They had not been a week from her,
    A week but barely three,
When word came to the carlin wife
    That her sons she'd never see.

'I wish the wind may never cease,
    Nor fashes in the flood,
Till my three sons come hame to me,
    In earthly flesh and blood.'

It fell about the Martinmas,
    When nights are long and mirk,
The carlin wife's three sons came hame,
    And their hats were of the birk.

It neither grew in dyke nor ditch,
    Nor yet in any sheugh;
But at the gates of Paradise,
    That birk grew fair eneugh.

'Blow up the fire, my maidens two,
    Bring water from the well;
For all my house shall feast this night,
    Since my three sons are well.'

And she has made to them a bed,
    She's made it large and wide,
And she's ta'en her mantle her about,
    Sat down at the bedside.

O, up then crew the red, red cock
    And up and crew the grey;
The eldest to the youngest said:
    ''Tis time we were away.'

The cocks they had not crawed but once,
    And dinged their breasts for day,
When the youngest to the eldest said:
    'Brother, we must away!'

'The cock doth craw, the day doth daw:
    The channerin' worm doth chide;
Gin we be missed out of our place,
    A sair pain we must bide.

'Fare ye well, my mother dear,
    Farewell to barn and byre!
And fare ye well, the bonny lass
    That kindles my mother's fire!'

Traditional

Babylon

As most representatives of the spirit world were enemies of the living,
so were the ghosts of dead men and women. Death chilled all human
affections; it turned love to hate; the deeper the love had been, the
deeper became the enmity fostered by the ghost. ... The most terrible

ghost in Babylonia was that of a woman who had died in childbed. She was pitied and dreaded; her grief had demented her; she was doomed to wail in the darkness; her impurity clung to her like poison. No spirit was more prone to work evil against mankind, and her hostility was accompanied by the most tragic sorrow.

From *Myths of Babylonia and Assyria* by Donald A. Mackenzie

'Mother, mother'

Mother, mother, thou art kind,
   Thou art standing in the room,
In a molten glory shrined
   That rays off into the gloom!
But thy smile is bright and bleak
Like cold waves – I cannot speak,
I sob in it, and grow weak.

Ghostly mother, keep aloof
   One hour longer from my soul,
For I still am thinking of
   Earth's warm-beating joy and dole!
On my finger is a ring
Which I still see glittering
When the night hides everything.

From 'Bertha in the Lane' by Elizabeth Barrett Browning, 1844

Nero's mother

Being terrified with her threats and violent shrewdness he determined to kill and dispatch her at once. . . .

Worse matter yet than all this and more horrible is reported beside, and that by authors of good credit who will stand to it; namely, that he ran in all haste to view the dead body of his mother when she was killed, that he handled every part and member of it, found fault with some and commended others, and being thirsty in the meantime took a draught of drink. Howbeit, notwithstanding he was heartened by the joyous gratulation of soldiers, senate, and people, yet could he not either for the present or ever after endure the worm and sting of conscience for this foul act, but confessed many a time that haunted and harried he was with the apparition of his mother's ghost, tormented also with the scourges and burning torches of the Furies. Moreover, with a sacrifice made by direction of magicians, he assayed to raise up her soul and spirit and to entreat the same to forgive him.

From the *History of Twelve Caesars* by Suetonius, c.AD 140,
translated by Philemon Holland, 1606

Anne Lisbeth

'Hang on, hang on!' the ghosts had cried in the stories she had heard. And as Anne Lisbeth repeated these words to herself, she suddenly remembered the dream she had had in the ditch digger's cottage. So real did it become to her that again she felt the weight of the other mothers clinging to her, while they screamed: 'Hang on! Hang on!'

And she remembered how the world had come to an end, and how the sleeves of her blouse had ripped, so that her child, who on the Day of Judgment had tried to save her, could no longer hold on to her. Her own child, the one she had borne but never loved, and had never even given a thought to. Now that child rested on the bottom of the sea, and his ghost could come and demand of her, 'Bury me in Christian soil. Hang on! Hang on!'

As these thoughts passed through her mind, fear bit her heels and she hurried on. Dread like a cold hand squeezed her heart so that it hurt. She looked out over the sea. A mist came rolling in; it obscured and changed the shapes of bushes and trees. She looked up at the moon. It appeared as a pale, pale disc. Her body felt heavy, as if she were carrying a great weight. 'Hang on! hang on!' the words echoed in her mind.

Again she turned to look at the moon, and now its white face seemed very close to her and the fog hung like a winding sheet from her shoulders. 'Hang on! hang on, bring me to my grave!' She expected to hear those words any moment.

There was a sound! What was it? It could not be frogs or the cry of a raven or a crow. A hollow voice said, 'Bury me, bury me.' She had heard it plainly. It was the voice of her child, the one who now rested on the bottom of the sea. He would never find peace until he was carried to the churchyard and there buried in hallowed ground. She would dig his grave. She walked in the direction where she thought a church stood, and now it seemed to her that her body felt lighter, that the burden was gone.

Hurriedly she turned and walked instead towards her home, but then the weight returned. 'Hang on, hang on!' The cry sounded again like the deep voice of some monstrous frog or frightened bird.

'Bury me, bury me.'

The fog was cold and wet, and her face and hands were cold and damp from fear. The world outside was pressing on her and she herself had become an empty void in which thoughts she had never had before were free to fly. . . . and her feelings so overpowered her that she fell to the ground and crawled on all fours like an animal.

'Bury me, bury me,' whispered the voice, and gladly would she have buried herself, if that would have meant the end of all memories.

It was her day of reckoning, and it brought her only fear and dread. All the superstitions she knew mixed as heat and icy coldness with her blood, and tales she had not remembered for years came back to her. As soundlessly as the clouds that pass by the pale moon, a spectre rushed by her. Four dark horses with fire coming from their nostrils drew a carriage in which sat the evil count who, more than a hundred years before, had lived and ruled in this district. Now at midnight he drove from the churchyard to his castle and back again. He was not pale as ghosts usually are described. No, his face was as black as burned-out coals. He nodded to Anne Lisbeth and waved.

'Hang on! hang on!' he shouted. 'Then you can again drive in a count's carriage and forget your own child!'

She ran and at last she reached the churchyard. The black crosses on the graves and the black ravens that lived in the church tower became one. All the crosses became ravens that cried and screamed at her. She remembered that unnatural mothers are called 'raven mothers', for that bird is known, to its shame, for not taking good care of its young. Would she become a black bird when she died: a raven?

She threw herself down on the ground and with her fingers dug in the hard earth until blood ran from her nails. And all the time she heard the voice saying, 'Bury me, bury me!' She feared that the cock would crow and the eastern sky grow red before she had finished her work; and then all would be lost.

The cock crowed and the sun rose. The grave was but half finished! A cold hand caressed her face and a voice sighed, 'Only half a grave.' It was the spirit of her son, who now had to return to the bottom of the sea. Anne Lisbeth sank to the ground and all thoughts and feelings left her.

It was almost noon when she awoke. Two young men had found her. She was not lying in the churchyard but on the beach. In front of her was the big hole she had dug. She had cut her hands on a broken glass, the stem of which had been forced down into a little square piece of wood that was painted blue.

Anne Lisbeth was sick. Her conscience had dealt the cards of superstition, and she had read them. She now believed that she had only half a soul; the ghost of her son had taken the other half with him, down to the bottom of the sea. She would not be able to enter heaven unless she could get back that part of her soul that lay beneath the deep waters of the ocean.

Anne Lisbeth was brought home, but she was no longer the woman she had been. Her thoughts were like threads, all tangled up in knots; only one idea was clear to her: that she must find again the ghost of her child, carry him to the churchyard, and bury him there, so that she could win back her soul.

Many a night she was missed at home, but they knew where they could find her: down on the beach, waiting for the ghost of her son to come. A year went by and then one night she disappeared, and this time they could not find her; all day they searched in vain.

Towards evening the bell ringer who had come to ring the bells for vespers saw her. In front of the altar lay Anne Lisbeth. She had been there since morning. She had no strength left but the light in her eyes was one of joy. The last of the sun's rays fell on her face and gave it the pink colour of health. The sun's rays were reflected in the brass clasps of the old Bible that lay upon the altar. It had been opened upon the page of the prophet Joel, where it is written: 'Rend your heart and not your garments, and turn unto the Lord your God.' This, they said, was quite by chance, as so much is in this world.

In Anne Lisbeth's sun-filled face one could see that she had found peace. She whispered that she was well, that she was not afraid any more. The ghost had come at last. Her son had been with her and said: 'You dug only half a grave for me, but for a whole year and a day you have buried me in your heart, and that is the right place for a mother to keep her child.' Then he had given her back the half of her soul that he had taken with him and led her up here to the church.

'Now I am in God's house,' she said, 'and here one is blessed.'

When the sun finally went down, Anne Lisbeth's soul went up to where fear is unknown and all struggles cease. And Anne Lisbeth had striven.

From 'Anne Lisbeth' by Hans Christian Andersen, 1855, translated from the Danish by Erik Christian Haugaard

The Cruel Mother

Sung by Mrs Bowring, Cerne Abbas, Dorset (H.E.D.H. 1907)

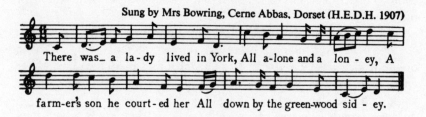

There was a la-dy lived in York, All a-lone and a lon - ey, A
farm-er's son he court-ed her All down by the green-wood sid - ey.

There was a lady lived in York,
    All alone and a loney,
A farmer's son he courted her
    All down by the greenwood sidey.

He courted her for seven long years.
At last she proved in child by him.

She pitched her knee against a tree,
And there she found great misery.

She pitched her back against a thorn,
And there she had her baby born.

She drew the fillet off her head.
She bound the baby's hands and legs.

She drew a knife both long and sharp.
She pierced the baby's innocent heart.

She wiped the knife upon the grass.
The more she wiped, the blood run fast.

She washed her hands all in the spring,
Thinking to turn a maid again.

As she was going to her father's hall,
She saw three babes a-playing at ball.

One dressed in silk, the other in satin,
The other star-naked as ever was born.

O, dear baby, if you was mine,
I'd dress you in silk and satin so fine.

O, dear mother, I once was thine.
You never would dress me coarse or fine.

The coldest earth it was my bed.
The green grass was my coverlet.

O, mother, mother, for your sin,
Heaven gate you shall not enter in.

There is a fire beyond hell's gate,
And there you'll burn both early and late.

Traditional English folk song, collected by Ralph Vaughan Williams
and A. L. Lloyd, 1959

Statement of the late Julia Herman, through the medium Bayrolles

The sum of what we knew at death is the measure of what we know afterward of all that went before. Of this existence we know many things, but no new light falls upon any page of that; in memory is written all of it that we can read. Here are no heights of truth overlooking the confused landscape of that dubitable domain. We still dwell in the Valley of the Shadow, lurk in its desolate places, peering from brambles and thickets at its mad, malign inhabitants. How should we have new knowledge of that fading past?

What I am about to relate happened on a night. We know when it is night, for then you retire to your houses and we can venture from our places of concealment to move unafraid about our old homes, to look in at the windows, even to enter and gaze upon your faces as you sleep. I had lingered long near the dwelling where I had been so cruelly changed to what I am, a we do while any that we love or hate remain. Vainly I had sought some method of manifestation, some way to make my continued existence and my great love and poignant pity understood by my husband and son. Always if they slept they would wake, or if in my desperation I dared approach them when they were awake, would turn toward me the terrible eyes of the living, frightening me by the glances that I sought from the purpose that I held.

On this night I had searched for them without success, fearing to find them; they were nowhere in the house, nor about the moonlit lawn. For, although the sun is lost to us forever, the moon, full-orbed or slender, remains to us. Sometimes it shines by night, sometimes by day, but always it rises and sets, as in that other life.

I left the lawn and moved in the white light and silence along the road, aimless and sorrowing. Suddenly I heard the voice of my poor husband in exclamations of astonishment, with that of my son in re-assurance and dissuasion; and there by the shadow of a group of trees they stood – near, so near! Their faces were toward me, the eyes of the elder man fixed upon mine. He saw me – at last, at last, he saw me! In the consciousness of that, my terror fled as a cruel dream. The death-spell was broken: Love had conquered Law! Mad with exultation I shouted – I *must* have shouted, 'He sees, he sees: he will understand!' Then, controlling myself, I moved forward, smiling and consciously beautiful, to offer myself to his arms, to comfort him with endearments, and, with my son's hand in mine, to speak words that should restore the broken bonds between the living and the dead.

Alas! alas! his face went white with fear, his eyes were as those of a hunted animal. He backed away from me, as I advanced, and at last turned and fled into the wood – whither, it is not given to me to know.

To my poor boy, left doubly desolate, I have never been able to im-part a sense of my presence. Soon he, too, must pass to his Life Invisible and be lost to me forever.

'The Moonlit Road' by Ambrose Bierce, 1893

A Chilly Night

I rose at the dead of night,
    And went to the lattice alone
To look for my Mother's ghost
    Where the ghostly moonlight shone.

My friends had failed one by one,
    Middle-aged, young, and old,
Till the ghosts were warmer to me
    Than my friends that had grown cold.

I looked and I saw the ghosts
    Dotting plain and mound:
They stood in the blank moonlight,
    But no shadow lay on the ground:
They spoke without a voice
    And they leaped without a sound.

I called: 'O my Mother dear,' –
  I sobbed: 'O my Mother kind,
Make a lonely bed for me
  And shelter it from the wind.

'Tell the others not to come
  To see me night or day:
But I need not tell my friends
  To be sure to keep away.'

My Mother raised her eyes,
  They were blank and could not see:
Yet they held me with their stare
  While they seemed to look at me.

She opened her mouth and spoke;
  I could not hear a word,
While my flesh crept on my bones
  And every hair was stirred.

She knew that I could not hear
  The message that she told
Whether I had long to wait
  Or soon should sleep in the mould.
I saw her toss her shadowless hair
  And wring her hands in the cold.

I strained to catch her words,
  And she strained to make me hear;
But never a sound of words
  Fell on my straining ear.

From midnight to the cockcrow
  I kept my watch in pain
While the subtle ghosts grew subtler
  In the sad night on the wane

From midnight to the cockcrow
  I watched till all were gone,
Some to sleep in the shifting sea
  And some under turf and stone:
Living had failed and dead had failed,
  And I was indeed alone.

Christina Rossetti, 1866

Night-town: mother and son

(The couples fall aside. Stephen whirls giddily. Room whirls back. Eyes closed, he totters. Red rails fly spacewards. Stars all around suns turn roundabout. Bright midges dance on wall. He stops dead.)

STEPHEN: Ho!

(Stephen's mother, emaciated, rises stark through the floor in leper grey with a wreath of faded orange blossoms and a torn bridal veil, her face worn and noseless, green with grave mould. Her hair is scant and lank. She fixes her bluecircled hollow eyesockets on Stephen and opens her toothless mouth uttering a silent word. A choir of virgins and confessors sing voicelessly.)

THE CHOIR:

Liliata rutilantium te confessorum . . .
Iubilantium te virginum . . .

(From the top of a tower Buck Mulligan, in particoloured jester's dress of puce and yellow and clown's cap with curling bell, stands gaping at her, a smoking buttered split scone in his hand.)

BUCK MULLIGAN: She's beastly dead. The pity of it! Mulligan meets the afflicted mother. *(He upturns his eyes)* Mercurial Malachi.

THE MOTHER: *(With the subtle smile of death's madness)* I was once the beautiful May Goulding. I am dead.

STEPHEN: *(Horrorstruck)* Lemur, who are you? What bogeyman's trick is this?

BUCK MULLIGAN: *(Shakes his curling capbell)* The mockery of it! Kinch killed her dogsbody bitchbody. She kicked the bucket. *(Tears of molten butter fall from his eyes into the scone)* Our great sweet mother! *Epi oinopa ponton.*

THE MOTHER: *(Comes nearer, breathing upon him softly her breath of wetted ashes)* All must go through it, Stephen. More women than men in the world. You too. Time will come.

STEPHEN: *(Choking with fright, remorse and horror)* They said I killed you, mother. He offended your memory. Cancer did it, not I. Destiny.

THE MOTHER: *(A green rill of bile trickling from a side of her mouth)* You sang that song to me. *Love's bitter mystery.*

STEPHEN: *(Eagerly)* Tell me the word, mother, if you know now. The word known to all men.

THE MOTHER: Who saved you the night you jumped into the train at Dalkey with Paddy Lee? Who had pity for you when you were sad among the strangers? Prayer is all powerful. Prayer for the suffering souls in the Ursuline manual, and forty days' indulgence. Repent, Stephen.

STEPHEN: The ghoul! Hyena!

THE MOTHER: I pray for you in my other world. Get Dilly to make you that boiled rice every night after your brain work. Years and years I loved you, O my son, my firstborn, when you lay in my womb.

ZOE: *(Fanning herself with the grate fan)* I'm melting!

FLORRY: *(Points to Stephen)* Look! He's white.

BLOOM: *(Goes to the window to open it more)* Giddy.

THE MOTHER: *(With smouldering eyes)* Repent! O, the fire of hell!

STEPHEN: *(Panting)* The corpsechewer! Raw head and bloody bones!

THE MOTHER: *(Her face drawing near and nearer, sending out an ashen breath)* Beware! *(She raises her blackened, withered right arm slowly towards Stephen's breast with outstretched fingers)* Beware! God's hand! *(A green crab with malignant red eyes sticks deep its grinning claws in Stephen's heart.)*

STEPHEN: *(Strangled with rage)* Shite! *(His features grow drawn and grey and old.)*

BLOOM: *(At the window)* What?

STEPHEN: *Ah non, par exemple!* The intellectual imagination! With me all or not at all. *Non serviam!*

FLORRY: Give him some cold water. Wait. *(She rushes out.)*

THE MOTHER: *(Wrings her hands slowly, moaning desperately)* O Sacred Heart of Jesus, have mercy on him! Save him from hell, O divine Sacred Heart!

STEPHEN: No! No! No! Break my spirit all of you if you can! I'll bring you all to heel!

THE MOTHER: *(In the agony of her deathrattle)* Have mercy on Stephen, Lord, for my sake! Inexpressible was my anguish when expiring with love, grief and agony on Mount Calvary.

STEPHEN: *Nothing!*

(He lifts his ashplant high with both hands and smashes the chandelier. Time's livid final flame leaps and, in the following darkness, ruin of all space, shattered glass and toppling masonry.)

*

STEPHEN: *(Murmurs)*

... shadows ... the woods.
... white breast ... dim ...

(He stretches out his arms, sighs again and curls his body. Bloom holding his hat and ashplant stands erect. A dog barks in the distance. Bloom tightens and loosens his grip on the ashplant. He looks down on Stephen's face and form.)

BLOOM: *(Communes with the night)* Face reminds me of his poor mother. In the shady wood. The deep white breast. Ferguson, I think I caught. A girl. Some girl. Best thing could happen him ... *(He murmurs)* ... swear that I will always hail, ever conceal, never reveal, any part or parts, art or arts ... *(He murmurs)* in the rough sands of the sea ... a cabletow's length from the shore ... where the tide ebbs ... and flows ...

[369]

(Silent, thoughtful, alert, he stands on guard, his fingers at his lips in the attitude of secret master. Against the dark wall a figure appears slowly, a fairy boy of eleven, a changeling, kidnapped, dressed in an Eton suit with glass shoes and a little bronze helmet, holding a book in his hand. He reads from right to left inaudibly, smiling, kissing the page.)

BLOOM: *(Wonderstruck, calls inaudibly)* Rudy!

RUDY: *(Gazes unseeing into Bloom's eyes and goes on reading, kissing, smiling. He has a delicate mauve face. On his suit he has diamond and ruby buttons. In his free left hand he holds a slim ivory cane with a violet bowknot. A white lambkin peeps out of his waistcoat pocket.)*

From Ulysses by James Joyce, 1922

'The other Roquebrune'

'My discovery of England,' writes Sebastian *(Lost Property)*, 'put new life into my most intimate memories . . . After Cambridge I took a trip to the Continent and spent a quiet fortnight at Monte Carlo. I think there is some Casino place there, where people gamble, but if so, I missed it, as most of my time was taken up by the composition of my first novel – a very pretentious affair which I am glad to say was turned down by almost as many publishers as my next book had readers. One day I went for a long walk and found a place called Roquebrune. It was at Roquebrune that my mother had died thirteen years before. I well remember the day my father told me of her death and the name of the pension where it occurred. The name was "Les Violettes". I asked a chauffeur whether he knew of such a house, but he did not. Then I asked a fruit-seller and he showed me the way. I came at last to a pinkish villa roofed with the typical Provence round red tiles and I noticed a bunch of violets clumsily painted on the gate. So this was the house. I crossed the garden and spoke to the landlady. She said she had only lately taken over the pension from the former owner and knew nothing of the past. I asked her permission to sit awhile in the garden. An old man naked as far down as I could see peered at me from a balcony, but otherwise there was no one about. I sat down on a blue bench under a great eucalyptus, its bark half stripped away, as seems to be always the case with this sort of tree. Then I tried to see the pink house and the tree and the whole complexion of the place as my mother had seen it. I regretted not knowing the exact window of her room. Judging by the villa's name, I felt sure that there had been before her eyes that same bed of purple pansies. Gradually I worked myself into such a state that for a moment the pink and green seemed to shimmer and float as if seen through a veil of mist. My mother, a dim slight figure in a large hat, went slowly up the steps which seemed to dissolve into water. A terrific bump made me regain consciousness. An orange had rolled down out of the paper bag on my lap. I picked it up and left the garden. Some months later in London I happened to meet a cousin of hers. A turn of the conversation led me to mention that I had visited the place where she had died. "Oh," he said, "but it was the other Roquebrune, the one in the Var."'

From *The Real Life of Sebastian Knight* by Vladimir Nabokov, 1945

Clearing

I

The ambulance, the hearse, the auctioneers
clear all the life of that loved house away.
The hard-earned treasures of some 50 years
sized up as junk, and shifted in a day.

A stammerer died here and I believe
this front room with such ghosts taught me my trade.
Now strangers chip the paintwork as they heave
the spotless piano that was never played.
The fingerprints they leave mam won't wipe clean
nor politely ask them first to wipe their boots,
nor coax her trampled soil patch back to green
after they've trodden down the pale spring shoots.

I'd hope my mother's spirit wouldn't chase
her scattered household, even if it could.
How could she bear it when she saw no face
stare back at her from that long polished wood?

II

The landlord's glad to sell. The neighbourhood,
he fears, being mostly black, 's now on the skids.
The gate my father made from bread-tray wood
groans at the high jinks of Jamaican kids.

Bless this house's new black owners, and don't curse
that reggae booms through rooms where you made hush
for me to study in (though I wrote verse!)
and wouldn't let my sister use the flush!

The hearse called at the front, the formal side.
Strangers used it, doctors, and the post.
It had a show of flowers till you died.
You'll have to use the front if you're a ghost,
though it's as flat and bare as the back yard,
a beaten hard square patch of sour soil.

Hush!
      Haunt me, and not the house!
          I've got to lard
my ghosts' loud bootsoles with fresh midnight oil.

Tony Harrison, 1981

They

I felt my relaxed hand taken and turned softly between the soft hands of
a child. So at last I triumphed. In a moment I would turn and acquaint
myself with those quick-footed wanderers . . .

The little brushing kiss fell in the centre of my palm – as a gift on
which the fingers were, once, expected to close: as the all-faithful half-
reproachful signal of a waiting child not used to neglect even when
grown-ups were busiest – a fragment of the mute code devised very
long ago.

Then I knew. And it was as though I had known from the first day
when I looked across the lawn at the high window.

I heard the door shut. The woman turned to me in silence, and I felt
that she knew.

What time passed after this I cannot say. I was roused by the fall of a
log, and mechanically rose to put it back. Then I returned to my place
in the chair very close to the screen.

'Now you understand,' she whispered, across the packed shadows.

'Yes, I understand – now. Thank you.'

'I – I only hear them.' She bowed her head in her hands. 'I have no
right, you know – no other right. I have neither borne nor lost – neither
borne nor lost!'

'Be very glad then,' said I, for my soul was torn open within me.
'Forgive me!'

She was still, and I went back to my sorrow and my joy.

'It was because I loved them so,' she said at last, brokenly. '*That* was
why it was, even from the first – even before I knew that they – they

[372]

were all I should ever have. And I loved them so!'

She stretched out her arms to the shadows and the shadows within the shadow.

'They came because I loved them – because I needed them. I – I must have made them come. Was that wrong, think you?'

From 'They' by Rudyard Kipling, 1904

A Revenant

Now she is here
Again, quick in a taste
Of lemon, not even so
Much as a bite, she is here
In a whiff

Of lemon peel, no way
Even to tell
Where from, the light
Saffron perhaps, a snowy
Touch of metal

Or, afloat
On a flood of being, me,
I had drawn
A tingle out, indistinct,
A distant signal

Flashing in the hotter rush
Of air tonight, mixed
Into it, funny,
Today, the wiggle
Of a child, head back

Shrimp bodysock, she
Did a glancing
Noonday
Dance across
A crack

In a paving stone, she
Shook

At the sky
Her fist
With a flower in it

Now so long dead
Another
Is here, I remember to be
In the taste
Or touch, or in the child

A wandering
Sensation, mutely
To learn my shape, later to flit
Ghostwise from a being
I will never know

Christopher Middleton, 1993

The Poor Thing

There was a man in the islands who fished for his bare bellyful, and
took his life in his hands to go forth upon the sea between four planks.
But though he had much ado, he was merry of heart; and the gulls
heard him laugh when the spray met him. And though he had little
lore, he was sound of spirit; and when the fish came to his hook in the
mid-waters, he blessed God without weighing. He was bitter poor in
goods and bitter ugly of countenance, and he had no wife.

It fell in the time of the fishing that the man awoke in his house
about the midst of the afternoon. The fire burned in the midst, and the
smoke went up and the rain came down by the chimney. And the man
was aware of the likeness of one that warmed his hands at the red
peats.

'I greet you,' said the man, 'in the name of God.'

'I greet you,' said he that warmed his hands, 'but not in the name of
God, for I am none of His; nor in the name of Hell, for I am not of Hell.
For I am but a bloodless thing, less than wind and lighter than a sound,
and the wind goes through me like a net, and I am broken by a sound
and shaken by the cold.'

'Be plain with me,' said the man, 'and tell me your name and of your
nature.'

'My name,' quoth the other, 'is not yet named, and my nature not yet
sure. For I am part of a man; and I was part of your fathers, and went

out to fish and fight with them in the ancient days. But now is my turn not yet come; and I wait until you have a wife, and then shall I be in your son, and a brave part of him, rejoicing manfully to launch the boat into the surf, skilful to direct the helm, and a man of might where the ring closes and the blows are going.'

'This is a marvellous thing to hear,' said the man; 'and if you are indeed to be my son, I fear it will go ill with you; for I am bitter poor in goods and bitter ugly in face, and I shall never get me a wife if I live to the age of eagles.'

'All this have I come to remedy, my Father,' said the Poor Thing; 'for we must go this night to the little isle of sheep, where our fathers lie in the dead-cairn, and to-morrow to the Earl's Hall, and there shall you find a wife by my providing.'

So the man rose and put forth his boat at the time of the sunsetting; and the Poor Thing sat in the prow, and the spray blew through his bones like snow; and the wind whistled in his teeth, and the boat dipped not with the weight of him.

'I am fearful to see you, my son,' said the man. 'For methinks you are no thing of God.'

'It is only the wind that whistles in my teeth,' said the Poor Thing, 'and there is no life in me to keep it out.'

So they came to the little isle of sheep, where the surf burst all about it in the midst of the sea, and it was all green with bracken, and all wet with dew, and the moon enlightened it. They ran the boat into a cove, and set foot to land; and the man came heavily behind among the rocks in the deepness of the bracken, but the Poor Thing went before him like a smoke in the light of the moon. So they came to the dead-cairn, and they laid their ears to the stones; and the dead complained withinsides like a swarm of bees: 'Time was that marrow was in our bones, and strength in our sinews; and the thoughts of our head were clothed upon with acts and the words of men. But now are we broken in sunder, and the bonds of our bones are loosed, and our thoughts lie in the dust.'

Then said the Poor Thing: 'Charge them that they give you the virtue they withheld.'

And the man said: 'Bones of my fathers, greeting! for I am sprung of your loins. And now, behold, I break open the piled stones of your cairn, and I let in the noon between your ribs. Count it well done, for it was to be; and give me what I come seeking in the name of blood and in the name of God.'

And the spirits of the dead stirred in the cairn like ants; and they spoke: 'You have broken the roof of our cairn and let in the noon between our ribs; and you have the strength of the still-living. But what virtue have we? what power? or what jewel here in the dust with us, that any living man should covet or receive it? for we are less than nothing. But we tell you one thing, speaking with many voices like bees, that the way is plain before all like the grooves of launching: So forth into life and fear not, for so did we all in the ancient ages.' And their voices passed away like an eddy in a river.

'Now,' said the Poor Thing, 'they have told you a lesson, but make them give you a gift. Stoop your hand among the bones without drawback, and you shall find their treasure.'

So the man stooped his hand, and the dead laid hold upon it many and faint like ants; but he shook them off, and behold, what he brought up in his hand was the shoe of a horse, and it was rusty.

'It is a thing of no price,' quoth the man, 'for it is rusty.'

'We shall see that,' said the Poor Thing; 'for in my thought it is a good thing to do what our fathers did, and to keep what they kept without question. And in my thought one thing is as good as another in this world; and a shoe of a horse will do.'

Now they got into their boat with the horseshoe, and when the dawn was come they were aware of the smoke of the Earl's town and the bells of the Kirk that beat. So they set foot to shore; and the man went up to the market among the fishers over against the palace and the Kirk; and he was bitter poor and bitter ugly, and he had never a fish to sell, but only a shoe of a horse in his creel, and it rusty.

'Now,' said the Poor Thing, 'do so and so, and you shall find a wife and I a mother.'

It befell that the Earl's daughter came forth to go into the Kirk upon her prayers; and when she saw the poor man stand in the market with only the shoe of a horse, and it rusty, it came in her mind it should be a thing of price.

'What is that?' quoth she.

'It is a shoe of a horse,' said the man.

'And what is the use of it?' quoth the Earl's daughter.

'It is for no use,' said the man.

'I may not believe that,' said she; 'else why should you carry it?'

'I do so,' said he, 'because it was so my fathers did in the ancient ages; and I have neither a better reason nor a worse.'

Now the Earl's daughter could not find it in her mind to believe him. 'Come,' quoth she, 'sell me this, for I am sure it is a thing of price.'

'Nay,' said the man, 'the thing is not for sale.'

'What!' cried the Earl's daughter. 'Then what make you here in the town's market, with the thing in your creel and nought beside?'

'I sit here,' says the man, 'to get me a wife.'

'There is no sense in any of these answers,' thought the Earl's daughter; 'and I could find it in my heart to weep.'

By came the Earl upon that; and she called him and told him all. And when he had heard, he was of his daughter's mind that this should be a thing of virtue; and charged the man to set a price upon the thing, or else be hanged upon the gallows; and that was near at hand, so that the man could see it.

'The way of life is straight like the grooves of launching,' quoth the man. 'And if I am to be hanged let me be hanged.'

'Why!' cried the Earl, 'will you set your neck against a shoe of a horse, and it rusty?'

'In my thought,' said the man, 'one thing is as good as another in this world; and a shoe of a horse will do.'

'This can never be,' thought the Earl; and he stood and looked upon the man, and bit his beard.

And the man looked up at him and smiled. 'It was so my fathers did in the ancient ages,' quoth he to the Earl, 'and I have neither a better reason nor a worse.'

'There is no sense in any of this,' thought the Earl, 'and I must be growing old.' So he had his daughter on one side, and says he: 'Many suitors have you denied, my child. But here is a very strange matter that a man should cling so to a shoe of a horse, and it rusty; and that he should offer it like a thing on sale, and yet not sell it; and that he should sit there seeking a wife. If I come not to the bottom of this thing, I shall have no more pleasure in bread; and I can see no way, but either I should hang or you should marry him.'

'By my troth, but he is bitter ugly,' said the Earl's daughter. 'How if the gallows be so near at hand?'

'It was not so,' said the Earl, 'that my fathers did in the ancient ages. I am like the man, and can give you neither a better reason nor a worse. But do you, prithee, speak with him again.'

So the Earl's daughter spoke to the man. 'If you were not so bitter ugly,' quoth she, 'my father the Earl would have us marry.'

'Bitter ugly am I,' said the man, 'and you as fair as May. Bitter ugly I am, and what of that? It was so my fathers –'

'In the name of God,' said the Earl's daughter, 'let your fathers be!'

'If I had done that,' said the man, 'you had never been chaffering with me here in the market, nor your father the Earl watching with the end of his eye.'

'But come,' quoth the Earl's daughter, 'this is a very strange thing, that you would have me wed for a shoe of a horse, and it rusty.'

'In my thought,' quoth the man, 'one thing is as good –'

'Oh, spare me that,' said the Earl's daughter, 'and tell me why I should marry.'

'Listen and look,' said the man.

Now the wind blew through the Poor Thing like an infant crying, so that her heart was melted; and her eyes were unsealed, and she was aware of the thing as it were a babe unmothered, and she took it to her arms, and it melted in her arms like the air.

'Come,' said the man, 'behold a vision of our children, the busy hearth, and the white heads. And let that suffice, for it is all God offers.'

'I have no delight in it,' said she; but with that she sighed.

'The ways of life are straight like the grooves of launching,' said the man; and he took her by the hand.

'And what shall we do with the horseshoe?' quoth she.

'I will give it to your father,' said the man; 'and he can make a kirk and a mill of it for me.'

It came to pass in time that the Poor Thing was born; but memory of these matters slept within him, and he knew not that which he had done. But he was a part of the eldest son; rejoicing manfully to launch the boat into the surf, skilful to direct the helm, and a man of might where the ring closes and the blows are going.

'The Poor Thing' from *Fables* by Robert Louis Stevenson, 1881

Anchyses

As for Anchyses syght yf yow desyre
Ile bee your guyde, Ile set yow on your way,
wee must beyond that knole, so mownting hyer
hee showd the shyning feelds that vnder lay,
It hapned at that tyme Eneas syre,
was in a vally making strawng survay
   of sowls, that showld heerafter lyve on earth,
   whose bodyes showld descend from his by berth./

I say by deep and wondrows speculacion
his childrens children yet vnborn wear seen,
theyr fortunes and theyr fates, theyr face theyr fashion,
the whyle his noble sonne marcht ore the green.
whome when hee saw, with deerest salutacion,
and tears, but tears of Ioy, that fell between
   and art thow come indeed sayd hee my sonne,
   and hath thy vertue this hard passage wonne?

Have I not Iust occasyon to reiyse
I, that have been by thee so deer respected,
to see thy person and to heer thy voyce?
Nor was thy comming meerly vnexspected,
for of this place, for this cawse made I choyse

forseing thow showldst hether bee dyrected,
    oh from what dawngers thow hast been exempted
    then cheefe, when thee the Lybian lady tempted.

Eneas thus replyde, your revrent ghost,
Deer Syre appeerd to mee in fearfull dreams,
Commawnding mee to search this hidden coast,
and leave my shipps in Tirrhen saltysh streams.
To fynde your wyshed presence I have crost
full many seas, and sayld by sundry realms.
    Oh let mee kysse your hands, let myne embracinge,
    seem to your sacred speryt no defasinge.

Thre sundry tymes the prince did thear endever
In open armes his syre to have embrast,
but thryse the towch his shaddow did dissever,
lyke wynd, or lyke a dream that soon ys past.

      Virgil's *Aeneid*, translated from the Latin by Sir John Harington, 1604

Travelling in the Family

To Rodrigo M. F. de Andrade

In the desert of Itabira
the shadow of my father
took me by the hand.
So much time lost.
But he didn't say anything.
It was neither day nor night.
A sigh? A passing bird?
But he didn't say anything.

We have come a long way.
Here there was a house.
The mountain used to be bigger.
So many heaped-up dead,
and time gnawing the dead.
And in the ruined houses,
cold disdain and damp.
But he didn't say anything.

The street he used to cross
on horseback, at a gallop.
His watch. His clothes.
His legal documents.
His tales of love-affairs.
Opening of tin trunks
and violent memories.
But he didn't say anything.

In the desert of Itabira
things come back to life,
stiflingly, suddenly.
The market of desires
displays its sad treasures;
my urge to run away;
naked women; remorse.
But he didn't say anything.

Stepping on books and letters
we travel in the family.
Marriages; mortgages;
the consumptive cousins;
the mad aunt; my grandmother
betrayed among the slave-girls,
rustling silks in the bedroom.
But he didn't say anything.

What cruel, obscure instinct
moved his pallid hand
subtly pushing us
into the forbidden
time, forbidden places?
I looked in his white eyes.
I cried to him: Speak! My voice
shook in the air a moment,
beat on the stones. The shadow
proceeded slowly on
with that pathetic travelling
across the lost kingdom.
But he didn't say anything.

I saw grief, misunderstanding
and more than one old revolt
dividing us in the dark.
The hand I wouldn't kiss,

the crumb that they denied me,
refusal to ask pardon.
Pride. Terror at night.
But he didn't say anything.

Speak speak speak speak.
I pulled him by his coat
that was turning into clay.
By the hands, by the boots
I caught at his strict shadow
and the shadow released itself
with neither haste nor anger.
But he remained silent.

There were distinct silences
deep within his silence.
There was my deaf grandfather
hearing the painted birds
on the ceiling of the church;
my own lack of friends;
and your lack of kisses;
there were our difficult lives
and a great separation
in the little space of the room

The narrow space of life
crowds me up against you,
and in this ghostly embrace
it's as if I were being burned
completely, with poignant love.
Only now do we know each other!
Eye-glasses, memories, portraits
flow in the river of blood.
Now the waters won't let me
make out your distant face,
distant by seventy years . . .

I felt that he pardoned me
but he didn't say anything.
The waters cover his moustache,
the family, Itabira, all.

Elizabeth Bishop, from the Portuguese of Carlos Drummond de Andrade,
in *Complete Poems*, 1983

The sons of Frederic, knight of Kelle

A citizen of Andernach named Erkinbert, the father of our monk John, going one day before light for a certain purpose, was met by someone on a very black war-horse from whose nostrils shot smoke and fire. . . . Now he appeared to be clothed in sheepskins and carried a great load of earth on his shoulders. To him Erkinbert said: 'Are you the lord Frederic?' And when he replied: 'I am,' he went on: 'Whence do you come and what mean these things which I see?' 'I,' said he, 'am in very great pains; those skins I took from a widow and now I feel them red-hot. Likewise I made an unjust claim to a portion of land, under whose weight I am now crushed. If my sons restore this property, they will much lighten my punishment.' And so he vanished from sight. When he told the sons next day their father's words, they preferred that he should remain for ever in his pains than themselves give up what had been left to them.

From *The Dialogue of Miracles* by Caesarius of Heisterbach, *c*.1220–35, translated by H. von E. Scott and C. C. Swinton Bland

What Ghosts Can Say

When Harry Wylie saw his father's ghost,
As bearded and immense as once in life,
Bending above his bed long after midnight,
He screamed and gripped the corner of the pillow
Till aunts came hurrying white in dressing gowns
To say it was a dream. He knew they lied.
The smell of his father's leather riding crop
And stale tobacco stayed to prove it to him.
Why should there stay such tokens of a ghost
If not to prove it came on serious business?
His father always had meant serious business,
But never so wholly in his look and gesture
As when he beat the boy's uncovered thighs
Calmly and resolutely, at an hour
When Harry never had been awake before.
The man who could choose that single hour of night
Had in him the ingredients of a ghost;
Mortality would quail at such a man.

An older Harry lost his childish notion
And only sometimes wondered if events
Could echo thus long after in a dream.
If so, it surely meant they had a meaning.
But why the actual punishment had fallen,
For what offense of boyhood, he could try
For years and not unearth. What ghosts can say –
Even the ghosts of fathers – comes obscurely.
What if the terror stays without the meaning?

Adrienne Rich, 1951

The Printery

Our house with its bougainvillea trellises,
the front porch gone, was a printery. In its noise
I was led up the cramped stair to its offices.

I saw the small window near which we slept as boys,
how close the roof was. The heat of the galvanize.
A desk in my mother's room, not that bed, sunlit,

with its rose quilt where we were forbidden to sit.
Pink handbills whirred under their spinning negative
and two girls stacked them from their retractable bed

as fast as my own images were reprinted
as I remembered them in an earlier life
that made the sheets linen, the machines furniture,

her wardrobe her winged, angelic mirror. The hum
of the wheel's elbow stopped. And there was a figure
framed in the quiet window for whom this was home,

tracings its dust, rubbing thumb and middle finger,
then coming to me, not past, but through the machines,
clear as a film and as perfectly projected.

as a wall cut by the jalousies' slanted lines.
He had done a self-portrait, it was accurate.
In his transparent hand was a book I had read.

'In this pale blue notebook where you found my verses' –
my father smiled – 'I appeared to make your life's choice,
and the calling that you practise both reverses

and honours mine from the moment it blent with yours.
Now that you are twice my age, which is the boy's,
which the father's?'

     'Sir' – I swallowed – 'they are one voice.'

In the printery's noise, and as we went downstairs
in that now familiar and unfamiliar house,
he said, in an accent of polished weariness,

'I was raised in this obscure Caribbean port,
where my bastard father christened me for his shire:
Warwick. The Bard's county. But never felt part

of the foreign machinery known as Literature.
I preferred verse to fame, but I wrote with the heart
of an amateur. It's that Will you inherit.

I died on his birthday, one April. Your mother
sewed her own costume as Portia, then that disease
like Hamlet's old man's spread from an infected ear,

I believe the parallel has brought you some peace.
Death imitating Art, eh?'

     At the door to the yard,
he said, 'I grew grapes here. Small, a little sour,

still, grapes all the same.'

     'I remember them,' I said.
'I thought they died before you were born. Are you sure?'
'Yes.' The furred nap like nettles, their gloves' green acid.

'What was Warwick doing, transplanting Warwickshire?'
I saw him patterned in shade, the leaves in his hair,
the vines of the lucent body, the swift's blown seed.

From *Omeros* by Derek Walcott, 1991

Stranraer Gardens

At about four I got up and went for a walk. I walked along the landing and looked in on my mum. She was lying with her nose in the air, giving out a light snuffling sound. Mrs Quigley and Emily were locked together in a rather awkward-looking clinch. Between them was Emily's teddy bear, whose name, in case any of you are interested, is Mr Porkerchee.

I went back to my room and looked down at Stranraer Gardens. Surely, I thought to myself, they wouldn't make him roam Stranraer Gardens? Death brought you some privileges, surely? He might not deserve the Elysian Fields, but he hardly deserved *that*.

And then I saw him. He was standing outside number 20. Everything about him said *ghost* in very large letters indeed. And, if he wasn't actually roaming, he looked like a man on the verge of roaming. He looked pretty condemned to wander to me.

He was wearing white, as ghosts tend to do. A kind of long smock, almost down to his ankles. He was barefoot, of course, and there was, you had to admit, a kind of ghostly yellowish glow about him – although that could have had something to do with the fact that he was standing under a sodium lamp.

The only other serious effect death seemed to have had on him was to deprive him of his glasses. But, I guess, Over There, you have no need of glasses. It certainly hadn't made him any more decisive. He was just hanging round looking vague – the way he used to when he was alive. Maybe, I thought to myself, he hadn't been assertive enough to get through to the Other Side. He looked a bit like one of those guys you see at airports, waiting for their luggage to come round on the carousel.

I just assumed it was an optical illusion – in a couple of minutes, I'd look back and it would be gone. Either that or we'd get a few special effects – a shooting star or a voice booming out round Stranraer Gardens telling us our days were numbered. But my dad proved to be as low-key posthumously as he had been when above, the sod.

I lay down on my bed, closed my eyes and counted to a hundred. Then, very slowly, I pulled myself up to the window and looked out. He was still there.

From *They Came from SW19* by Nigel Williams, 1992

The Erl-king

Who rides so late through the grisly night?
'Tis a father and child, and he grasps him tight;
He wraps him close in his mantle's fold,
And shelters the boy from the piercing cold.

'My son, why thus to my arm dost cling?'
'Father, dost thou not see the Erl-king?
The king with his crown and his long black train!'
'My son, 'tis a streak of the misty rain!

'Come hither, thou darling! come, go with me!
Fine games know I that I'll play with thee;
Flowers many and bright do my kingdoms hold,
My mother has many a robe of gold.

'Oh father, dear father! and dost thou not hear
What the Erl-king whispers so low in mine ear?'
'Calm, calm thee, my boy, it is only the breeze,
As it rustles the wither'd leaves under the trees!

'Wilt thou go, bonny boy! wilt thou go with me?
My daughters shall wait on thee daintilie;
My daughters around thee in dance shall sweep,
And rock thee, and kiss thee, and sing thee to sleep!'

'O father, dear father! and dost thou not mark
Erl-king's daughters move by in the dark!'
'I see it, my child; but it is not they,
'Tis the old willow nodding its head so grey!

'I love thee! thy beauty, it charms me so;
And I'll take thee by force, if thou wilt not go!'
'O father, dear father! he's grasping me –
My heart is as cold as cold can be!'

The father rides swiftly – with terror he gasps –
The sobbing child in his arms he clasps;
He reaches the castle with spurring and dread;
But, alack! in his arms the child lay dead!

Johann Wolfgang Goethe, 1782, translated from the German
by Theodore Martin

The July Ghost

He described the boy. Blond, about ten at a guess, he was not very good at children's ages, very blue eyes, slightly built, with a rainbow-striped tee shirt and blue jeans, mostly though not always – oh, and those football practice shoes, black and green. And the other tee shirt, with the ships and wavy lines. And an extraordinarily nice smile. A really *warm* smile. A nice-looking boy.

He was used to her being silent. But this silence went on and on and on. She was just staring into the garden. After a time, she said, in her precise conversational tone,

'The only thing I want, the only thing I want at all in this world, is to see that boy.'

She stared at the garden and he stared with her, until the grass began to dance with empty light, and the edges of the shrubbery wavered. For a brief moment he shared the strain of not seeing the boy. Then she gave a little sigh, sat down, neatly as always, and passed out at his feet.

After this she became, for her, voluble. He didn't move her after she fainted, but sat patiently by her, until she stirred and sat up; then he fetched her some water, and would have gone away, but she talked.

'I'm too rational to see ghosts, I'm not someone who would see anything there was to see, I don't believe in an after-life, I don't see how anyone can, I always found a kind of satisfaction for myself in the idea that one just came to an end, to a sliced-off stop. But that was myself; I didn't think *he* – not *he* – I thought ghosts were – what people *wanted* to see, or were afraid to see . . . and after he died, the best hope I had, it sounds silly, was that I would go mad enough so that instead of waiting every day for him to come home from school and rattle the letter-box I might actually have the illusion of seeing or hearing him come in. Because I can't stop my body and mind waiting, every day, every day, I can't let go. And his bedroom, sometimes at night I go in, I think I might just for a moment forget he *wasn't* in there sleeping, I think I would pay almost anything – anything at all – for a moment of seeing him like I used to. In his pyjamas, with his – his – his hair . . . ruffled, and his . . . you said, his . . . that *smile*.'

From 'The July Ghost' by A. S. Byatt, 1987

'Her'

A footstep, a low throbbing in the walls,
A noise of falling weights that never fell,
Weird whispers, bells that rang without a hand,
Door-handles turn'd when none was at the door,
And bolted doors that open'd of themselves;
And one betwixt the dark and light had seen
Her, bending by the cradle of her babe.

From *The Ring* by Alfred Lord Tennyson, 1887

Return of My Mother From the Dead

Yes, I've seen dead people come back. I saw my mother when I was eleven. She had died and left a little baby boy. The next morning after birthing it she died about nine o'clock. The fourth day after, I was laying down in bed – it was about ten o'clock. I had put the baby's nightclothes on, and gave it its milk bottle and laid it on my arm, just like I'd seen mother do it. There wasn't nothing burning but a little tin lamp, and I had blowed it, and that made the house dark.

The mother came in and looked at the mantelpiece, as if she was looking for some medicine. Her robe she had on – you could call it a dress but it reached the floor – was so white it lit up the house just like as if I had the lamp on. That's what made me look, to see what it was lit up the house so bright. Her back was to me, but I could tell her shape. It scared me so I hollered like something was killing me, and got out and into the bed with my grandmother and my little cousin – I just slided right down between them, like a rat. Soon as I hollered the light went out. I reckon she discovered she had frightened me to death.

Mother come back after that baby. It died the next day. It got to foaming at the mouth and couldn't take its little bottle. My grandmother told me it was dying.

Grandma saw the light as it went out. She told me it was her Annie come back to see about the baby. Mother knew we couldn't raise it – it was too much of a burden to us that year; I didn't have no experience. Wasn't nobody to take care of it but me and my daddy.

You don't hardly never see a spirit's face. You know him by his voice or his shape or by what he's doing; he does what he was in the custom of doing before he died. I've seen several spirits, but sleeping or awake, I never saw one in the face.

Mary Robertson, aged 89, recorded by Richard M. Dorson
in *American Negro Folktales*, 1956

She is mine

BELOVED, she my daughter. She mine. See. She come back to me of her own free will and I don't have to explain a thing. I didn't have time to explain before because it had to be done quick. Quick. She had to be safe and I put her where she would be. But my love was tough and she back now. I knew she would be. Paul D ran her off so she had no choice but to come back to me in the flesh. I bet you Baby Suggs, on the other side, helped. I won't never let her go. I'll explain to her, even though I don't have to. Why I did it. How if I hadn't killed her she would have died and that is something I could not bear to happen to her. When I explain it she'll understand, because she understands everything already. I'll tend her as no mother ever tended a child, a daughter.

I AM BELOVED and she is mine. . . .

I come out of blue water   after the bottoms of my feet swim away from me   I come up   I need to find a place to be   the air is heavy   I am not dead   I am not   there is a house   there is what she whispered to me   I am where she told me   I am not dead   I sit   the sun closes my eyes   when I open them I see the face I lost   Sethe's is the face that left me   Sethe sees me see her and I see the smile   her smiling face is the place for me   it is the face I lost   she is my face smiling at me   doing it at last   a hot thing   now we can join   a hot thing

From *Beloved* by Toni Morrison, 1987

Travelling Clothes

The stepmother took the red-hot poker and burned the orphan's face with it because she had not raked the ashes. The girl went to her mother's grave. In the earth her mother said: 'It must be raining. Or else it is snowing. Unless there is a heavy dew tonight.'

'It isn't raining, it isn't snowing, it's too early for the dew. My tears are falling on your grave, mother.'

The dead woman waited until night came. Then she climbed out and went to the house. The stepmother slept on a feather bed, but the burned child slept on the hearth among the ashes. When the dead woman kissed her, the scar vanished. The girl woke up. The dead woman gave her a red dress.

'I had it when I was your age.'

The girl put the red dress on. The dead woman took worms from her eyesockets; they turned into jewels. The girl put on a diamond ring.

'I had it when I was your age.'

They went together to the grave.

'Step into my coffin.'

'No,' said the girl. She shuddered.

'I stepped into *my* mother's coffin when I was your age.'

The girl stepped into the coffin although she thought it would be thedeath of her. It turned into a coach and horses. The horses stamped, eager to be gone.

'Go and seek your fortune, darling.'

From 'Ashputtle' by Angela Carter, 1987

'Bear up, Bessie lass!'

There was a woman at Horbury Bridge, near Wakefield, who kept a little shop. [When she] was a girl of sixteen her mother died, and she went into a situation in the same hamlet, where she was very unhappy because unkindly treated.

One night she left the house, ran to the churchyard, and, kneeling by her mother's grave, told her the tale of her sorrows. Then she saw the vaporous form of her mother standing or floating above the grave-mound. As the woman described it, it was as if made out of fog and moonshine, but the face was distinct. And she heard the apparition say: 'Bear up, Bessie lass! It's no but for a little while, and then thou'lt be right.' Whereat the figure slowly dissolved and disappeared.

From *A Book of Folk-lore* by Sabine Baring-Gould, 1913

Fourteen

LOVE

But first let yawning Earth a Passage rend;
And let me through the dark Abyss descend;
First let avenging *Jove*, with Flames from high,
Drive down this Body, to the neather Sky,
Condemn'd with Ghosts in endless Night to lye;
Before I break the plighted Faith I gave;
No; he who had my Vows, shall ever have;
For whom I lov'd on Earth, I worship in the Grave.

JOHN DRYDEN

I know, although when looks meet
I tremble to the bone,
The more I leave the door unlatched
The sooner love is gone,
For love is but a skein unwound
Between the dark and dawn.

A lonely ghost the ghost is
That to God shall come;
I – love's skein upon the ground,
My body in the tomb –
Shall leap into the light lost
In my mother's womb.

But were I left to lie alone
In an empty bed.
The skein so bound us ghost to ghost
When he turned his head
Passing on the road that night.
Mine must walk when dead.

W. B. YEATS

Quia amore langueo

In a tabernacle of a toure,
As I stode musing on the mone,
A crowned quene, most of honoure,
Apered in ghostly sight full sone.
She made compleint, thus, by her one:
'For mannes soule was wrapped in wo
I may nat leve mankinde alone,
Quia amore langueo.

*

'Why was I crowned and made a quene?
Why was I called of mercy the welle?
Why shuld an erthly woman bene
So high in Heven above aungell?
For thee, mankinde, the truthe I tell.
Thou aske me helpe, and I shall do
That I was ordeined – kepe thee fro hell –
Quia amore langueo.

'Nowe man have minde on me for ever,
Loke on thy love thus languishing.
Late us never fro other dissever:
Mine helpe is thine owne, crepe under my wing.
Thy sister is a quene, thy brother is a king,
This heritage is tailed – sone come therto:
Take me for thy wife and lerne to sing,
Quia amore langueo.'

Anon., c.1400

Paolo and Francesca

After I listened to my instructor
   naming the ancient women and knights,
   I felt bewildered, lost in thought.
I said, 'Poet, I'd appreciate it
   if I spoke to those two together,
   who seem so weightless on the wind.'
He says, 'Just wait till they blow

closer to us, then you invoke them
by their driving love; they'll come.'
When the wind bent them near us
I spoke up: 'Oh vexed spirits,
come and talk to us, if God allows!'
Just like doves summoned by desire
sweep across the sky on impulse,
gliding towards their happy nest,
so these came from the Dido group
and to us through the brutal air,
so strong my compassionate cry.
'Oh gracious, good-natured soul,
visiting through this black weather
those like us who bloodied earth,
if the cosmic king was our friend
we'd pray to him for your peace,
since our evil rouses your pity.
Whatever you want to hear and say,
we can speak with you and listen
while the wind keeps low as now.
The town sits where I was born
on the coast, where Po runs down
with his streams to final peace.
Love, swift in seizing noble hearts,
it took this man with the loveliness
taken from me, and still it hurts.
Love insists the loved loves back,
and pleased me with him so much
that it's still with me, as you see.
Love brought us both to one death:
Caina awaits him, our assassin.'
These were the words they spoke.
After I'd heard these hounded souls,
I looked at the ground so long
the poet asked me 'What's wrong?'
And I said in reply, 'Oh dear,
how many sweet thoughts or hopes
led these to that awful moment!'
Then I turned to them and said,
'Francesca, these torments of yours
dismay me to the point of tears.
But tell me: when sighs were sweet,
by what means did love arrange it
that you knew its dubious desires?'

She says, 'The worst thing there is
  is to remember the happy times
  in misery; your master knows that.
But if you're keen to know them,
  these first rootings of our love,
  I'll talk even while I'm in tears.
We were reading one day for fun
  how Lancelot was seized by love:
  we were alone, but didn't suspect.
Several times the book made us pale,
  making us look in each other's eyes,
  but only once it became too much.
When we read of that adorable smile
  and how the great lover kisses it,
  this man, who'll always be by me,
he kissed my mouth all quivering.
  Both book and author were panders:
  we didn't read any more that day.'
While one of the ghosts told us this
  the other wept – I felt so awful
  I fainted as if I'd actually died,
and down I went like a dead body.

From *L'Inferno* by Dante Alighieri, *c*.1310, translated from the Italian
by Steve Ellis

Nastagio's Lesson

When Lauretta was silent, Filomena, at the queen's command, began
thus:

Charming ladies, as pity is commended in us, so divine justice rigidly
punishes cruelty in you. To display this to you and cause you to drive it
wholly from you, I desire to tell you a tale no less full of compassion
than of delight.

In Ravenna, that most ancient city of Romagna, there were of old
many nobles and gentlemen, among whom was a young man named
Nastagio degli Onesti, who became exceedingly rich on the death of his
father and an uncle. As happens to young men without a wife, he fell in
love with a daughter of Messer Paolo Traversaro, a girl of far more
noble birth than he, whom he hoped to win by his actions. But however
fair and praiseworthy they were, they not only failed to please her but
actually seemed to displease her, so cruelly, harshly, and unfriendly did
the girl behave, perhaps on account of her rare beauty, perhaps because

her lofty and disdainful nobility of birth made her despise him and everything he liked.

This was so hard for Nastagio to bear that for very grief he often desired to slay himself. But, dreading to do this, he very often determined to leave her or, if he could, to hate her as she hated him. But in vain, for it seemed that the less hope he had, the more his love grew.

As the young man continued to love and to spend money recklessly, his friends and relatives felt that he was wasting both himself and his possessions. So they often advised and begged him to leave Ravenna, and to go and live somewhere else for a time, to diminish his love and his expense. Nastagio several times made mock of this advice; but unable to say 'No' to their repeated solicitations, he agreed to do it. He made great preparations, as if he were going to France or Spain or some other far off land, mounted his horse, and left Ravenna accompanied by many of his friends. He went to a place about three miles from Ravenna, called Chiassi; and having set up tents and pavilions there, told his friends he meant to stay there and that they should return to Ravenna. There Nastagio led the most extravagant life, inviting different parties of people to dine or sup, as he had been accustomed to do.

Now, in very fine weather about the beginning of May, he began to think of his cruel lady, and ordered his attendants to leave him alone so that he could dream of her at his ease; and in his reverie his footsteps led him into the pine woods. The fifth hour of the day was already spent, and he was a good half-mile inside the woods, forgetful of food and everything else, when suddenly he thought he heard a loud lamentation and the wild shrieks of a woman. Breaking off his sweet reverie, he raised his head to see what it was, and to his surprise found himself in the pine forest. But, in addition, as he looked in front of him he saw coming towards him a very beautiful girl, naked, with disordered hair, and all scratched by the thorns and twigs of the brambles and bushes in the wood. She was weeping and calling for mercy. Beside her he saw two very large, fierce mastiffs, savagely pursuing her, and frequently snapping cruelly at her; and behind her on a black horse was a dark knight, with grief and anger in his face, with a sword in his hand, who often threatened her with death in dreadful and insulting terms.

This aroused astonishment and terror in his soul, and finally compassion for the unfortunate lady, from which was born the desire to set her free from such agony and such a death, if he could. But, finding himself unarmed, he ran to tear off a tree bough in place of a cudgel, and began to advance towards the dogs and the knight. But the knight saw him, and called to him from a distance:

'Nastagio, don't meddle here, let me and these dogs do what this wicked woman has deserved.'

As he spoke the dogs seized the girl by the thighs, bringing her to the ground, and the knight dismounted from his horse. Nastagio went up to him, and said:

'I do not know who you are, though you seem to know me; but I tell you it is baseness in an armed knight to want to kill a naked woman, and to have set dogs at her, as if she were a wild beast. I shall defend her as far as I can.'

Then said the knight:

'Nastagio, I am of the same country as yourself, and you were still a little child when I, whose name was Messer Guido degli Anastagi, was more deeply in love with this woman than you now are with your Traversaro. Owing to her cruelty and pride, my misfortune caused me in despair to kill myself with the sword you see in my hand, and I am damned to eternal punishment. Not long afterwards, she, who had rejoiced exceedingly at my death, died also, and died unrepentant, believing that she had not sinned but done well; but for the sin of her cruelty and of her rejoicing at my torments, she too was and is damned to the punishments of hell. When she descended into hell, the punishment imposed upon us was that she should fly from me and that I, who once loved her so much, should pursue her as a mortal enemy, not as a beloved woman. As often as I catch her I kill her with the very sword with which I slew myself, and split her open, and drag out (as you will see) that hard cold heart, wherein love and pity could never enter, together with her entrails, and give them to these dogs to eat.

'After no long space of time, in accordance with the justice and the will of God, she rises up again as if she had not been dead, and once more begins her anguished flight, and I and the dogs pursue her. Every Friday at this hour I catch up with her here and slaughter her as you will see. And do not think that we rest on other days. I catch her in other places where she thought or wrought cruelly against me. Having changed from a lover to an enemy, as you see, I am condemned in this way to pursue her for as many years as the months she was cruel to me. Now let me execute divine justice, and strive not to oppose what you cannot prevent.'

Nastagio was terrified by these words, and there was scarcely a hair of his body which did not stand on end. He drew back and gazed at the miserable girl, awaiting fearfully what the knight would do. When the knight had done speaking, he rushed like a mad dog at the girl with his sword in his hand, while she, held on her knees by the mastiffs, shrieked for mercy. But he thrust his sword with all his strength through the middle of her breast until it stood out behind her back. When the girl received this thrust, she fell forward still weeping and shrieking. The knight took a dagger in his hand, slit her open, took out her heart and everything near it, and threw them to the mastiffs who hungrily devoured them at once.

But before long the girl suddenly rose to her feet as if nothing had happened, and began to run towards the sea, with the dogs continually snapping at her. The knight took his sword, remounted his horse and followed; and in a short time they were so far away that Nastagio lost sight of them. After seeing these things, Nastagio hesitated a long time between pity and fear; but after some time it occurred to him that it might be useful to him, since it happened every Friday. So, having marked the place, he returned to his servants, and in due course sent for many of his relatives and friends, to whom he said:

'You have long urged me to refrain from loving my fair enemy and to cease my expense. I am ready to do so, if you will dine with me, and bring Messr Paolo Traversaro, his wife, his daughter, all their women relatives, and any other women you like. Why I want this you will see later.'

They thought this a small thing to do. So they returned to Ravenna, and invited those whom Nastagio wanted. And although it was hard to get the girl whom Nastagio loved, still she went along with the rest. Nastagio made preparations for a magnificent feast, and had the tables set among the pines near the place where he had seen the massacre of the cruel lady. He placed the men and women at table in such a manner that the girl he loved was exactly opposite the place where this would happen.

The last course had arrived when they all began to hear the despairing shrieks of the pursued lady. Everyone was astonished and asked what it was. Nobody knew. They stood up to look, and saw the agonized girl and the dogs and the knight. And in a very short time they all arrived in front of them. Great was the uproar against knight and dogs, and many started forward to help the girl. But the knight, speaking to them as he had spoken to Nastagio, not only made them draw back, but filled them with astonishment and terror. He did what he had done before; and all the women, many of whom were relatives of the suffering girl and of the knight, and remembered his love and death, wept as wretchedly as if it had been done to themselves.

When the massacre was over, and the lady and the knight had gone, those who had seen it fell into different sorts of discourse. But the most frightened was the cruel lady beloved by Nastagio, who had distinctly seen and heard everything, and knew that these things came nearer to her than to anyone else, for she remembered the cruelty with which she had always treated Nastagio. So that in her mind's eye she already seemed to be flying from his rage and to feel the mastiffs at her side.

Such fear was born in her from this that, to avoid its happening to her, she could scarcely wait for that evening to change her hate into love and to send a trusted maidservant secretly to Nastagio, begging him to go to see her, because she was ready to do anything he pleased.

Nastagio replied that this was a happiness to him but that he desired his pleasure with honour, which was to take her as his wife, if she would agree. The girl knew that she herself had been the only obstacle to this hitherto, and replied that she was willing. So making herself the messenger, she told her father and mother that she was willing to marry Nastagio, which greatly delighted them. Next Sunday Nastagio married her and made a wedding feast, and lived happily with her for a long time.

Nor was this the only good which resulted from this terrifying apparition, for all the ladies of Ravenna took fear, and became far more compliant to the pleasures of the men than they had ever been before.

From *The Decameron* by Giovanni Boccaccio (1349–51), translated from the Italian by Richard Aldington

'*I daily doom'd to follow, she to fly*'

Short was her Joy; for soon th' insulting Maid
By Heav'n's Decree in the cold Grave was laid,
And as in unrepenting Sin she dy'd,
Doom'd to the same bad Place, is punish'd for her Pride;
Because she deem'd I well deserv'd to die,
And made a Merit of her Cruelty.
There, then, we met; both try'd and both were cast,
And this irrevocable Sentence pass'd:
That she whom I so long pursu'd in vain,
Should suffer from my Hands a lingring Pain:
Renew'd to Life, that she might daily die,
I daily doom'd to follow, she to fly;
No more a Lover but a mortal Foe,
I seek her Life (for Love is none below).

From 'Theodore and Honoria' by John Dryden, 1700

The Dweller in the Ilsenstein

Hast thou never seen the beautiful maiden sitting on the Ilsenstein? Every morning with the first beams of the sun, she opens the rock and goes down to the Ilse to bathe in its clear cold waters. True, the power of seeing her is not granted to every one, but those who have seen her, praise her beauty and benevolence. She often dispenses the treasures contained in the Ilsenstein; and many families owe their prosperity to the lovely maiden.

Once, very early in the morning, a charcoal-burner, proceeding to the forest, saw the maiden sitting on the Ilsenstein. He greeted her in a friendly tone, and she beckoned to him to follow her. He went, and they soon stood before the great rock. She knocked thrice, and the Ilsenstein opened. She entered, and brought him back his wallet filled, but strictly enjoined him not to open it till he reached his hut. He took it with thanks. As he proceeded, he was struck by the weight of the wallet, and would gladly have seen what it contained. At length, when he came to the bridge across the Ilse, he could no longer withstand his curiosity. He opened it, and saw in it acorns and fir-cones. Indignant he shook the cones and acorns from the bridge down into the swollen stream, when he instantly heard a loud jingling as the acorns and cones touched the stones of the Ilse, and found to his dismay that he had shaken out gold. He then very prudently wrapped up the little remnant that he found in the corners of the wallet, and carried them carefully home; and even this was enough to enable him to purchase a small house and garden.

But who is this maiden? Listen to what our fathers and mothers have told us. At the Deluge, when the waters of the North Sea overflowed the valleys and plains of Lower Saxony, a youth and a maiden, who had been long attached to each other, fled from the North country towards the Harz mountains, in the hope of saving their lives. As the waters rose they also mounted higher and higher, continually approaching the Brocken, which in the distance appeared to offer them a safe retreat. At length they stood upon a vast rock, which reared its head far above the raging waters. From this spot they saw the whole surrounding country covered by the flood, and houses, and animals, and men had disappeared. Here they stood alone and gazed on the foaming waves, which dashed against the foot of the rock. The waters rose still higher, and already they thought of fleeing farther over a yet uncovered ridge of rock, and climbing to the summit of the Brocken, which appeared like a large island rising above the billowy sea.

At this moment the rock on which they stood trembled under their feet and split asunder, threatening every instant to separate the lovers. On the left side towards the Brocken stood the maiden, on the right the youth; their hands were firmly clasped in each other's; the precipice inclined right and left outwards; the maiden and the youth sank into the flood. The maiden was called Ilse, and she gave her name to the beautiful Ilsenthal, to the river, which flows through it, and to the Ilsenstein, in which she still dwells.

From Müllenhof's *Sagen, Märchen und Lieder*, 1845, translated by Benjamin Thorpe

Fatimah

Once there was a girl called Fatimah. Every day she goes to school and looks thinner and paler until her mother asks harshly, 'Why do you look so weak?' and swears at her, 'Why have you got like that?' The girl says, 'Whenever I reach the bridge on the way to school, I hear someone tell me I will meet a dead man.' When her mother sees her losing weight, she takes her on a picnic, to make her happy, out on the desert plain. Looking round they see a house, but only the door. The mother tries it, but it will not open. Later, the girl pushes the door; it opens easily and in she goes. Suddenly, it closes behind her, and however much her mother tries to open it, she can't. She waits for many days until the girl tells her, 'Go back, for God has written thus in my face.'

She walks round the house and sees a bunch of keys: all the doors are locked. One by one, she unlocks the doors. The first room is full of gold and jewellery. In the second is a horse, but instead of straw, bones are spread around him. In the third is everything a house might need. Thus she opens all the doors, and all have something. But the seventh door is covered and when she looks inside she finds a dead king, his body pierced with needles from head to toe. Every day, she takes out the needles, one by one, until just one is left, on the end of his nose, but at last she gives up, and sighs, for he cannot be brought to life.

Later, she sees some gypsies from the terrace and asks them to sell her a girl. They agree and she lifts the gypsy girl up with a rope and makes her the housekeeper. One day she goes to the baths, saying, 'Look after the house.' When the gypsy explores, she finds the fallen man with the needle in the tip of his nose. She takes out the needle; the King comes to life, sneezes, arises and declares, 'You are my Halal, my lawful wife.' When Fatimah hears this, she hides herself away: the gypsy becomes the King's wife, and now Fatimah is the housekeeper.

Later, when the King is going to the city, he asks what they want. The wife asks for jewellery, Fatimah for a stone knife. When the King is coming home he remembers her request, but when he goes to buy the stone knife, the shopkeeper says, 'Beware of the person you are taking this to. She is in despair and will tell her despair to that stone, then kill herself.' On his return, he gives the presents, but he follows his housekeeper and hears her tell her story to the stone – what has happened to her, how she came here, what she has done. Just as she is about to kill herself, the King grasps her hand from behind, saying, 'Don't do it – I realise now that it was my fault.' The girl becomes his wife and makes the gypsy her housekeeper. Thus Fatimah spends her life with the King.

Told by Atool Mohamed Zoone in Iraqi Kurdistan, 1993,
collected by Shukria Rasool, translated by Aram Mohamed

'The marquis was not surprised'

The marquis was not surprised at the silence that reigned in the princess's apartment. Concluding her, as he had been advertised, in her oratory, he passed on. The door was ajar; the evening gloomy and overcast. Pushing open the door gently, he saw a person kneeling before the altar. As he approached nearer, it seemed not a woman, but one in a long woollen weed, whose back was towards him. The person seemed absorbed in prayer. The marquis was about to return, when the figure, rising, stood some moments fixed in meditation, without regarding him. The marquis, expecting the holy person to come forth, and meaning to excuse his uncivil interruption, said:

'Reverend father, I sought the Lady Hippolita.'

'Hippolita!' replied a hollow voice; 'camest thou to this castle to seek Hippolita?' And then the figure, turning slowly round, discovered to Frederic the fleshless jaws and empty sockets of a skeleton, wrapt in a hermit's cowl.

'Angels of peace protect me!' cried Frederic, recoiling.

'Deserve their protection,' said the spectre.

Frederic, falling on his knees, adjured the phantom to take pity on him.

'Dost thou not remember me?' said the apparition. 'Remember the wood of Joppa!'

'Art thou that holy hermit?' cried Frederic, trembling; 'can I do aught for thy eternal peace?'

'Wast thou delivered from bondage,' said the spectre, 'to pursue carnal delights? Hast thou forgotten the buried sabre, and the behest of Heaven engraven on it?'

'I have not, I have not,' said Frederic; 'but say, blest spirit, what is thy errand to me? what remains to be done?'

'To forget Matilda,' said the apparition, and vanished.

From *The Castle of Otranto* by Horace Walpole, 1764

Fair Imogine

And now had the marriage been bless'd by the priest;
    The revelry now was begun:
The tables they groan'd with the weight of the feast;
Nor yet had the laughter and merriment ceased,
    When the bell of the castle toll'd – 'one!'

Then first with amazement Fair Imogine found
    That a stranger was placed by her side:
His air was terrific; he utter'd no sound;
He spoke not, he moved not, he look'd not around,
    But earnestly gazed on the bride.

His vizor was closed, and gigantic his height;
    His armour was sable to view:
All pleasure and laughter were hush'd at his sight;
The dogs, as they eyed him, drew back in affright;
    The lights in the chamber burnt blue!

His presence all bosoms appear'd to dismay;
    The guests sat in silence and fear:
At length spoke the bride, while she trembled: – 'I pray,
'Sir Knight, that your helmet aside you would lay,
    'And deign to partake of our cheer.' –

The lady is silent: the stranger complies,
    His vizor he slowly unclosed:
Oh! then what a sight met Fair Imogine's eyes!
What words can express her dismay and surprise,
    When a skeleton's head was exposed!

All present then utter'd a terrified shout;
    All turn'd with disgust from the scene.
The worms they crept in, and the worms they crept out,
And sported his eyes and his temples about,
    While the spectre address'd Imogine:

'Behold me, thou false one! behold me!' he cried;
    'Remember Alonzo the Brave!
'God grants, that, to punish thy falsehood and pride,
'My ghost at thy marriage should sit by thy side,
'Should tax thee with perjury, claim thee as bride,
    'And bear thee away to the grave!'

Thus saying, his arms round the lady he wound,
    While loudly she shriek'd in dismay;
Then sank with his prey through the wide-yawning ground:
Nor ever again was Fair Imogine found,
    Or the spectre who bore her away.

Not long lived the Baron: and none since that time
    To inhabit the castle presume;
For chronicles tell, that, by order sublime,
There Imogine suffers the pain of her crime,
    And mourns her deplorable doom.

At midnight four times in each year does her sprite,
    When mortals in slumber are bound,
Array'd in her bridal apparel of white,
Appear in the hall with the skeleton-knight,
    And shriek as he whirls her around.

While they drink out of skulls newly torn from the grave,
    Dancing round them pale spectres are seen:
Their liquor is blood, and this horrible stave
They howl:– 'To the health of Alonzo the Brave,
    And his consort, the False Imogine!'

From 'Alonzo the Brave and Fair Imogine' in *The Monk*
by Matthew Gregory Lewis, 1795

Golden Hair

Once upon a time there was a young peasant maiden who had beautiful long golden hair. And the wicked Count Rinaldo fell in love with that golden hair and said he would take the maiden for his bride.

'Ah!' said Golden Hair's mother. 'Now our little daughter will be a countess. How fine that is!'

'Oh ho!' said Golden Hair's father. 'Count Rinaldo shall have her, yes, he shall have her; but he shall pay me a bag of gold.'

But Golden Hair loved a peasant lad called Pietro. She would have nothing to do with the wicked Count.

Her mother wept and scolded, her father cursed and raged, and the wicked Count said, 'Bah! I will soon remove that worm out of my path!'

So the Count lay in wait for Pietro on a dark night, thinking to kill him. But when the Count fell on Pietro with his sword, Pietro drew his hunting knife to defend himself; and it wasn't Pietro who was killed in that struggle, but the Count.

Then Pietro fled to a far country, for the Count's people were after him to kill him. But before he went he managed to see Golden Hair and he said to her, 'Do not despair, my beloved! Wait for me, though it be one year, or two, or three. I will work hard and make a home for you. And one night I will come to fetch you and take you to our home.'

'I will wait,' said Golden Hair.

And she waited. One year passed, two years passed, three years passed. And after the three years, one day as Golden Hair was walking through the market, there came a little lad who thrust a letter into her hand and disappeared among the crowd.

The letter said, 'Our home is ready, Golden Hair. Look for me tonight between midnight and cockcrow. Look for me on a grey horse in the street outside your window.'

That night Golden Hair sat at her window, watching and waiting. She heard the church clock strike midnight – and surely she heard something else? Yes, the muffled steps of a horse down there in the street. And yes, the merest whisper of a voice: 'Golden Hair, Golden Hair, come down and go with me!'

'I come, I come, Pietro! Ah, how long I have waited!'

'Quick, quick, I have come to fetch you to our home.'

Golden Hair crept downstairs, opened the house door quietly – oh, how quietly – and stepped out into the night: all silent, all dark, the moon hidden behind a black cloud; the glimmer of a grey horse, the dusky shape of a rider muffled in a cloak, the whisper of a voice: 'Quick, quick, up behind me, Golden Hair!'

The rider reached down a hand. Golden Hair grasped it and sprang up behind him. In a moment they were off: *patata, patata, patata*, the horse going like the wind.

On, on, on, Golden Hair with her arms clasped round the body of the cloaked rider; on, on, on, clouds racing over the sky, the moon shining out bright and clear between them; on, on, on, *patata, patata, patata, faster, faster, faster, and faster* – on into a country Golden Hair had never seen before.

See, now they were passing a churchyard, the white gravestones gleaming in the moonlight; and hark, a loud voice calling from among the graves, 'The clouds part, the light of the moon shines clear like day. A youth rides with his maiden. Living maiden, are you not afraid?'

And Golden Hair called back, 'What should I fear when I have plighted my troth?'

On, on, on, *patata, patata, patata, go faster, go faster, go faster!* The world flying away under the horse's hoofs. See, now they were passing another churchyard, and again a loud voice called from among the graves, 'The moon shines bright as day. A youth rides with his maiden. Living maiden, are you not afraid to ride with the dead?'

And Golden Hair called back, 'What should I fear? I do not ride with the dead, I ride with my lover.'

'Ha! ha! ha! Ha! ha! ha!' Up from the graveyard rose shouts of laughter, and from the cloaked rider came a laugh louder than all the rest. 'Truly you ride with your lover, but truly you ride with the dead!'

The rider flung his cloak from his head and turned, and leered at Golden Hair.

And it was not Pietro. It was the ghost of Count Rinaldo.

'In hell I have burned, in hell I have waited,' screamed the ghost. 'In life you escaped me; in death you are mine!'

'Help, help, help!' Golden Hair slid from the horse, but the ghost seized her by her long hair.

'Help! Help! Help!' Was there no help for Golden Hair whirled along by the hair of her head by the side of the galloping horse? *Patata, patata, patata, go faster, go faster, go faster!* Towns, plains and mountains rushing to meet them, vanishing behind them, and there, at the world's end, the iron gates of the City of the Dead drawing nearer and nearer.

'Pietro! Pietro! Help! Pietro! Pietro! Pietro! Help! Help'

And far away, Pietro riding through the night towards Golden Hair's village, heard that cry, swung round his horse, and galloped in pursuit.

'Golden Hair, Golden Hair, I am coming, my beloved, I am coming!'

Patata, patata, patata, go faster, go faster, go faster! Two riders, two grey horses galloping through the night towards the ends of the earth; see, the glow of a great fire over there beyond the ends of the earth, and rising dark and huge against the glow of that fire, the iron gates of the City of the Dead. And see, ahead of Pietro, a glitter of golden hair swinging wildly from the saddle of a galloping horse.

'Pietro! Pietro!'

Patata, patata, patata, go faster, go faster, go faster!

The moon shone clear from a black cloud. Pietro lashing his willing horse, was galloping nearer, ever nearer to the ghostly rider on the ghostly horse. But the huge iron gates of the City of the Dead were also drawing nearer, and those iron gates were slowly opening.

But Pietro was now abreast of the ghostly rider, and Pietro leaned from the saddle, drew his hunting knife, slashed through the golden hair clutched in the ghost's hand, snatched up his beloved and set her on his own horse, just as the iron gates of the City of the Dead swung wide open and the ghost, still clutching the golden hair, galloped through.

The iron gates shut with a clang behind the ghostly horse and the ghostly rider. Yes, Count Rinaldo had the golden hair, but he had nothing else. And since it was the golden hair that Count Rinaldo fell in love with, why then – let him be satisfied!

But Pietro carried Golden Hair away to his home in a far country, and there they married, and lived in peace and happiness ever after.

Corsican folk tale, retold by Ruth Manning-Saunders, 1968

The Highwayman

And still of a winter's night, they say, when the wind is in the trees,
When the moon is a ghostly galleon tossed upon cloudy seas,
When the road is a ribbon of moonlight over the purple moor,
A highwayman comes riding –
   Riding – riding –
A highwayman comes riding, up to the old inn-door.

Over the cobbles he clatters and clangs in the dark inn-yard.
He taps with his whip on the shutters, but all is locked and barred.
He whistles a tune to the window, and who should be waiting there
But the landlord's black-eyed daughter,
   Bess, the landlord's daughter,
Plaiting a dark red love-knot into her long black hair.

From 'The Highwayman' by Alfred Noyes, 1917

Consumed

Dec. 20th. I have been again; I have heard the music; I have been inside the church; I have seen Her! I can no longer doubt my senses. Why should I? Those pedants say that the dead are dead, the past is past. For them, yes; but why for me? – why for a man who loves, who is consumed with the love of a woman? – a woman who, indeed – yes, let me finish the sentence. Why should there not be ghosts to such as can see them? Why should she not return to the earth, if she knows that it contains a man who thinks of, desires, only her?

From *Amour Dure* by Vernon Lee, 1890

O'Tei

Immediately, – and in the unforgotten voice of the dead, – she thus made answer: –

'My name is O-Tei; and you are Nagao Chōsei of Echigo, my promised husband. Seventeen years ago, I died in Niigata: then you made in writing a promise to marry me if ever I could come back to this world in the body of a woman; – and you sealed that written promise with your seal and put it in the *butsudan*, beside the tablet inscribed with my name. And therefore I came back.' . . .

From 'The Story of O'Tei', translated from the Japanese by
Lafcadio Hearn, in *Kwaidun*, 1907

'Open the door to me Oh'

Oh, open the door, some pity to shew,
   If love it may na be, Oh;
Tho' thou hast been false, I'll ever prove true,
   Oh, open the door to me, Oh.

Cauld is the blast upon my pale cheek,
   But caulder thy love for me, Oh:
The frost that freezes the life at my heart,
   Is nought to my pains frae thee, Oh.

The wan moon sets behind the white wave,
   And time is setting with me, Oh:
False friends, false love, farewell! for mair
   I'll ne'er trouble them, nor thee, Oh.

She has open'd the door, she has open'd it wide,
   She sees his pale corse on the plain, Oh:
My true love! she cried, and sank down by his side,
   Never to rise again, Oh.

Robert Burns, *Poems*, 1793

Isabella

It was a vision. – In the drowsy gloom,
    The dull of midnight, at her couch's foot
Lorenzo stood, and wept: the forest tomb
    Had marred his glossy hair which once could shoot
Lustre into the sun, and put cold doom
    Upon his lips, and taken the soft lute
From his lorn voice, and past his loamèd ears
Had made a miry channel for his tears.

Strange sound it was, when the pale shadow spake;
    For there was striving, in its piteous tongue,
To speak as when on earth it was awake,
    And Isabella on its music hung.
Languor there was in it, and tremulous shake,
    As in a palsied Druid's harp unstrung;
And through it moaned a ghostly under-song,
Like hoarse night-gusts sepulchral briars among.

Its eyes, though wild, were still all dewy bright
    With love, and kept all phantom fear aloof
From the poor girl by magic of their light,
    The while it did unthread the horrid woof
Of the late darkened time – the murderous spite
    Of pride and avarice, the dark pine roof
In the forest, and the sodden turfed dell,
Where, without any word, from stabs he fell.

Saying moreover, 'Isabel, my sweet!
    Red whortle-berries droop above my head,
And a large flint-stone weighs upon my feet;
    Around me beeches and high chestnuts shed
Their leaves and prickly nuts; a sheep-fold bleat
    Comes from beyond the river to my bed:
Go, shed one tear upon my heather bloom,
And it shall comfort me within the tomb.

'I am a shadow now, alas! alas!
    Upon the skirts of human-nature dwelling
Alone. I chant alone the holy mass,
    While little sounds of life are round me knelling,
And glossy bees at noon do fieldward pass,
    And many a chapel bell the hour is telling,
Paining me through: those sounds grow strange to me,
And thou art distant in humanity.

'I know what was, I feel full well what is,
    And I should rage, if spirits could go mad;
Though I forget the taste of earthly bliss,
    That paleness warms my grave, as though I had
A seraph chosen from the bright abyss
    To be my spouse: thy paleness makes me glad;
Thy beauty grows upon me, and I feel
A greater love through all my essence steal.'

The Spirit mourn'd 'Adieu!' – dissolved and left
    The atom darkness in a slow turmoil;
As when of healthful midnight sleep bereft,
    Thinking on rugged hours and fruitless toil,
We put our eyes into a pillowy cleft,
    And see the spangly gloom froth up and boil:
It made sad Isabella's eyelids ache,
And in the dawn she started up awake –

From 'Isabella or The Pot of Basil' by John Keats, 1818

Cathy

This time I remembered I was lying in the oak closet, and I heard distinctly the gusty wind, and the driving of the snow; I heard also the fir-bough repeat its teasing sound, and ascribed it to the right cause; but it annoyed me so much that I resolved to silence it, if possible; and, I thought, I rose and endeavoured to unhasp the casement. The hook was soldered into the staple; a circumstance observed by me when awake, but forgotten.

'I must stop it, nevertheless!' I muttered, knocking my knuckles through the glass, and stretching an arm out to seize the importunate branch; instead of which, my fingers closed on the fingers of a little, ice-cold hand!

The intense horror of nightmare came over me: I tried to draw back my arm, but the hand clung to it, and a most melancholy voice sobbed –

'Let me in – let me in!'

'Who are you!' I asked, struggling, meanwhile, to disengage myself.

'Catherine Linton,' it replied, shiveringly (why did I think of *Linton*? I had read *Earnshaw* twenty times for Linton); 'I'm come home: I'd lost my way on the moor!'

As it spoke, I discerned, obscurely, a child's face looking through the window. Terror made me cruel; and, finding it useless to attempt shaking the creature off, I pulled its wrist on to the broken pane, and rubbed

[409]

it to and fro till the blood ran down and soaked the bedclothes; still it wailed, 'Let me in;' and maintained its tenacious grip, almost maddening me with fear.

'How can I?' I said at length. 'Let *me* go, if you want me to let you in!'

The fingers relaxed, I snatched mine through the hole, hurriedly piled the books up in a pyramid against it, and stopped my ears to exclude the lamentable prayer.

I seemed to keep them closed above a quarter of an hour; yet the instant I listened again, there was the doleful cry moaning on!

'Begone!' I shouted, 'I'll never let you in, not if you beg for twenty years!'

'It's twenty years,' mourned the voice; 'twenty years. I've been a waif for twenty years!'

Thereat began a feeble scratching outside, and the pile of books moved as if thrust forward.

I tried to jump up, but could not stir a limb; and so yelled aloud, in a frenzy of fright.

He got on to the bed, and wrenched open the lattice, bursting, as he pulled at it, into an uncontrollable passion of tears.

'Come in! come in!' he sobbed. 'Cathy, do come! Oh! do – *once* more! Oh! my heart's darling! hear me *this* time, Catherine, at last!'

The spectre showed a spectre's ordinary caprice: it gave no sign of being; but the snow and wind whirled wildly through, even reaching my station, and blowing out the light.

From *Wuthering Heights* by Emily Brontë, 1847

'What cares it for Byron?'

Well sleep the dead: in holy ground
Well sleeps the heart of iron;
The worm that pares his sister's cheek,
What cares it for Byron?

Yet when her night of death comes round,
They ride and drive together;
And ever, when they ride and drive,
Wilful is the weather.

O mighty winds, in spectre coach,
Fast speeds the heart of iron;

On spectre-steed, the spectre-dame –
Side by side with Byron.

Oh, Night doth love her! Oh, the clouds
They do her form environ!
The lightning weeps – it hears her sob –
'Speak to me, Lord Byron!'

On winds, on clouds they ride, they drive –
Oh, hark, thou heart of iron!
The thunder whispers mournfully,
'Speak to her, Lord Byron!'

                                        Ebenezer Elliott, 1846

An Invite to Eternity

Wilt thou go with me sweet maid
Say maiden wilt thou go with me
Through the valley depths of shade
Of night and dark obscurity
Where the path hath lost its way
Where the sun forgets the day
Where there's no life nor light to see
Sweet maiden wilt thou go with me

Where stones will turn to flooding streams
Where plains will rise like ocean waves
Where life will fade like visioned dreams
And mountains darken into caves
Say maiden wilt thou go with me
Through this sad non-identity
Where parents live and are forgot
And sisters live and know us not

Say maiden wilt thou go with me
In this strange death of life to be
To live in death and be the same
Without this life, or home, or name
At once to be, & not to be
That was, and is not – yet to see
Things pass like shadows – and the sky
Above, below, around us lie

The land of shadows wilt thou trace
And look – nor know each others face
The present mixed with reasons gone
And past, and present all as one
Say maiden can thy life be led
To join the living with the dead
Then trace thy footsteps on with me
We're wed to one eternity

John Clare, 1848

Sweetheart

Sweetheart, when in the utter grave
    you lie at last, I'll follow
and make the love I did not have
    your blanket and your pillow.

I'll tremble, weep and clasp my proud,
    my pale, my cold, my still one;
and if warm blood disturb the shroud,
    I'll die myself and fill one.

When all the ghosts at midnight twirl,
    we will not join the flurry,
but lie, a sweetheart with his girl,
    and leave the dead to worry.

And when they throng to Gabriel
    the damned and the forgiven,
we'll say, 'If where we lie is Hell,
    we want no other heaven.'

Intermezzo xxii by Heinrich Heine 1823, translated by Humbert Wolfe

'O that 'twere possible'

O that 'twere possible
After long grief and pain
To find the arms of my true love
Round me once again!

When I was wont to meet her
In the silent woody places
By the home that gave me birth,
We stood tranced in long embraces
Mixt with kisses sweeter sweeter
Than anything on earth.

A shadow flits before me,
Not thou, but like to thee:
Ah Christ, that it were possible
For one short hour to see
The souls we loved, that they might tell us
What and where they be.

From 'Maud' by Alfred Lord Tennyson, 1855

Princess Purple Jade

Fu-ch'ai, King of the land of Wu, had a little daughter who was called
Purple Jade. She was eighteen years old and of perfect beauty. At her
father's court there dwelt also a youth by the name of Han Chung, who
was a year older than she was and who for his profession had learned
the Taoist doctrines. Now the girl fell in love with him, and before long
secret love letters were passing to and fro, and finally she promised the
youth that she would be his wife.

But one day Chung had to prepare for his departure, for he wanted
to go to the east to complete his education in the lands of Ch'i and Lu.
So he sent a messenger to the girl's parents and asked for their
daughter's hand in marriage. The King was merely irritated and re-
jected the request. But when the youth departed alone, Purple Jade's
heart broke for love. Her corpse was carried out in front of the palace
and buried with all due pomp. Three years passed before Han Chung
returned home to the land of Wu and asked the King and Queen about
their daughter. They answered: 'Because we were so terribly angry,
and did not comply with your wishes, she died from the pangs of love.
Her body is already buried.'

When the youth heard this, the tears burst from his eyes and pain
gnawed at his vitals. He bought a sacrificial animal and bales of silk and
went out to the grave, to offer them to the dead person. When he
arrived at that place Purple Jade's soul rose up out of the vault and became visible to the young man. With tears in her eyes, she approached
him and sobbed: 'After you left me that time, I realized that I was going

[413]

to have to renounce my life's dearest wish, for I loved you, a mere retainer of my royal parents, and I could not imagine that fate would ever bring us together again after this separation. What else could I do but die?'

She turned her head away and sang:

> 'On the southern slopes flocks of crows make their home,
> On the northern slopes people set nets to catch them.
> But when they fly, inaccessible on the winds,
> Of what use then are nets and bird traps?
> My heart wanted to follow your course
> For your words without number flowed mightily,
> But then in the pangs of love I caught a fatal fever
> And my young flesh and blood sank into the brown earth.
> A life unlived –
> Is there anything worse on earth?
> The noblest of all feathered creatures
> Are love-birds: the phoenix and the pheasant.
> If once they lose their loved ones
> Their hearts bleed for three years
> And even with hosts of other birds around there
> They remain mourning in loneliness.
> So I too appear in my lowly shape
> To you, my beloved, in all your splendour.
> My body is distant, my heart so near.
> How could I so suddenly forget you?'

After she had sung this, she broke out again in loud weeping and asked Chung to accompany her back into her funeral vault. But the young man hesitated and said: 'Life and death go separate ways. I am afraid to heap up yet more guilt upon myself, and so I dare not meet your wishes.' But Purple Jade replied: 'I know only too well that life and death go separate ways, but if we part at this hour we shall never in all eternity meet again. Are you perhaps afraid that I am some evil spirit and want to do you harm? Truly, I want only the best for you. How can you fail to trust me?'

Chung was touched by her words and followed her back into the funeral vault. Purple Jade gave him wine to drink and pleaded with him to stay with her three days and three nights. In this time they celebrated their nuptials in exact accordance with ritual custom. As the hour of their separation drew near, she gave him as a farewell present a gleaming pearl an inch across and said: 'My name is forgotten among the living, my wishes were not fulfilled – what else can I say to you? Think of me from time to time with love. And if you should go again sometimes to my father's palace, continue to honour him as a great king.'

When Chung left the tomb he went at once to the King and informed him in person of what he had experienced with Purple Jade. However, the King did not believe his words and shouted in the greatest fury: 'My little daughter is dead, and now you come along with some lying tale, to smear her departed spirit with filth! You have nothing else in your head but breaking open graves and looting valuables and then inventing ghost stories as an excuse.'

And he had him arrested on the spot by the guards.

Chung, however, managed to escape from the prison. He rushed to Purple Jade's tomb and told her what had happened. Then she said: 'Do not worry. I will myself go to my royal father and tell him the truth.'

And indeed some days later, just as the King was busy dressing, Purple Jade's spirit appeared before him. Terrified and shocked, his feelings alternated between joy and uneasiness.

'For what reason have you wakened to life again?' he asked.

Thereupon the girl bent her knee and said: 'Once, my royal father, a young and learned man came to you and begged you passionately for your daughter's hand. After I had left this world he returned from afar. At my tomb, where he offered up a sacrifice and prayed, we met again, because our love had been pure unto death. It was there I gave him the pearl as a present. He never broke open my grave. I should not like you to stain your royal office with murder.'

In an adjoining room the women heard the conversation. But when they hurried out and tried to seize the apparition, it faded away as light as smoke.

'Princess Purple Jade' by Chao Yen, China, c.AD 40; translated from a German
version by Christopher Leverson

Aeneas finds Creusa . . .

Then, with ungovern'd Madness, I proclaim,
Through all the silent Streets, *Creusa*'s Name.
Creusa still I call: At length she hears;
And suddain, through the Shades of Night appears.

Appears, no more *Creusa*, nor my Wife:
But a pale Spectre, larger than the Life.
Aghast, astonish'd, and struck dumb with Fear,
I stood; like Bristles rose my stiffen'd Hair.
Then thus the Ghost began to sooth my Grief:
Nor Tears, nor Cries can give the dead Relief;
Desist, my much lov'd Lord, t' indulge your Pain:

You bear no more than what the Gods ordain.

I trust our common Issue to your Care,
She said: And gliding pass'd unseen in Air.
I strove to speak, but Horror ty'd my Tongue;
And thrice about her Neck my Arms I flung;
And thrice deceiv'd, on vain Embraces hung.
Light as an empty Dream at break of Day,
Or as a blast of Wind, she rush'd away.

From *Virgil's Aeneis* by John Dryden, 1697

The gilt sandal

While we were exchanging these words the sons of Eucrates came in
upon us from the palaestra, one already of age, the other about fifteen
years old, and after greeting us sat down upon the couch beside their
father; a chair was brought in for me. Then, as if reminded by the sight
of his sons, Eucrates said: 'As surely as I hope that these boys will be a
joy to me' – and he laid his hand upon them – 'what I am about to tell
you, Tychiades, is true. Everyone knows how I loved their mother, my
wife of blessed memory; I made it plain by what I did for her not only
while she was alive but even when she died, for I burned on the pyre
with her all the ornaments and the clothing that she liked while she
lived. On the seventh day after her death I was lying here on the couch,
just as I am now, consoling my grief; for I was peacefully reading Plato's book about the soul. While I was thus engaged, Demaenete herself
in person came in upon me and sat down beside me, just as Eucratides
here is sitting now' – with a gesture toward the younger of his sons,
who at once shuddered in a very boyish way; he had already been pale
for some time over the story. 'When I saw her,' Eucrates continued, 'I
caught her in my arms with a cry of grief and began to weep. She
would not permit me to cry, however, but began to find fault with me
because, although I had given her everything else, I had not burned one
of her gilt sandals, which, she said, was under the chest, where it had
been thrown aside. That was why we did not find it and burned only
the one. We were continuing our conversation when a cursed toy dog
that was under the couch, a Maltese, barked, and she vanished at his
barking. The sandal, however, was found under the chest and was
burned afterwards.

'Is it right, Tychiades, to doubt these apparitions any longer, when
they are distinctly seen and a matter of daily occurrence?' 'No, by

Heaven,' I said: 'those who doubt and are so disrespectful toward truth deserve to be spanked like children, with a gilt sandal!'

From the *Philopseudes* of Lucian; translated from the Greek by A. H. Harman

'Methought I saw my late espoused Saint'

Methought I saw my late espoused Saint
  Brought to me like *Alcestis* from the grave,
  When *Joves* great Son to her glad Husband gave,
  Rescu'd from death by force though pale and faint.
Mine as whom washt from spot of child-bed taint,
  Purification in the old Law did save,
  And such, as yet once more I trust to have
Full sight of her in Heaven without restraint,
Came vested all in white, pure as her mind:
  Her face was vail'd, yet to my fancied sight,
  Love, sweetness, goodness, in her person shin'd
So clear, as in no face with more delight.
  But O as to embrace me she enclin'd
  I wak'd, she fled, and day brought back my night.

John Milton, 1658

The Wind at the Door

As day did darken on the dewless grass,
  There, still, wi' nwone a-come by me
  To stay a-while at hwome by me
  Within the house, all dumb by me,
I zot me sad as the eventide did pass.

An' there a win'blast shook the rattlèn door,
  An' seemed, as win' did mwoan without,
  As if my Jeäne, alwone without,
  A-stannèn on the stwone without,
Wer there a-come wi' happiness oonce mwore.

I went to door; an' out vrom trees above
  My head, upon the blast by me,
  Sweet blossoms wer a-cast by me,

As if my Love, a-past by me,
Did fling em down – a token ov her love.

'Sweet blossoms o' the tree where I do murn,'
I thought, 'if you did blow vor her,
Vor apples that should grow vor her,
A-vallen down below vor her,
O then how happy I should zee you kern!'

But no. Too soon I voun my charm a-broke.
Noo comely soul in white like her –
Noo soul a-steppèn light like her –
An' nwone o' comely height like her
Went by; but all my grief ageän awoke.

William Barnes, c.1860

The Voice

Woman much missed, how you call to me, call to me,
Saying that now you are not as you were
When you had changed from the one who was all to me,
But as at first, when our day was fair.

Can it be you that I hear? Let me view you, then,
Standing as when I drew near to the town
Where you would wait for me: yes, as I knew you then,
Even to the original air-blue gown!

Or is it only the breeze, in its listlessness
Travelling across the wet mead to me here,
You being ever dissolved to wan wistlessness,
Heard no more again far or near?

Thus I; faltering forward,
Leaves around me falling,
Wind oozing thin through the thorn from norward,
And the woman calling.

Thomas Hardy, 1925

The Delegate

In the garden (it was always a garden)
there is the punishment of remembrance.
I pray you love, remember. And quote me
the many things which might come to you
on your own death bed.
          I was there
even in our worst hour – the wreaths
and the mis-named name competing with
the other mourners' flowers upon
the crematorium slabs. I am divided
into an infinity of myself, pieces
for everywhere – especially that damp day,
that insistence on seriousness.
We shall never be so serious again.
But this frees you for levity today,
and perhaps a little licenced selfishness.
Take this gift of despair – what can
a ghost give but remembrance and
forgetfulness in the right proportions?

Never to puff up those sloping headlands
watching the children ahead negotiating
the lanes of the wide bay: never
the afternoon sun straining
the bedroom light to a tint distinctly
like gin: never more the in-flight panic,
refusing to see omens in our food
or the number of letters in the month.
          These *nevers*
are just parts of my docility
as I go back. I am always receding,
my ambition is to accomplish
non-existence, to go out and close the door
on ever having been.
          I am doing it in death
as I did in life – but it's so hard.
I cannot forget unless you remember,
pin down each day and weighted eye
with exact remorse. After fifteen years'
convergence, now we may draw apart
and face our different exits.

So I am your delegate
at the screaming hours: I walk alone
among the plains of hell. We dream here
in the skin of our deeds: such changes
as the schoolgirl saw in her body
are metamorphoses of the gods.
                    First I went back,
a quick change in the early morning
with my blood running into frost.
Now the reduction is set at smaller things –
I may even become the healthy strider
or flamenco dancer, but I must reduce, reduce,
become so small that I escape the eye
of god. There is no peace here, or on earth.
                    You will know
how the mind works at poems, feels ideas
as tissue – but, alas, the ceremony here
is different. I am not what you remember,
the snapshots in time and sunshine,
nor even the angry and accusing face
at breakfast, the suddenly delivered tone
of hope along a Venetian calle on a Sunday –
                    I am made fiction
by my needs: the brain changing in the garden
to a bush of thorns, a dream looking for
its dreamer, murder always at the end
of every vista. A letter now, headed
'Malcontenta, Orto Chiuso', a puff-adder's face
as I prop myself against the dying mirror
viewing disgust with satisfaction.
                    Breaking an egg-cup,
learning to give up, crying at the sight
of a withered seahorse pinned to the wall:
all those afternoons of hope and all those gardens,
no wonder I cannot escape now.
                    After a year in office,
your delegate has found this court
a place of ashes and the matches
played by moonlight cruel games.
But I have an immense truth to give you –
In the end, we are condemned
only for our lack of talent.
                    There is no morality,
no metered selfishness, or cowardly fear.

What we do on earth is its own parade
and cannot be redeemed in death. The pity
of it, that we are misled. By mother,
saying her sadness is the law, by love,
hiding itself in evenings of ethics,
by despair, turning the use of limbs
to lockjaw.
                    The artist knows this.
He is being used despite himself. The truth
is a story forcing me to tell it. It is not
my story or my truth. My misery
is on a colour chart – even my death
is a chord among the garden sounds.
                    And in this garden, love,
there will be forgiveness, when
we can forgive ourselves. 'Remember me,
but ah forget my fate.' Tell me like music
to the listeners. 'I would not know her in that dress.'

The days I lived through change to words
which anyone may use. When you arrive
I shall have done your work for you.
                    Forgetting will not be hard,
but you must remember still. Evenings
and mad birds cross your face,
                    everything must be re-made.

Peter Porter, 1978

Reincarnations

The kitten that befriends me at its gate
Purrs, rubs against me, until I say goodbye,
Stroking its coat, and asking 'Why? Why? Why?'
For now I know the shame of being late
Too late. She waits for me at home
Tonight, in the house-shadows. And I must mourn
Until Equator crawls to Capricorn
Or murder in the sun melts down
The Arctic and Antarctica. When bees collide
Against my study's windowpane, I let them in.
She nurtures dignity and pride;
She waters in my eye. She rustles in my study's palm;

She is the flower on the geranium.
Our little wooden train runs by itself
Along the windowsill, each puff-puff-puff
A breath of secret, sacred stuff.
I feel her goodness breathe, my Lady Christ.
Her treasured stories mourn her on their shelf,
In spirit-air, that watchful poltergeist.

From *Elegies* by Douglas Dunn, 1985

'Caro piccolo insetto'

Dear little insect
whom they used to call 'Fly,' for some reason,
this evening when it was almost dark
while I was reading Deuteronomy
you reappeared next to me,
but you were not wearing glasses
you couldn't see me
nor could I, without that glittering,
recognise you in the dusk.

From 'Xenia I' by Eugenio Montale, 1962, translated by Jonathan Burnham

Kutoka Kaburini

Once upon a time there was a married couple who lived in peace and loved each other dearly. One day the husband said: 'I love you so much, that on the day I die I will come out of my grave and appear to you.' The wife promised him too that she would come back to him after her death. After many years the husband fell ill and died. Neighbours and relatives gathered and wept bitterly. The wife too cried, and remembered the promises they had made to each other. The dead husband was duly buried, but after the funeral the wife of the deceased refused to go home. She stayed and lingered at the graveyard. The relatives returned home, but she remained near the grave, singing softly to herself. Suddenly she saw the soil of the grave splitting open: her dead husband rose up and came towards her. She was overjoyed on seeing him back, and they went home together.

Now the mother of that woman lived in the same house, and she was mourning her beloved son-in-law, when suddenly, to her dismay, she heard her daughter chattering and laughing in the conjugal bedroom. The old lady went and reprimanded her daughter, saying: 'Your husband has died, and now you are laughing as if you are glad!' Her daughter said: 'He is not dead, he is here!' The mother entered the room, and there she saw the man she knew was dead, standing near her daughter.

Not long after that the daughter fell ill and died. All the people of the village cried, but the husband did not. He was silent. After the funeral he stayed on near the grave, singing quietly and reciting poetry. And lo! the sand of the grave parted and there appeared his wife: so they went home together. That evening the mother came along and saw them there, sitting together, and they were all very happy.

Jan Knappert, *Myths and Legends of the Swahili,* 1970

'Hey, wait'

Now this pool the girl's bathing-party was going to was Tigilau's pool; the pool was called Tāneonu'ulua. The girl walked on, and began to stride out. Tigilau's village was full of his concubines; the women had many children. A breeze blew towards the sea, carrying the fragrance of the girl's outfit to the village, where it spread, just like the day – that day was different inside the village of Tigilau and his harem. When she reached the village, the girl's outfit was so fragrant, it was like the pervasive perfume of turmeric. And what happened? A woman grabbed one child, hit another child, and kept on hitting another child; they were surprised and furious, but the girl had done nothing – the girl was simply going to bathe. Manuoleuma arrived, took off her outfit and put it on a rock, then plunged down into the water and bathed. She jumped out again, came and put on her outfit, and walked back. Tigilau couldn't restrain himself; he looked out – okaoka, what a beautiful girl; the girl's body was like the rising moon, beautifully ruddy all over, and her outfit so fragrant.

And what happened? Tigilau stood, and ran out in pursuit of the girl, but the girl began to step out so as to increase her pace, remembering the instructions to her to take care not to be disobedient. The girl had gone quite a long way in her walking, having already passed through the village, and so it was that she came to the forest. The girl heard a man calling. *Hey, wait.*

But the girl just kept on walking. Again came the call. *Hey, wait.*

The girl turned around. And so it was here that the girl was caught, it was here that Tigilau stopped the girl in her tracks, at that place. The

[423]

two of them remained here. And what happened? Tigilau used the girl's leg as a pillow, and the man went to sleep, while the girl stayed sitting up. When the girl heard that he was asleep, she reached out and gently lowered the head to the ground, and then fled. She fled back home, only to find the aunt staring at her. The girl tried to go into the house, but the woman said, *'Isa! Disobedient pig! Get away with you. Get away; you are forbidden to live in this place any longer. I told you to be obedient, but I saw you. Get away; this place is forbidden to you.'*

The girl turned and left, suddenly aware of her parents; she went off, going to her parents. The girl was about to go through the door of their house, when she fell dead.

This Tigilau suddenly awoke – there was no girl there. He ran off in pursuit of her. He went to the place where the aunt was, but there was nobody, just a mountain. Then he came down to the girl's parents; when he arrived, the girl's funeral rites were in progress. Tigilau looked – Manuoleuma's funeral rites were being held. Tigilau saw this, and sat outside the house. (And now I'm going to sing the story.)

> Tānconu'ulua was where you were bathing, Manuoleuma.
> I called out once, but you took no notice, Manuoleuma.
> I called a second time, and you turned around, Manuoleuma.
> We slept in the togālito bushes, Manuoleuma.
> We slept and slept, then you fled back, Manuoleuma.
> Here is your belt of striped tapa which I brought, Manuoleuma.
> Here is your floral necklace which I brought, Manuoleuma.
> I visited the mountain, but you weren't there, Manuoleuma.
> I visited the valley, but you weren't there, Manuoleuma.

From inside her house, the aunt looked out, and was heartbroken out of sympathy towards Tigilau, because, despite the painful heat of the sun in the day, the man would not stop weeping outside, out of grief for the girl. So the aunt came straightaway, bringing some tree-leaves. Standing outside, she cried, *'Isa! Disobedient pig! Sit up at once! Don't you realise that Tigilau is about to be burnt by the sun, and how would that be?'*

The girl sat up, alive again because the aunt came and restored the girl.

And so what happened? Tigilau and the girl lived together here; he didn't return to his family and his harem, but married Manuoleuma and they lived here, in that place.

The story is finished.

From *Fāgogo, Fables from Samoa*, translated by Richard Moyle, 1981

'Women'

A number of men there be yet liuing, who haue been haunted by their wiues after their death, about forswearing themselues, and vndooing their children, of whom they promised to be carefull fathers: whereof I can gather no reason but this, that Women are borne to torment a man both aliue and dead.

From The Terrors of the Night by Thomas Nashe, 1594

The Ghost

(After Sextus Propertius)

A ghost is someone: death has left a hole
For the lead-coloured soul to beat the fire:
   Cynthia leaves her dirty pyre
   And seems to coil herself and roll
      Under my canopy,
Love's stale and public playground, where I lie
And fill the run-down empire of my bed.
I see the street, her potter's field, is red
And lively with the ashes of the dead;

But she no longer sparkles off in smoke:
It is the body carted to the gate
   Last Friday, when the sizzling grate
   Left its charred furrows on her smock
      And ate into her hip.
A black nail dangles from a finger-tip
And Lethe oozes from her nether lip.
Her thumb-bones rattle on her brittle hands,
As Cynthia stamps and hisses and demands:

'Sextus, has sleep already washed away
Your manhood? You forget the window-sill
   My sliding wore to slivers? Day
   Would break before the Seven Hills
      Saw Cynthia retreat
And climb your shoulders to the knotted sheet.
You shouldered me and galloped on bare feet

[425]

To lay me by the crossroads. Have no fear:
Notus, who snatched your promise, has no ear.

'But why did no one call in my deaf ear?
Your calling would have gained me one more day.
   Sextus, although you ran away
    You might have called and stopped my bier
      A second by your door.
No tears drenched a black toga for your whore
When broken tilestones bruised her face before
The Capitol. Would it have strained your purse
To scatter ten cheap roses on my hearse?

'The State will make Pompilia's Chloris burn:
I knew her secret when I kissed the skull
   Of Pluto in the tainted bowl.
   Let Nomas burn her books and turn
      Her poisons into gold:
The finger-prints upon the potsherd told
Her love. You let a slut, whose body sold
To Thracians, liquefy my golden bust
In the coarse flame that crinkled me to dust.

'If Chloris' bed has left you with your head,
Lover, I think you'll answer my arrears:
   My nurse is getting on in years,
   See that she gets a little bread –
      She never clutched your purse;
See that my little humpback hears no curse
From her close-fisted friend. But burn the verse
You bellowed half a lifetime in my name:
Why should you feed me to the fires of fame?

'I will not hound you, much as you have earned
It, Sextus: I shall reign in your four books –
   I swear this by the Hag who looks
   Into my heart where it was burned:
      Propertius, I kept faith;
If not, may serpents suck my ghost to death
And spit it with their forked and killing breath
Into the Styx where Agamemnon's wife
Founders in the green circles of her life.

'Beat the sycophant ivy from my urn,
That twists its binding shoots about my bones

Where apple-sweetened Anio drones
Through orchards that will never burn
  While honest Herakles,
My patron, watches. Anio, you will please
Me if you whisper upon sliding knees:
"Propertius, Cynthia is here:
She shakes her blossoms when my waters clear."

'You cannot turn your back upon a dream,
For phantoms have their reasons when they come:
  We wander midnights: then the numb
  Ghost wades from the Lethean stream;
    Even the foolish dog
Stops its hell-raising mouths and casts its clog;
At cock-crow Charon checks us in his log.
Others can have you, Sextus; I alone
Hold: and I grind your manhood bone on bone.'

Robert Lowell, 1946

Margaret's Complaint

This is the dumb and dreary hour,
  When injur'd ghosts complain;
When yauning graves give up their dead
  To haunt the faithless swain.

Bethink thee, WILLIAM, of thy fault,
  Thy pledge, and broken oath:
And give me back my maiden vow,
  And give me back my troth.

Why did you promise love to me,
  And not that promise keep?
Why did you swear my eyes were bright,
  Yet leave those eyes to weep?

How could you say my face was fair,
  And yet that face forsake?
How could you win my virgin heart,
  Yet leave that heart to break?

Why did you say, my lip was sweet,
  And made the scarlet pale?

And why did I, young, witless maid!
   Believe the flattering tale?

That face, alas! no more is fair;
   Those lips no longer red:
Dark are my eyes, now clos'd in death,
   And every charm is fled.

The hungry *worm* my *sister* is;
   This *winding-sheet* I wear:
And cold and weary lasts our *night*,
   Till that *last morn* appear.

From 'William and Margaret' by David Mallet, in *The Plain Dealer*, 24 July 1724

Sweet William's Ghost

There came a ghost to Marjorie's door,
   Wi' many a grievous groan,
And aye he tirled at the pin,
   But answer made she none.

'O say, is that my father?
   Or is't my brother John?
Or is it my true love Willy,
   From Scotland new come home?'

'Tis not thy father, Marjorie,
   Nor yet thy brother John;
But 'tis thy true love Willy,
   From Scotland new come home.

'O Marjorie sweet! O Marjorie dear!
   For faith and charitie,
Will ye gie me back my faith and troth
   That I gave once to thee?'

'Thy faith and troth thou gavest to me,
   And again thou'lt never win,
Until thou come within my bower
   And kiss me cheek and chin.'

'My lips they are sae bitter,' he says,
  'My breath it is sae strang,
If ye get ae kiss from me to-night,
  Your days will not be lang.

'The cocks are crawing, Marjorie –
  The cocks are crawing again;
The dead wi' the quick they mustna stay,
  And I must needs begone.'

She follow'd him high, she follow'd him low,
  Till she came to yon churchyard green;
And there the deep grave opened up,
  And young William he lay down.

'What three things are these, sweet William,
  That stand beside your head?'
'O it's three maidens, Marjorie,
  That once I promised to wed.'

'What three things are these, sweet William,
  That stand close at your side?'
'O it's three babes,' he says, 'Marjorie,
  That these three maidens had.'

'What three things are these, sweet William,
  That lie close at your feet?'
'O it's three hell-hounds, Marjorie,
  That's waiting my soul to keep.'

And she took up her white, white hand,
  And struck him on the breast;
Saying, 'Have here again thy faith and troth,
  And I wish your soul good rest.'

Traditional

Sonnet

Oh! for some honest Lovers ghost,
  Some kind unbodied post
  Sent from the shades below,
  I strangely long to know
Whether the nobler Chaplets wear,

Those that their mistresse scorn did bear,
　　Or those that were us'd kindly.

For what-so-e'er they tell us here
　　To make those sufferings dear,
　　'Twill there I fear be found,
　　That to the being crown'd,
T'have lov'd alone will not suffice,
Unlesse we also have been wise,
　　And have our Loves enjoy'd.

From *Fragmenta Aurea* by Sir John Suckling, 1646

'I long to talke'

I long to talke with some old lovers ghost,
　　Who dyed before the god of Love was borne:
I cannot thinke that hee, who then lov'd most,
　　Sunke so low, as to love one which did scorne.
But since this god produc'd a destinie,
And that vice-nature, custome, lets it be;
　　I must love her, that loves not mee.

From 'Love's Deitie' by John Donne, in *Poems*, 1635

The Apparition

When by thy scorne, O murdresse, I am read,
And that thou thinkst thee free
From all solicitation from mee,
Then shall my ghost come to thy bed,
And thee, fain'd vestall, in worse armes shall see;
Then thy sicke taper will begin to winke,
And he, whose thou art then, being tyr'd before,
Will, if thou stirre, or pinch to wake him, thinke
　　Thou call'st for more,
And in false sleepe will from thee shrinke,
And then poore Aspen wretch, neglected thou
Bath'd in a cold quicksilver sweat wilt lye
　　A veryer ghost than I;
What I will say, I will not tell thee now,
Lest that preserve thee; and since my love is spent,

I had rather thou shouldst painfully repent,
Than by my threatnings rest still innocent.

From *Songs and Sonets* by John Donne, 1593–1601

Caisho's mistress

Sir John Burroughes being sent envoy to the Emperor by King Charles I, did take his eldest son Caisho Burroughes along with him, and taking his journey through Italy, left his son at Florence, to learn the language; where he having an intrigue with a beautiful courtisan (mistress of the Grand Duke), their familiarity became so public, that it came to the Duke's ear, who took a resolution to have him murdered; but Caisho having had timely notice of the Duke's design, by some of the English there, immediately left the city without acquainting his mistress with it, and came to England; whereupon the Duke being disappointed of his revenge, fell upon his mistress in most reproachful language; she on the other side, resenting the sudden departure of her gallant, of whom she was most passionately enamoured, killed herself. At the same moment that she expired, she did appear to Caisho, at his lodgings in London; Colonel Remes was then in bed with him, who saw her as well as he; giving him an account of her resentments of his ingratitude to her, in leaving her so suddenly, and exposing her to the fury of the Duke, not omitting her own tragical exit, adding withal, that he should be slain in a duel, which accordingly happened; and thus she appeared to him frequently, even when his younger brother (who afterwards was Sir John) was in bed with him. As often as she did appear, he would cry out with great shrieking, and trembling of his body, as anguish of mind, saying, O God! here she comes, she comes, and at this rate she appeared till he was killed; she appeared to him the morning before he was killed. Some of my acquaintance have told me, that he was one of the most beautiful men in England, and very valiant, but proud and blood-thirsty.

From *Miscellanies* by John Aubrey, 1696

The Ghost

Like angels fierce and tawny-eyed,
Back to your chamber I will glide,
And noiselessly into your sight
Steal with the shadows of the night.

And I will bring you, brown delight,
Kisses as cold as lunar night
And the caresses of a snake
Revolving in a grave. At break

Of morning in its livid hue,
You'd find I had bequeathed to you
An empty place as cold as stone.

Others by tenderness and ruth
Would reign over your life and youth,
But I would rule by fear alone.

From *Les Fleurs du Mal* by Charles Baudelaire, 1857;
translated by Roy Campbell

Modern Love

At dinner, she is hostess, I am host.
Went the feast ever cheerfuller? She keeps
The Topic over intellectual deeps
In buoyancy afloat. They see no ghost.
With sparkling surface-eyes we ply the ball:
It is in truth a most contagious game:
HIDING THE SKELETON, shall be its name.
Such play as this the devils might appal!
But here's the greatest wonder: in that we,
Enamoured of an acting nought can tire,
Each other, like true hypocrites, admire;
Warm-lighted looks, Love's ephemerioe,
Shoot gaily o'er the dishes and the wine.
We waken envy of our happy lot.
Fast, sweet, and golden, shows the marriage-knot.
Dear guests, you now have seen Love's corpse-light
    shine.

From *Modern Love* by George Meredith, 1862

After Death

The curtains were half drawn, the floor was swept
    And strewn with rushes, rosemary and may
    Lay thick upon the bed on which I lay,

Where through the lattice ivy-shadows crept.
He leaned above me, thinking that I slept
  And could not hear him, but I heard him say,
  'Poor child, poor child': and as he turned away
Came a deep silence, and I knew he wept.
He did not touch the shroud, or raise the fold
  That hid my face, or take my hand in his,
    Or ruffle the smooth pillows for my head:
    He did not love me living; but once dead
  He pitied me; and very sweet it is
To know that he is warm though I am cold.

Christina Rossetti, 1862

The Wardrobe

A woman stood there, a lady, tall, lean, and old. She wore a cap with a large pale-lilac bow and an old-fashioned, faded black gown. She had a sunken birdlike face and on her brow there was an eruption, a sort of fungus growth. It was rather repulsive.

'Good evening,' said van der Qualen. 'The rooms?'

The old lady nodded; she nodded and smiled slowly, without a word, understandingly, and with her beautiful long white hand made a slow, languid, and elegant gesture towards the next, the left-hand door. Then she retired and appeared again with a key. 'Look,' he thought, standing behind her as she unlocked the door; 'you are like some kind of banshee, a figure out of Hoffmann, madam.' She took the oil lamp from its hook and ushered him in.

It was a small, low-ceiled room with a brown floor. Its walls were covered with straw-coloured matting. There was a window at the back in the right-hand wall, shrouded in long, thin white muslin folds. A white door also on the right led into the next room. This room was pathetically bare, with staring white walls, against which three straw chairs, painted pink, stood out like strawberries from whipped cream. A wardrobe, a washing-stand with a mirror. . . . The bed, a mammoth mahogany piece, stood free in the middle of the room.

Piece by piece he put down his good, unobtrusive grey suit on the red chair beside the bed; but then as he loosened his braces he remembered his hat and overcoat, which still lay on the couch. He fetched them into the bedroom and opened the wardrobe. . . . He took a step backwards and reached behind him to clutch one of the large dark-red mahogany

[433]

balls which ornamented the bedposts. The room, with its four white walls, from which the three pink chairs stood out like strawberries from whipped cream, lay in the unstable light of the candle. But the wardrobe over there was open and it was not empty. Somebody was standing in it, a creature so lovely that Albrecht van der Qualen's heart stood still a moment and then in long, deep, quiet throbs resumed its beating. She was quite nude and one of her slender arms reached up to crook a forefinger round one of the hooks in the ceiling of the wardrobe. Long waves of brown hair rested on the childlike shoulders – they breathed that charm to which the only answer is a sob. The candlelight was mirrored in her narrow black eyes. Her mouth was a little large, but it had an expression as sweet as the lips of sleep when after long days of pain they kiss our brow. Her ankles nestled and her slender limbs clung to one another.

Albrecht van der Qualen rubbed one hand over his eyes and stared ... and he saw that down in the right corner the sacking was loosened from the back of the wardrobe. 'What –' said he ... 'won't you come in – or how should I put it – out? Have a little glass of cognac? Half a glass?' But he expected no answer to this and he got none. Her narrow, shining eyes, so very black that they seemed bottomless and inexpressive – they were directed upon him, but aimlessly and somewhat blurred, as though they did not see him.

'Shall I tell you a story?' she said suddenly in a low, husky voice.

'Tell me a story,' he answered. He had sunk down in a sitting posture on the edge of the bed, his overcoat lay across his knees with his folded hands resting upon it. His mouth stood a little open, his eyes half-closed. But the blood pulsated warm and mildly through his body and there was a gentle singing in his ears. She had let herself down in the cupboard and embraced a drawn-up knee with her slender arms, while the other leg stretched out before her. Her little breasts were pressed together by her upper arm, and the light gleamed on the skin of her flexed knee. She talked ... talked in a soft voice, while the candle-flame performed its noiseless dance.

Two walked on the heath and her head lay on his shoulder. There was a perfume from all growing things, but the evening mist already rose from the ground. So it began. And often it was in verse, rhyming in that incomparably sweet and flowing way that comes to us now and again in the half-slumber of fever. But it ended badly; a sad ending: the two holding each other indissolubly embraced and, while their lips rest on each other, one stabbing the other above the waist with a broad knife – and not without good cause. So it ended. And then she stood up with an infinitely sweet and modest gesture, lifted the grey sacking at the right-hand corner – and was no more there.

From now on he found her every evening in the wardrobe and

listened to her stories – how many evenings? How many days, weeks, or months did he remain in this house and in this city? It would profit nobody to know. Who would care for a miserable statistic? And we are aware that Albrecht van der Qualen had been told by several physicians that he had but a few months to live. She told him stories. They were sad stories, without relief; but they rested like a sweet burden upon the heart and made it beat longer and more blissfully. Often he forgot himself. – His blood swelled up in him, he stretched out his hands to her, and she did not resist him. But then for several evenings he did not find her in the wardrobe, and when she came back she did not tell him anything for several evenings and then by degrees resumed, until he again forgot himself.

How long it lasted – who knows? Who even knows whether Albrecht van der Qualen actually awoke on that grey afternoon and went into the unknown city; whether he did not remain asleep in his first-class carriage and let the Berlin–Rome express bear him swiftly over the mountains? Would any of us care to take the responsibility of giving a definite answer? It is all uncertain. 'Everything must be in the air . . .'

From 'The Wardrobe' by Thomas Mann, 1899, anonymous translation

'Desire is a sacred thing'

I had fought too much, even against the most imposing circumstances, to use any more violence for love. Desire is a sacred thing, and should not be violated.

'Hush!' I said to myself. 'I will sleep, and the ghost of my silence can go forth, in the subtle body of desire, to meet that which is coming to meet it. Let my ghost go forth, and let me not interfere. There are many intangible meetings, and unknown fulfilments of desire.'

So I went softly to sleep, as I wished to, without interfering with the warm, crocus-like ghost of my body.

And I must have gone far, far down the intricate galleries of sleep, to the very heart of the world. For I know I passed on beyond the strata of images and words, beyond the iron veins of memory, and even the jewels of rest, to sink in the final dark like a fish, dumb, soundless, and imageless, yet alive and swimming.

And at the very core of the deep night the ghost came to me, at the heart of the ocean of oblivion, which is also the heart of life. Beyond hearing, or even knowledge of contact, I met her and knew her. How I know it I don't know. Yet I know it with eyeless, wingless knowledge.

[435]

For man in the body is formed through countless ages, and at the centre is the speck, or spark, upon which all his formation has taken place. It is even not himself, deep beyond his many depths. Deep from him calls to deep. And according as deep answers deep, man glistens and surpasses himself.

Beyond all the pearly mufflings of consciousness, of age upon age of consciousness, deep calls yet to deep, and sometimes is answered. It is calling and answering, new-awakened God calling within the deep of man, and new God calling answer from the other deep. And sometimes the other deep is a woman, as it was with me, when my ghost came.

Women were not unknown to me. But never before had woman come, in the depths of night, to answer my deep with her deep. As the ghost came, came as a ghost of silence, still in the depth of sleep.

I know she came. I know she came even as a woman, to my man. But the knowledge is darkly naked as the event. I only know, it was so. In the deep of sleep a call was called from the deeps of me, and answered in the deeps, by a woman among women. Breasts or thighs or face, I remember not a touch, no, nor a movement of my own. It is all complete in the profundity of darkness. Yet I know it was so.

I awoke towards dawn, from far, far away. I was vaguely conscious of drawing nearer and nearer, as the sun must have been drawing towards the horizon, from the complete beyond. Till at last the faint pallor of mental consciousness coloured my waking.

And then I was aware of a pervading scent, as of plum-blossom, and a sense of extraordinary silkiness – though where, and in what contact, I could not say. It was as the first blemish of dawn.

And even with so slight a conscious registering, *it* seemed to disappear. Like a whale that has sounded to the bottomless seas. That knowledge of *it*, which was the mating of the ghost and me, disappeared from me, in its rich weight of certainty, as the scent of the plum-blossom moved down the lanes of my consciousness, and my limbs stirred in a silkiness for which I have no comparison.

As I became aware, I also became uncertain. I wanted to be certain of *it*, to have definite evidence. And as I sought for evidence, *it* disappeared, my perfect knowledge was gone. I no longer knew in full.

Now as the daylight slowly amassed, in the windows from which I had put back the shutters, I sought in myself for evidence, and in the room.

But I shall never know. I shall never know if it was a ghost, some sweet spirit from the innermost of the ever-deepening cosmos; or a woman, a very woman, as the silkiness of my limbs seems to attest; or a dream, a hallucination! I shall never know.

From 'Glad Ghosts' by D. H. Lawrence, 1926

Ghosts

The terrace is said to be haunted.
By whom or what nobody knows; someone
Put away under the vines behind dusty glass
And rusty hinges staining the white-framed door
Like a nosebleed, locked; or a death in the pond
In three feet of water, a courageous breath?
It's haunted anyway, so nobody mends it
And the paving lies loose for the ants to crawl through
Weaving and clutching like animated thorns.
We walk on to it,
Like the bold lovers we are, ten years of marriage,
Tempting the ghosts out with our high spirits,
Footsteps doubled by the silence. . . .

. . . and start up like ghosts ourselves
Flawed lank and drawn in the greenhouse glass:
She turns from that, and I sit down,
She tosses the dust with the toe of a shoe,
Sits on the pond's parapet and takes a swift look
At her shaking face in the clogged water,
Weeds in her hair; rises quickly and looks at me.
I shrug, and turn my palms out, begin
To feel the damp in my bones as I lever up
And step toward her with my hints of wrinkles,
Crows-feet and shadows. We leave arm in arm
Not a word said. The terrace is haunted,
Like many places with rough mirrors now,
By estrangement, if the daylight's strong.

Peter Redgrove, 1961

Girls in their Seasons

Girls in their seasons. Solstice and equinox,
This year, make reincarnate
Spry ghosts I had consigned to fate,
Left soaking at the ends of bars,
Pasted in dying calendars
Or locked in clocks.

[437]

I can no longer walk the streets at night
But under a lamp-post by a bistro,
To the sound of a zither,
I see one standing in an arc of snow,
Her collar up against the wintry weather
Smoking a cigarette.

Or, as now, slumped by a train window,
The hair of another flies in the air-stream.
This one is here in an advisory
Capacity, reminding me
Of a trip I took last winter
From dream into bad dream.

Their ghosts go with me as I hurtle north
Into the night,
Gathering momentum, age,
Know-how, experience (I travel light) –
Girls, you are welcome to my luggage
For what it is worth.

No earthly schedule can predict
Accurately our several destinations.
All we can do is wash and dress
And keep ourselves intact.
Besides which, this is an express
And passes all the stations.

Now we are running out of light and love,
Having left far behind
By-pass and fly-over.
The moon is no longer there
And matches go out in the wind.
Now all we have

Is the flinty chink of Orion and the Plough
And the incubators of a nearby farm
To light us through to the land of never-never.
Girls all, be with me now
And keep me warm
Before we go plunging into the dark for ever.

Derek Mahon, 1968

Fifteen

VANISHINGS

Cold graves, we say? It shall be testified
  That living men who burn in heart and brain,
    Without the dead were colder. If we tried
  To sink the past beneath our feet, be sure
  The future would not stand.

ELIZABETH BARRETT BROWNING

The glow-worm shows the matin to be near,
And gins to pale his ineffectual fire:
Adieu, adieu! Hamlet, remember me.

WILLIAM SHAKESPEARE

The day was breaking. In the disfigured street
He left me, with a kind of valediction,
And faded on the blowing of the horn.

T. S. ELIOT

I can call up old ghosts
and they will come.
But my art limps –
I cannot send them home.

STEVIE SMITH

Devil's Batch

A belated farm labourer passing late at night through Devil's Batch, and knowing it to have an uncanny reputation, saw a dark figure in front of him and anxiously asked the time.

'Past midnight, and time you left this place to Those to Whom it Belongs,' said a deep, cold voice. Then the vision clanked away, the starlight shining on his armour as he moved.

From 'Somerset Folklore' by Ruth L. Tongue, 1965

Euthymus fights Lycas

In that and the next Olympiad Euthymus won the crown for boxing. His statue is by Pythagoras, and most well worth seeing it is. On his return to Italy, Euthymus fought with the Hero. The facts about the Hero were these. In his wanderings after the taking of Ilium, Ulysses, it is said, was driven by the winds to various cities of Italy and Sicily, and amongst the rest he came with his ships to Temesa. There a tipsy sailor of his ravished a maiden, for which offence he was stoned to death by the natives. Ulysses thought nothing of the fellow's loss and sailed away; but the ghost of the murdered man began to kill the people of Temesa, sparing neither old nor young, and he never left off till the people were fain to flee from Italy altogether; but the Pythian priestess bade them not to abandon Temesa, but to appease the Hero and build him a temple in a precinct of his own, and to give him every year the fairest maiden in Temesa to wife. They did as the god bade them, and had nothing more to fear from the ghost. But Euthymus chanced to come to Temesa at the very time when the people were paying the usual respects to the ghost; and learning how matters stood, he desired to go into the temple and behold the maiden. When he saw her he was first touched with pity, and then he fell in love with her, and the girl swore she would be his wife if he saved her. So Euthymus put on his armour, and awaited the assault of the ghost; and he had the best of it in the fight, and the Hero, driven from the land, plunged into the sea and vanished. Euthymus had a splendid wedding, and the men of that country were rid of the ghost for ever. I have heard say that Euthymus lived to extreme old age, and that he escaped death, but took leave of the world in some other way. I have been told by a man who made a trading voyage to Temesa, that the town is inhabited to this day. That is what I have heard; and I have seen a picture, which was a copy of an old painting. It was like this. There was a youth Sybaris, and a river Calabrus, and a spring Lyca, and moreover a hero's shrine, and the city of Temesa; and there, too, was the ghost which Euthymus expelled. The ghost was of a horrid black colour, and his whole appearance was most dreadful, and he wore a wolfskin. The writing on the picture gave him the name of Lycas. So much for that.

From *Pausanias's Description of Greece*, c.160 AD; translated by J. G. Frazer, 1898

The Arunta chase away the ghosts

No one may mention the name of the deceased during the period of mourning for fear of disturbing and annoying the ghost, who is believed to be walking about at large. Some of the relations of the dead man, it is true, such as his parents, elder brothers and sisters, paternal aunts, mother-in-law, and all his sons-in-law, whether actual or possible, are debarred all their lives from taking his name into their lips; but other people, including his wife, children, grandchildren, grandparents, younger brothers and sisters, and father-in-law, are free to name him so soon as he has ceased to walk the earth and hence to be dangerous. Some twelve or eighteen months after his death the people seem to think that the dead man has enjoyed his liberty long enough, and that it is time to confine his restless spirit within narrower bounds. Accordingly a grand battue or ghost-hunt brings the days of mourning to an end. The favourite haunt of the deceased is believed to be the burnt and deserted camp where he died. Here therefore on a certain day a band of men and women, the men armed with shields and spear-throwers, assemble and begin dancing round the charred and blackened remains of the camp, shouting and beating the air with their weapons and hands in order to drive away the lingering spirit from the spot he loves too well. When the dancing is over, the whole party proceed to the grave at a run, chasing the ghost before them. It is in vain that the unhappy ghost makes a last bid for freedom, and, breaking away from the beaters, doubles back towards the camp; the leader of the party is prepared for this manœuvre, and by making a long circuit adroitly cuts off the retreat of the fugitive. Finally, having run him to earth, they trample him down into the grave, dancing and stamping on the heaped-up soil, while with downward thrusts through the air they beat and force him under ground. There, lying in his narrow house, flattened and prostrate under a load of earth, the poor ghost sees his widow wearing the gay feathers of the ring-neck parrot in her hair, and he knows that the time of her mourning for him is over. The loud shouts of the men and women shew him that they are not to be frightened and bullied by him any more, and that he had better lie quiet. But he may still watch over his friends, and guard them from harm, and visit them in dreams.

From *The Golden Bough* by J. G. Frazer, 1911

But, look, the morn

BERNARDO: It was about to speak when the cock crew.
HORATIO: And then it started like a guilty thing
Upon a fearful summons. I have heard
The cock, that is the trumpet to the morn,
Doth with his lofty and shrill-sounding throat
Awake the god of day; and at his warning,
Whether in sea or fire, in earth or air,
The extravagant and erring spirit hies
To his confine; and of the truth herein
This present object made probation.
MARCELLUS: It faded on the crowing of the cock.
Some say that ever 'gainst that season comes
Wherein our Saviour's birth is celebrated,
The bird of dawning singeth all night long;
And then, they say, no spirit can walk abroad;
The nights are wholesome; then no planets strike,
No fairy takes, nor witch hath power to charm,
So hallow'd and so gracious is the time.
HORATIO: So have I heard and do in part believe it.
But, look, the morn in russet mantle clad,
Walks o'er the dew of yon high eastern hill;
Break we our watch up; and by my advice
Let us impart what we have seen to-night
Unto young Hamlet.

From *Hamlet* by William Shakespeare, 1603–4

'When, Goddess'

When, Goddess, thou liftst up thy wakened Head,
    Out of the Mornings purple bed,
    Thy Quire of Birds about thee play,
And all the joyful world salutes the rising day.

The Ghosts, and Monster Spirits, that did presume
   A Bodies Priv'lege to assume,
   Vanish again invisibly,
And Bodies gain agen their visibility.

From 'Hymn to Light' by Abraham Cowley, in *Works*, 1668

'The golden lyre'

But when thro' all th' infernal bounds,
Which flaming Phlegeton surrounds,
   Love, strong as Death, the Poet led
   To the pale nations of the dead,
What sounds were heard,
What scenes appear'd,
   O'er all the dreary coasts!
     Dreadful gleams,
     Dismal screams,
     Fires that glow,
     Shrieks of woe,
     Sullen moans,
     Hollow groans,
And cries of tortur'd ghosts!

But hark! he strikes the golden lyre;
And see! the tortur'd ghosts respire,
   See, shady forms advance!
   Thy stone, O Sysiphus, stands still,
   Ixion rests upon his wheel,
   And the pale spectres dance!
The Furies sink upon their iron beds,
And snakes uncurl'd hang list'ning round their heads.

From 'Ode on St Cecilia's Day' by Alexander Pope, 1713

Rahero

And fear, there where she sat, froze the woman to stone:
Not fear of the crazy boat and the weltering deep alone;
But a keener fear of the night, the dark, and the ghostly hour,

And the thing that drove the canoe with more than a mortal's power
And more than a mortal's boldness. For much she knew of the dead
That haunt and fish upon reefs, toiling, like men, for bread,
And traffic with human fishers, or slay them and take their ware,
Till the hour when the star of the dead goes down, and the morning
   air
Blows, and the cocks are singing on shore.

From 'The Song of Rahero', in *Ballads* by Robert Louis Stevenson, 1888

The Two Corpses

A soldier had obtained leave to go home on furlough – to pray to the holy images, and to bow down before his parents. And as he was going his way, at a time when the sun had long set, and all was dark around, it chanced that he had to pass by a graveyard. Just then he heard that some one was running after him, and crying:

'Stop! you can't escape!'

He looked back and there was a corpse running and gnashing its teeth. The Soldier sprang on one side with all his might to get away from it, caught sight of a little chapel, and bolted straight into it.

There wasn't a soul in the chapel, but stretched out on a table there lay another corpse, with tapers burning in front of it. The Soldier hid himself in a corner, and remained there hardly knowing whether he was alive or dead, but waiting to see what would happen. Presently up ran the first corpse – the one that had chased the Soldier – and dashed into the chapel. Thereupon the one that was lying on the table jumped up, and cried to it:

'What hast thou come here for?'

'I've chased a soldier in here, so I'm going to eat him.'

'Come now, brother! he's run into my house. I shall eat him myself.'

'No, I shall!'

'No, I shall!'

And they set to work fighting; the dust flew like anything. They'd have gone on fighting ever so much longer, only the cocks began to crow. Then both the corpses fell lifeless to the ground, and the Soldier went on his way homeward in peace, saying:

'Glory be to Thee, O Lord! I am saved from the wizards!'

Russian folk tale, collected by Afanasief, 1863,
translated by W. R. S. Ralston

[444]

'Throw him back again'

One day a number of brothers had climbed into a great tree, when the youngest made a mis-step, and falling to the ground, was killed. The other brothers, who could not see what had happened because of the thick foliage, called out, 'What was that which fell?' The ghost of the dead brother, however, still stood in the tree and said, 'I stepped on a dead branch which broke,' and thus lying to his brothers, he descended from the tree before them, wrapped his body in leaves, and hid it. When his brothers came down, the ghost went along with them, but on the way he suddenly said, 'Oh! I forgot and left something at that tree. Wait for me till I get it.' Accordingly they waited while the ghost went back, picked up his body, and brought it along, but hid it again before he came to the place where his brothers were. Then they all went on toward the village; but after a while he repeated the trick several times until his brothers, becoming suspicious, watched and found out how they had been deceived. Thereupon they all fled, and coming to the village, cried out, 'We have seen something mysterious. Shut your doors.' So all the people obeyed, all but an old woman and her grandson, for she had not heard the warning and left her door open.

By and by the ghost came, carrying his body on his back. He tried to throw his corpse into the first house, but it struck against the closed door and fell down again; so he picked it up and cast it at the next with like result. Thus he tried them all until he came to the last house, in which the old woman lived; and here, because the door was open, the ghost succeeded and threw his body into the house. Quickly the old woman seized the bundle and tossed it out again, but the ghost caught it and hurled it back. Thus they continued to send the body to and fro; but at last the old woman seized her grandson by mistake and threw him out, at which the ghost cried, 'That is great! Now you have given me something to eat.' The old woman then said, 'Throw him back again,' but the ghost replied, thinking to cheat her, 'Do you first throw out my body. Then I will throw him back.' So they argued until dawn was near, when the old woman shouted, 'The dawn is coming. Does that mean something for you or for me?' Since the ghost replied, 'For me!' the woman delayed until the day had come. The light of the sun put the ghost in danger, so he threw the grandson back and received his own body in return; but being no longer able to conceal himself, he was changed into a wild *taro*-plant, while his body became a piece of bark.

A Kai tale from Papua New Guinea, from *Oceanic Mythology*
by R. B. Dixon, 1916

The Grey Cock

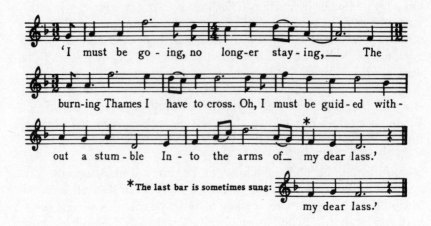

'I must be go-ing, no long-er stay-ing,— The
burn-ing Thames I have to cross. Oh, I must be guid-ed without a stum-ble In-to the arms of— my dear lass.'

*The last bar is sometimes sung:

my dear lass.'

'I must be going, no longer staying,
The burning Thames I have to cross.
Oh, I must be guided without a stumble
Into the arms of my dear lass.'

When he came to his true love's window,
He knelt down gently on a stone,
And it's through a pane he whispered slowly:
'My dear girl, are you alone?'

She rose her head from her down-soft pillow,
And snowy were her milk-white breasts,
Saying: 'Who's here, who's there at my bedroom window,
Disturbing me from my long night's rest?'

'Oh, I'm your love and don't discover,
I pray you rise, love, and let me in,
For I am fatigued from my long night's journey.
Besides, I am wet into the skin.'

Now this young girl rose and put on her clothing.
She quickly let her own true love in.
Oh, they kissed, shook hands, and embraced together,
Till that long night was near an end.

'O Willie dear, O dearest Willie,
Where is that colour you'd some time ago?'
'O Mary dear, the clay has changed me.
I'm but the ghost of your Willie O.'

'Then O cock, O cock, O handsome cockerel,
I pray you not crow until it is day.
For your wings I'll make of the very first beaten gold,
And your comb I'll make of the silver grey.'

But the cock it crew, and it crew so fully.
It crew three hours before it was day.
And before it was day, my love had to go away.
Not by the light of the moon or the light of day.

Then it's 'Willie dear, O dearest Willie,
Whenever shall I see you again?'
'When the fish they fly, love, and the sea runs dry, love,
And the rocks they melt in the heat of the sun.'

Traditional English folk song, collected by Ralph Vaughan Williams
and A. L. Lloyd, 1959

The Corpse-Rider

The body was cold as ice; the heart had long ceased to beat: yet there
were no other signs of death. Nobody even spoke of burying the
woman. She had died of grief and anger at having been divorced. It
would have been useless to bury her – because the last undying wish of
a dying person for vengeance can burst asunder any tomb and rift the
heaviest graveyard stone. People who lived near the house in which
she was lying fled from their homes. They knew that she was only
waiting for the return of the man who had divorced her.

At the time of her death he was on a journey. When he came back
and was told what had happened, terror seized him. 'If I can find no
help before dark,' he thought to himself, 'she will tear me to pieces.' It
was yet only the Hour of the Dragon; but he knew that he had no time
to lose.

He went at once to an *inyōshi*, and begged for succor. The *inyōshi*
knew the story of the dead woman; and he had seen the body. He said

to the supplicant: – 'A very great danger threatens you. I will try to save you. But you must promise to do whatever I shall tell you to do. There is only one way by which you can be saved. It is a fearful way. But unless you find the courage to attempt it, she will tear you limb from limb. If you can be brave, come to me again in the evening before sunset.' The man shuddered; but he promised to do whatever should be required of him.

At sunset the *inyōshi* went with him to the house where the body was lying. The *inyōshi* pushed open the sliding-doors, and told his client to enter. It was rapidly growing dark. 'I dare not!' gasped the man, quaking from head to foot; – 'I dare not even look at her!' 'You will have to do much more than look at her,' declared the *inyōshi*; – 'and you promised to obey. Go in!' He forced the trembler into the house and led him to the side of the corpse.

The dead woman was lying on her face. 'Now you must get astride upon her,' said the *inyōshi*, 'and sit firmly on her back, as if you were riding a horse. . . . Come! – you must do it!' The man shivered so that the *inyōshi* had to support him – shivered horribly; but he obeyed. 'Now take her hair in your hands,' commanded the *inyōshi*, – 'half in the right hand, half in the left. . . . So! . . . You must grip it like a bridle. Twist your hands in it – both hands – tightly. That is the way! . . . Listen to me! You must stay like that till morning. You will have reason to be afraid in the night – plenty of reason. But whatever may happen, never let go of her hair. If you let go, – even for one second, – she will tear you into gobbets!'

The *inyōshi* then whispered some mysterious words into the ear of the body, and said to its rider: – 'Now, for my own sake, I must leave you alone with her. . . . Remain as you are! . . . Above all things, remember that you must not let go of her hair.' And he went away, – closing the doors behind him.

Hour after hour the man sat upon the corpse in black fear; – and the hush of the night deepened and deepened about him till he screamed to break it. Instantly the body sprang beneath him, as to cast him off; and the dead woman cried out loudly, 'Oh, how heavy it is! Yet I shall bring that fellow here now!'

Then tall she rose, and leaped to the doors, and flung them open, and rushed into the night, – always bearing the weight of the man. But he, shutting his eyes, kept his hands twisted in her long hair, – tightly, tightly, – though fearing with such a fear that he could not even moan. How far she went, he never knew. He saw nothing: he heard only the sound of her naked feet in the dark, – *picha-picha, picha-picha*, – and the hiss of her breathing as she ran.

At last she turned, and ran back into the house, and lay down upon the floor exactly as at first. Under the man she panted and moaned till the cocks began to crow. Thereafter she lay still.

But the man, with chattering teeth, sat upon her until the *inyōshi* came at sunrise. 'So you did not let go of her hair!' – observed the *inyōshi*, greatly pleased. 'That is well ... Now you can stand up.' He whispered again into the ear of the corpse, and then said to the man: – 'You must have passed a fearful night; but nothing else could have saved you. Hereafter you may feel secure from her vengeance.'

Japanese folk tale, from Shadowings by Lafcadio Hearn, 1900

The Ghost's Leavetaking

Enter the chilly no-man's land of about
Five o'clock in the morning, the no-color void
Where the waking head rubbishes out the draggled lot
Of sulfurous dreamscapes and obscure lunar conundrums
Which seemed, when dreamed, to mean so profoundly much,

Get ready to face the ready-made creation
Of chairs and bureaus and sleep-twisted sheets.
This is the kingdom of the fading apparition,
The oracular ghost who dwindles on pin-legs
To a knot of laundry, with a classic bunch of sheets

Upraised, as a hand, emblematic of farewell.
At this joint between two worlds and two entirely
Incompatible modes of time, the raw material
Of our meat-and-potato thoughts assumes the nimbus
Of ambrosial revelation. And so departs.

Chair and bureau are the hieroglyphs
Of some godly utterance wakened heads ignore:
So these posed sheets, before they thin to nothing,
Speak in sign language of a lost otherworld,
A world we lose by merely waking up.

Trailing its telltale tatters only at the outermost
Fringe of mundane vision, this ghost goes
Hand aloft, goodbye, goodbye, not down
Into the rocky gizzard of the earth,
But toward a region where our thick atmosphere

Diminishes, and God knows what is there.
A point of exclamation marks that sky
In ringing orange like a stellar carrot.
Its round period, displaced and green,
Suspends beside it the first point, the starting

Point of Eden, next the new moon's curve.
Go, ghost of our mother and father, ghost of us,
And ghost of our dreams' children, in those sheets
Which signify our origin and end,
To the cloud-cuckoo land of color wheels

And pristine alphabets and cows that moo
And moo as they jump over moons as new
As that crisp cusp towards which you voyage now.
Hail and farewell. Hello, goodbye. O keeper
Of the profane grail, the dreaming skull.

Sylvia Plath, 1958

The Haunted Chamber

Each heart has its haunted chamber,
　　Where the silent moonlight falls!
On the floor are mysterious footsteps,
　　There are whispers along the walls!

*

What are ye, O pallid phantoms!
　　That haunt my troubled brain?
That vanish when day approaches,
　　And at night return again?

What are ye, O pallid phantoms!
　　But the statues without breath,
That stand on the bridge over-arching
　　The silent river of death.

Henry Wadsworth Longfellow, 1841

Of a Prodigy

I know of a strange portent that occurred in Wales. William Laudun, *or* Landun, an English knight, strong of body and of proved valour came to Gilbert Foliot, then Bishop of Hereford, now of London, and said: 'My Lord, I come to you for advice. A Welshman of evil life died of late unchristianly enough in my village, and straightway after four nights took to coming back every night to the village, and will not desist from summoning singly and by name his fellow-villagers, who upon being called at once fall sick and die within three days, so that now there are very few of them left.' The bishop, marvelling, said: 'Peradventure the Lord has given power to the evil angel of that lost soul to move about in the dead corpse. However, let the body be exhumed, cut the neck through with a spade, and sprinkle the body and the grave well with holy water, and replace it.' When this was done, the survivors were none the less plagued by the former illusion. So one night when the summoner had now left but few alive, he called William himself, citing him thrice. He, however, bold and quick as he was, and awake to the situation, darted out with his sword drawn, and chased the demon, who fled, up to the grave, and there, as he fell into it, clave his head to the neck. From that hour the ravages of that wandering pestilence ceased, and did no more hurt either to William himself or to any one else. The true facts of his death I know, but not the cause.

From *De Nugis Curialium* by Walter Map, *c.*1180, translated by M. R. James

'Old Molly Lee'

'Old Molly Lee', who used to sell milk at Burslem in the Staffordshire Potteries, had the reputation of being a witch, and after her death it was commonly reported that she used to be seen about the streets, with her milk-pail on her head, wandering about, and repeating:

> 'Weight and measure sold I never,
> Milk and water sold I ever.'

She came so often, both by day and night, that at last the inhabitants of Burslem begged the neighbouring clergy to try to lay her ghost. So six of them met, and brought a stone pig-trough, which was really an ancient stone coffin, into Burslem Church. They 'prayed and prayed' that her spirit might have rest from its torment, and at last they saw her hovering in the air up in the roof of the church, and as they continued to pray, the appearance came lower and lower, till it entered the pig-trough itself, face downwards. Then they lifted the trough, and carried it to her grave in the churchyard, and so her ghost was laid. But three of the parsons died after the experience, and the other three were long before they recovered their full strength.

From *Shropshire Folk-lore*, 1883, summarised by K. M. Briggs

Of the laying of ghosts and the Red Sea

The ceremony must be performed in Latin; a language that strikes the most audacious ghost with terror. A ghost may be laid for any term less than a hundred years and in any place or body, full or empty; as, a solid oak – the pommel of a sword – a barrel of beer, if a yeoman or simple gentleman, a pipe of wine, if an esquire or justice. But of all place the most common, and what a ghost least likes, is the Red Sea; it being related in many instances, that ghosts have most earnestly besought the exorcists not to confine them in that place. It is nevertheless considered as an indisputable fact, that there are an infinite number laid there, perhaps from it being a safer prison than any other nearer at hand, though neither history nor tradition gives us any instance of ghosts escaping or returning from this kind of transportation before their time.

Captain Francis Grose, 1775

West Country pools

Local clergy, in remote parts, were driven by the plight of their desperate parishioners to devise a method of 'laying' spirits – a method which owed little or nothing to Church teaching. Although it would be difficult to prove that such ceremonies were actually performed, the belief that they were is found in many parts of England:

A ghost harasses his family, the vicar is appealed to, he comes with his Bible and 'reads the ghost down' – either he gains sufficient control of it to dismiss it to a distant part of the parish to perform an endless task and then to return home at 'a cockstride a year', or he reduces it to such a small size it can walk into a bottle or snuff box, which is hastily closed and thrown into deep water. In other cases he may throw a handful of earth from a graveyard into its face, and this transforms it into an animal, such as a black horse or dog. In this guise the ghost is manageable, and can be led to a suitable point of entry to the underworld and thrown in. Often an assistant is needed. At Cranmere Pool, an innocent boy, duly blessed, rode the horse to the Pool, slipped off at the last moment, removing the bridle, and the horse plunged head first into the Pool. Near Lustleigh, the boy was ordered to ride the horse as hard as he could down the hill to the River Wrey. As the horse rode to jump it, it melted away, and the boy landed heavily the other side, still clutching the empty reins. At Otterton, the horse was simply driven into the sea. In Somerset a grey horse was backed into a pond. Only one instance of a black hound is known, that of Knowles, the weaver of Dean Combe (near Buckfastleigh). Here the ghost was not pushed into the Hound's Pool of the Dean Burn, but was given a perforated nutshell and ordered to bale out the pool. To this day, the locals say that the pool sometimes makes a strange grinding sound – and this is the Hound scraping the bottom.

From 'West Country Entrances to the Underworld' by Theo Brown, 1975

Post Mortem

About three months after Mola Ndive died, I saw his ghost walking along the road leading to the Engelberg Mission School in Bonjongo. It was about 8.30 in the morning as I was hurrying to school. My pencil had dropped through a hole in the pocket of my shirt. I was sure I had put it there when I started off, so I retraced my steps looking and searching the ground before me. I had walked about ten yards when I came face to face with a man carrying a climbing rope over his shoulder. There was no possibility that I was mistaken about who or what I saw. There was Mola Ndive himself in the flesh, very much alive, tall, stoopy and grey haired. He still wore that old bush shirt torn at the back and the striped piece of loin cloth around his waist. This was not a case of mistaken identity, and I'll tell you why. I was ten years old when it happened and in Standard Four. Mola Ndive was my mother's half-brother, from the same father. He lived a couple of houses away from our home and I saw him everyday when he came for his dinner. He had a swelling, the size of a basket ball between his legs. That ball still hung there. There was no mistake whatsoever about his real identity.

Others had identified him at various times and places. There had been reports of knockings at night in the family house where the widow had been staying until the traditional funeral rites were performed. All these visits were preceded by the endless whining and barking of dogs – a sure sign that something mysterious and weird was around.

Then something else happened. This time the widow had sworn that he walked into the bedroom and asked her to turn over so that they should sleep. Her loud screams for help had aroused the household and the neighbours around the house. She had been so terrified that she clung to the first person who came to her rescue like a frightened child.

[453]

She had received a terrible shock that kept her temporarily dumb for three days. They had searched in vain – Mola Ndive's ghost had vanished.

Mola Ndive had died from what was clearly a case of strangulated hernia. He had survived a number of mild attacks merely by squeezing the enlarged scrotum. This time the attack was severe and required some emergency operation. Nothing could be done to save him. They would have been obliged to carry him to the local hospital eight miles away on some improvised stretcher made from a piece of bed sheet and two stout poles, through a hilly and difficult terrain. But they had waited too long and he had died. . . .

The frequent appearances of Mola Ndive's ghost affected the daily lives of the village community. The men had to accompany their wives to their farms. It had been rumoured that Mola Ndive had developed certain vices since his death. That he had become a sex maniac. He had molested his wife on many occasions. The villagers had to retire early to the safety of their homes as the ghost normally started its prowls at nine o'clock. If one had to travel at night one had to carry a burning kerosene lantern. It was believed that ghosts only haunted in the dark and were afraid of lights.

*

The village council met a few days later. Also at the meeting was Misole, from the village of Bomboko. His mission was to put Mola Ndive's roving ghost finally to rest. When the meeting ended, a date had been fixed for the operation. It was arranged that Misole would be accompanied by six others who would assist with the digging and hauling up of the coffin.

It was past midnight when the little party arrived at the grave side. All was quiet around except for the weird chanting of the witch doctor and the sound of the muffled gong. One of the men carried a loaded dane gun and a matchet. The others shovels and picks. The last carried the juju-bag and a lighted torch of bamboo fronds.

Misole first encircled the grave with some white powder, drove a rattle-spear into the ground beside the grave and ordered the men to start digging. It was hard work and the shovels changed hands as the digging progressed. Forty-five minutes later they hit the coffin. Two stout ropes were thrown in and they all assisted in hauling the coffin to the surface. It was intact. There was no smell of festering human flesh and its weight indicated that the corpse was still inside.

Misole then took over. He tapped the coffin several times with the spear, chanting as he did so. Then he nodded. The others understood and started opening the lid. It was a grisly, hair-raising affair. There in the coffin was a fresh corpse as it had been laid there three months

[454]

before, its eyes closed and beads of sweat on the forehead. The flaming torch was brought closer and the body examined. The white hand-kerchief which was used to hold up the lower jaw to prevent it from gaping had been removed. There was a slight twitching of the skin above the temple. The group gazed in complete horror as the witch doctor addressed the corpse. 'At last we have caught up with you, you son of the devil. Why have you continued to harass the living? Why have you refused to die? Open those evil eyes, quick,' he commanded. The eyes opened. There was a slight movement amongst those who stood looking. Misole raised his hand and went on: 'Now you will be destroyed . . . destroyed, and may you sleep for ever.' He ordered them to take the corpse out of the coffin. They raised the motionless corpse with its eyes still open and placed it on the ground beside the grave; and the post-mortem began.

It was quick work. Two four-inch steel nails were handed to Misole. 'May these eyes never see again,' he murmured as he prepared to drive them into both eyes. The corpse's face twitched up again and there was a slight quivering of the mouth. Then its mouth opened. 'Don't please don't.' It was a frightened, hoarse plea. 'Shut up,' the witch doctor ordered. There were tears mixed with blood as the nails pierced the eyes. Then he took the cutlass. One straight longitudinal stroke re-vealed the heart still beating. 'May the heart of the evil one never beat again,' he pronounced, as he removed it. The corpse was then laid in the coffin on its face and shot through the back with the dane gun. The coffin was lowered again, and the earth filled in once again.

The group with the witch doctor at the rear, walked back to the vil-lage in silence, their heads straight before them. The assignment had been carried out. It was a successful post-mortem. Mola Ndive's ghost never appeared again.

From 'Post Mortem' by Ndeley Mokoso, 1987

Weak

'I never realized,' said Clayton . . . 'the poor sort of thing a ghost might be,' and he hung us up again for a time, while he sought for matches in his pocket and lit and warmed to his cigar.

'I took an advantage,' he reflected at last.

We were none of us in a hurry. 'A character,' he said, 'remains just the same character for all that it's been disembodied. That's a thing we too often forget. People with a certain strength or fixity of purpose may have ghosts of a certain strength and fixity of purpose – most haunting ghosts, you know, must be as one-idea'd as monomaniacs and as obsti-nate as mules to come back again and again. This poor creature wasn't.'

He suddenly looked up rather queerly, and his eye went round the room. 'I say it,' he said, 'in all kindliness, but that is the plain truth of the case. Even at the first glance he struck me as weak.'

He punctuated with the help of his cigar.

'I came upon him, you know, in the long passage. His back was towards me and I saw him first. Right off I knew him for a ghost. He was transparent and whitish; clean through his chest I could see the glimmer of the little window at the end. . . .

'I thought: "Good Lord! Here's a ghost at last! And I haven't believed for a moment in ghosts during the last five-and-twenty years!"'

'Um,' said Wish.

'I suppose I wasn't on the landing a moment before he found out I was there. He turned on me sharply, and I saw the face of an immature young man, a weak nose, a scrubby little moustache, a feeble chin. So for an instant we stood – he looking over his shoulder at me – and re-garded one another. Then he seemed to remember his high calling. He turned round, drew himself up, projected his face, raised his arms, spread his hands in approved ghost fashion – came towards me. As he did so his little jaw dropped, and he emitted a faint drawn-out "Boo." No, it wasn't – not a bit dreadful. I'd dined. I'd had a bottle of cham-pagne, and being all alone, perhaps two or three – perhaps even four or five – whiskies, so I was as solid as rocks and no more frightened than if I'd been assailed by a frog. "Boo," I said. "Nonsense. You don't belong to *this* place. What are you doing here?"

'I could see him wince. "Boo – oo," he said.

'"Boo – be hanged! Are you a member?" I said; and just to show I didn't care a pin for him I stepped through a corner of him and made to light my candle. "Are you a member?" I repeated, looking at him side-ways.

'He moved a little so as to stand clear of me, and his bearing became crestfallen. "No," he said, in answer to the persistent interrogation of my eye; "I'm not a member – I'm a ghost."

'"Well, that doesn't give you the run of the Mermaid Club. Is there anyone you want to see, or anything of that sort?" And doing it as steadily as possible for fear that he should mistake the carelessness of whisky for the distraction of fear, I got my candle alight. I turned on him, holding it. "What are you doing here?" I said.

'He had dropped his hands and stopped his booing, and there he stood, abashed and awkward, the ghost of a weak, silly, aimless young man. "I'm haunting," he said.

'"You haven't any business to," I said, in a quiet voice.

'"I'm a ghost," he said, as if in defence.

'"That may be, but you haven't any business to haunt here. This is a respectable private club; people often stop here with nursemaids and children, and, going about in the careless way you do, some poor little mite could easily come upon you and be scared out of her wits. I suppose you didn't think of that?"

'"No sir," he said, "I didn't."

'"You should have done. You haven't any claim on the place, have you? Weren't murdered here, or anything of that sort?"

'"None, sir; but I thought as it was old and oak-panelled –"

'"That's *no* excuse," I regarded him firmly. "Your coming here is a mistake," I said, in a tone of friendly superiority. I feigned to see if I had my matches, and then looked up at him frankly. "If I were you I wouldn't wait for cock-crow – I'd vanish right away."

'He looked embarrassed. "The fact *is*, sir –" he began.

'"I'd vanish," I said, driving it home.

'"The fact is, sir, that – somehow – I can't."

'"You *can't?*"'

From 'The Inexperienced Ghost' by H. G. Wells, 1903

'Put out the candle'

Like flames they cover him.
'Oh, I am ashamed of the woes that consume me.
No man must see me. I will put out the candle!' he said;
For a foolish man is like a summer moth that flies into the flame.
The wind that blew out the candle
Carried him away. In the darkness his ghost has vanished.
The shadow of his ghost has vanished.

From *Tsunemasa*, a Nōh play by Seami, mid-fourteenth century, translated from the Japanese by Arthur Waley

At Home

When I was dead, my spirit turned
　　To seek the much-frequented house.
I passed the door, and saw my friends
　　Feasting beneath green orange-boughs;
From hand to hand they pushed the wine,
　　They sucked the pulp of plum and peach;
They sang, they jested, and they laughed,
　　For each was loved of each.

I listened to their honest chat.
   Said one: 'To-morrow we shall be
Plod plod along the featureless sands,
   And coasting miles and miles of sea.'
Said one: 'Before the turn of tide
   We will achieve the eyrie-seat.'
Said one: 'To-morrow shall be like
   To-day, but much more sweet.'

'To-morrow,' said they, strong with hope,
   And dwelt upon the pleasant way:
'To-morrow,' cried they one and all,
   While no one spoke of yesterday.
Their life stood full at blessed noon;
   I, only I, had passed away:
'To-morrow and to-day,' they cried;
   I was of yesterday.

I shivered comfortless, but cast
   No chill across the tablecloth;
I all-forgotten shivered, sad
   To stay and yet to part how loth:
I passed from the familiar room,
   I who from love had passed away,
Like the remembrance of a guest
   That tarrieth but a day.

Christina Rossetti, 1866

The Visitor

No, no, do not beguile me, do not come
Between me and my ghost, that cannot move
Till you are gone,
And while you gossip must be dumb.
Do not believe I do not want your love,
Brother and sister, wife and son.
But I would be alone
Now, now and let him in,
Lest while I speak he is already flown,
Offended by the din
Of this half-uttered scarcely-whispered plea

(So delicate is he).
No more, no more.
Let the great tidings stay unsaid,
For I must to the door,
And oh I dread
He may even now be gone
Or, when I open, will not enter in.

Edwin Muir, 1949

A renunciation

He stood gazing long and earnestly in the direction taken by the
departing footsteps, and doing so, his attention was attracted by the
flight of a bird which came swooping towards him from the depths of
the woodland glade. Nearer and nearer it came, uttering a strange,
shrill cry, as if to attract his attention; and then, after circling in the air
above his head, came fluttering down, and lighted upon the gate-post at
his elbow. It was Dorothy's parrot. But what did it mean by this
unusual freak of familiarity? Paul spoke to the bird, which pleased it;
and when he put out his hand to smooth its feathers, the parrot lifted its
wings, and with a loud cackle exhibited a note which had been carefully
tied beneath one of them. Henley relieved the animal of its burden, and
discovered that the note was addressed to himself. When he looked
around again, the parrot had flown away. This is what the note contained:

GUIR HOUSE

MY OWN DEAR COMRADE – I call you my own because you are all that
I ever had, but even now the memory of our few brief interviews is all
that is left to me, for I must go without you. So happy was I when we
first met, that I don't mind telling you, since we shall not meet again,
how, in anticipation, I rested in your dear arms and felt your loving
caresses; for you were all the world to me then – the only world I had
ever known – and the break of day seemed close at hand. But soon the
thought of drawing you down into that awful abyss 'twixt heaven and
earth, which has whirled its black shadows about me for more than a
century, seized me, and I could not willingly make a thrall of the one I
loved; and so I leave you to those for whom you are fitted, while I shall
continue my solitary life as before. You say that you are lonely without
me! But what is your loneliness to mine? I, who never had a comrade;
who never felt the joy of friendship; and who was dazed with the sudden flush of love, of hunger satisfied, of companionship! Have you ever
felt the want of these, dear Paul? Have you ever known what it is to be

[459]

alone – to live in an empty world – and that, not for a time, but for ages? Yes, you will say, you understand it, and that you pity me, and yet you do not know its meaning; for you at least can live out the life for which God and nature have fitted you, while I am fit for nothing. You know not what it is to be shunned; to be avoided; to be feared! You go your way, and smile and nod to those you meet, and they are pleased to see you. You are welcome among your friends, as they to you. Live on in that precious state, and feel blessed and happy, for there are worse conditions, although you know it not.

And now I am going to tell you a strange thing. It is this: I have shadowed your life from the hour of your birth. I have watched your career, and where able have guided and helped you, knowing that you were one whom I could love. I have helped to make you what you are, and therefore my right of possession is doubly founded, even though my love be too great to lead you astray. Gradually I led you up to the hour when all was ripe, and then mentally impressed you with the letter which you thought you received, and which I knew would affect you through your strongest characteristics – love of adventure, and – curiosity – as well as from the fact that you were susceptible to mental influence. You came and I was happy – more happy than you will ever know – until my unsated Karma thwarted my plan, and showed that while seeking my own peace, I might possibly endanger yours. That ended all. I could go no further. But even now, as before, I shall come to you in spirit, during the still hours of night; for my love is more intense and strangely different from that which waking men are wont to feel. It is that which sometimes comes in dreams. Do you not know what I mean?

You will feel bewildered on reading this, and at a loss to understand many things, but remember that your inward or spiritual sight has been opened through the power of hypnotism, and you must not judge things as in your normal state.

When you reached our little station of Guir, you were expecting to find me there, and expectation is the proper frame of mind in which to produce a strong impression; and therefore, although you did not know what I was like, Ah Ben and I together easily made you see me as I was, together with the cart and horse; and although you actually got into the stage which was waiting, you thought you were in the cart with me. The incident of the broken spring was merely suggested as a fitting means to bring you back physically from the coach to the cart, where for the first time, in the moonlight, you saw me in semi-material form, visible as a shadow to some men, but wholly so to you. Had I appeared thus at the station, I should have alarmed all who saw me, and so I came to you only. The two worlds are so closely intermingled that men often live in one while their bodies are in another, and to those who are susceptible, the immaterial can be made more real than the other. I know these things, because, while at home in neither, I have been in both.

And now, dear comrade, think sometimes of her who loves you, and to whom you have been the only joy; and she will be with you always, although you may not know it, except in your dreams.

[460]

One more word. Think happily of the dead, for they are happy, and in a way you can not understand. If you love them truly, rejoice that they have gone, for what you call their death is but their birth, with powers transcending those of their former state, as light transcends the darkness. Disturb them not with idle yearnings, lest your thought unsettle the serenity of their lives. Let the ignorance which has ruined me be a warning. Some day I shall complete my term of loneliness, and begin life anew. We will know each other then, dear Paul, as here. Remember, I shall always be your spirit guide.   DOROTHY

Henley folded the letter and looked about him in bewilderment, and with a sense of loneliness he had never known before. He thought he could realize the emptiness of life, the dissociation with all things, of which Dorothy had spoken. He was adrift, without anchor in either world. Heart-broken and crushed, he determined to find the girl at all hazards, and bounded down the garden path in search of Ah Ben, who alone could help him. At the last of the boxwood trees he stopped, and then, *in an agony of horror, beheld the roofless ruin of the old house as Ah Ben had shown it to him.* The crumbling walls and broken belfry, half hidden amid the encroaching trees, were all that was left of Guir House and its spacious grounds. Heaps of stone and piles of rubbish beset his path, and the open portals, choked with wild grass and bushes, showed glimpses of the sky beyond. In a panic of terror lest his reason had gone, Paul flew madly on in the direction from which Dorothy had first brought him. But not an indication of what once were ornamental grounds remained. Beyond, an unbroken forest was upon every side, and the growth was wild and dense. On he rushed, with both hands pressed tightly against his head, neither knowing nor caring whither he went. But at last two shadowy forms emerged from a dense thicket of calmia upon his left, and Paul felt that their influence was kindly, and that they had come to guide him back into the world he had left behind.

From *The Ghost of Guir House* by Charles Willing Beale, 1901

'Love, Ambition, Poesy'

So, ye three Ghosts, adieu! Ye cannot raise
    My head cool-bedded in the flowery grass;
For I would not be dieted with praise,
    A pet-lamb in a sentimental farce!
Fade softly from my eyes, and be once more
    In masque-like figures on the dreamy urn.
        Farewell! I yet have visions for the night,
And for the day faint visions there is store.

Vanish, ye Phantoms! from my idle sprite,
Into the clouds, and never more return!

From *Ode on Indolence* by John Keats, *c.*1819

The poet Guido Guincelli introduces Dante
to Arnaut Daniel

Then I: 'Your verse, forged sweetly link by link,
 Which while our modern verse shall last in song,
 Must render precious even the very ink.'

And he: 'Oh brother, I can show among
 Our band' (he pointed out a spirit in front)
 'A better craftsman of his mother tongue.

Love rhyme or prose in language of Romaunt
 He topped them all; and let the fools proclaim
 Him of Limoges to be of more account!

They, caring less for truth than common fame,
 Pronounce off-hand, not waiting to be told
 What art and reason have to say to them.'

*

Then, to make room for neighbours pressing on
 Perhaps, he vanished through the flame, even as
 Through a deep pool a fish slips and is gone.

I to that soul he'd shown advanced a pace,
 Begging he would vouchsafe his name to me
 Who hoped to write it in an honoured place;

And he at once made answer frank and free:
 'Sae weel me likes your couthie kind entreatin',
 I canna nor I winna hide fra' ye;

I'm Arnaut, whae gae singin' aye and greetin';
 Waeful; I mind my fulish deeds lang syne,
 Lauchin' luik forrit tae the bricht morn's meeting.'

Pray ye the noo, by yonder micht that fine
　　Sall guide ye till the top step o' the stair,
　　Tak' timely thocht for a' my mickle pine' –

Then veiled him in the fires that find them there.

From *Il Purgatorio*, by Dante Alighieri, *c.*1310–20, translated from the Italian by
Dorothy L. Sayers

'Like a convalescent, I took the hand'

Like a convalescent, I took the hand
stretched down from the jetty, sensed again
an alien comfort as I stepped on ground.

to find the helping hand still gripping mine,
fish-cold and bony, but whether to guide
or to be guided I could not be certain.

for the tall man in step at my side
seemed blind, though he walked straight as a rush
upon his ash plant, his eyes fixed straight ahead.

Then I knew him in the flesh
out there on the tarmac among the cars,
wintered hard and sharp as a blackthorn bush.

His voice eddying with the vowels of all rivers
came back to me, though he did not speak yet,
a voice like a prosecutor's or a singer's.

cunning, narcotic, mimic, definite
as a steel nib's downstroke, quick and clean,
and suddenly he hit a litter basket

with his stick, saying, 'Your obligation
is not discharged by any common rite.'
What you must do must be done on your own

So get back in harness. The main thing is to write
for the joy of it. Cultivate a work-lust
that imagines its haven like your hands at night

[463]

dreaming the sun in the sunspot of a breast.
You are fasted now, light-headed, dangerous.
Take off from here. And don't be so earnest,

let others wear the sackcloth and the ashes.
Let go, let fly, forget.
You've listened long enough. Now strike your note.'

It was as if I had stepped free into space
alone with nothing that I had not known
already. Raindrops blew in my face

as I came to. 'Old father, mother's son,
there is a moment in Stephen's diary
for April the thirteenth, a revelation

set among my stars – that one entry
has been a sort of password in my ears,
the collect of a new epiphany,

the Feast of the Holy Tundish.' 'Who cares,'
he jeered, 'any more? The English language
belongs to us. You are raking at dead fires,

a waste of time for somebody your age.
That subject people stuff is a cod's game,
infantile, like your peasant pilgrimage.

You lose more of yourself than you redeem
doing the decent thing. Keep at a tangent.
When they make the circle wide, it's time to swim.

out on your own and fill the element
with signatures on your own frequency,
echo soundings, searches, probes, allurements,

elver-gleams in the dark of the whole sea.'
The shower broke in a cloudburst, the tarmac
fumed and sizzled. As he moved off quickly

the downpour loosed its screens round his straight walk.

From Station Island by Seamus Heaney, 1984

My Sad Captains

One by one they appear in
the darkness: a few friends, and
a few with historical
names. How late they start to shine!
but before they fade they stand
perfectly embodied, all

the past lapping them like a
cloak of chaos. They were men
who, I thought, lived only to
renew the wasteful force they
spent with each hot convulsion.
They remind me, distant now.

True, they are not at rest yet,
but now that they are indeed
apart, winnowed from failures,
they withdraw to an orbit
and turn with disinterested
hard energy, like the stars.

Thom Gunn, 1961

'Who is the third?'

Who is the third who walks always beside you?
When I count, there are only you and I together
But when I look ahead up the white road
There is always another one walking beside you
Gliding wrapt in a brown mantle, hooded
I do not know whether a man or a woman
– But who is that on the other side of you?

From *The Waste Land* by T. S. Eliot, 1923

'When a man is overcome by fear'

When a man is overcome by fear he sometimes trembles and shudders at a circumstance which ought to fill him with joy. We have an example of this in the disciples of Our Lord Jesus Christ, who, being in their boat in the midst of the Sea of Galilee, and tossed with the waves, for the wind was contrary, about the fourth watch of the night saw Our Lord, Who came to them walking upon the sea. And they were troubled, saying: It is an apparition. And they cried out in fear. And immediately Jesus spoke to them, saying: *Be of good heart: it is I, fear ye not.* And as S. Luke in his twenty-fourth chapter, verses 36–44, after the Resurrection when the eleven were gathered together and Jesus stood in the midst of them, they being troubled and frightened, supposed that they saw a spirit. And He said unto them: Why are you troubled, and why do thoughts arise in your hearts? See My hands and feet, that it is I Myself; handle, and see: for a spirit hath not flesh and bones, as you see Me to have. But while they yet believed not, and wondered for joy, He said: Have you here anything to eat? And He ate a piece of broiled fish and a honeycomb. Thus we learn that fear made the very disciples believe that they saw a ghost when it was their Master.

From 'A Treatise of Ghosts' by Father Noël Taillepied, 1588,
translated by M. Summers

The Road to Emmaus

And, behold, two of them went that same day to a village called Emmaus, which was from Jerusalem *about* threescore furlongs.

And they talked together of all these things which had happened.

And it came to pass, that, while they communed *together* and reasoned, Jesus himself drew near, and went with them.

But their eyes were holden that they should not know him.

And he said unto them, What manner of communications *are* these that ye have one to another, as ye walk, and are sad?

And the one of them, whose name was Cleopas, answering said unto him, Art thou only a stranger in Jerusalem, and hast not known the things which are come to pass there in these days?

And he said unto them, What things? And they said unto him, Concerning Jesus of Nazareth, which was a prophet mighty in deed and word before God and all the people:

And how the chief priests and our rulers delivered him to be condemned to death, and have crucified him.

But we trusted that it had been he which should have redeemed Israel: and beside all this, to day is the third day since these things were done.

Yea, and certain women also of our company made us astonished, which were early at the sepulchre;

And when they found not his body, they came, saying, that they had also seen a vision of angels, which said that he was alive.

And certain of them which were with us went to the sepulchre, and found *it* even so as the women had said: but him they saw not.

Then he said unto them, O fools, and slow of heart to believe all that the prophets have spoken:

Ought not Christ to have suffered these things, and to enter into his glory?

And beginning at Moses and all the prophets, he expounded unto them in all the scriptures the things concerning himself.

And they drew nigh unto the village, whither they went: and he made as though he would have gone further.

But they constrained him, saying, Abide with us: for it is toward evening, and the day is far spent. And he went in to tarry with them.

And it came to pass, as he sat at meat with them, he took bread, and blessed *it*, and brake, and gave to them.

And their eyes were opened, and they knew him; and he vanished out of their sight.

And they said one to another, Did not our heart burn within us, while he talked with us by the way, and while he opened to us the scriptures?

And they rose up the same hour, and returned to Jerusalem, and found the eleven gathered together, and them that were with them,

Saying, The Lord is risen indeed, and hath appeared to Simon.

And they told what things *were done* in the way, and how he was known of them in breaking of bread.

And as they thus spake, Jesus himself stood in the midst of them, and saith unto them, Peace *be* unto you.

But they were terrified and affrighted, and supposed that they had seen a spirit.

And he said unto them, Why are ye troubled? and why do thoughts arise in your hearts?

Behold my hands and my feet, that it is I myself: handle me, and see; for a spirit hath not flesh and bones, as ye see me have.

And when he had thus spoken, he shewed them *his* hands and *his* feet.

And while they yet believed not for joy, and wondered, he said unto them, Have ye here any meat?

And they gave him a piece of a broiled fish, and of an honeycomb.

And he took *it*, and did eat before them.

And he said unto them, These *are* the words which I spake unto you, while I was yet with you, that all things must be fulfilled, which were written in the law of Moses, and *in* the prophets, and *in* the psalms, concerning me.

Then opened he their understanding, that they might understand the scriptures,

And said unto them, Thus it is written, and thus it behoved Christ to suffer, and to rise from the dead the third day:

And that repentance and remission of sins should be preached in his name among all nations, beginning at Jerusalem.

And ye are witnesses of these things.

And, behold, I sent the promise of my Father upon you: but tarry ye in the city of Jerusalem, until ye be endued with power from on high.

And he led them out as far as to Bethany, and he lifted up his hands, and blessed them.

And it came to pass, while he blessed them, he was parted from them, and carried up into heaven.

And they worshipped him, and returned to Jerusalem with great joy:

And were continually in the temple, praising and blessing God. Amen.

St Luke XXIV

Offa

And it seemed, while we waited, he began to walk towards us   he vanished

he left behind coins, for his lodging, and traces of red mud.

'*Mercian Hymns*, xxx' by Geoffrey Hill, 1971

Acknowledgments

Ghosts appeal to all ages and much fun has come from discussions with my family – Steve, Tom, Hannah, Jamie and Luke (they all had suggestions, and Hannah did heroic photocopying). Several friends directed me to sources, including A. S. Byatt, Agnes Cardinal, John Gross, Nick Humphrey, Ian Hunt, Elene Kolb, Julian Loose, Blake Morrison, Peter Raby, Francis Spufford, Sarah Nash, Jane Turner and Michael Wood. I am particularly indebted to Josephine Lee, who sent hard-to-find spectres by post, with uncanny perception, and to Hermione Lee, whose knowledge and humour added greatly to the pleasure of my work.

My colleagues at Chatto have been tremendous and I'd like to take a rare opportunity to thank them: Carmen Callil, who commissioned *The Chatto Book of Ghosts*; Jonathan Burnham, my understanding editor, and translator of Montale; Barry Featherstone, who masterminded production with immense patience; Humphrey Stone, who designed the text; Julian Abela-Hyzler, who illustrated the cover; Alison Samuel and Jenny Chapman, whose enthusiasm spurred me on; Simon Armitage, who appears sporadically (but not spectrally) and Sophie Martin and Sara Holloway, (who do the hard work). My affectionate thanks, too, to Rowena Skelton-Wallace, the nicest possible person to share an office with, and to Rosemary Davidson, who never fails to make me laugh, and is *still* finding ghosts in the press. Finally, Mark Bell has been indispensable. He encouraged the first notion, found brilliant extracts, commented on the 'first cut', and copy-edited the typescript. My gratitude knows no bounds.

For permission to reprint copyright material the author and the publishers gratefully acknowledge the following:

Peter Ackroyd: *Hawksmoor*, 1983, by permission of Hamish Hamilton Ltd; Opal Palmer Adisa: 'Duppy Get Her', 1989, by permission of HarperCollins Publishers Ltd; Isabel Allende: *The House of the Spirits*, 1985, by permission of Jonathan Cape Ltd; Anthony Alpers: *Maori Myths*, 1964 by permission of David Higham Associates; Hans Christian Andersen: 'Anne Lisbeth', translated by Erik Christian Haugaard, by permission of Victor Gollancz Ltd; W. H. Auden: 'Five Songs: V', *Collected Poems*, 1976, by permission of Faber & Faber Ltd; John Banville: *Ghosts*, 1993, by permission of Secker & Warburg; Charles Baudelaire: 'Don Juan in Hell' and 'The Ghost' from 'Les

Fleurs du Mal' translated by Roy Campbell, (Harvill Press 1953) by permission of Aitken, Stone & Wylie Ltd; Samuel Beckett: *Watt*, published by John Calder (Publishers) Ltd. Copyright © Samuel Beckett, 1953, 1963, 1970, 1976, 1978 and 1981. Reprinted by permission of The Samuel Beckett Estate and the Calder Educational Trust, London; R. M. Berndt: 'Wonguri–Madjigai Song Cycle', *Oceania* 19.1, 1948, by permission of University of Sydney Press; Elizabeth Bishop: 'The Wit' and 'Travelling in the Family', *Complete Poems*, 1983, by permission of Chatto & Windus Ltd; Carmen Blacker and Theo Brown, from *The Folklore of Ghosts*, ed. H. R. Ellis Davidson and W. M. Russell, 1981, by permission of the Folklore Society; Elizabeth Bowen: 'Hand in Glove', by permission of Jonathan Cape Ltd; Dee Brown: *Bury My Heart at Wounded Knee*' (Barrie & Jenkins, 1971), by permission of Peters, Fraser & Dunlop; Katharine M. Briggs: *A Dictionary of British Folk Tales*, 1971, by permission of Routledge & Kegan Paul Ltd; Katharine M. Briggs and Ruth L. Tongue: *Folktales of England*, 1965, by permission of Routledge Kegan Paul; Georg Büchner: *Woyzeck*, translated by John Holmstrom, 1963, by permission of Penguin Books Ltd; John A. Burrison, Debby Creecy, Sharon McParland, Nan Gilmer Lang: *Storytellers: Folktales and Legends from the South*, © 1989, by permission of University of Georgia Press; A. S. Byatt: 'The July Ghost' from *Sugar and Other Stories*, 1987, and *Angels and Insects*, 1992, by permission of Chatto & Windus Ltd; Italo Calvino: *Italian Folklore*, 1956, translated from the Italian by George Martin, 1980, by permission of Harcourt Brace Jovanovich Inc.; Bo Carpelan: 'They are alive', 1973, trans. Anne Born, 1987 by permission of Forest Books Ltd; Angela Carter: *The Passion of New Eve* (Virago, 1982), and 'Ashputtle', from *The Virago Book of Ghost Stories*, 1987, by permission of Rogers, Coleridge & White; C. P. Cavafy: 'To Call Up the Shades', *Collected Poems*, translated by Edmund Keely and Phillip Sherrard, ed. George Savidis, 1984, by permission of Chatto & Windus Ltd; Noël Coward: *Blithe Spirit*, 1941, *The Plays of Noël Coward*, 1942, by permission of Heinemann Ltd; Stephanie Dalley: 'The Descent of Ishtar' and 'Gilgamesh' from *Myths from Mesopotamia*, 1989, by permission of Oxford University Press; Dante Alighieri: *The Divine Comedy: Purgatory*, translated by Dorothy L. Sayers, (Penguin Books, 1955), by permission of David Higham Associates Ltd; *Hell*, translated by Steve Ellis, 1994, by permission of Chatto & Windus Ltd; Walter de la Mare: 'The Listeners', and 'The Song of the Soldiers', from *Collected Rhymes and Verses*, 1970, by permission of The Society of Authors; Douglas Dunn: 'Supreme Death' and 'Home Again' from *Collected Poems*, 1986, by permission of Faber & Faber Ltd; *Eirik's Saga*, translated by Magnus Magnusson and Hermann Pálsson, 1965, by permission of Penguin Books Ltd; T. S. Eliot: extracts from *The Waste Land* (1923); from *The Four Quartets* (1943); and *The Family Reunion* (1939), by permission of Faber & Faber Ltd; D. J. Enright: 'Guest', *Collected Poems*, (Oxford University Press 1981), by permission of Watson, Little, Ltd; *Eyrbyggia Saga*, translated by Hermann Pálsson and Paul Edwards, 1989, by permission of Penguin Books Ltd; R. C. Finucane: *Appearances of the Dead*, 1982, by permission of Prometheus Books Inc.; Robert Frost: 'The Witch of Coos', *Complete Poems*, by permission of Jonathan Cape Ltd;

John Fuller: 'Hauntings', *The Mechanical Body*, 1991, by permission of Chatto & Windus Ltd; Kathleen Gallagher: 'Ghosts', *Poems* (1989), by permission of Forest Books Ltd; Jane Gardam: 'The Weeping Child', *Black Faces, White Faces* (1975), by permission of Hamish Hamilton Ltd; William Gibson: *Mona Lisa Overdrive* (1989), by permission of Shelley Power Literary Agency Ltd; William Golding: 'The Ladder and the Tree' from *The Hot Gates* (1965), by permission of Faber & Faber Ltd; Celia Green and Charles McCreery: *Apparitions* (1975), by permission of Hamish Hamilton Ltd; Thom Gunn: 'My Sad Captains', *My Sad Captains and Other Poems* (1961), by permission of Faber & Faber Ltd; Tony Harrison: 'Clearing', *Selected Poems*, (Penguin Books, 1984), by permission of Peters, Fraser & Dunlop Ltd; L. P. Hartley: *Eustace and Hilda*, 1947, by permission of Bodley Head Ltd; Seamus Heaney: 'Station Island', *Collected Poems*, 1984, by permission of Faber & Faber Ltd; Hermann Hesse: *Steppenwolf*, 1927, translated by Joseph Mileck and Horst Franz, 1963, by permission of Suhrkamp Verlag; Geoffrey Hill: 'Funeral Music' (Sonnet 8), from *King Log*, 1968, *Mercian Hymns*, 1971, by permission of Penguin Books Ltd; Henrik Ibsen: *Ghosts*, translated by Peter Watts, 1984, by permission of Penguin Books Ltd; Alois Jirásek: *Old Czech Legends*, translated by Marie K. Holeček, 1992, © UNESCO, by permission of Forest Books Ltd; Jan Knappert: *Myths and Legends of the Swahilis* (Heinemann Educational, 1970), by kind permission of the author; *Laxdaela Saga*, translated by Magnus Magnusson and Hermann Pálsson, 1969, by permission of Penguin Books Ltd; Christopher Leverson: *The Golden Casket: Chinese Stories of Five Millennia*, 1965, by permission of Carl Hanser Verlag; Arnold Lobel, 'Days with Frog and Toad' by permission of Puffin Books Ltd; Robert Lowell: 'The Ghost', *Poems 1939–49*, 1950, by permission of Faber & Faber Ltd; Tom Lowenstein: *The Things that Are Said of Us*, 1992, © The Regents of the University of California, 1992; Norman MacCaig: 'High Street, Edinburgh', *Collected Poems*, 1993, by permission of Chatto & Windus Ltd; Louis MacNeice, 'The Taxis', *Selected Poems, 1988*, by permission of Faber & Faber Ltd; Derek Mahon: 'Girls in their Seasons', *Night Crossing*, 1968, by permission of Oxford University Press; David Malouf: 'Elegy: The Absences', *Collected Poems*, 1992, by permission of Chatto & Windus Ltd; Thomas Mann: 'The Wardrobe', from *Little Herr Friedman and Other Stories*, 1961 by permission of Secker & Warburg; Ruth Manning Saunders: 'Golden Hair', from *The Book of Ghosts and Goblins*, 1968, by permission of David Higham Associates; Christopher Middleton: 'A Revenant', *The Balcony Tree*, 1993, by permission of Carcanet Press Ltd; Ndeley Mokoso: 'Post Mortem', *Man Pass Man and Other Stories*, 1987, by permission of Longman Group UK Ltd; Blake Morrison: 'Whinny Moor', *The Ballad of the Yorkshire Ripper*, 1989, by permission of Chatto & Windus Ltd; Toni Morrison: *Beloved*, 1989, by permission of Chatto & Windus Ltd; Richard Moyle: *Fagogo: Fables from Samoa*, (Auckland University Press 1981), by kind permission of the author; Edwin Muir: 'The Visitor', *Collected Poems 1921–51*, by permission of Faber & Faber Ltd; Haruki Murakami: *A Wild Sheep Chase*, 1989, translated by Alfred Birnbaum, by permission of Kodansha and Penguin Books Ltd; Vladimir Nabokov: *The Real Life of Sebastian Knight*, 1945, by permission of New Directions Inc.; Alfred Noyes: 'The

Highwayman', *Collected Poems*, 1963, by permission of John Murray Ltd; Ben Okri: *Songs of Enchantment*, 1993, by permission of Jonathan Cape Ltd; Pliny the Younger: *Letters*, translated by Betty Radice, by permission of Penguin Books Ltd; Sylvia Plath: 'November Graveyard', 'The Ghost's Leavetaking', *Collected Poems*, edited by Ted Hughes, 1981, by permission of Faber & Faber Ltd; Plautus: 'The Ghost', *Comedies*, translated by E. F. Watling, 1964, by permission of Penguin Books Ltd; Peter Porter: 'The Delegate', *The Cost of Seriousness*, 1978, by permission of Oxford University Press; Terry Pratchett: *Wyrd Sisters*, 1988, by permission of Victor Gollancz Ltd; S. S. Prawer: 'The Two Grenadiers' (Heine) in *The Penguin Book of Lieder*, 1964, by permission of Penguin Books Ltd; Herbert Read: 'To a Conscript of 1940', *Collected Poems*, 1946, by permission of Faber & Faber Ltd; Peter Redgrove: 'Ghosts', *The Moon Disposes: Poems 1954–87*, 1987, by permission of Routledge & Kegan Paul Ltd; Adrienne Rich, 'What Ghosts Can Say', *A Change of World*, 1951, by permission of W. W. Norton Inc.; Anne Rice: *The Queen of the Damned*, 1989, by permission of Rogers, Coleridge & White; Rainer Maria Rilke: 'Orpheus, Eurydice, Hermes', *New Poems*, translated by J. B. Leishmann, by permission of Chatto & Windus Ltd; Michèle Roberts: *Daughters of the House*, 1992, by permission of Virago Press Ltd; Theodore Roethke: 'The Visitant', *The Waking* (1953) (*Collected Poems*, 1968), by permission of Faber & Faber Ltd; Siegfried Sassoon: 'Repression of War Experience', *Poems*, 1917, by permission of George Sassoon, and *Memoirs of an Infantry Officer*, 1930, by permission of Faber & Faber Ltd; George F. Schultz: *Vietnamese Legends*, 1965, by permission of Charles E. Tuttle Inc; Orson Scott Card: 'Malpractice', 1977, in *Maps in a Mirror*, 1990, by permission of Legend, Random House UK; D. Shay, *Making Ghostbusters* (New York 1985), by permission of the author. Stevie Smith, 'Animula, Vagula, Blandula', 'Old Ghosts', from *The Complete Poems of Stevie Smith*, by permission of James MacGibbon; James Thurber, *My Life and Hard Times*, 1933, by permission of Hamish Hamilton Ltd; Ruth L. Tongue: 'Somerset Folklore', *County Folklore*, VIII, 1965, by permission of the Folklore Society; Marina Tsvetayeva: *Poems for Alexander Blok*, 1921, in *Selected Poems* translated by Elaine Feinstein, 1971, by permission of Oxford University Press; Amos Tutuola: *The Palm Wine Drinkard*, 1952, by permission of Faber & Faber Ltd; Ralph Vaughan Williams and A. L. Lloyd: *The Penguin Book of English Folksongs*, 1959, by permission of The English Folk Dance and Song Society; Virgil: *The Aeneid*, translated by Robert Fitzgerald, 1983, by permission of HarperCollins Ltd; Derek Walcott: *Omeros*, 1990, by permission of Faber & Faber Ltd; Rebecca West: *The Fountain Overflows*, 1956, by permission of Macmillan Publishers Ltd; Nigel Williams: *They Came from SW19*, 1992, by permission of Faber & Faber; William Carlos Williams: 'The Yachts', by permission of Carcanet Press Ltd; Judith Wright: 'The Dead Astronaut', 1970, *Collected Poems*, 1972, by permission of Angus & Robertson and Carcanet Press Ltd.

Chatto & Windus apologise for any errors or omissions in the above list and would be grateful to be notified of any corrections.

Index

The End . . .

'Frog,' asked Toad
'was that a true story?'
'Maybe it was
and maybe it wasn't,
said Frog.
Frog and Toad sat
close by the fire.
They were scared.
The teacups shook
in their hands.
They were having the shivers.
It was a good, warm feeling.

From 'Shivers' in *Days with Frog and Toad* by Arnold Lobel, 1979